CAREER OPPORTUNITIES IN BANKING, FINANCE, AND INSURANCE

Second Edition

CAREER OPPORTUNITIES IN BANKING, FINANCE, AND INSURANCE

Second Edition

THOMAS FITCH

Foreword by
Robert R. Johnson, Ph.D., CFA
Managing Director, CFA and
CGIPS Programs Division
CFA Institute

Ferguson
An imprint of Infobase Publishing

Ferguson
An imprint of Infobase Publishing
132 West 31st Street
New York NY 10001

ISBN-10: 0-8160-6473-3
ISBN-13: 978-0-8160-6473-1

Library of Congress Cataloging-in-Publication Data
Fitch, Thomas P.
    Career opportunities in banking, finance, and insurance / Thomas Fitch; foreword by Robert R. Johnson.—2nd ed.
        p. cm.
    Includes index.
    ISBN 0-8160-6473-3 (hc : alk. paper) 1. Financial services industry—Vocational guidance. 2. Finance—Vocational guidance. 3. Banks and banking—Vocational guidance. I. Title.
    HG173.F55 2007
    332.023'73—dc22   2006012802

Ferguson books are available at special discounts when purchased in bulk quantities for businesses, associations, institutions, or sales promotions. Please call our Special Sales Department in New York at (212) 967-8800 or (800) 322-8755.

You can find Ferguson on the World Wide Web at http://www.fergpubco.com

Cover design by Nora Wertz

Printed in the United States of America

VB Hermitage 10 9 8 7 6 5 4 3 2 1

This book is printed on acid-free paper.

CONTENTS

FOREWORD

The fact that you have opened *Career Opportunities in Banking, Finance, and Insurance* indicates that you are at a crossroads in your professional development. The career path you choose will affect many aspects of your life, and it is an honor to be invited to address a few words to you at this critical point. I have been privileged to participate in the investment profession as a practitioner, as an academic, and currently as the individual at CFA Institute responsible for the Chartered Financial Analyst (CFA) program and the newly created Certificate in Global Investment Performance Standards (CGIPS) program. Growing up in Omaha, Nebraska, provided me with an excellent opportunity to follow closely one of the premier investment professionals of all time, Warren Buffett. I certainly share Mr. Buffett's enthusiasm and passion for this profession, and I hope that you find it both challenging and rewarding.

The only constant in the finance and investment industry is change. Every day is a new adventure, without routine or agenda. Security prices are set by the market and often overreact to news, behaving quite irrationally. For many, such unpredictability can be extremely stressful. I embrace it. Nothing is more fulfilling than thorough due diligence resulting in correctly valuing a security, and nothing is more exhilarating than making investment decisions on the basis of the best information available.

The industry's structure is also constantly evolving. The growth of hedge funds, independent research boutiques, and private client assets are three examples that have dramatically altered the landscape of the investment profession over the last 10 years. Hundreds of high-profile portfolio managers and investment bankers have abandoned large employers over the last decade, opting for the flexibility and favorable fee structures of the hedge fund environment. This exodus has exacerbated the unfortunate decline in investment time horizons. Most alternative strategies, while valuable in a total portfolio context, focus on short-term asset mispricings and arbitrage opportunities. By their nature, they are fostering a culture of "What have you done for me lately?" and a concentration on absolute return rather than relative return (employing an appropriate benchmark). This contradicts what we teach in the CFA program, using a disciplined process to construct risk-adjusted, client-appropriate portfolios.

New instruments and new analytical techniques also create new career opportunities. For example, the field of investment performance evaluation and presentation is emerging as a respected specialization. Because performance measurement is central to investment operations from asset gathering through feedback on results, performance analysts are well positioned to contribute to their firm's success.

The conflicts of interest inherent in a firm that conducts both investment banking and investment research were ultimately exposed in the early 21st century. The "Chinese walls" that brokerage firms claimed protected research analysts from the pressure to rate investment banking clients positively were significantly abused. Eliot Spitzer, New York's attorney general, led a charge to eradicate this bias by requiring more separation between the two business units. In 2003, Spitzer brokered a deal between the Securities and Exchange Commission and the brokerage firms mandating that an independent research alternative be offered. Independent research boutiques, firms dedicated to providing unbiased, value-added research, have exploded in popularity since the ruling and have reshaped the relational dynamics between investment management firms ("buy-side") and brokerage firms ("sell-side"). Buy-side firms now funnel trade commission dollars based on merit rather than give them to a few very large brokerage houses in which traders have global relationships. Further, trade dollars are bifurcated between firms that offer the best execution of trades (pure trade commission) and the firms that provided the research that led to the trade (flat fees). This "unbundling" of fees continues to gain momentum and is sure to have lasting implications on the industry.

The growth in private wealth is pressuring investment professionals to be versed in a much broader body of knowledge. The global surge in high–net worth individuals demands a competency in local tax law and regulation, estate planning, and alternative perceptions of risk in order to design successful, tax-efficient investment strategies. Moreover, traditional private wealth managers are increasingly applying institutional principles such as portfolio theory, asset allocation, and multimanager strategies to individual investment portfolios. The line between institutional and private wealth money management will continue to blur as best practices are shared across both markets.

So what makes a good investor in this complex environment? What is the recipe for success? Unfortunately, there is no magic formula. Successful investing requires a strong educational foundation, hard work, and the ability to adapt to the structural changes described above. Of course, we believe the CFA program is the place to start. The CFA charter is a measure of competence and integrity that is globally recognized as the highest achievement in the investment profession. The rigorous program that the *Economist* has referred to as the "gold standard" equips charterholders with a practitioner-oriented and relevant body of knowledge that will serve as their ethical and educational foundation when they begin applying their skills.

In today's highly connected world, investors have access to all public information available on a security almost immediately. Additionally, Regulation Fair Disclosure (Reg FD), introduced in October 2000 to eliminate rampant selective disclosure by firms to their large investors, has leveled the playing field. Today's skilled investor no longer possesses an information edge but rather can quickly separate opinion from fact, material from nonmaterial, and important information from irrelevant when filtering today's copious news flow. Timing remains critical in the analysis of data, but it is the interpretation of that data that separates average from great investors.

The most celebrated investors also remain steadfast in their valuation methodologies throughout a cycle. In fact, the most serious red flag for consultants is "style creep" by a manager when his or her strategy is out of favor. A consistent and disciplined application of investment process and style is paramount. There will continue to be periods of "irrational exuberance" and bubbles as crowd mentality attracts inexperienced and speculative investors to the latest investment theme or fad. The 17th-century Dutch tulip craze, the 18th-century South Sea bubble, railroads and canals in the 19th century, and dot-coms in the late 20th century are all examples of short-term mispricings of asset values. Do not ever be fooled into thinking that "It's different this time" or that the business cycle is obsolete. The present value of future cash flows will always be the ultimate value of an investment.

Most important, remember our fundamental mission as privileged members of the investment profession. We are fiduciaries, possessing a heightened responsibility to act with loyalty, prudence, and care when managing other's assets. Regrettably, this duty has been overshadowed in recent years by corporate malfeasance, investor and client focus on short-term profits, and an irresponsible financial media. It is easy to allow the relationship with your client to become highly impersonal and get lost in the process. However, behind the financial statements, spreadsheets, portfolio models, and trading systems is a retirement fund or a college savings account or an educational endowment. As professionals in a position of trust, we are responsible for protecting that wealth. As underscored in the CFA Institute *Standards of Practice Handbook,* we must always place the interests of clients above our own.

So far I have focused only on careers in investment management and securities analysis. There are many other fields in banking and insurance where the opportunities for a rewarding career are just as plentiful. Financial industry deregulation has broken down many of the barriers that traditionally separated the fields of banking, insurance, and asset management. For example, commercial banks can now market a broader array of products to their customers (such as annuities, mutual funds, and insurance) than previously was allowed.

As financial services companies become more interconnected, the job-related skills you develop in one area of the industry are often transferable into another field. People who have investment analyst training can readily move into marketing, client servicing, investor relations, or senior management. Those who have experience in investment management may find an equally rewarding career at a commercial bank, life insurance company, or mortgage banking firm.

This is an exciting time to be embarking on a career in finance. I wish you the best of luck in finding a fulfilling career in a wonderful industry.

—Robert R. Johnson, Ph.D., CFA
Managing Director, CFA and
CGIPS Programs Division,
CFA Institute

February 1, 2006

INDUSTRY OUTLOOK

Financial services companies in the United States are a major industry group, providing five to six million full-time jobs. Banks, insurance companies, and securities firms offer good to excellent employment prospects in many job classifications, including many opportunities in the emerging new economy—the online world of Internet banking, brokerage and e-commerce financial services. Employment prospects for many traditional jobs, such as bank tellers and customer service employees, also is likely to remain strong over the next five to 10 years. Banking, brokerage, and insurance are service sector industries; quality of service is frequently the reason customers give for selecting their service provider or changing financial institutions.

Employment opportunities in the financial services industries reflect the broader economic themes in the United States and around the world. The dominant industry trends, globalization and consolidation, have created a financial services industry with a small number of very large service providers and a much larger number of smaller firms competing in regional and local markets. While this consolidation trend is likely to continue, if not accelerate, over the next several years, the financial services industry is a very dynamic, competitive, market. As financial companies create newer products and more innovative ways to service their customers, the impact on the employment picture is creation of many new job opportunities.

The financial services industry continues to attract a diverse group of people. Employment opportunities will vary by size of institution and market niche. International banking talent is in high demand at money center banks servicing the global economy. Regional banks, super-regionals, and money center banks are looking to increase their fee-based investment, lending, and finance operations. Many want to hire experts who can help transform traditional business groups into new entities, leveraging online and Internet technology to stay abreast of e-commerce developments.

Focused banks, brokerage firms, and insurance companies will continue to do well in this dynamic market and create more jobs. Recruiting skilled professionals to fill expected job vacancies is becoming a major challenge for financial institutions and corporations. Many are looking to hire younger candidates with non-traditional backgrounds, or who have come from organizations they would not have looked at in the past.

The future of financial services is in new business services, even as it goes through a period of consolidation. One out of every five commercial banks owns a full-service brokerage firm. Many financial services companies specializing in a particular niche, such as retail banking, credit cards, or international banking, are positioned to weather the financial storms resulting from mergers, acquisitions, market globalization, and increased price competition among major players.

Brief History

Banking and finance in the United States have had a long history of expansion and diversification. Through much of the 20th century banks, securities firms, and insurance companies were fierce competitors, motivated by two ambitions: to capitalize on an expanding economy following the end of World War II, and an even stronger desire to keep other financial services firms from invading their turf. This protectionist outlook, which persisted through much of the last 50 years of the 20th century, has its origins in financial legislation of the 1930s, measures that were enacted to put the country back on its feet economically and stabilize the financial system.

The primary catalyst of the 1930's financial legislation, which set in place the financial industry structure that lasted for the next 60 years, was the stock market collapse in 1929 and the Great Depression. Following the stock market collapse, the U.S. banking system was in near total disarray. In 1930 more than 1,300 U.S. commercial banks had failed, wiping out their depositors' savings. By 1933 an additional 7,000 banks had closed their doors. The bank failures of the early 1930s sent the U.S. economy into a vicious cycle, deepening the effects of the Depression. Businesses went into bankruptcy, laid off their workers, and defaulted on their bank loans. Individuals could not withdraw funds from their banks because the banks did not have enough cash on hand to distribute.

In 1933 Congress intervened in the growing economic crisis, passing the Glass-Steagall Act. The Glass-Steagall Act, also known as the Banking Act of 1933, did much to restore public confidence in the banking system. A new federal agency, the Federal Deposit Insurance Corp., was created to provide deposit insurance for banking customers. The FDIC was given authority to set operating standards for banks holding federally insured deposits, and also to inspect financial records of banks to ensure compliance with these standards. The Glass-Steagall Act is best remembered, though, for the permanent separation it imposed between commercial banking (lending and deposit taking) and investment banking (securities underwriting). Banks were prevented from underwriting revenue bonds for municipalities and common stocks for corporations. Commercial banks that owned investment banking subsidiaries were required to divest their securities operations.

The Glass-Steagall barriers remained more or less intact for the next 66 years, despite numerous attempts to modernize the financial system. In the 1970s Congress began periodically debating financial reform legislation that would roll back or remove altogether the Glass-Steagall limitations, but all of the reform bills eventually failed because they lacked the necessary votes for passage. In 1987 the Federal Reserve Board, exercising its own authority when Congress failed to act, determined that banks could underwrite and deal in commercial paper (short-term unsecured obligations issued by corporations), as long as the underwriting was done by a separate company and commercial paper issuance did not exceed 5 percent of bank revenue. This limit was raised to 10 percent in 1989, and finally was lifted in 1999, to 25 percent in 1996, and the list of eligible securities expanded to include common stocks and corporate bonds. Commercial banks are drawn to the underwriting business for several reasons. By underwriting securities, banks can more easily diversify their revenue sources, can earn additional fee income, and they can offer commercial loan customers additional services—a kind of "one stop shopping" for all banking and banking-related services.

Besides securities underwriting, banks have long had an interest in selling insurance products such as variable annuities through branch banking offices, but until recently were prohibited by banking legislation from doing so. In 1996 a ruling by the U.S. Supreme Court cleared away much of the legal uncertainty about the insurance market. The Supreme Court determined that annuities were investment products rather than insurance, giving banks access to one of the fastest growing markets in financial services.

In November 1999, the Gramm-Leach-Bliley Act was passed, effectively repealing the depression-era Glass-Steagall Act. A complex piece of legislation, Gramm-Leach-Bliley allows banks, insurance companies, and securities firms to affiliate with one another, through common ownership, and to enter each other's businesses. The financial modernization act preserves the current financial regulatory system, and gives the Federal Reserve Board the power to regulate financial holding companies, a new type of financial corporation created by the Gramm-Leach-Bliley Act. More than 550 financial holding companies were in existence in 2006, according to the Federal Reserve. In insurance sales, the law also preserves the authority of states to regulate insurance, but requires state insurance departments to treat bank-affiliated firms selling insurance on the same basis as other insurance agents.

The Gramm-Leach-Bliley Act, a milestone piece of legislation, provides consumers with access to a wider array of services through their current financial services provider. American families count a wide range of financial products toward their household net worth, including insurance and mutual funds.

Nearly 57 million U.S. households, fully half, own common stocks directly or through mutual funds, according to a survey by the Investment Company Institute and the Securities Industry Association in the first quarter of 2005. Between 60 percent and 70 percent of American households own some form of life insurance, according to insurance industry sources.

Financial deregulation in the emerging new economy will affect different segments of the industry in different ways. How well banks, insurance companies and other financial services firms respond to the opportunities and challenges presented by the expected convergence of banking, finance and insurance, will largely determine the longterm viability of many firms and the employment opportunities they might offer in the future.

The financial scandals triggered by the stock market meltdown of 2000–02 resulted in efforts to restore accountability in financial reporting by public corporations and a sense of fairness in the way companies release sensitive information to the public. The Sarbanes-Oxley Act of 2002, called the most sweeping change in the enforcement of securities laws since the Securities and Exchange Commission and the present-day system of securities regulation were created back in the 1930s, ushered in several new changes. Sarbanes-Oxley required accounting firms inspecting a company's financial reports to affirm that the issuing company's numbers were accurate and that the company had sufficient financial controls in place to prevent any manipulation of the data. This financial controls oversight, spelled out in Section 404 of Sarbanes-Oxley, created a whole new industry for consulting firms and accountants specializing in Sarbanes-Oxley audits. Internal auditors suddenly were given a new mission, in addition to their normal auditing functions. A new, independent, regulatory body was created—the Public Company Accounting Oversight Board—and charged with enforcing the accounting controls put into place by Sarbanes-Oxley.

Banks

U.S. commercial banks make loans to businesses and consumers, accept deposits, and offer an array of related banking services, including trust and advisory services, safe deposit boxes, securities custody, and underwriting. Thrift institutions, a category of financial institutions that includes savings and loan associations (S&Ls), savings banks, and credit unions, also offer banking services. There is no functional difference between commercial banks and thrift institutions for most routine banking services, such as home mortgages and rates offered on certificates of deposit or other interest-bearing accounts.

Compared with the banking systems in most countries, the U.S. banking industry is highly fragmented. Several thousand commercial banks compete for a piece of the business and consumer market, but the 10 largest banks dominate the industry and hold the largest portion of total banking assets. As of January 2006, these large banks owned 74 percent of U.S. banking industry assets.

The U.S. banking industry is consolidating, as larger, better-capitalized banks acquire smaller ones. The Federal Deposit Insurance Corp. reports a decline in the number of insured banks from 14,625 in 1975 to 14,500 in 1984, 9,940 in 1995, and 7,748 as of December 31, 2005. Consolidation allows banks to compete more freely, improve efficiency, boost fee-income generating opportunities and withstand competition from other financial services providers. Other benefits of bank mergers are expanded delivery networks, geographic and product diversification, and greater convenience for consumers. Banking legislation enacted in 1994 has allowed banks to open branch offices across state lines, moving the industry closer to nationwide interstate banking, and banks have since been busy consolidating their branch office networks.

Over time, savings and loan associations will become more like banks. Savings and loans, the fourth largest group of financial institutions, have gone through a rapid transition in the last 20 years. S&Ls, originally chartered in the 1930s for the purpose of originating home mortgages and promoting consumer savings, are a fast-shrinking industry. In 1990 the number of federally regulated thrift institutions (S&Ls and federal savings banks) stood at 2,616, dropping to 1,108 by December 31, 2005.

Among the factors driving this consolidation are the liquidation of insolvent S&Ls under a federally funded bailout in 1989, and acquisitions by commercial banks. Competition from mortgage bankers and mortgage brokers in the thrifts core business, home mortgages, has led many thrifts to try to become commercial banks and offer consumer and business loans, checking accounts and credit cards. In 1985 S&Ls produced 40 percent of the total mortgages in the United States, compared to 38 percent originated by mortgage bankers. By 2005 savings associations originated 26 percent of new and refinanced mortgage loans, compared with a 18 percent market share by commercial banks and 56 percent by mortgage bankers. But S&Ls trying to diversify by adding new lines of business will need to attract bankers with the necessary loan management skills. Consumer and business loans require different types of expertise than mortgage lending.

Employment Outlook

The banking industry employed over two million salaried workers in 2005, making it the largest industry in the financial services sector of the economy. Commercial banks account for the most jobs—1.6 million full-time positions, according to the American Bankers Association. The remainder were in savings and loan associations, savings banks, and credit unions. Clerical and administrative support positions accounted for the largest number of banking positions—about seven out of every 10 jobs. Bank tellers, who process routine deposits and account withdrawals for banking customers, accounted for one of four jobs in banking. Executive, managerial, and administrative employees accounted for 25 percent of banking positions.

Employment opportunities in most banking occupations will grow at a slower rate than all occupations through 2014. This decrease in employment growth is attributable to industry downsizing, shedding of unprofitable business units, and financial institution mergers. However, the pace of downsizing is expected to slow down as banks begin putting more emphasis on retaining employees. A number of banking occupations is projected to grow at a much faster pace over the next several years. Among these are customer service representatives who handle sales and marketing in branch bank offices, loan officers who develop new business and evaluate loan applications, and financial services sales representatives who sell mutual funds and investment products. Banks will also look to hire people with sales and marketing experience, particularly those with experience selling investment products and insurance. In the near term, for the next three or four years, community banks and thrift institutions may offer somewhat greater employment opportunities than large regional banks, which have mature branch banking systems and generally fewer employment opportunities.

Financial Managers and Finance Companies

There are two broad categories of finance companies: consumer finance companies and diversified financial services companies. Consumer finance companies are very similar to banks. They issue loans and lines of credit, record interest income and loan origination fees, establish reserves for potential loan defaults, and compete with each other, and with banking institutions, for a share of the multi-billion dollar consumer finance market.

Consumer finance companies are somewhat less regulated than banks, and they generally prefer to focus their lending activities on specific market niches such as credit cards and home equity credit. Examples are Associates First Capital Corp. and General Motors Acceptance Corp.

Diversified financial services companies are either large financial conglomerates, such as Citigroup, or are companies that do not fit easily into another industry grouping. Fannie Mae, a publicly owned corporation chartered to help moderate-income consumers become homeowners, is another diversified financial services company. Both consumer finance companies and diversified financial services companies are going through a period of consolidation, creating financial conglomerates of increasing size. Financial conglomerates have a distinct size advantage over smaller finance companies: they can borrow funds at very low cost; they can leverage their distribution channels by offering a wide array of products to large numbers of consumers. Finance companies, like banks, employ larger numbers of credit analysts, loan counselors and loan collectors, and customer service representatives. The largest finance companies have hundreds of service employees working in centralized customer service centers that are often staffed 24 hours a day, seven days a week.

Employment Outlook

Almost every corporation, organization, or government agency has one or more financial managers who oversee the preparation of financial reports, direct cash management activities, and manage investments. Financial managers in all industries including consumer finance, held about 528,000 jobs in 2004, according to the U.S. Labor Department. The job outlook is good for those with the right skills. As in most financial occupations, expertise in accounting and a working knowledge of information systems are fundamental to on-the-job performance. While mergers and corporate downsizing will continue to affect employment of financial managers, the need for financial expertise will keep the profession growing about as fast as average for all occupations through 2014.

Investment Services and Securities

The investment services sector has enjoyed a growth spurt in employment through the 1990s as the result of increased popularity of investment products like mutual funds and a rising stock market. While the stock market downturn in 2000–01 has erased much of the recent employment gains, employment in the industry is still near record levels. In 2004 there were 767,000 people employed in the securities industry, compared to 426,900 in 1989, according to the U.S. Department of Labor's Bureau of Labor Statistics.

Employment growth in investment services and securities can be linked to the explosive growth of financial products over the past 30 years and to a desire by consumers, especially those approaching their retirement years, for putting their financial assets in stocks or stock mutual funds over low-yielding fixed-income securities and bank deposits. Nearly three-fourths of Americans' liquid financial assets today are invested in securities-related products, such as stocks, bonds, and mutual funds (73 percent); the balance is in bank deposits and certificates of deposit, according to Federal Reserve data. This preference for owning securities as opposed to federally insured deposit accounts is a remarkable transformation, considering that in 1975 more than half of Americans' assets were in bank deposits (55 percent). The total market value of financial

assets grew from $1.7 trillion at the end of 1975 to $16.6 trillion in the third quarter of 2004, a tenfold increase since 1975, after reaching a peak of $19.3 trillion in the first quarter of 2000.

The investment services industry has two main segments: investment management, which provides investment and advisory services for individual and institutional investors; and the securities industry, which offers investment banking and brokerage services. Investment management firms oversee the investment of pools of savings such as employee retirement plans and mutual funds. The term "investment management" is very inclusive, since every type of financial institution is involved in some form of investment management activity.

Investment management firms benefited from extraordinarily favorable economic conditions in the 1990s—low inflation, low interest rates, and an exceptionally strong stock market. The result was a surge in the number of investment advisory firms and in total assets managed. Mutual funds, the largest investment services group, report sales and performance data to the Securities and Exchange Commission; fund companies represent a burgeoning portion of the investment services market. Investable assets managed by mutual fund companies grew to $9.1 trillion by January 2006 from just under $1 trillion at year-end 1990. According to the investment Company Institute, an industry professional association, there were 8,044 mutual funds in the United States in 2005, or nearly triple the number of funds in existence a decade earlier.

Changing population demographics is the primary driver behind the increase in sales of investment products. The aging of the baby boomer generation, the 81 million people born between 1946 and 1964, is largely responsible for baby boomers shifting assets from bank deposits into securities. Investment management is not a capital intensive business. It is a service business, so a mutual fund company's employees are its most important asset. Key employees in a mutual fund company are portfolio managers and investment analysts who formulate investment strategy and make decisions about portfolio holdings. Mutual funds also employ securities traders, sales people, and marketing professionals, in addition to the various clerical support staff who perform administrative functions.

Brokerage Services and Investment Banking

The securities industry, consisting of brokerage services and investment banking, is one of the oldest in the country. It is even older than the country itself, going back to the colonial days when traders bought and sold stock certificates under the legendary buttonwood tree, near the present-day site of the New York Stock Exchange. The securities industry is very concentrated. The 280 largest firms, members of the New York Stock Exchange, collectively hold about 70 percent of the industry's total assets, according to Standard & Poor's Corp.

Securities firms perform a wide range of client services, including the following: executing trades of stocks, bonds, commodities, and options; conducting company and industry research; underwriting new offerings of securities (investment banking); advising corporate clients and government agencies on investment strategy. Most securities firms also own a brokerage affiliate, which performs the actual buying or selling of securities for individual investors, corporate clients, and government agencies. Securities firms have been classified as belonging to one of the groups outlined below:

- National full-service firms, also known as "wirehouses," offer a complete range of financing and brokerage services and have extensive branch office networks. Examples are Merrill Lynch & Co. and A.G. Edwards.
- Large investment banks, such as Goldman Sachs Group Inc., serving corporations and other institutional clients; these have limited branching networks.
- Regional brokers or full-service broker-dealers with branch networks in a limited geographic region, which service mainly retail clients. An example is Morgan-Keegan, Inc.
- New York City–based regional brokers, which service domestic and international clients. An example is Gruntal, Inc.
- Discount brokers, who service the investment needs of retail investors.

Employment Outlook

Employment in the investment services and securities industries is projected to grow about 10 percent, a faster rate than for all occupations through 2014. The primary drivers of job growth are increasing investments in securities and commodities. People saving for their retirement years have shifted a significant portion of their assets from traditional savings products such as bank savings accounts and certificates of deposit to market- sensitive investments to lock in the higher rates of return available in common stocks. This trend may continue as long as interest rates remain relatively low on competing, but lower risk, savings and bank CD accounts.

The need for skilled financial managers to manage mutual fund portfolios, analyze investment securities for fund managers, manage portfolio risk, and maintain compliance with industry regulations will create employment opportunities. Financial services sales representatives, who are often employed by commercial banks or other depository financial institutions, will also be in demand. Also contributing to increased job growth is the increased "globalization" of the securities industry, as securities exchanges around the world link up to provide greater access to securities listed on local or regional stock exchanges.

The stock market bubble of 2000–02 took its toll on securities industry employment as investors retreated from technology stocks, which took the worst beating, for the relative safety of dividend-paying stocks and fixed-income securities. Between 2001 and 2003 the securities industry went through one of its worst contractions. The industry lost 83,100 jobs nationwide between the peak of 840,900 in March 2001 and the low of 757,800 in May 2003, according to the Securities Industry Association. After bottoming in May 2003, the industry has regained a total of 41,100 jobs—a 5.4 percent increase over an 18-month period to 798,900 in November 2004, or a recovery of less than half the job losses from peak to trough.

Insurance

The insurance industry provides financial protection against various kinds of losses, such as accidental death, fire, sickness and injury, or loss of income. The industry has two main components: insurance carriers (also called *insurers*) that underwrite insurance policies, assuming financial risk; and insurance agents or brokers who sell insurance policies to businesses and individuals. Insurance carriers are generally large companies, although many small insurers actively compete for a piece of the insurance market. Insurance agents and brokers are generally employees of small companies or are self-employed professionals.

Insurance carriers offer a variety of insurance policies. Many have expanded their product offerings to include investment products and advisory services, largely in response to the competitive threat from banks and other financial intermediaries. Life insurers today offer tax deferred annuities, estate planning, and tax planning services in addition to providing death-benefit coverage. Some property and casualty insurers, notably personal lines carriers, have expanded to the retirement savings market to compensate for slower growth rates in auto insurance and other traditional business lines.

The 1999 financial modernization legislation, leveling the competitive playing field in financial services, will encourage insurers to look for new ways to cut operating expenses and distribute insurance products through alternative channels. Some insurers are exploring direct marketing and Internet-based distribution, while others are looking to expand their distribution channels by selling insurance through bank branch offices. If successful, these alternative sales channels, bypassing the traditional agent-broker distribution network, could mean that at least some insurance sales and marketing positions will be created outside the traditional insurance industry.

The insurance industry employed about 2.3 million workers in 2004, including both insurance carriers and agents and brokers, according to the Bureau of Labor Statistics. Insurance carriers, located mostly in urban centers, have large corporate staffs and provide about seven out of every 10 insurance jobs. This portion of the insurance industry is dominated by very large companies; insurers employing 250 or more workers account for more than half of all jobs at insurance carriers. Insurers with 50 or more employees account for 80 percent of the insurance carrier positions.

Insurance workers who work directly with the public—agents, brokers, and claims adjusters—are located through out the country. These workers typically work in much smaller organizations. Approximately 40 percent work in agencies or insurance brokerage offices with fewer than 10 employees. Another 30 percent are employed by organizations with 10 to 49 employees.

Administrative support workers, including clerical employees, account for four out of 10 insurance jobs. Executives, administrators, managerial, and sales workers hold most of the remaining jobs. Entry-level clerical positions generally require a high school diploma, whereas executive and managerial positions require some specialized industry knowledge and a college degree.

One of the fastest growing fields in insurance is the business of alternative risk transfer. This type of insurance provides loss protection for a variety of risks that only a short time ago were thought to be uninsurable. Alternative risk transfer insurance often combines some form of event- related risk, such as weather-related risk or merger and acquisition risk, with a conventional business insurance policy in a single comprehensive policy.

Employment Outlook

Employment opportunities in insurance are projected to grow about 10 percent, a slower rate than in all industries through 2014, according to the Bureau of Labor Statistics, despite an expected increase in demand, especially for long-term healthcare insurance, annuities, and other investment products. Overall employment growth will be limited by insurance company mergers, computerization, and a trend toward direct sales and telephone marketing. Even so, thousands of job openings will be created as current employees retire or leave the field.

Employment opportunities for claims professionals, risk managers, and specialists in alternative risk transfer are expected to grow at an above average rate over the next several years as companies strive to improve customer service. Claims examiner and claims inspection positions require frequent contact with policyholders and are difficult to automate.

HOW TO USE THIS BOOK

The job descriptions in this book provide an overview and discussion of more than 80 positions involving banking, insurance, and finance. They are divided into six categories: Banking, Accounting and Corporate Finance, Insurance, Investment Banking and Securities, Money Management, and Supervisory Agencies.

Employers often have different job descriptions for the same position, so there can be wide differences in position responsibilities from one employer to another. A company's size, organizational structure, management style, and other factors determine specific job requirements—the duties an employee is expected to perform. The position descriptions on the following pages are intended as generic descriptions, based on publicly available information and interviews with industry experts. Each entry is organized as follows:

Career Profile

The entry begins with a section that briefly summarizes key aspects of the position, including duties, salary range, employment and advancement prospects, education, experience, skills, and personality traits.

Career Ladder

This section indicates the location of the position within a typical career path, such as Bank Teller, Teller Supervisor, Assistant Branch Manager, and Branch Office Manager. Not all the positions listed in a career ladder are discussed separately in the book. Some organizations, typically larger financial institutions, have many grades or steps within each level of the ladder.

Position Description

This section describes in detail the tasks associated with the position, the typical workplace, and how the position relates to other positions. Bulleted lists are often used to summarize important tasks or concentrations.

Salaries

This is an *approximate* indication of what an individual may expect to earn in this position in 2007. Generally, this reflects a range from entry level to moderately experienced. Highly experienced individuals or those with highly specialized skills may earn considerably more. The factors that determine how much money a person will earn in this position may include:

- the educational qualifications and experience of the individual at the time of hiring—higher education and more experience generally bring a higher starting salary

- whether the individual has particular skills that are high in demand
- the number of workers competing for openings (which can be influenced by educational trends and geographical concentration)
- economic growth and wage inflation

You can refine this analysis by consulting the latest salary surveys on the World Wide Web (see Appendix VII: Internet Resources).

Employment Prospects

This section treats many of the above factors from the point of view of how they affect the applicant's chances of being hired. Technological changes have reduced demand for some positions, such as loan processing clerks in banking. On the other hand, the growing complexity of the financial services industry has driven up demand for positions such as financial analyst or risk analyst. The discussion also includes trends that may influence future demand for the position and ways in which applicants might improve their prospects.

Advancement Prospects

The opportunities to move up the career ladder from this position are discussed in this section. The typical paths to advancement such as through greater specialization, going into independent practice, or going into management, are also reviewed.

Education and Training

This covers the level of education or training likely to be required by prospective employers, such as high school graduate, two-year college (associate degree), four-year college (B.A. or B.S. degree), or graduate degree (M.S. or M.B.A.), as well as recommended courses or subject areas. Additional training or industry certification is included where appropriate.

Experience, Skills, and Personality Traits

Experience and demonstrable skills are often as important as education. This section summarizes the intellectual and social skills as well as the kind of personality traits that are most likely to lead to success in such a position.

Unions and Associations

Most positions discussed in this book are professional or specialist positions and may have professional organizations devoted to them. This section characterizes the kind of associations that a person in this position may wish to join, with some examples given. Appendix III lists many more organizations broken down into categories.

Tips for Entry

This final section gives a series of suggestions that can help an individual prepare for entry into the position. The first suggestions are geared to high school or college students who are still choosing courses, internships, or work-study opportunities. Later suggestions give pointers for gaining work experience for the résumé, and, eventually, entry-level positions.

Other Resources in This Book

The appendixes that follow the job descriptions contain additional resources that can help with career research and job hunting. Appendix I and Appendix II list colleges and universities offering four-year and graduate degree programs. The other appendixes feature selected professional trade associations and organizations, federal agencies, industry periodicals and career-related books, and tips on how to use the Internet during a job search.

ACKNOWLEDGMENTS

Employment opportunities in financial services are as varied as the industry itself. The task of putting together a representative sampling of job descriptions in banking, insurance, securities, and money management is a neverending one. The key players—the banks, insurance companies, securities firms, and others—are constantly adjusting in what is now a global services market, creating new positions with new requirements and refining older ones. The pages that follow are a collaborative effort with assistance from numerous individuals and many different sources. The author gratefully acknowledges the organizations that contributed research materials, job descriptions, salary data, and other information useful to the preparation of this book.

Thanks to the following: American Credit Alliance; American Bankers Association's Center for Banking Information; America's Community Bankers; ACTEX, An Actuarial Recruiter; Association for Financial Professionals; NBY Jaywalk Inc.; Bank Administration Institute; Beardsley Brown & Bassett; Capital Markets Credit Analysts Society; The CFA Institute; The College of Insurance; Crown Advisors; Credit Suisse First Boston; The Delves Group; The Financial Planning Association; Liberty Mutual Group; The Institute of Internal Auditors; Mortgage Bankers Association of America; National Association of Enrolled Agents; New Alliance Bank; New York State Department of Insurance; Prudential Financial Services; Ruzek O'Malley Burns; Securities Industry Association; TIS Consulting and Publishing; Warburg Dillon Read; The Westminster Group; Williams Financial Group.

In addition to the companies and organizations cited above, the following provided research information and employment surveys or made other contributions. Their contributions are gratefully acknowledged: *ABA Banking Journal; American Banker;* American Institute of Banking; Insurance Information Institute; Alliance of American Insurers; National Association of Colleges and Employers; Center for Futures Education, Inc.; Robert Half International; and the U.S. Department of Labor's Bureau of Labor Statistics.

BANKING

ACCOUNT EXECUTIVE, BANKING

CAREER PROFILE

Duties: Solicits residential mortgage loans originated by mortgage brokers and correspondent financial institutions; builds broker network through networking, cold calling, and prospecting

Alternate Title(s): Wholesale Account Manager, Mortgage Broker Channel Manager

Salary Range: $50,000 to $100,000

Employment Prospects: Good

Advancement Prospects: Fair

Prerequisites:

Education or Training—Four-year college degree

Experience—Three to five years of mortgage banking experience with emphasis on sales

Special Skills and Personality Traits—Detailed knowledge of the mortgage origination process, including deal structuring and underwriting; working knowledge of PC software programs; ability to work independently; excellent communication skills

CAREER LADDER

```
┌─────────────────────────────────┐
│  Group or Division Sales Manager │
└─────────────────────────────────┘

┌─────────────────────────────────┐
│      Regional Sales Manager      │
└─────────────────────────────────┘

┌─────────────────────────────────┐
│        Account Executive         │
└─────────────────────────────────┘
```

Position Description

The mortgage Account Executive is responsible for developing and managing the national or regional sales efforts of a mortgage broker network or third-party channel. In mortgage banking, the account executive acts as a primary liaison with mortgage brokers and correspondent financial institutions (mortgage originators that sell their loan production to larger financial institutions). The Account Executive, or account manager, is responsible for generating quality loans through the mortgage broker network. Account Executives maintain regular contacts with wholesale loan customers to provide advice regarding bank products, sales presentations, rates, and fees; to answer technical questions; and to act as a liaison for underwriting and funding. In addition, Account Executives provide management with market data and cross-sell other bank products and services.

Mortgage brokers are independent sales companies that originate residential mortgages for sale to mortgage companies, banks, savings associations, or mortgage banking subsidiaries of investment banks. The 53,000 operating mortgage brokerage firms in the United States accounted

for 68 percent of residential mortgage loan originations in 2004, according to Wholesale Access, a mortgage industry research firm. About 47 percent of this loan production was in subprime loans and "Alt A" loans (higher-quality loans with minor defects in title or loan documentation). The average mortgage brokerage sold its loan production to 13 wholesale financial institutions. About two-thirds of the residential mortgage loans originated in 2005 were originated by independent mortgage brokers that sell their loan production to larger financial institutions (known as wholesale mortgage companies) that in turn package residential mortgage loans into pools for sale or securitization in the secondary mortgage market.

The Account Executive maintains daily contact with sources of loan production, including correspondent financial institutions or mortgage brokers, to ensure a smooth flow of loan applications and closed loans (completed loan packages) to the company. The Account Executive takes mortgage applications from wholesale source clients; assists clients in reviewing, credit grading, pricing, and structuring of subprime mortgage loans; and answers client questions about the status of loans during loan processing. The Account Executive keeps mortgage brokers informed about current rates and mortgage programs available and pre-underwrites loans to expedite loan processing.

Salaries

Account Executives receive a base salary plus commissions in the first year, averaging $50,000. Second-year potential income is $65,000 to $80,000. Top-producing Account Executives can earn $100,000 or more within five years.

Employment Prospects

Demand for mortgage wholesale Account Executives is tied to the fortunes of the mortgage industry. Demand is higher in periods of strong mortgage production in subprime loans, as in 2004–05, when subprime originations boomed while higher-credit quality mortgages (prime mortgages) lagged. Subprime lending is less sensitive to the interest rate than prime mortgages are and more tied to borrower needs to refinance higher-cost consumer credit loans. Demand for Account Executives may lag if residential mortgage production begins to decline.

Most of the employment opportunities for wholesale mortgage Account Executives are with the top 200 U.S. mortgage companies, which have extensive nationwide or multistate mortgage production networks. The mortgage origination business is highly concentrated among the largest mortgage companies, according to the industry research firm Wholesale Access. The 25 largest mortgage firms account for about 80 percent of the high-quality prime mortgage market (loans to home owners considered average or above average credit risks in their ability to repay a home mortgage). Another 100 banking companies are significant players in the subprime residential mortgage market, and these firms also purchase most of their loan production from mortgage brokers.

Advancement Prospects

Account Executives advance in their career by meeting sales goals. They can potentially advance into more senior positions such as area manager or district manager, in charge of a larger geographic territory. Another option is to take a position with a larger mortgage company, with a correspondent increase in base compensation, commission revenue, and other employee benefits.

Education and Training

Some college courses are normally required, and most financial institutions prefer a four-year degree with courses in business, marketing, or finance. Applicants should also have working knowledge of residential mortgage loan production, deal structuring, and underwriting.

Experience, Skills, and Personality Traits

Three to five years of experience in direct sales and marketing of wholesale mortgage lending products to the mortgage broker community is a minimum qualification. Prior experience in mortgage banking, preferably with subprime mortgage loans, is generally a requirement, as is some prior experience in financial sales. A detailed knowledge of subprime mortgage production is important, as is a proven track record of originating subprime loans. Other important skills are an ability to make marketing presentations, an ability to analyze and evaluate sales situations, strong written and oral communication skills, strong client relation skills, and an ability to work closely with prime Account Executives in the local market. Proficiency with MS Office Suite and sales force automation software is also required.

Unions and Associations

There are no unions or associations for mortgage banking account executives.

Tips for Entry

1. Bank Web sites are a good place to start looking for open positions.
2. Business networking through local or state chapters of mortgage banking or mortgage brokerage associations such as the National Association of Mortgage Brokers can also lead to opportunities in the field.
3. Experience in sales or marketing is a transferable skill, so personal contacts with prior employers can produce job referrals.

BANK TELLER

CAREER PROFILE

Duties: Handles all forms of customer transactions; processes deposits and cashes checks; receives customer inquiries and refers service requests to appropriate bank departments

Alternate Title(s): Branch Sales Associate, Financial Associate

Salary Range: $17,475 to $20,878

Employment Prospects: Good

Advancement Prospects: Fair

Prerequisites:

Education or Training—High school degree or equivalent; on-the-job training provided by financial institutions

Experience—Increasing levels of responsibility; prior experience in bookkeeping or accounting; or handling cash and working with the public a plus

Special Skills and Personality Traits—Attention to detail; pleasant, courteous personality; good telephone skills; aptitude with mathematics; working knowledge of cash handling and transaction processing in a retail environment

CAREER LADDER

Assistant Branch Manager or Branch Manager

Teller Supervisor

Teller

Position Description

Bank Tellers cash checks, make deposits and withdrawals, and handle a variety of other transactions for bank customers. Tellers are employed by commercial banks, finance companies, savings and loan associations, and credit unions. They generally work a 35-hour to 40-hour week; working evenings and Saturdays is often required. Tellers are supervised by head tellers or teller supervisors, who monitor their work and help tellers fix accounting discrepancies in their daily cash drawer. Tellers are becoming increasingly involved in marketing of financial products. Tellers identify cross-selling opportunities, or sales of additional products to bank customers. Tellers refer new business customers and loan customers to customer service representatives.

In large financial institutions, Bank Tellers identified by the type of financial transaction they handle. Note tellers receive and issue promissory notes and record these transactions in a ledger. Foreign banknote tellers work in the exchange department, where they count out foreign currencies exchanged for dollars. They may also sell foreign currency and traveler's checks. Collection and exchange tellers accept payments made in forms other than cash, such as contracts, mortgages, or government securities.

Their duties include:

- handling customer transactions such as checking or savings deposits, check cashing, and savings withdrawals
- selling money orders and official bank checks
- selling and redeeming U.S. savings bonds
- preparing coin and currency for retail customers
- accepting credit card, mortgage, and loan payments
- accepting utility payments
- accepting bankcard deposits from retail merchants
- balancing automated teller machines and replenishing ATM cash
- processing ATM deposits

- promoting banking services and answering customer inquiries
- referring loan requests to the appropriate banking department
- balancing cash drawer daily

The Bank Teller's job is an entry level position. Starting tellers are either recruited from outside the financial institution, usually through newspaper advertisements, or are promoted from clerical positions. This is a good job for individuals who are detail oriented and like working with people.

Salaries

Teller salaries vary according to the financial institution's size and location, formal education, training, and experience. Annual salaries for Bank Tellers ranged from $17,475 to $20,878 according to America's Community Bankers, a banking trade association. The median bank teller salary in 2004 was $19,138; the highest annual salary was $59,488. Fringe benefits of Bank Tellers are usually very good. In addition to salary, full-time tellers receive health insurance coverage, employer-paid education and training, and can participate in their employer's 401 (k) savings plan. About one-fourth of tellers employed are part-time tellers, who provide additional staffing during peak banking hours. Part-time tellers are paid an hourly rate but do not receive benefits such as employer-paid health insurance.

Employment Prospects

Tellers are hired as new employees or are promoted from clerical or bookkeeping positions. Over the next several years there will be a decline in the total number of teller jobs as consumers do more of their banking at automated teller machines, instead of the teller window. However, teller turnover is high in most regions of the country Financial institutions are continually hiring new Bank Tellers to replace tellers lost through job turnover or promotion to other positions in banking, especially in urban areas.

Individuals with previous experience handling cash in banking or who have worked in customer service positions in other industries are the most desirable candidates. Many financial institutions maintain evening and weekend hours in retail branches, which means there are plenty of opportunities for part-time tellers, especially for evenings, Saturdays, and Sundays, in supermarket and shopping mall branch offices.

Advancement Prospects

Advancement can be to a position of increased responsibility such as head teller in a branch office or collection teller in the corporate services department. Banks tend to promote internally when filling vacancies for teller supervisor and customer service representative positions. Tellers may also find opportunities for advancement in clerical positions in the lending or deposit services departments, credit card department, auditing, and bank trust departments.

Education and Training

Initial teller training is usually provided by the bank in a format which combines classroom instruction and branch observation and instruction. Most tellers receive at least one week of on-the-job training shortly after being hired. Many banks provide or make available continuing training to enhance skills and knowledge in sales skills, product knowledge, and supervisory skills. Banks also pay tuition costs for classes taken after banking hours at the American Institute of Banking, the educational affiliate of the American Bankers Association, or banking courses sponsored by Bankers Training & Consulting Company, a division of Bank Administration Institute (http://www.bankerstraining.com).

Experience, Skills, and Personality Traits

The teller position requires good communication skills, both written and verbal. Also important are good people management skills, good telephone skills, an aptitude for mathematics and problem solving, great attention to detail, and ability to handle large amounts of cash in a safe and accurate manner. Also important in today's banking world is familiarity with computer systems and an ability to use computer terminals to process transactions and get access to account information. A knowledge of basic accounting is important in balancing the teller's cash drawer daily. Bank Tellers should have a working knowledge of the transaction processing systems used in a retail branch banking office. This knowledge is typically acquired through on-the-job training and is not a condition of employment.

Unions and Associations

Bank Tellers can join organizations such as American Institute of Banking, the educational affiliate of the American Bankers Association. The AIB offers correspondence courses in banking and classroom training at local colleges and universities.

Tips for Entry

1. Prior experience handling cash or serving customers in retail or service industry, or experience in an insurance agency is helpful.
2. There are often more opportunities for part-time and supermarket tellers than full-time Bank Tellers.
3. Financial institutions in urban markets are always looking for bilingual tellers.
4. Check job listings in local newspapers, or the Web sites of local banks, for Bank Teller opportunities.

CUSTOMER SERVICE REPRESENTATIVE, BANKING

CAREER PROFILE

Duties: Opens deposit accounts for bank customers; interviews customers to obtain financial information and explain services available; help customers resolve account problems; may help customers complete loan applications

Alternate Title(s): Customer Service Clerk, Financial Services Representative, New Accounts Representative

Salary Range: $20,800 to $26,533

Employment Prospects: Excellent

Advancement Prospects: Good

Prerequisites:

Education or Training—High school diploma or equivalent; must go through teller training and CSR training

Experience—Previous banking experience useful but not required; one year customer service and sales experience; previous banking experience a plus

Special Skills and Personality Traits—Must be able to interview customers and communicate information clearly; know how to open accounts and be familiar with the bank's consumer deposit products; must be familiar with bank deposit and credit products and bank procedures for opening new accounts; have general understanding of required consumer disclosures; pass the selection process

CAREER LADDER

```
┌─────────────────────────────┐
│   Assistant Branch Manager   │
│      or Branch Manager       │
└─────────────────────────────┘

┌─────────────────────────────┐
│ Customer Service Representative │
└─────────────────────────────┘

┌─────────────────────────────┐
│         Bank Teller          │
└─────────────────────────────┘
```

Position Description

Customer Service Representatives perform functions such as opening new checking or savings accounts and retirement accounts, assisting customers with queries about bank services, and helping customers resolve account problems. They work in branch offices of financial institutions or in customer service centers where they answer customer telephone requests.

Customer Service Representatives assist banking customers by answering questions about their accounts and available banking services. They greet prospective customers and gather information from the customer needed to open an account. If the customer is opening a new deposit account, they may accept the initial deposit and set up the account by entering the necessary account information into a computer terminal.

They usually work with deposit-account customers, but may also provide information on home mortgages, equity credit lines, and credit cards. They may help customers fill out loan applications or refer an application to the loan department. Customer Service Representatives may also cross-sell additional banking services to customers who have only one or two banking accounts, for example, offering to take a credit card application for a customer who has a checking account or savings account.

Being a Customer Service Representative may be a full-time or part-time job, depending on the size of the branch office. Small branches may staff the CSR position with part-time employees and schedule working hours according to customer activity.

Duties performed include the following:

- interviewing customers to obtain personal financial information and explain available services
- opening new deposit accounts and accepting loan applications
- answering customer questions and investigating account errors
- presenting funds received from customers to a bank teller for deposit and obtaining receipt for the customer
- assisting customer in filling out loan applications
- obtaining credit records from a credit reporting agency
- admitting customers to safe deposit vault
- executing wire transfers of funds

Salaries

Salaries for Customer Service Representatives in banking averaged between $20,800 and $26,533 in 2004, according to America's Community Bankers, a banking trade group. Customer Service Representatives may also qualify for incentive compensation for new accounts opened or meeting performance goals. Average annual salary for full-time service representatives, including incentive or bonus pay, was $24,521 in 2003.

Employment Prospects

Customer Service Representatives work in commercial banks, savings and loan associations, and credit unions. The CSR position is a trainee position in most financial institutions. Job growth in larger institutions may be limited due to industry mergers; however some jobs will be created from employee turnover. Newly created financial institutions will also have a continuing need for Customer Service Representatives. Most CSRs are newly hired employees or are promoted from bank teller or other clerical positions.

Advancement Prospects

Depending on their experience and qualifications, Customer Service Representatives have several advancement options in banking. They can advance to more senior branch office positions such as assistant branch manager and branch offi-

cer manager. Another alternative is advancement to a position in loan operations or item processing (check clearing) operations.

Education and Training

Employers require Customer Service Representatives to have a high school degree or equivalent diploma. Many prefer candidates with some college courses in business, marketing, or related fields. Financial institutions provide on-the-job training to new employees, and also sponsor continuing education courses at organizations such as American Institute of Banking.

Experience, Skills, and Personality Traits

Applicants generally need at least six months experience in retail banking, starting as a branch office bank teller. Most financial institutions also require some sales experience in cross-marketing (selling) financial products or services. Customer Service Representatives should have good telephone skills and interpersonal skills, and be able to assist customers in resolving routine account problems.

Unions and Associations

Customer Service Representatives might belong to banking associations such as the American Institute of Banking (the educational affiliate of the American Bankers Association) or America's Community Bankers. AIB has state chapters offering continuing education courses in most states. These groups offer networking opportunities, continuing education, and other professional services and support.

Tips for Entry

1. Take an employment application directly from the hiring financial institution.
2. Network with other professionals to learn about currently available job openings.
3. Courses in retail banking and consumer lending (available from American Institute of Banking) can provide you with valuable knowledge about a career in retail banking.
4. To learn more about banking opportunities in your state, visit Web sites such as http://www.careerbuilder.com or http://www.Nationjob.com.

PERSONAL BANKER

CAREER PROFILE

Duties: Services high-net-worth accounts; manages business and individual customer deposit and loan portfolio; refers business to investment management, trust, and other departments as needed

Alternate Title(s): Private Banker, Relationship Banker

Salary Range: $30,000 to $75,000 and up

Employment Prospects: Good

Advancement Prospects: Good

Prerequisites:

Education or Training—Bachelor's degree with courses in accounting and finance; additional training provided by financial institution

Experience—Three to six years of retail banking experience, or related financial services experience marketing financial services

Special Skills and Personality Traits—Excellent written and verbal communication skills; good organizational and customer service skills; ability to handle multiple tasks in a busy environment; strong sales experience; experience dealing with public accounting and law firms; knowledge of consumer banking, credit and business banking services; experience handling trusts, investments, tax insurance, real estate management, estate planning and financial planning; formal credit training

Special Requirements—Series 7 registered representative and Series 63 brokerage licenses are required in some situations

CAREER LADDER

```
┌─────────────────────────────────┐
│   Personal Banking Supervisor   │
└─────────────────────────────────┘

┌─────────────────────────────────┐
│        Personal Banker          │
└─────────────────────────────────┘

┌─────────────────────────────────┐
│     Consumer Loan Officer       │
└─────────────────────────────────┘
```

Position Description

Personal Bankers provide customized banking services to high-net worth businesses and individuals. They act as a financial adviser in helping clients develop an overall wealth management strategy. Business development efforts may include loan generation, and trust and investment management referrals. They manage all aspects of a client portfolio, including investments and insurance. Personal Bankers must build a portfolio of regular clients, much like stock brokers do in the securities industry.

Personal Bankers work a standard 35- to 40-hour week, usually working in branch offices or central office locations. Some may work evenings and weekends to service customers who prefer meeting their banking officer after working hours.

Their duties include:

- opening, closing, and servicing customer accounts
- writing individual profiles of current and prospective customers
- actively cross-selling banking products such as loans and retirement accounts to customers serviced
- calling on customers at home during evenings and weekends
- referring clients to trust management, investment department (mutual funds), and loan departments

- processing loan documents
- resolving client problems such as checking account overdrafts
- recommending other banking services as needed
- representing the bank at community civic club and service club events.

Personal Bankers are sometimes referred to as private bankers. Personal Bankers may work from an office or from their homes. They typically manage 75 to 125 account relationships. They spend much of their day on the road traveling to meet clients, and they stay in contact with their offices and clients via laptop computer, cellular phone, or pager.

Salaries
Salaries of Personal Bankers vary with experience, academic background, and size of financial institution. Larger banks that have trust departments and retail brokerage operations often pay the highest salaries. Salaries of Personal Bankers increase with on-the-job experience. Personal bankers with one to three years of experience earned salaries between $30,000 and $50,000 in 2005, according to Robert Half International Inc., a staffing services firm. Personal Bankers with three or more years of experience earned between $35,000 and $50,000 annually. Private bankers servicing high-net-worth customers earn higher salaries, ranging from $45,000 to $75,000. Private bankers may receive incentive bonuses as part of compensation and the use of a company car.

Employment Prospects
There are good employment opportunities for Personal Bankers. Opportunities for experienced Personal Bankers should grow slightly faster then the job growth in the overall economy. Financial institution services catering to the high–net worth market have become very competitive in the last 10 years. Individuals with prior lending experience with business customers, or trust account customers, should be in greatest demand. Many financial institutions promote employees with prior customer service experience to Personal Banker and private banker positions.

Advancement Prospects
Personal Bankers can advance to positions of increased responsibility, by taking on a larger client base (or manag-

ing a more select group of clients) or moving up to aa management position in retail banking. Another option is taking a sales and marketing position in a bank's trust department or retail brokerage subsidiary.

Education and Training
There is no specific academic program for a career in personal banking. A four-year degree with courses in accounting, finance, marketing, and communication is a general requirement. Also helpful are courses in the liberal arts since Personal Bankers work on a regular basis with a more exclusive group of bank customers.

Experience, Skills, and Personality Traits
Prior lending experience in retail banking is considered essential to the position. Experience in sales or marketing trust department products is also a preferred qualification. Personal Bankers need to have excellent communication and organizational skills since they spend much of their day working independently.

Special Requirements
In some financial institutions a brokerage registered representative license (Series 7 Exam) and financial adviser license (Series 63 Exam) are required for Personal Bankers who sell investment products in addition to bank deposit accounts and loans.

Unions and Associations
Personal Bankers can join professional associations such as the American Bankers Association for networking and career advancement opportunities.

Tips for Entry
1. If you have prior lending experience, your customer experience and contacts can open the door to an interview.
2. Networking is key to success in this position, much like any sales job. Attend meetings of local civic organizations to learn about job opportunities.
3. Follow newspaper ads and apply directly to the financial institution advertising the position.
4. Take college courses in business and marketing to gain insights into small business management.

BRANCH MANAGER, BANKING

CAREER PROFILE

Duties: Managing customer relationships; opening new accounts and originating loans; handling customer service problems; supervising branch employees

Alternate Title(s): Branch Sales Manager

Salary Range: $35,402 to $50,283

Employment Prospects: Good

Advancement Prospects: Excellent

Prerequisites:

Education or Training—Four-year college degree with emphasis in business or finance preferred; two-year degree may be acceptable with related work experience

Experience—Three to five years in banking or financial services industry

Special Skills and Personality Traits—Knowledge of banking and consumer protection regulations, consumer and small business lending; willingness to meet sales goals; good computer skills (word processing and spreadsheet software programs); must have prior experience in banking or related financial services industry; meet specified position requirements

Special Requirements—Series 7 securities brokerage license preferred

CAREER LADDER

```
┌─────────────────────────────┐
│      Regional Manager       │
└─────────────────────────────┘

┌─────────────────────────────┐
│       Branch Manager        │
└─────────────────────────────┘

┌─────────────────────────────┐
│   Assistant Branch Manager  │
└─────────────────────────────┘
```

Position Description

A Branch Manager in banking is responsible for overseeing all the activities in a branch office, including opening new accounts, loan origination, and solving customer problems. The manager is responsible for establishing relationships with business and retail customers, and increasing the total deposits in the branch office under their supervision. The Branch Manager may be employed by a commercial bank, credit union, finance company, savings and loan association, or savings bank.

The business of banking is changing, largely a result of recent financial modernization allowing banks to sell a greater variety of financial products and intensifying competition for market share among all financial institutions. The new environment will add new responsibilities to the Branch Manager's job. Branch Managers will become more

directly involved in the sale of insurance and investment products, authorized by the 1999 Financial Services Modernization Act (the Gramm-Leach-Bliley Act), the federal legislation permitting bank affiliations with insurance companies and brokerage firms.

While the overall financial services market is changing, banking Branch Managers will still devote much of their day to marketing conventional banking services to current and prospective customers. These services may include checking accounts, savings accounts, certificates of deposit, residential mortgages, equity credit lines, retirement accounts, checking overdraft protection, credit cards, automated teller machine cards, bill payment services, online banking accounts, and other banking products. In addition, the manager may also sell non-bank financial products (not backed by federal deposit insurance) such as annuities, life insurance, and mutual funds, if the manager is licensed to sell investment and insurance products.

In servicing the financial needs of business customers, the manager is responsible for identifying new business lending opportunities, including loans guaranteed by the federal Small Business Administration, and referring prospective business loan customers to the commercial loan department. The manager is responsible for servicing the checking and other deposit accounts of commercial loan customers with accounts at their branch. In addition, the manager refers new mortgage loan customers to the mortgage department, and identifies opportunities for customer referrals to the bank's trust department. The manager may schedule meetings in their branch between a trust account officer and bank customers asking for help with their investments.

The Branch Manager directs and coordinates activities in their branch to implement the bank's policies, including procedures and practices concerning bank lines of credit, consumer loans, commercial loans, and real estate loans. Throughout their work, Branch Managers are responsible for supervision and training of branch office staff, including tellers, sales associates, and customer service representatives.

Branch Managers fulfill various duties in their jobs, including the following:

- Examining, evaluating, and processing loan applications
- Talking to customers to resolve complaints and account problems
- Approving checking account overdrafts by business and retail customers
- Interviewing and hiring branch employees
- Evaluating branch office income and expenses
- Recommending new loan opportunities or customer relationships to bank management or the board of directors
- Evaluating weekly or monthly sales data and report sales results to bank management
- Planning and developing policies and procedures to carry out management directives
- Conducting annual job performance reviews of branch employees
- Contacting customers, prospective customers, and civic organizations to promote goodwill and generate new business opportunities
- Preparing financial and regulatory reports as required by the bank's internal auditor, board of directors, and state and federal banking regulatory agencies

Salaries

Salaries are determined by several factors, including years of experience, geographic location, and customer deposits at the branch office managed. In 2004, Branch Managers of banking branch offices with deposits of $15 to $25 million earned between $35,402 and $46,224 in base salary annually; managers of $25 to $50 million branch offices earned between $38,815 and $50,283, according to America's Community Bankers. Commissions and incentive bonuses provide additional compensation. For example, the average annual salary, including commissions, for managers of $25 to $50 million deposit bank branches was $47,807. Branch Managers working in metropolitan areas such as Atlanta, Chicago, Los Angeles, or New York generally earn higher salaries than managers in non-metropolitan areas, in some regions over $60,000.

In addition to their base salary, branch managers may receive incentive compensation for loan referrals resulting in new commercial loans or mortgages. Incentive compensation may be a flat fee or a percentage of the dollar value of new loans or deposits. Branch Managers may also receive brokerage commissions from sales of annuities and mutual funds. Branch Managers are salaried employees, and typically do not received overtime wages; however, managers may received paid compensation for working Saturday mornings, when many customers do their routine banking activities. Managers of supermarket branch offices typically are compensated with paid days off for working a weekend shift.

Employment Prospects

Employment opportunities for banking branch office managers are expected to grow about as fast as average through 2014 and possibly faster than average in markets with above-average population growth. There are two main drivers behind this trend. Banks are refocusing their attention on serving customers through networks of conveniently located branch offices, countering the potential downsizing effects of bank mergers. Second, banks are adding investment services and insurance to their service offerings as they try to capture a greater share of their customers' total finances. Financial managers with sales experience in either of these markets—and the licenses to sell securities or insurance— will find greater opportunities in the years ahead. Employment opportunities in banking are sensitive to changes in the overall economy, which could mean fewer available jobs if the economy begins to slow, but the longer term outlook remains quite positive.

Advancement Prospects

Experienced Branch Managers have several career advancement options. A Branch Manager can move up to a larger branch office, where he or she will manage a larger staff and take on responsibility for more bank deposits and customer accounts. Another option is managing two or more branch offices (a branch "cluster"), often with an upward adjustment in salary. Branch Managers with several years of experience can move on to become market managers, or regional managers, and oversee all the branch offices in a specified geographic market.

Education and Training

Banking attracts a diverse group of people. Most banks look for applicants who are detail oriented and have a strong work ethic; a high grade point average (GPA) in college is less important than a general understanding of business. Applicants must have at least a high school diploma and two years of college. Increasingly, banks want Branch Manager applicants to have a bachelor's degree with an emphasis in accounting, finance, or marketing. Some banks may hire applicants with an associate's degree and some experience as an assistant Branch Manager or a closely related occupation in retail banking. Applicants who have completed employer-sponsored training programs in sales or marketing of financial products are sought-after candidates for branch management positions.

Special Requirements

As banks today are becoming more general financial services marketing firms, more banks are starting to require managers to have brokerage licenses (typically a Series 7 license issued by the National Association of Securities Dealers), which authorizes Branch Managers to sell registered securities such as annuities and mutual funds.

Experience, Skills, and Personality Traits

Prior financial industry experience is a requirement in branch management positions. Most applicants selected to manage a branch office have a minimum of three to five years of retail banking experience in a branch office, usually working as an assistant Branch Manager. Many Branch Managers start their careers as tellers or customer service representatives, moving up to more senior positions as they gain experience.

Because Branch Managers spend much of their day helping customers get the loans and investments they want, excellent customer service skills, quantitative problem solving skills, self-management skills, and a solid understanding of banking are essential parts of the manager's job. Also important are an ability to supervise subordinates, a willingness to meet Sales goals, strong written and verbal communication skills, and familiarity with word processing and spreadsheet accounting computer programs. Applicants must have no criminal records.

Unions and Associations

Branch Managers represent their financial institution in the local community, and frequently attend events sponsored by a local chamber of commerce, civic organization, or community group. Managers may also participate as members in local civic organizations, frequently assuming leadership roles. These events provide a setting to meet informally with current and prospective customers, answer questions about account servicing issues, and present opportunities to gather market intelligence about new companies coming into the community, companies that might need financing or other bank services sometime in the future.

Financial institutions such as banks also provide employee training through associations. Many commercial banks sponsor employee training programs offered through the American Institute of Banking, the educational affiliate of the American Bankers Association. Participating banks pay the training costs of employees attending AIB sponsored programs.

Tips for Entry

1. Gain experience while attending college through summer employment as a bank teller or customer service representative in a branch office.
2. Earn a bachelor's degree in accounting, finance, or business marketing as more financial institutions are making a college degree a requirement.
3. Learn about the banking profession and requirements for entry by talking to bankers at job fairs sponsored by a chamber of commerce or university in your area.
4. If you have on-the-job experience in sales or marketing of insurance and investment services, your selling skills are equally applicable to a career in banking.

REGIONAL MANAGER, BANKING

CAREER PROFILE

Duties: Manages a group of regional branch offices for a financial institution

Alternate Title(s): Area Manager, District Manager

Salary Range: $51,168 to $70,000

Employment Prospects: Fair

Advancement Prospects: Poor

Prerequisites:

Education or Training—Four-year college degree

Experience—Five to eight years of experience in banking or financial services marketing

Special Skills and Personality Traits—Excellent communication skills; good management and interpersonal skills; working knowledge of financial institution operating policies and procedures

CAREER LADDER

```
┌─────────────────────────────────┐
│     Regional Vice President      │
└─────────────────────────────────┘

┌─────────────────────────────────┐
│        Regional Manager          │
└─────────────────────────────────┘

┌─────────────────────────────────┐
│         Branch Manager           │
└─────────────────────────────────┘
```

Position Description

A Regional Manager supervises a group of branch offices of commercial banks and savings institutions. The Regional Manager is the banking executive responsible for deposit and loan growth in the group, usually five to 15 branch offices. In commercial banks the Regional Manager also works closely with commercial loan officers and business development officers to establish new customer accounts and new commercial loans. This person reports to the branch administration manager or a regional vice president.

Regional Managers help branch managers meet performance objectives, such as total sales per branch office or new accounts opened. They monitor the budgets of branch offices in their region, and approve staffing changes and annual employee performance reviews. They make recommendations for marketing programs that may be required to reach goals for deposit growth or loan growth.

Regional Managers may also:

- approve or disapprove loans
- recommend loans to the bank's loan committee for approval
- accompany branch managers on sales calls to prospective customers

- monitor loan applications in the area for loan quality and compliance with bank policy
- identify and help develop new business relationships
- coordinate the administrative needs of branches
- prepare administrative reports of deposit and loan activity
- supervise clerical support staff reporting to the Regional Manager

Regional banking managers represent their financial institution in the local community, and they frequently attend events sponsored by a local chamber of commerce, civic organization, or community group. They may also participate as members in local civic organizations, frequently assuming leadership roles. These events provide a setting to meet informally with current and prospective customers, answer questions about account servicing issues. They also present opportunities to gather market intelligence about new companies coming into the community that might need financing or other bank services sometime in the future.

Managers and banking officers work long hours, up to 50 hours a week, including evening meetings and weekends. They work in an office setting, but frequently travel to branch offices managed.

Salaries

Regional banking managers receive an annual salary. Salaries in 2004 ranged from $51,168 to $70,000, excluding sales commissions, according to America's Community Bankers, a banking trade association. The median salary was $63,336. In addition to salary, Regional Managers usually receive annual performance bonuses for reaching sales goals and/or stock options. Average annual earnings of regional banking managers in 2004, including commissions and incentive pay, were $71,041, according to America's Community Bankers.

Employment Prospects

There are good prospects for employment, but these are mainly in small regional banks or start-up banks and credit unions. Mergers of commercial banks that shrank the total number of banks in the 1990s will probably continue, but with fewer layoffs than in the past because more of the mergers will occur across state lines.

In addition, banks are placing more emphasis on retaining experienced managers in a tight labor market. Over the next several years the number of position openings is expected to be matched by the number of qualified applicants.

Advancement Prospects

Many financial management positions in banking are filled by promotion of experienced, technically skilled professionals. Advancement for Regional Managers is rated fair to poor only because of industry consolidation and competition for top jobs in marketing and branch administration. Advancement to more senior management positions may be accelerated by special study, but the competition is often intense.

Banks offer numerous opportunities to take classes, with tuition expenses paid by the employer, at local colleges or universities or at banking industry schools such as American Institute of Banking, affiliated with the American Bankers Association, or the Institute for Financial Education, now part of the Bank Administration Institute.

Education and Training

A four-year college degree with an emphasis in business administration or the liberal arts is good preparation for the position. Some financial institutions prefer candidates with a post-graduate business degree such as a master's of business administration. College-level courses in accounting, finance, economics, or marketing are very helpful. Also helpful are courses in communication and public speaking.

Experience, Skills, and Personality Traits

Prior sales management experience and general banking experience is considered a requirement for the position. Typically, Regional Managers have at least five to eight years experience in marketing, administration, and staff management. Regional Managers should have excellent communication skills, and good management and interpersonal skills.

Regional Managers are often called to deal with personnel issues, including hiring branch managers and disciplining employees. A sense of tact and diplomacy is useful dealing with problem situations and maintaining the bank's public image with its customers.

A working knowledge of financial institution policies and procedures is generally required. Regional Managers need to be very familiar with procedures for approving loans, acquiring deposits, and the reporting requirements of state and federal banking supervisory agencies.

Unions and Associations

Regional Managers in financial services can participate in state chapters of the American Bankers Association for career advancement opportunities and networking. They often serve as instructors in ABA's educational affiliate, the American Institute of Banking. AIB has several hundred chapters across the United States.

Tips for Entry

1. Broaden your skills in marketing, sales management, project management, and communication.
2. Attend local job fairs and talk to bankers in your area.
3. Check newspaper ads and Internet job listings and post your résumé in an online career center; apply directly to the hiring insitution.
4. Attending employer-sponsored training or seminars in marketing non-bank financial products can be a useful career-building experience.
5. Banking industry jobs clearinghouses such as Bank Administration Institute's Bank Job Search (http://www.bankjobsearch.com) are other useful resources.

BANK CARD MANAGER

CAREER PROFILE

Duties: Reviews, rejects, or accepts bank credit card and debit card applications; develops bank card marketing goals for the financial institution

Alternate Title(s): Credit Card Manager, Bank Card Program Manager

Salary Range: $25,000 to $79,000

Employment Prospects: Good

Advancement Prospects: Fair

Prerequisites:

    Education or Training—Undergraduate degree in business, finance, or related field

    Experience—Five to seven years experience in credit or consumer lending

    Special Skills and Personality Traits—Good managerial, communication, and organizational skills; teamwork management; strong knowledge of financial institution products, policies, and procedures; detailed knowledge of bank card risk management, credit scoring, and bank card credit operations

CAREER LADDER

```
┌─────────────────────────────────┐
│   Consumer Lending Director      │
└─────────────────────────────────┘

┌─────────────────────────────────┐
│      Bank Card Manager           │
└─────────────────────────────────┘

┌─────────────────────────────────┐
│   Bank Card Marketing Manager    │
└─────────────────────────────────┘
```

Position Description

The Bank Card Manager has overall responsibility for managing the operation of the bank card department in a financial institution. They work in commercial banks, savings associations, and credit unions. Job responsibilities may vary by institution, but in general, the manager is responsible for bank card marketing to new customers to meet sales targets for bank card accounts and credit card loan volume. The Bank Card Manager is usually responsible for financial institution relations with card accepting retail merchants and outside service firms that play a role in processing merchant sales receipts.

The manager reviews credit limit increases, name changes, and internal procedures relating to credit risk management. He or she manages compliance with federal and state consumer protection laws and regulations, and prepares management reports on credit card sales volume, card delinquencies, and charge-offs to the credit department and senior management.

The Bank Card Manager oversees cardholder acquisition or marketing promotions to prospective cardholders through direct mail, telemarketing, or Internet marketing via the financial institution's Web site. The Manager also deals on a regular basis with credit reporting agencies that run background credit checks on prospective new accounts, and the financial institution's collection department for recovery of past-due credit card loans.

Bank Card Managers also work closely with the bank's checking account department or deposit services group in managing the issuing bank's debit card program. Non-cash payment cards, including bank-issued credit cards and debit cards, account for an increasing percentage of retail merchant transactions and are gradually replacing retail payments by check or cash. Innovative new card products such as gift cards, merchant reward cards, and payroll cards will provide new opportunities for Bank Card Managers to create customized card programs linking a bank-issued card with some form of cardholder incentive to promote new card programs at the retail point of sale.

Salaries

Salaries for Bank Card Managers are about average for middle management executives in banking, ranging from $25,000 to $79,000 or more. The middle 50 percent had salaries between $25,000 and $42,945, and the highest reported salary was $79,364 in 2004, according to a survey by America's Community Bankers. Annual earnings may be supplemented by incentive bonuses for reaching sales goals. As in other banking positions, compensation is based on qualifications, experience, and the issuing bank's deposit base and credit card portfolio. Larger financial institutions located in or near metropolitan centers issue more cards and have more complex card management programs than rural or community banks do.

Employment Prospects

Employment opportunities for Bank Card Managers are expected to grow somewhat slower than job prospects for commercial loan officers and mortgage lenders through 2014. This is a maturing industry, with limited job growth outside the top five card-issuing banks. Offsetting this outlook, some job opportunities will result from financial innovations such as payroll cards and gift cards as banks discover new ways to replace cash and paper checks with plastic payment cards. Growth in finance company credit card programs will create additional job opportunities. Most financial institutions with the legal authority to offer bank cards have already done so. Financial industry consolidation will reduce the number of jobs being created; many positions will become available through retirements and managers moving to jobs outside banking.

The bank credit card industry is highly concentrated; the top 10 financial institutions in the United States control about 90 percent of the bank-issued credit cards outstanding. Historically, the credit card business has been a low-profit margin business with some risk of losses to bad debt write-offs. Further consolidation is possible as banks look for opportunities to reduce or sell their low-margin business segments to larger financial institutions.

Advancement Prospects

Bank Card Managers generally advance to senior lending positions in consumer banking or product management when vacancies occur. Another option is taking a position in bank card operations or marketing with a bank card service company. Today non-bank service corporations perform much of the labor-intensive back office processing of merchant sales receipts, operating under contractual agreements with card-issuing financial institutions. Bank Card Managers may also find opportunities for advancement in nonfinancial companies that process bank card transactions submitted by card-honoring retail merchants.

Education and Training

An undergraduate degree is required. Financial institutions look for individuals with academic backgrounds in accounting, finance, or marketing. Some prior experience in retail banking is usually required.

Experience, Skills, and Personality Traits

Five to seven years experience in bank card management, credit card marketing, or a related field is usually required. Important job skills include strong managerial, communications, and public relations skills, a strong attention to detail, and strong leadership skills. Team leadership and motivation skills are also valuable assets in this position. The position requires a detailed understanding of financial institution products, policies, and procedures, plus an understanding of statistical methods (credit or loan scoring) financial institutions employ to evaluate credit risk and to make credit decisions.

Unions and Associations

Bank Card Managers can become members of various organizations, such as the American Bankers Association or Consumer Bankers Association for networking opportunities and career advancement.

Tips for Entry

1. Bank Card Managers are often recruited from outside the bank; recruiting firms can put you in contact with potential employers.
2. Attending regional or national meetings of financial industry trade associations can lead to job interviews.
3. Check out employment listings in banking industry Web sites, such as American Bankers Association's jobs clearinghouse.

CONSUMER LOAN OFFICER

CAREER PROFILE

Duties: Evaluates applications for consumer loans and lines of credit; interviews loan applicants and requests copies of credit reports; may recommend terms of loans; informs prospective borrowers of loan commitments

Alternate Title(s): Retail Lender, Consumer Loan Specialist

Salary Range: $29,775 to $41,360

Employment Prospects: Good

Advancement Prospects: Good

Prerequisites:

Education or Training—Four-year degree in business administration, accounting, or finance, or general degree with equivalent experience

Experience—Two to four years of experience in a lending or sales environment

Special Skills and Personality Traits—Excellent interviewing, organizational, and analytical skills; good computer skills; good cross-selling and marketing skills; must be familiar with federal and state laws and regulations governing consumer loans, such as the Fair Credit Reporting Act and Truth in Lending Act

CAREER LADDER

```
┌─────────────────────────────┐
│  Manager, Loan Department    │
└─────────────────────────────┘

┌─────────────────────────────┐
│   Consumer Loan Officer      │
└─────────────────────────────┘

┌─────────────────────────────┐
│         Loan Clerk           │
└─────────────────────────────┘
```

Position Description

Consumer Loan Officers work in commercial banks, credit unions, and savings institutions. They assist financial institution customers applying for loans and lines of credit by interviewing the customer and gathering all information necessary to approve the request. Consumer Loan Officers process requests for auto loans, education loans, home improvement loans, credit cards, and overdraft lines of credit. Consumer loans, unlike home mortgages or home equity credit lines, are usually not secured by a lien on the borrower's home.

After completing the loan application forms, the loan officer begins the process of verifying and analyzing the application to determine the borrower's creditworthiness. The loan officer may request a copy of the applicant's credit report from a credit bureau. The loan officer may consult with his or her supervisor before approving a loan request. If the loan is approved, the loan officer arranges a repayment schedule and notifies the customer.

Their duties include:

- interviewing loan applicants in person or by telephone
- ordering copies of credit bureau reports
- notifying applicants of the loan decision
- explaining repayment terms of the loan such as interest rate, late fees, and other costs
- coordinating and completing loan closings and disbursements
- corresponding with customers, applicants, or creditors to resolve questions regarding applicant information
- managing a delinquent account file on past-due loans and contacting past-due customers
- marketing or cross-selling banking services to current loan customers

Consumer Loan Officers work in an office setting, normally working 35 to 40 hours a week. They may work from branch offices or service customers from a central office location. The position involves minimal travel to visit customers during evenings and weekends.

Salaries

Salaries of Consumer Loan Officers vary according to financial institution, geographic region, and job responsibilities. Salaries earned by Consumer Loan Officers in 2004 ranged from $29,775 to $41,360, according to a survey by America's Community Bankers. Loan Officers in larger financial institutions earned higher salaries than those employed in smaller banks. The median annual salary was $36,249. Some financial institutions may also offer incentive bonuses to reach sales goals. In addition to salary, loan officers usually receive benefits including pensions or employee savings plans, paid health insurance, free checking accounts, and reduced-rate loans on home mortgages.

Employment Prospects

Employment opportunities for Consumer Loan Officers should grow as fast as average through 2012, according to the U.S. Department of Labor. Among the factors influencing job growth is the increasing variety and complexity of consumer loans. Employment opportunities are still subject to the upturns and downturns in the economy, which could dampen opportunities in some regions of the country. College graduates and persons with sales or lending experience will have the best job prospects.

Advancement Prospects

Advancement for Consumer Loan Officers is generally to positions of increased responsibility. A loan officer with a successful track record in new loan production may be promoted to manage a group of lenders. Loan officers demonstrating leadership potential can also move into senior management positions such as management of a loan department (loan supervisor) or head of retail banking.

Education and Training

A four-year undergraduate degree with an emphasis in business administration or equivalent courses is a requirement for the position. Courses in the liberal arts are also helpful. Financial institutions provide continuous on-the-job training through career advancement programs, providing training to keep up with industry trends and changes in bank regulation.

Experience, Skills, and Personality Traits

At least two years of experience in lending or in a financial environment, such as a loan processing department or branch office, is a general requirement for the position. Consumer Lenders spend much of their time interviewing customers, and need excellent interviewing and organizational skills, and good marketing or cross-selling skills. Also important are good word processing and computer skills for processing loan documents. Consumer Loan Officers should have a working knowledge of federal and state regulations dealing with consumer credit, such as disclosure of interest rates and loan repayment terms. Also essential is having some working knowledge of financial institution processes and procedures in pre-screening and approving loans, and knowledge of automated loan scoring (credit scoring) routinely used in processing consumer loan applications.

Unions and Associations

Consumer Loan Officers can become members of several banking associations, such as the American Bankers Association, America's Community Banks, the Consumer Bankers Association. Credit union Loan Officers can join trade groups such as Credit Union National Association for career advancement education and networking.

The American Institute of Banking, affiliated with the American Bankers Association, offers correspondence courses and classroom courses at local colleges and universities.

Tips for Entry

1. Expand your contact network through on-the-job experience while attending college.
2. Check help-wanted ads for entry-level positions and apply directly to the financial institution posting the ad.
3. Sales experience or credit experience in any industry is helpful to a career in retail banking.
4. Periodically check out job opportunities at the American Bankers Association's Web site or other jobs clearinghouses.
5. Taking banking school courses at American Institute of Banking or similar organization can improve your chances of getting hired.

COMMERCIAL LOAN OFFICER

CAREER PROFILE

Duties: Examines and evaluates applications for business loans and lines of credit; approves loans up to a designated dollar amount; contacts prospects for new loans

Alternate Title(s): Commercial Lender, Commercial Account Officer

Salary Range: $45,000 to $69,943

Employment Prospects: Good

Advancement Prospects: Good

Prerequisites:

Education or Training—Four-year degree with courses in finance, accounting, and economics

Experience—Two to four years lending experience

Special Skills and Personality Traits—Excellent leadership, management, and interpersonal skills; knowledge of lending procedures, state and federal laws covering lending, ability to use spreadsheet software, word processing in written presentations

CAREER LADDER

```
┌─────────────────────────────────┐
│   Manager, Loan Department       │
└─────────────────────────────────┘

┌─────────────────────────────────┐
│   Commercial Loan Officer        │
└─────────────────────────────────┘

┌─────────────────────────────────┐
│   Credit Analyst                 │
└─────────────────────────────────┘
```

Position Description

Commercial Loan Officers evaluate and approve non-real estate commercial loans originated by commercial banks and other financial institutions. Business loans are an important source of income to banks, and commercial lenders facilitate this process by seeking potential borrowers and assisting them in applying for loans. Loan officers gather information about clients and businesses to ensure that the lender has adequate information regarding the quality of the loan and the probability of repayment.

Commercial lenders in many financial institutions perform a dual role, acting as lender and salesperson. They will contact businesses to determine their need for loan financing. If the business is seeking new funding, the loan officer will try to persuade the business to obtain financing from their institution. Following the initial contact, the loan officer will guide the borrower through the loan approval process. The loan officer obtains basic information about the borrower's financial condition and may help the borrower fill out the loan applications.

The loan officer's job involves considerable travel. Commercial Loan Officers frequently work away from their offices and use laptop computers, cellular phones, and pagers to stay in contact with their offices and clients. Most loan officers work a standard 40-hour week, but they may work longer hours depending on the number of clients serviced and seasonal demand for loans. Loan officers are often busiest during periods of low interest rates, when demand for financing is highest.

Their duties include:

• identifying new business loan and line of credit customers to help the bank achieve its goals for new loan production and asset growth

• approving loan applications based on a thorough analysis of the applicant's credit history, current financial condition, and projected income or earnings

• structuring loans to meet the needs of the borrower and meeting the bank's guidelines for asset-liability management

• documenting new loans in accordance with relevant legal requirements

• monitoring the borrower's financial status, including deposit accounts, and reporting any irregularities to bank management

- analyzing the applicant's financial status, credit history, and assets owned to determine feasibility of granting a loan
- negotiating credit terms, such as costs, loan repayment, and collateral specifications
- interviewing applicant and requests specified information for loan application
- approving loans within specified limits
- referring high-value loans (loans exceeding personal lending authority) to loan committee for approval
- contacting applicant or creditors to resolve questions regarding application information
- ensuring loan documents are complete and accurate according to policy and banking regulations
- computing loan payment schedule
- submitting application to credit analysis for verification and recommendation
- ensuring legal transfer of pledged collateral to the bank

Salaries

Salaries of Commercial Loan Officers vary according to financial institution. Some loan officers are paid commissions based on loan origination volume, while others are salaried employees. Some loan officers may be paid a base salary with an incentive bonus for meeting loan origination targets. Salaries earned by commercial loan officers ranged from $45,000 to $69,993 in 2004, according to America's Community bankers, a banking trade association. The median annual earnings of Commercial Loan Officers was $54,446.

Employment Prospects

Employment opportunities for loan officers are determined to a large degree by economic growth. The U.S. Department of Labor forecasts average growth through 2012. Job growth will be driven by a growing population, continued economic expansion, as well as growth in the complexity and variety of loans originated. Many of these openings, however, will be created by bankers retiring or leaving the industry.

Advancement Prospects

Advancement for Commercial Loan Officers is generally done by assuming positions of increased responsibility. A Commercial Loan Officer in originating new loans with a successful track record may be promoted to manage loan portfolios of major loan customers, and service bigger loans. Advancement beyond the loan officer position could be to a position supervising other lenders and clerical staff. Lenders with leadership ability could also move into management positions, such as management of a loan department.

Education and Training

An undergraduate degree is a requirement for the position. College courses in business, finance, and marketing are helpful as are courses in social science and the liberal arts. Financial institutions provide extensive on-the-job training

through career advancement programs which provide skills training in credit analysis and credit management.

Experience, Skills, and Personality Traits

Commercial Loan Officers should have at least one to two years experience, preferably in commercial loans or consumer loans. The position requires good managerial, communication, and sales skills, as well as negotiating skills. Completion of professional certification courses and programs enhances your employment and advancement opportunities. The position requires an understanding of financial analysis, general literacy with computer spreadsheet programs, and a detailed understanding of bank policies and procedures for commercial loans. Knowledge of loan scoring (credit scoring) may also be required.

Special Requirements

Industry certifications are available, though these are not generally requirements for job entry. The American Institute of Banking, affiliated with the American Bankers Association, offers correspondence courses, and college and university classes. Completion of these courses enhances an individual's employment and advancement opportunities. Eligible certifications include the Certified Lender–Business Banker designation awarded by the American Bankers Association.

Unions and Associations

Commercial Loan Officers can belong to professional organizations, including the American Bankers Association and the Risk Management Association (formerly Robert Morris Associates), and join special interest groups devoted to career advancement and networking issues. As representatives of their employers, loan officers often attend local chamber of commerce and community group meetings and they may join these organizations as members.

Tips for Entry

1. Get some on-the-job experience in banking by working part time in a bank's credit department or in a branch office while attending college.
2. Sales experience, especially with a financial organization, can become helpful to a career in banking; part of the lender's job is selling the bank to its customers.
3. Check out job opportunities on the Internet by visiting the American Bankers Association's career Web site (http://www.aba.careersite.com) and other job clearinghouses.
4. As in other financial careers, contacts gained from informal networking are very useful in banking. College associations with community links can be a good place to start.
5. Some financial institutions have on-campus recruiting programs—another potential source of job leads.

COMMERCIAL LOAN WORKOUT OFFICER

CAREER PROFILE

Duties: Responsible for maintenance, security, and sale of real estate obtained through foreclosure; conducts foreclosure appraisal; renegotiates terms and conditions of loans

Alternate Title(s): Real Estate Owned Manager

Salary Range: $60,000 to $82,000

Employment Prospects: Good

Advancement Prospects: Good

Prerequisites:

Education or Training—Undergraduate degree in business administration, finance, or equivalent courses

Experience—Five to seven years experience commercial lending, commercial real estate, or sales experience helpful

Special Skills and Personality Traits—Excellent interpersonal, organizational, and project management skills; strong negotiating and analytical skills; must have thorough knowledge of real estate project finance, accounting, bankruptcy law, and commercial law dealing with real estate projects.

CAREER LADDER

```
┌──────────────────────────────────┐
│   Senior Commercial Loan Officer  │
└──────────────────────────────────┘

┌──────────────────────────────────┐
│  Commercial Loan Workout Officer  │
└──────────────────────────────────┘

┌──────────────────────────────────┐
│     Commercial Loan Officer       │
└──────────────────────────────────┘
```

Position Description

When commercial loans deteriorate or go past due, the Commercial Loan Workout Officer gets involved in negotiating the sale or resolution of property acquired through foreclosure. They design and implement a workout (rescheduled) loan payment plan, or, if the problem loan cannot be fixed, develop appropriate plans and budgets to manage and dispose of foreclosed properties that become non-earning assets of the bank. They may request on-site inspections, engineering studies, or construction bids to bring an unfinished project to completion. They oversee the analysis of properties and corresponding markets to recommend appropriate disposition strategies, in accordance with bank policy.

Commercial Loan Workout Officers maintain bank relationships with commercial real estate brokers, potential purchasers, title and escrow companies, court-appointed receivers, property management companies, and other vendor firms that may become involved in a loan workout

situation. In some situations, the loan workout officer may negotiate bank financing for a troubled project, for example a bank loan to a company in bankruptcy reorganization, allowing the borrower to bring the project to completion.

In their administrative duties, Loan Workout Officers direct and coordinate the activities of staff employees, and prepare reports and forecasts detailing the management and disposition of real estate owned. They analyze financial statements, business history, and creditworthiness of potential buyers. They supervise all sales negotiations with potential purchasers and their agents. This is a good job for an individual who has strong organizational and negotiating skills.

Bad real estate loans nearly brought the banking industry to its knees during the 1990–91 recession, when there was a glut of foreclosed properties. But problem loans can surface even during the good times. Bankers go to great lengths to try to avoid foreclosing, or seizing a borrower's mortgaged property or pledged collateral, because they do not want to be in the property management business. Bankers also want to avoid any "lender liability" lawsuits from borrowers claiming they were coerced into doing something they did not want to do and consequently suffered a loss.

In loan workouts, almost everything is negotiable: loan length, interest rates, payment schedules, and technical loan covenants (i.e., debt-to-equity ratios). Each loan workout is different. An entire set of new loan documents may be needed, or, if the changes are minor, amendments to existing loan agreements will be sufficient. Borrowers may be asked to pay renewal or rollover fees to the lender for changes in the loan terms. Some lenders require borrowers to pay any lender's attorney's fees incurred in the workout. The written documents of a workout can be just as comprehensive as the original loan documents.

Salaries

Loan Workout Officers earn salaries ranging from $60,000 to $82,000. Compensation may include incentive bonuses for meeting goals for disposition of troubled real estate.

Employment Prospects

Commercial Loan Workout Officers are in demand when times are bad, which often happens after a period of rapid growth in loan portfolios or immediately after a recession. Problem loans may not come to light until two or three years after they were made, or after they have been "seasoned" a bit. So there will always be some need for loan specialists who can try to restructure a loan by extending the payment schedule or, if necessary, allowing the borrower to skip a few payments or temporarily reduce the interest rate.

Loan workout is also a training area where newly minted loan officers learn how to write good loans by first learning what can go wrong when a loan is made. Spending some time in the loan workout area is an excellent way to learn what can go wrong in a loan. After spending several months or a year working on problem loans, the workout officer is ready to move on to become a full-fledged loan officer and begin calling on bank customers for new loan business. Larger financial institutions have full-time workout specialists to handle the routine number of problem loans.

Advancement Prospects

Commercial Loan Workout Officers generally advance to positions of increased responsibility in the loan department. Individuals with strong leadership skills could move into a management slot and manage the loan department and eventually move up into senior management. Some workout officers prefer to stay as commercial lenders because the position is high paying and they like the challenge of the job.

Commercial Loan Workout Officers, after a career in banking, can also move on to a career in consulting. They offer advice, for a fee, to financial institutions or to their loan customers on the best ways to restructure a problem loan and avoid further trouble years down the road. Workout consultants are often retired senior loan officers.

Education and Training

An undergraduate degree is required. Financial institutions look for individuals with academic backgrounds in business management, finance, or equivalent courses. Some Loan Workout Officers also have law degrees.

Experience, Skills, and Personality Traits

Five to seven years' experience in commercial lending is generally a minimum requirement for the position. Related experience in real estate appraisal, construction, or finance is considered helpful.

Important skills in this position include strong interpersonal, organizational, and management skills. Also important is having strong negotiating skills, because the workout officer is responsible for recovering the financial institution's investment in the project. Excellent communication and leadership skills are also valuable. Individuals in this position should have a thorough understanding of real estate, finance, accounting, and state laws (the Uniform Commercial Code) dealing with rights of creditors in commercial loans. Also important is a detailed understanding of federal and state bankruptcy laws.

Unions and Associations

Commercial Loan Workout Officers can become members of the American Bankers Association or Risk Management Association (formerly Robert Morris Associates) for networking and career advancement opportunities.

Tips for Entry

1. Networking at local or regional bank association meetings can lead to job tips.
2. Some of the best opportunities can also be found on banking industry Web sites.
3. Take college courses in finance and accounting to get a well-rounded background in credit management.
4. Internship programs can be the key to landing employment following college graduation.
5. Loan workout managers with good track records can apply their skills in related industries such as commercial finance.

SMALL-BUSINESS BANKER

CAREER PROFILE

Duties: Originates business loans guaranteed by the U.S. Small Business Administration

Alternate Title(s): Small-Business Lender

Salary Range: $45,500 to $100,000

Employment Prospects: Very good

Advancement Prospects: Good

Prerequisites:

Education or Training—Four-year degree preferred

Experience—Two to five years of experience in lending to small business owners

Special Skills and Personality Traits—Excellent verbal and written communication skills; good analytical and negotiating skills; formal credit training; must be familiar with banking products and services

Special Requirements—Certification optional

CAREER LADDER

```
┌─────────────────────────────────┐
│     Head, Commercial Lending     │
└─────────────────────────────────┘

┌─────────────────────────────────┐
│     Small-Business Banker        │
└─────────────────────────────────┘

┌─────────────────────────────────┐
│       Commercial Lender          │
└─────────────────────────────────┘
```

Position Description

Small-Business Bankers originate commercial loans to small business owners, usually companies with annual sales under $10 million. Small-Business lenders are responsible for processing small business loans guaranteed by the Small Business Administration and servicing loans to existing business customers. They make sales marketing calls on current banking customers, and assist customers in obtaining SBA loans. The position reports to a senior loan officer, or in small banks, directly to the bank president.

The Small Business Administration, a federal agency established in 1953, is the largest source of business credit to the 25 million small business in the United States. The SBA does not make loans directly to qualified businesses. Instead, it guarantees loans for working capital or equipment financing (up to $750,000) that has been originated by approved financial institutions. There are two types of SBA lenders. SBA *certified lenders* collect loan documents and perform the initial credit analysis, but do not approve loans. SBA *preferred lenders*—a much smaller group—have authority to approve loans acting on behalf of the SBA, dramatically cutting the waiting period to get financing so borrowers get their money much faster.

Small-Business Bankers prepare loan documentation, collect all the necessary documentation, and process loans according to credit terms of the lender and the Small Business Administration. They coordinate loan closings and recording of liens with outside attorneys, other financial institutions, title companies, appraisers, and other professionals.

SBA lenders also:

- arrange loan servicing with the loan servicing and administration department
- process loan advances to borrowers and loan paydowns
- update bank records for all SBA loan participations sold in the secondary loan market
- present a favorable image of the bank in the community

Small-Business Bankers usually work a 40-hour week in an office setting. They may work on weekends filling out loan forms or visit customers during evenings. Most customer contact occurs during normal business hours. As representatives of their employers in the community, small business loan officers often attend after hours meetings of local business groups and civic associations. They may join these organizations as members.

Salaries

Salaries are generally comparable to commercial loan officer salaries. Actual salaries vary according to job function. Small-Business Bankers who perform loan analysis in addition to making sales calls usually receive a salary plus an annual bonus for meeting loan production goals. Loan officers whose job responsibility is primarily business development or marketing may receive a draw against commissions (advance payments of expected future earnings) instead of salary. Salaries of Small-Business Bankers with one to three years' experience were between $45,500 and $70,000 in 2005, according to Robert Half International Inc. Bankers with three to five years' experience earned $61,750 to $88,500, and bankers with five or more years' experience earned $80,000 to $100,000 annually. Highest salaries are paid by financial institutions in the Northeastern U.S. or on the West Coast. Benefits in addition to salary usually include employer-paid health and life insurance, tuition reimbursement for education expenses, and participation in employer-sponsored retirement plans.

Employment Prospects

Demand is high for people with good skills and some experience with SBA loans. Because SBA loans are backed financially by the Small Business Administration, financial institutions have an incentive to recruit business lenders who know how to make loans meeting the SBA loan approval guidelines.

Advancement Prospects

With experience, a Small-Business Banker can advance to more senior administrative positions in the SBA lending group, such as construction and loan funding supervisor. One may provide administrative support for more complex types of business loans.

Education and Training

A four-year degree is preferred for the position, although qualified individuals with a high school degree or some college experience may also be considered. College-level courses in accounting, finance, or related areas are very useful. Formal credit training is required, and most people entering this field have attended industry-sponsored training programs in credit analysis and commercial loan underwriting, usually given by banking schools or seminars.

Special Requirements

Available certifications include the Certified Lender–Business Banker certification from the American Bankers Association. While there are no licensing requirements for the position, industry certification is helpful.

Experience, Skills, and Personality Traits

Two or more years experience in bank commercial lending, or marketing or selling financial services products or commercial loans is recommended. An ability to analyze financial statements and extract key information from financial reports is crucial to job performance. Strong personal computer skills and knowledge of financial spreadsheet programs is also important. A thorough understanding of financial products and services and some working knowledge of SBA loan processing software is needed.

Unions and Associations

Small-Business Bankers can become members of professional associations such as the American Bankers Association or the Risk Management Association (formerly Robert Morris Associates) for networking and career advancement opportunities. They can also join special interest groups focusing on lending to small businesses and minority-owned businesses.

Tips for Entry

1. While attending college, get practical experience through part-time or summer employment in a bank credit department.
2. Take courses in business administration and marketing to learn the fundamentals of managing a business.
3. Participate in activities of local business and civic associations to get insights into the local job market and make contacts with bankers in your area.
4. Post your résumé in an online job clearinghouse such as American Bankers Association's job bank (http://www.aba.careersite.com).
5. Your college's career center can help arrange on-campus interviews with interested employers.

LOAN PROCESSOR

CAREER PROFILE

Duties: Reviews applications for credit cards and loans; processes loan payments to insure payments are properly received and recorded; maintains records of customer account activity

Alternate Title(s): Credit Clerk, Loan Service Clerk, Loan Service Counselor

Salary Range: $16,000 to $45,000

Employment Prospects: Good

Advancement Prospects: Fair

Prerequisites:

Education or Training—High school diploma or equivalent

Experience—Six months to one year experience in a credit card or loan processing environment

Special Skills and Personality Traits—Good organizational and analytical skills; good attention to details; working knowledge of financial institution products and services; complete in-house training program

CAREER LADDER

```
┌─────────────────────────────────────┐
│   Credit Manager or Loan Officer     │
└─────────────────────────────────────┘

┌─────────────────────────────────────┐
│          Loan Processor              │
└─────────────────────────────────────┘

┌─────────────────────────────────────┐
│        Loan Clerk Trainee            │
└─────────────────────────────────────┘
```

Position Description

Loan Processors process loan and credit applications for major consumer purchases, such as homes, motor vehicles, or home appliances. Most work in commercial banks, credit unions, savings associations, and mortgage companies, performing a variety of clerical functions. Some are employed in credit bureaus, where they verify and update information for credit reports.

Loan Processors interview applicants or review credit applications to obtain personal and financial data. They contact the applicant if information is missing from the application and call employers to verify salaries. They review completed loan applications and calculate debt-to-income ratios to see whether the applicants meet the minimum guidelines for a loan. Loan Processors usually make credit approval decisions for credit card applications on their own. Large amount loans, such as mortgages, are sent to a loan underwriter for approval.

Statement clerks answer customer telephone inquiries and attempt to reconcile account discrepancies or resolve complaints. Loan Processors obtain and process the mort-gage-related documents needed for real estate settlement. They make sure that all legal documents are accurate and correctly signed. Loan Processors also check to see that all loan conditions for settlement have been satisfied.

Their duties include:

- verifying that loan records contain proper signatures, dates, and other data
- processing paperwork for loan payments or fees
- handling changes of address notifications
- maintaining and setting up files on each loan and ensuring that all information is complete
- answering telephone queries from customers regarding outstanding balance on loans and loan payoff amount
- contacting customers about overdue accounts
- contacting credit bureaus to obtain updated information
- presenting loan application and supporting documents to an underwriter for final decision on the loan
- notifying customers of acceptance or rejection of their credit application

Loan Processors usually work a standard 35- to 40-hour week. However, they may work overtime during particularly busy periods. Loan Processors handling residential real estate during peak periods—spring and summer months and the end of each month—often work overtime during these periods. Loan Processors in large financial institutions may be expected to work evenings and weekends.

Salaries

Most Loan Processors work full time, but employers also hire part-time workers. Annual salaries of full-time Loan Processors and loan counselors vary between $16,000 and $45,000, according to EZDesk, a mortgage industry information clearing house. The average annual salary of Loan Processors and loan closing officers in 2004, including commissions and bonuses, was $38,103, according to America's Community Bankers.

Employment Prospects

This is an entry-level position. New applicants will face competition because many individuals have the desired basic qualifications. Employers often promote current employees, such as tellers or customer service representatives, to loan service positions. The employment outlook for experienced processors and counselors is good over the next several years because financial institutions will increasingly emphasize service to retain their customer base. This outlook assumes that consumer demand for credit is steady and the economy remains healthy.

Employment opportunities in some positions may become limited due to financial industry consolidation and the growing use of automation in approving and servicing loans.

Advancement Prospects

Advancement is to a position with increased responsibility or a managerial position. Loan Processors and counselors may get promoted to loan officer, loan servicing supervisor, or credit manager. Another advancement option is moving to a loan collector position and contacting customers who are past-due on their loans. Advancement generally requires taking banking or credit courses, often paid for by the employer, to increase job-related skills.

Education and Training

A high school diploma or graduate equivalent degree is the minimum requirement for Loan Processors. Financial institutions provide new employees with on-the-job training, and periodic training as needed when they update loan processing policies and procedures. Most employers provide informal training for new employees, covering such things as credit policies and procedures and how to access records on the lender's computer system.

Experience, Skills, and Personality Traits

Loan Processors have considerable contact with customers. This position requires excellent verbal and written communication skills, excellent telephone skills, and careful attention to detail. Job applicants must be able to follow procedures accurately, be familiar with operating policies and procedures and any government regulations pertaining to credit approval and loan processing.

Loan Processors are expected to become familiar with the financial institution's policies and procedures after completion of an in-house training program.

Unions and Associations

Loan Processors may become members of professional associations such as the American Bankers Association or the American Institute of Banking, the educational affiliate of the ABA, for career advancement and skills improvement.

Tips for Entry

1. Many banks have their loan servicing done by service firms working under contractual agreement. Look for opportunities with outsourcing firms.
2. Take courses in mathematics and economics to gain an understanding of the fundamentals of credit.
3. Check newspaper ads for position openings and apply directly to the employer.
4. Any experience in a financial institution involving public contact, such as teller or customer service representative, can build valuable experience for this position.

LOAN COLLECTOR

CAREER PROFILE

Duties: Contacts loan customers with delinquent accounts; initiates appropriate collection action; maintains record of collection efforts

Alternate Title(s): Loan Counselor, Loan Adjuster, Repayment Specialist

Salary Range: $24,499 to $33,869

Employment Prospects: Good

Advancement Prospects: Fair

Prerequisites:

Education or Training—High school diploma or equivalent; successful completion of in-house training program

Experience—Two to three years' experience in credit and collections

Special Skills and Personality Traits—Good oral, written, and interpersonal skills; attention to detail and ability to meet deadlines; working understanding of the Fair Debt Collection Act and federal and state laws regarding debt collection activities; successful completion of in house training program

CAREER LADDER

```
┌─────────────────────────────┐
│    Collection Supervisor    │
└─────────────────────────────┘

┌─────────────────────────────┐
│        Loan Collector       │
└─────────────────────────────┘

┌─────────────────────────────┐
│      Loan Service Clerk     │
└─────────────────────────────┘
```

Position Description

Collectors review delinquent loan and credit accounts and contact customers to collect past-due payments. Loan Collectors, also called loan counselors, loan adjusters, or repayment specialists, can make arrangements for extensions or revisions of credit terms. If a satisfactory solution cannot be worked out, they locate assets pledged as loan collateral and attempt to take possession of the collateral. They may order foreclosure on unpaid real estates mortgages, or arrange liquidation of dealer inventory. If the loan is a credit card extension of credit, they can attempt to cancel the card.

They may refer uncollected accounts to independent collectors, retained by the bank to collect some portion of the debt. In the financial services industry, Collectors are employed in credit card, consumer loan, commercial loan, and mortgage loan departments.

Specific job duties include the following:

• contact credit bureaus for customer reports, check customer references, and update customer addresses

• ensure payments are properly credited to customer accounts and financial institution records
• prepare status reports on delinquent accounts and rate accounts according to financial institution procedures
• forward financial information to credit bureaus
• order liquidations, foreclosures, and repossessions when necessary

Salaries

Salaries of Loan Collectors vary by financial institution, location, and the number of accounts handled. Collectors are generally salaried employees. Annual salaries of banking collection officers in 2004 ranged from $24,499 to $33,869 according to a survey by America's Community Bankers. The median salary earned by bank Loan Collectors was $29,475.

Employment Prospects

Loan Collectors are typically promoted from clerical positions and learn on the job. Employment prospects are closely tied to growth in the economy, which means that demand for collectors increases in proportion to loan volume. Much of this growth in jobs, however, may occur from employee turnover. Collectors with the required knowledge and experience may be hired from the outside.

In the mortgage industry, loan servicing after closing (the collection and processing of mortgage payments from borrowers) is performed by a small group of companies that handle servicing for mortgage originators. These companies try to control their servicing costs through productivity improvements and application of computer technology, allowing loan servicers to process more loans per employee every year. Mortgage servicing employees handled a workload of 1,188 loans in 2004, up from 1,043 in 2003, according to the Mortgage Bankers Association of America. Further improvements in productivity can impose limits on future job growth, although normal attrition from employees leaving for other positions will create job vacancies.

Advancement Prospects

The Loan Collector position has limited advancement prospects. Generally, collectors advance by taking on positions of increased responsibility. A collector with a successful collection rate may be promoted to manage a group of collectors and clerical staff. Collectors with credit experience could advance to become lending officers.

Education and Training

A high school or equivalent degree is required. The collector position is an entry-level position in many financial institutions. Financial institutions generally provide their own in-house training to qualified candidates.

Experience, Skills, and Personality Traits

The position requires good telephone skills, and good oral and written communication skills. Also important is having good attention to detail, ability to meet deadlines, and a sense of tact when dealing with customers.

Loan Collectors should have a working knowledge of the Fair Debt Collection Practices Act, and federal and state regulations of debt collection activities. Collectors must pass the selection process and complete an in-house training program.

Unions and Associations

Loan Collectors can become members of banking associations such as the American Bankers Association and take continuing education courses to advance their careers. The American Institute of Banking, the educational affiliate of the ABA, provides correspondence courses and courses at local colleges and universities.

Tips for Entry

1. Consider part-time employment to gain experience.
2. Attend classes of American Institute of Banking to learn more about the field.
3. Job experience as a bank teller or customer service representative can help build your knowledge and skills for this position.

CREDIT ANALYST

CAREER PROFILE

Duties: Reviews a bank's loan portfolios for accuracy and completeness of loan files; reviews loans for compliance with federal and state banking regulations; may assist in calculation of bank reserves for loan losses and regulatory capital

Alternate Title(s): Financial Analyst, Loan Review Analyst, Loan Underwriter

Salary Range: $32,203 to $49,086

Employment Prospects: Good

Advancement Prospects: Fair

Prerequisites:

Education or Training—Four-year degree with courses in accounting, economics, and finance

Experience—One to three years' experience, preferably in a credit or lending environment

Special Skills and Personality Traits—Good managerial, communications, and public relations skills; extensive knowledge of financial statement analysis and spreadsheet accounting programs; working knowledge of loan collections, loan workout, and loan review procedures; accounting principles and regulatory guidelines for commercial loans, loan collection, and loan workout procedures; familiarity with financial institution lending policies and procedures

CAREER LADDER

```
┌─────────────────────────────────────┐
│   Loan Review Department Director     │
└─────────────────────────────────────┘

┌─────────────────────────────────────┐
│    Credit Administrative Manager      │
└─────────────────────────────────────┘

┌─────────────────────────────────────┐
│           Credit Analyst              │
└─────────────────────────────────────┘
```

Position Description

Credit Analysts evaluate credit quality of mortgages, commercial loans, and consumer loans, and assign risk ratings. They work in the audit department or credit department of financial institutions and commercial finance companies. They work closely with other members of the lender's credit department and loan officers. Credit Analysts work a standard 35- to 40-hour week in a central office location. Occasional travel may be required to inspect a borrower's property or examine loan collateral.

Analysts examine loan portfolios to determine whether loans meet the lending institution's guidelines for loan originations and that loan files contain all the necessary documents, and comply with banking regulations. They identify problem loans, such as past-due loans and loans with insuf-

ficient collateral. They write up a summary of their analysis if loan repayment becomes doubtful and report these findings to the bank's asset-liability committee, senior loan committee and board of directors. They may also act as senior credit analyst and coordinate credit reviews of commercial loans. Banks rely on the data gathered by the loan review analyst in calculating their loan loss reserves (funds set aside to cover possible loan losses), as stipulated by federal banking regulations.

Duties performed include the following:

• selecting loans to evaluate for credit risk, taking into account the borrower's credit history, type of business, and loan amount, plus information provided by credit reporting agencies

- verifying the value of collateral by calling appraisers and auction houses for current values of machinery and equipment
- contacting real estate appraisers for new real estate appraisals
- evaluating loans to determine if lenders have stayed within the guidelines of their lending authority
- identifying loans to be placed on the "watch" list of loans to be monitored and describing deficiencies in these loans
- assigning risk ratings indicating a borrower's financial strength, and explaining reasons for assigning adverse ratings
- auditing financial institution branches for loan quality
- providing quarterly reports to the board of directors
- conducting research on lending-related issues as needed

Salaries

Salaries of Credit Analysts range from $32,203 to $49,086. Many banks have multiple positions in this job category, starting more junior or entry-level positions. Annual compensation, including salary, increases with job experience and qualifications. The average annual salary for commercial real estate Credit Analysts, including commissions or bonuses, was $41,194 in 2004, according to America's Community Bankers.

Employment Prospects

There are good employment opportunities for individuals with some experience in credit analysis, commercial lending, or loan collection and loan workout. Financial institutions also hire recent college graduates as trainees for entry-level positions in loan analysis or loan review departments. Job prospects in this field should grow about as fast as opportunities for loan officers over the next several years.

Advancement Prospects

Credit Analysts can advance to management positions, such as manager of the loan review department. Other advancement options might be moving to positions of increased responsibility, such as loan workout manager or manager of the credit and collections department. Advancement to more senior positions may require upgrading job skills to stay current with industry trends and changes in banking regulation. An M.B.A. or master's degree may be required for advancement to management positions.

Education and Training

The minimum education for this position is a four-year college degree in accounting or finance, or a related field. Col-

lege courses in business, finance, and marketing are helpful as are courses in social science and the liberal arts. Financial institutions provide extensive on-the-job training through career advancement programs which provide skills training in credit analysis and credit management. Credit Analysts without college degrees have often advanced through the ranks of the organization, acquiring experience in various other occupations, such as branch office manager or credit analyst.

Experience, Skills, and Personality Trait

Individuals should have one to three years industry experience, including experience analyzing loans and working with commercial loan officers. Prior experience in a bank's credit department is often a prerequisite to becoming a loan review analyst. Other important job skills are good communication and interpersonal, as Credit Analysts have a high level of contact with senior management and with banking customers.

Credit Analysts must have thorough knowledge of the analytical methods employed in financial statement analysis, including ratio analysis, trend analysis, and cash flow analysis, plus a knowledge of general accounting principles. Also important is a strong understanding of financial institution policies and procedures in approving business loans and excellent skills in using spreadsheet accounting programs.

Unions and Associations

Credit Analysts can become members of state banking associations affiliated with the American Bankers Association and other banking trade associations. These associations are useful for personal networking, upgrading job skills through seminars and association-sponsored banking schools, and keeping up with industry trends. Some have job postings of currently available positions on their Internet Web sites.

Tips for Entry

1. Get some on-the-job experience in banking by working part time in a branch office or loan department while attending college.
2. Take courses in accounting, business administration, or finance or courses to improve your computer skills working with spreadsheet accounting programs.
3. Check out job opportunities on the Internet by visiting the Bank Administration Institute's career center (http://www.BankJobSearch.com) or the American Bankers Association's career Web site (http://www.aba.careersite.com).

MORTGAGE BROKER

CAREER PROFILE

Duties: Works on behalf of clients seeking mortgage financing; arranges mortgage loans at best available rate and terms

Alternate Title(s): None

Salary Range: $60,000 to $80,000

Employment Prospects: Good

Advancement Prospects: Good

Prerequisites:

Education or Training—Four-year college degree

Experience—Two to five years' mortgage lending experience

Special Skills and Personality Traits—Excellent communication and negotiating skills; good organizational and computer skills

Special Requirements—State licensing required; background checks conducted in some states

CAREER LADDER

```
┌─────────────────────────────────┐
│   Manager, Mortgage Brokerage   │
└─────────────────────────────────┘

┌─────────────────────────────────┐
│        Mortgage Broker          │
└─────────────────────────────────┘

┌─────────────────────────────────┐
│        Office Manager           │
└─────────────────────────────────┘
```

Position Description

Mortgage Brokers are the middlemen in the mortgage lending industry. They contact borrowers seeking mortgage financing and negotiate loans with mortgage lenders. Mortgage Brokers use their network of contacts with mortgage lenders to negotiate financing at the best interest rate and terms.

The business of brokering mortgage loans is tied to the fortunes of the residential mortgage market. When mortgage interest rates hit a 45-year low, as they did in 2001 through 2005, there is very strong demand for mortgage loans—and also for Mortgage Brokers. Rapidly rising rates in an industry as cyclical as mortgage lending would have the opposite effect, reducing market demand for brokers. Wholesale Access, a mortgage industry research firm, reports that there were 53,000 mortgage brokerages operating in 2004, up from 44,000 in 2002. The average firm generated $34.5 million in mortgage loans in 2004 and employed about eight Mortgage Brokers.

Brokers work on a commission basis only; effectively they are an unpaid sales force for mortgage lenders—until they bring in a customer. A Mortgage Broker hired by a lender is paid at the time of loan closing, when mortgage contracts are finalized and money passes from the buyer of the mortgaged property to the seller. Brokers save money for their clients by arranging financing at a lower cost than would be possible if the loan were made directly by the mortgage lender, without using an intermediary to broker the loan. By providing borrowers with financing at wholesale prices, Mortgage Brokers are able to save their clients money. Brokers maintain contacts with a large number of lenders, so they can shop around for the best rate and mortgage terms. Brokers work to understand the borrower's financial situation and personal goals. Every mortgage borrower is different, so there is not one loan package that's right for everyone. Many home mortgage borrowers have special needs, such as a desire to buy a home with little or no money down. Others may have less than perfect credit, which makes them a high-risk borrower from the typical lender's perspective. Even if the borrower's loan application is turned down, the Mortgage Broker will continue to work on their behalf.

In residential mortgage lending, the Mortgage Broker performs a number of services that normally would be done by the lender. Among these are the following:

- obtaining credit reports
- providing a good faith estimate of the loan and appraisal costs

- arranging for other work, such as property inspections and appraisals

Brokers are paid for their work by collecting a loan origination fee, or broker's commission at loan closing time. Mortgage Brokers are no longer the "lender of last resort" in the complex, and constantly changing, world of mortgage finance. Financial services companies, including commercial banks and thrift institutions, employ Mortgage Brokers to locate qualified borrowers and reduce their loan origination costs. Brokers bring to the table an in-depth knowledge of the many different types of mortgage rarely found at the local bank.

There is a great deal of specialization in the mortgage brokerage field. Many brokers specialize in commercial or industrial property and multi-family residential property. Some commercial brokers specialize their work according to transaction size or the number of lenders they work with.

Developing and maintaining relationships with mortgage lenders is an important aspect of a Mortgage Broker's job. Mortgage Brokers starting their careers spend much of their time building a contact file of mortgage lenders and prospective clients. Brokers can work 40- to 50-hour weeks, or longer, in the first few years of starting a career.

This is a good career choice if you are sates oriented, have good math ability, and enjoy helping people meet their financial goals.

Salaries

Mortgage Brokers are normally paid commissions rather than salary. Typically, this commission is in the form of a draw or advance against anticipated future commission earnings. Some brokers may receive a base salary plus commission. However, the trend in the industry over the last several years has been toward performance-based broker compensation, and a gradual reduction in base salaries. Experience and geographic location, among other factors determine salaries. Brokers working in the Northeastern United States or in metropolitan areas have higher earnings than brokers in non-metropolitan areas.

Mortgage Brokers entering the field directly from college can earn salaries of $60,000 to $80,000, plus an annual performance bonus of 10 to 15 percent. There may also be a signing bonus paid at the time of hiring. Experienced commercial Mortgage Brokers can earn up to $300,000 a year in total compensation.

Employment Prospects

Employment opportunities for Mortgage Brokers will likely grow about as fast as average over the next decade. Market demand for Mortgage Brokers rises and falls with growth in mortgage originations, which impacts both the total number of brokerage firms operating in any year and the employment opportunities in each firm. A sharp downturn in originations would definitely have a negative impact on employment prospects for someone entering the business for the first time.

On the other hand, Mortgage Brokers have become indispensable intermediaries in the mortgage origination cycle and, due to their close contact with mortgage borrowers, have become very adept at finding mortgage financing matching almost any borrower's needs. Mortgage Brokers accounted for 68 percent of mortgage loan originations in 2004, according to Wholesale Access, a figure indicative of their gateway position in the mortgage industry. Mortgage brokerage firms have also been able to survive as independently owned and managed companies, bucking the mortgage industry's general trend toward consolidation since the mid-1990s, which means continued demand for Mortgage Brokers into the foreseeable future.

Advancement Prospects

Mortgage Brokers usually advance their careers and salaries by taking on more complex projects, usually commercial projects, requiring more job-related experience. Residential Mortgage Brokers with leadership skills might advance into management positions, such as office manager. Mortgage Brokers seeking career stability might move into mortgage banking, which has an additional source of income—the servicing fees mortgage bankers collect for processing mortgage payments from borrowers.

Education and Training

Mortgage Brokers come from varied academic backgrounds. A four-year college degree with courses in business, finance, or other related courses is generally the minimum education requirement. Continuing education beyond college is required to maintain professional competency in the field, and is also a prerequisite in some states to the brokerage licensing exam.

The National Association of Mortgage Brokers or the Institute for Financial Education, now part of Bank Administration Institute, both offer continuing education and correspondence courses to Mortgage Brokers.

Special Requirements

Mortgage Brokers must pass a written exam and obtain a state license, usually from the state banking department or chief regulator of financial institutions. Mortgage Broker regulations vary widely from state to state. Some states issue licenses to individual brokers while others license brokerage offices. A number of states have stringent educational requirements, requiring brokers to attend professional training courses, while others require that brokers maintain a surety bond or pass a background investigation.

Experience, Skills, and Personality Traits

Two to five years experience in financial services marketing is a general requirement for the position. Mortgage Brokers should have strong written, interpersonal, and negotiating skills. Some knowledge of computers and computer programs used in business, such as word processing and financial spreadsheet programs, is also useful. Mortgage Brokers should be entrepreneurial in personality, goal oriented, and willing to work long hours.

Unions and Associations

Mortgage Brokers can become members of the National Association of Mortgage Brokers for career development and professional networking through state chapters of the association.

Tips for Entry

1. Take college-level courses in economics, finance, and related areas to get a good academic background in business and finance.
2. Licensing requirements for Mortgage Brokers can vary widely. Check into the education requirements of the state where you plan to work and take college courses in those subjects.
3. Contact industry associations such as the National Association of Mortgage Brokers (http://www.namb.org) for possible job leads.

REAL ESTATE APPRAISER

CAREER PROFILE

Duties: Examines and estimates the value of various types of income-producing commercial property; prepares reports of findings for use by investment staff

Alternate Title(s): Staff Appraiser

Salary Range: $53,125 to $74,550

Employment Prospects: Good

Advancement Prospects: Good

Prerequisites:

Education or Training—Four-year degree preferred

Experience—Six months to one year of experience assessing real estate

Special Skills and Personality Traits—Strong interpersonal and management skills; ability to gather and analyze facts and make valuation judgments based on past experience an attention to unusual details

Special Requirements—Real estate appraisal license; industry certification usually required for commercial appraisals

CAREER LADDER

```
┌─────────────────────────────────────┐
│   Certified Residential Appraiser    │
└─────────────────────────────────────┘

┌─────────────────────────────────────┐
│   Licensed Residential Appraiser     │
└─────────────────────────────────────┘

┌─────────────────────────────────────┐
│          Trainee Appraiser           │
└─────────────────────────────────────┘
```

Position Description

Real Estate Appraisers analyze and determine the replacement cost for commercial and residential properties and their contents. Appraisers work for commercial banks, thrift institutions, insurance companies, and independent appraisal firms.

Bank appraisers conduct onsite inspections of residential and commercial properties offered as collateral for a mortgage loan. Residential property appraisers gather and analyze data such as sales of comparable properties, legal descriptions and land values to determine a fair market appraisal value. They may inspect properties under construction, inspect properties for casualty losses, and inspect properties before and after a foreclosure action. They may recommend repair and rehabilitation work if necessary to bring mortgaged properties in conformance with local building codes.

Commercial appraisers advise on the estimated value of income-producing property. They determine the appropriate valuation methodology, select independent appraisal firms to conduct inspections, review internal and third-party apprais-

als, and prepare appraisals on selected properties. They read blueprints and specifications, and make estimates of earnings power of income-producing properties such as apartment buildings and commercial offices. They may identify gaps in insurance and make recommendations on additional insurance needed to protect against losses. Appraisers prepare reports based on their findings for use by lenders, investment officers, and others. Commercial bank appraisers submit their written reports to the bank's loan committee, which approves or declines commercial mortgage applications.

Duties typically performed include the following:

- managing on-site property appraisals
- submitting reports on the physical condition of properties
- making recommendations for repairs or replacement of mechanical systems such as heating, plumbing, and air conditioning in commercial buildings
- maintaining a basic knowledge of local real estate market conditions, construction expenses, and property improvement expenses

- reporting results of appraisal inspections to supervisors
- testifying in court as to the value of a piece of property
- researching public records of sales, leases, outstanding liens, and property tax assessments relating to an individual property
- supervising clerical staff

Appraisers spend much of their time out of the office visiting and inspecting properties.

This is a good career path if you are attentive to details and like the challenge of handling a diverse group of assignments.

Salaries

Commercial appraisal firms usually pay a base salary or a draw against commissions earned, plus commissions. Appraisers working in financial institutions earned salaries of $53,125 to $74,550 in 2004, according to a survey by American Community Bankers. Often there is a signing bonus paid to experienced appraisers. In addition to salary, top firms provide health insurance and pension benefits. Appraisers who work as independent contractors pay their own social security taxes and insurance premiums.

Employment Prospects

Employment opportunities for Real Estate Appraisers are expected to grow faster than average for other occupations through 2014. Demand for appraisals is strongest in active markets such as the east and west coasts of the United States and major metropolitan markets. While the real estate market itself is highly cyclical, wider use of mortgage financing with more affordable payment schedules—such as longer-term 40-year loans and mortgages—counters the effects of rising home prices. These so-called affordability mortgages could soften the impact of housing market downturns on property appraisals. But newer technology will have some impact on overall employment opportunities, notably the greater use of computer models, which offer faster appraisals at lower cost than a full property inspection by a certified property appraiser. Computer-based automated valuation models, or AVMs, have been used most often in second-lien mortgages and refinancings but may cut into first lien mortgages taken out for home purchase as the models become more refined and accuracy improves. Appraisers may find the best opportunities as independent fee appraisers because banks and other mortgage lenders are increasingly contracting their appraisals to independent appraisal firms.

Advancement Prospects

Advancement is usually to a management or supervisory position. In banking, a Real Estate Appraiser could advance to senior appraiser and supervise day-to-day performance of one or more appraisers. With additional job experience an appraiser could become chief appraiser, becoming responsible for directing appraisal policy and managing the appraisal staff.

Education and Training

A four-year college degree in business, finance, or a related field is required. Individuals entering this position have successfully completed a series of qualifying exams or have begun studying for these exams. Working as an insurance appraiser requires specialized training, and completion of a certification program in claims management. Appraisers are expected to upgrade their knowledge of property valuation and construction practices by attending conferences, reading trade journals, and utilizing other available resources.

Special Requirements

Specialized certification is required to become a Real Estate Appraiser. Certification is issued after the individual completes a series of qualifying exams. In addition, a real estate appraisal license is required in most states. The top qualification is the Master Senior Appraiser, awarded by the American Institute of Real Estate Appraisers. Industry certification is recognized as a mark of outstanding ability and is very helpful in career advancement. Certifications available to appraisers are the Master Certified Appraiser from the Appraisal Institute and the Certified International Property Specialist.

Experience, Skills, and Personality Traits

This position requires the ability to gather and analyze factual information, read blueprints and architectural drawings, and perform mathematical calculations. Real Estate Appraisers need to make valuation estimates and judgments based on previous real estate experience. Appraisers must also be alert to minor details such as a deterioration in maintenance that could affect adversely impact the resale value of property pledged as loan collateral.

Unions and Associations

Real Estate Appraisers often join one or more professional associations. Appraisers can become members of the American Institute of Real Estate Appraisers (The Appraisal Institute), the Society of Real Estate Appraisers, and the American Society of Appraisers.

Tips for Entry

1. Attend meetings of trade associations to expand networking opportunities.
2. Read up on real estate construction trends in trade journals such as *Appraisal Today.*
3. Some college courses in finance and accounting will be helpful.
4. Summer employment or part-time employment in a bank mortgage department or the investment department in an insurance company may also be helpful.

LETTER OF CREDIT MANAGER

CAREER PROFILE

Duties: Reviews applications for documentary credit financing in international trade; negotiates between parties for acceptable terms

Alternate Title(s): Letter of Credit Negotiator, Documentary Credit Specialist

Salary Range: $51,000 to $85,000

Employment Prospects: Good

Advancement Prospects: Good

Prerequisites:

Education or Training—Four-year college degree in finance or economics

Experience—Two to four years' experience processing documentary credit agreements

Special Skills and Personality Traits—Ability to analyze data, negotiate contracts, make decisions involving financial risk; good analytical and data gathering skills; working knowledge of international bank operations, payment systems, and letter of credit issuance procedures

Special Requirements—Professional certification usually required for advancement

CAREER LADDER

```
┌─────────────────────────────────┐
│     Trade Finance Officer       │
└─────────────────────────────────┘

┌─────────────────────────────────┐
│   Letter of Credit Manager      │
└─────────────────────────────────┘

┌─────────────────────────────────┐
│      Document Examiner          │
└─────────────────────────────────┘
```

Position Description

Letter of Credit Managers play a key role in international finance, issuing, and amending letters of credit financing the import or export of goods. (Letters of credit support international trade because the issuing bank, acting on behalf of its customer, offers its own credit and reputation to finance the transaction; a letter of credit is equivalent to a bank loan.) They examine trade documents relating to letters of credit and arrange financing terms for clients. They are employed in money center commercial banks and regional banks with customers active in international trade, and corporations with active trading desks such as commodity traders and energy companies.

The Letter of Credit Manager is responsible for administering letters of credit, reviewing letters and amending them as required. They contact correspondent financial institutions, usually foreign banks, suppliers, and other parties, to obtain documents needed to authorize the requested financing. They check the client's credit rating and may request increasing the amount of collateral or decreasing the loan amount accordingly. They also specify the method of payment, and contact the foreign bank when the loan has gone unpaid for a specified period of time, and initiate collection procedures.

Specific duties include:

• drafting, preparing, and updating letters of credit
• negotiating loan renewals, credit lines, and collection of past due loans
• ensuring that letters of credit are in compliance with banking regulations and financial institution policies
• making recommendations for improving policies supporting letter of credit financings
• answering customer inquiries regarding bank policy and specific letter of credit financings

- maintaining letter of credit files and status reports
- determining payment details in accordance with letter of credit agreements

Letter of Credit Managers work in an office setting, 35 to 40 hours a week with minimal travel. This can be a good career choice if you have good negotiating skills, financial aptitude, and an interest in a career in international trade.

Salaries

Salaries of Letter of Credit Managers are comparable to those earned by international banking officers. Managers can earn annual salaries of $51,000 to $85,000 and up, higher in banking centers like New York City where the cost of living is much higher than in other regions. Compensation in addition to salary usually includes employer-provided medical insurance, life and disability insurance, and participation in savings and pension plans.

Employment Prospects

This is not an entry-level position. Individuals are promoted from more junior positions such as letter of credit clerk or document examiner. Most positions are in financial institutions in New York City, Los Angeles, and other international banking centers, or in financial institutions that have made trade finance a specialty business. The recent surge in cross-border trade, aided to a large extent by the relaxation of trade barriers and creation of international free trade zones (the North American Free Trade region being one example), should provide ample opportunities for entry over the next decade.

Advancement Prospects

Advancement is usually to a more senior position in the international banking department, such as international banking officer, or operations manager supervising a team of letter of credit specialists. Another option for a Letter of Credit Manager would be to become a trade finance officer in a multi-national corporation, taking their knowledge of trade finance into the corporate world.

Education and Training

The position requires a four-year degree with courses in finance, economics, international finance, or other related courses. Courses in financial analysis and management of credit risk are also important, as are introductory courses in financial spreadsheet programs, which are widely used in evaluating a borrower's financial condition.

Special Requirements

Available certifications include Certified Documentary Credit Specialist, from the International Financial Services Association, Certified International Trade Finance Specialist, from the International Import-Export Institute.

Experience, Skills, and Personality Traits

Key job-related skills in this position are an ability to follow procedures, maintain accurate records, and analyze financial information. Excellent negotiating and interpersonal communication skills are also important because the Letter of Credit Manager provides the same services as a bank lender, but to a more specialized customer group. Letter of Credit negotiators need to have a working knowledge of legislative codes governing letters of credit, including the Uniform Customs and Practice for Commercial Documentary Credits (UCP), which are maintained by the International Chamber of Commerce.

Unions and Associations

Letter of Credit Managers can become members of the International Financial Services Association for networking and career advancement opportunities at ISFA-sponsored seminars and conferences.

Tips for Entry

1. Take courses in international finance and banking to understand how letters of credit work in financing world trade.
2. Read up on industry trends and current employment opportunities in industry trade journals such as *Documentary Credit World* published by the International Financial Services Association.
3. As in other financial careers, internships and summer employment opportunities provide a great opportunity to make preliminary contacts with potential employers.
4. Take a course or two in financial spreadsheets and become computer literate in financial analysis.

FINANCIAL SERVICES SALES REPRESENTATIVE

CAREER PROFILE

Duties: Sells investments and related services to banking customers

Alternate Title(s): Financial Services Officer, Investment Products Account Executive

Salary Range: $27,288 to $46,500

Employment Prospects: Very good

Advancement Prospects: Fair

Prerequisites:

Education or Training—Four-year college degree

Experience—One to two years sales or marketing experience

Special Skills and Personality Traits—Strong communication and interpersonal skills; good computer skills; ability to work independently and achieve goals

Special Requirements—Securities licenses required to sell insurance, mutual funds, and annuities

CAREER LADDER

```
┌─────────────────────────────────┐
│   Director, Investment Services   │
└─────────────────────────────────┘

┌─────────────────────────────────┐
│   Sales Manager, Investments      │
└─────────────────────────────────┘

┌─────────────────────────────────┐
│   Financial Services              │
│   Sales Representative            │
└─────────────────────────────────┘
```

Position Description

Financial Services Sales Representatives work in commercial banks, savings and loan associations, and other financial institutions. They sell annuities, brokerage accounts, mutual funds, and other investments to banking customers. They may also discuss conventional banking services such as cash management, deposit accounts, and lines of credit.

The duties of Financial Services Sales Representatives are similar to those of retail stockbrokers. They contact potential clients, explain the services available, and try to determine the customers' banking and other financial needs. They explain the differences between bank accounts, which are backed by federal deposit insurance, and investment products, which are uninsured and subject to market risk.

Financial Services Sales Representatives help clients set up an investment plan for future needs, such as college education or retirement savings. They give advice on the appropriate mix of investments to achieve short-term and long-term goals, and assist clients in setting up IRA accounts and other investment accounts to meet investment objectives. They may recommend specific investments to purchase.

Financial Services Sales Representatives, also called account executives or sales associates, work in customer service call centers or bank branch offices. Call center representatives service banking customers contacting the bank's call center with service questions. Branch officer representatives sell accounts to walk-in banking customers. They may work evenings meeting current or potential clients and attend civic functions or trade association meetings to meet potential clients.

Financial deregulation is changing how banks market investment products, making it easier to sell investments directly to the public through branch banking offices. The Gramm-Leach-Bliley Act of 1999 eliminated numerous legal barriers and gave banks more flexibility in marketing non-banking investment products (annuities, insurance, and mutual funds), using their current employees as a salesforce.

Many of the largest banks now sell investment services through two distinct sales-channels: bank-owned brokerage firms and financial institution branch offices. Sales through branch offices probably has the greatest potential for future growth, considering that banks own far more retail branch offices than brokerage offices. According to the ABA Banking Journal, a banking trade publication, at least 46 of the 60 largest U.S. retail banks now sell investments through licensed bankers.

Financial Services Sales Representatives work a 40-hour week and spend much of their time on the phone contacting clients and making appointments. They often receive client referrals from other bank employees, so their career development is somewhat less stressful in the early years than it is for licensed stockbrokers who have to build a client base from scratch. On the other hand, Financial Services Sales Representatives are less highly compensated than stockbrokers.

Salaries
Financial Services Sales Representatives receive a base salary plus commission. They may also receive a performance bonus if they Teach sales goals. Branch sales representatives earn lower commissions than licensed brokers, usually about 5 to 10 percent of the commission revenue their sales generate. (For comparison, full-time brokers receive about 38 percent of commission dollars.) Annual compensation for Financial Services Sales Representatives in 2004 was between $27,228 and $46,500, according to America's Community Bankers, a banking trade group. The average annual salary, including brokerage commissions, was $45,256.

Employment Prospects
Employment prospects for Financial Services Sales Representatives working in banking organizations are expected to grow about as fast as all job opportunities through 2014, according to the Bureau of Labor Statistics. Growth in personal incomes and expected growth in the variety of investment products being sold through banks will stimulate demand for sales representatives licensed to sell investment products through banks. Sales representatives who have brokerage or insurance licenses will be most in demand.

Advancement Prospects
Financial Services Sales Representatives usually advance by increasing the number and size of accounts they handle. With experience, people in sales marketing positions can become eligible for promotion. A successful individual might become a sales manager for investment sales through a group of branch offices. Eventual promotion might be to director of investment services, with responsibility for all investment products sold through a bank.

Financial representatives who excel in their jobs can advance their careers by becoming full-fledged brokers and taking the Series 7 Registered Representative Exam. The Series 7 Exam takes about two years of preparation and is considered very difficult; most people fail to get a passing grade the first time they take the exam.

Education and Training
Banks and other financial institutions prefer to hire college graduates for financial services sales positions. While there is no ideal academic background for a career in sales, courses in accounting, business administration, the liberal arts, and marketing are excellent preparation. Financial Services Sales Representatives learn the details of their jobs through on-the-job training and classroom instruction under the supervision of bank officers. Financial institutions provide entry-level training lasting anywhere from four months to approximately two years, depending on the range of services offered. Afterward, continuous training is given periodically in new products or key job-related skills.

Special Requirements
State licenses are required to sell mutual funds, annuities, and insurance. Background checks may also be conducted. Sales Representatives selling registered securities such as mutual funds or annuities must achieve a passing grade on the Uniform Securities State Law Exam, known as a Series 63 Exam. This exam requires less preparation time than the Series 7 Registered Representative Exam required for licensed securities brokers. Additional state licenses are required to sell life insurance. In some states, securities salespeople must pass a background check and post a personal bond, a specific amount of money held by someone else.

Experience, Skills, and Personality Traits
Many people enter this field from other careers. Employers look for people who have worked in sales before, such as insurance or real estate, but personal qualities are often as important to eventual success as education or experience. Individuals should have strong verbal and written communication skills, some knowledge of office computers and common word processing and spreadsheet programs, and a desire to succeed in this very competitive field. Self-confidence and an ability to work independently and handle rejection are very important personality traits.

Unions and Associations
Financial Services Sales Representatives can participate in state chapter meetings of various banking organizations, such as the American Bankers Association, for career advancement and networking. The Institute of Certified Bankers, an ABA affiliate, has training courses and certification programs for bankers who advise clients on personal investments.

Available certifications include the Certified IRA Services Professional and Certified Retirement Services Professional from the Institute of Certified Bankers.

Tips for Entry

1. College courses in business administration, economics, or finance are good preparation for a career in financial sales.
2. If you have a track record in sales, that can work to your advantage. Some employers prefer hiring people who have sales experience.
3. As in other financial positions, contact development and networking are crucial to success. Your college placement office may be of assistance in arranging on-campus interviews.
4. Part-time or summer employment in a bank branch office can produce practical experience and valuable contacts with industry decision makers.

INVESTMENT PORTFOLIO MANAGER, BANKING

CAREER PROFILE

Duties: Assists in determining investment policy for bank-owned securities; monitors cash requirements

Alternate Title(s): Director Investment Portfolio Management

Salary Range: $65,763 to $78,405

Employment Prospects: Fair

Advancement Prospects: Good

Prerequisites:

Education or Training—Four-year degree with courses in accounting and finance

Experience—Four to six years' experience in bank investments and funding

Special Skills and Personality Traits—Excellent management, organizational, analytical, and communication skills; working knowledge of asset-liability modeling software; knowledge of federal and state capital adequacy regulations of banks and thrift institutions

CAREER LADDER

```
┌─────────────────────────────────┐
│           Treasurer             │
└─────────────────────────────────┘

┌─────────────────────────────────┐
│  Investment Portfolio Manager   │
└─────────────────────────────────┘

┌─────────────────────────────────┐
│     Asset-Liability Analyst     │
└─────────────────────────────────┘
```

Position Description

Years ago commercial banks and thrift institutions worried a great deal about the impact to earnings from rising interest rates. Then banks discovered they could minimize the downside risk by carefully managing their customer deposits (liabilities to a bank) and assets (principally loans) to be assured of adequate funding to meet business goals for loan growth and earnings. Managing the asset-liability mix is the responsibility of the Investment Portfolio Manager.

Without asset-liability management, a bank might find the rate of interest it pays depositors holding Certificates of Deposit (CDs) is rising faster than interest it earns from making loans. Earnings would begin to deteriorate, and the bank would eventually have to stop making new loans. Asset-liability management keeps the two sides of the balance sheet in a state of equilibrium. Sometimes an imbalance is tolerated for a brief period, such as when a bank wants to increase its deposits or market share to boost its local market share.

The Investment Portfolio Manager, working with the bank's chief financial officer or treasurer, helps decide how the bank will invest its portfolio of bonds and other readily marketable securities. The manager also advises senior management on the effectiveness of the bank's investment policy. He or she may serve as a member of the bank's Asset-Liability Management Committee (ALCO), the management committee given formal responsibility for determining investment policy.

Other duties of the Investment Portfolio Manager include:

- updating the asset-liability model
- contributing to asset allocation decisions of the bank
- computing the bank's net interest income and capital reserves
- measuring interest rate risk on the balance sheet
- recommending transactions to reduce interest rate exposure
- preparing interest rate analyses under different interest rate scenarios

- supervising a staff of one to three financial analysts
- assisting in preparation of the annual budget and quarterly financial reports to bank regulatory agencies and the board of directors

Bank investment officers work in an office setting and typically work a 35- to 40-hour week using computers and telephones, with minimal travel. This is a good career choice if you are analytical, have an aptitude for figures, and good problem-solving ability.

Salaries

Salaries of bank investment officers are based on qualifications and experience. Annual salaries of investment officers in 2004 ranged from $65,763 to $78,405 according to a survey by America's Community Bankers. Compensation in addition to salary typically includes paid vacations and health benefits and participation in employer-sponsored retirement plans. Salaries are highest in financial institutions located in urban centers in the Northeast or the West Coast. The average annual salary in 2004, including commissions, was $89,768.

Employment Prospects

This is not an entry-level position. Employment opportunities for Portfolio Managers and banking professionals with good risk measurement or trading skills are expected to be positive through 2014. Individuals with strong quantitative skills and an aptitude for problem solving will find above average demand for their skills.

Advancement Prospects

Investment Portfolio Managers can advance to more senior positions in bank management, such as treasurer or chief financial officer. Other advancement options could include taking a position with a financial consulting firm, assisting banks in developing asset-liability models and risk management systems.

Education and Training

An undergraduate degree is a minimum requirement for all employees. Most people entering this field have a four-year college degree with a major in accounting, business administration, finance, or economics. Graduate work in finance or an M.B.A. is preferred, particularly in larger financial institutions. Courses in writing, communication, and computer science are also helpful.

Special Requirements

Available certifications include the Chartered Financial Analyst from Association for Investment Management and Research, and Fellow in Risk Management from Global Association of Risk Professionals.

Experience, Skills, and Personality Traits

A minimum of five years of experience in financial analysis, financial modeling, risk management, and analysis is mandatory. A candidate for this position must be organized and resourceful. He or she must have excellent management, organizational, analytical, and communication skills to effectively perform the required duties of the job and communicate results to senior management and the board of directors.

The position requires a working knowledge of asset-liability management software, bank investment policy, and government regulations affecting bank investments and capital reserves. Specific job requirements will vary by size of institution. A professional designation such as chartered financial analyst (CFA) is helpful. Excellent personal computer skills, particularly in handling financial spreadsheets, is a near universal requirement.

Unions and Associations

Bank investment officers can become members of several professional associations for networking and career advancement opportunities. Among these are American Bankers Association, Association for Investment Management and Research, Bank Administration Institute, and Global Association of Risk Professionals.

Tips for Entry

1. Take finance and accounting courses while in college. Some colleges also offer degree programs in banking.
2. Look into work-study, internship, or summer employment opportunities to gain practical experience and make industry contacts.
3. Check financial employment Web sites such as American Bankers Association's job bank or Asset-Liability Management Jobs (http://www.almprofessional.com/ jobs.asp).
4. Working in the credit department or risk management department of a bank can provide valuable experience leading to opportunities in more senior positions.

TRUST OFFICER

CAREER PROFILE

Duties: Manages trust accounts for financial institution clients; structures investment portfolios according to client instructions or court decision; prepares reports on investment performance

Alternate Title(s): Personal Trust Administrator, Trust Account Officer

Salary Range: $47,343 to $73,063

Employment Prospects: Good

Advancement Prospects: Good

Prerequisites:

Education or Training—Four-year degree in finance or a related field

Experience—Two to four years' experience in trust account management or related experience; knowledge of federal and state trust laws and regulations governing administration of trusts and the institution's trust policies and procedures

Special Skills and Personality Traits—Ability to collect and analyze financial data, make judgments based on experience, make decisions involving financial risk, and provide information and advice to bank trust clients

CAREER LADDER

```
┌─────────────────────────────┐
│  Trust Department Manager    │
└─────────────────────────────┘

┌─────────────────────────────┐
│       Trust Officer          │
└─────────────────────────────┘

┌─────────────────────────────┐
│      Financial Analyst       │
└─────────────────────────────┘
```

Position Description

Trust Officers manage the assets of a trust account according to the terms of the trust. The Trust Officer directs and coordinates activities relating to creating and administering personal and corporate trusts, and trusts established by a will or court order. Trust Officers may be designated by the type of trust account managed, for example a corporate Trust Officer or personal Trust Officer. Trust Officers generally work in an office setting, and work a 40-hour week, although they may arrange client meetings on evenings and weekends.

Their duties include:

• directing disbursement of funds according to conditions of a trust or needs of a beneficiary
• ensuring that surpluses are invested according to terms of a trust and wishes of a trust client
• preparing federal and state tax returns for trust accounts
• interviewing trust beneficiaries to locate sources of trust assets
• negotiating with public agencies such as the Social Security Administration and Workers Compensation Commission to accumulate all eligible assets into a trust
• consulting with client attorneys regarding trust conditions and duration of trust

Salaries

Salaries earned by banking Trust Officers can vary according to the size of institution, geographic location, level of education, and experience. Salaries vary from $47,343 to $73,063, according to the Bank Administration Institute. The average annual salary including commissions, for personal Trust Officers was $61,708.

Employment Prospects

Trust management positions are usually filled through promotion of bank employees with trust operations experience. Career opportunities in trust services should grow about as fast as industry average through 2014. Banking industry consolidation may reduce job opportunities in some markets, and some job openings will occur as a result of Trust Officers leaving the banking industry.

Advancement Prospects

Trust Officers have several advancement options. They may advance to become a portfolio manager within the trust department, or become a trust department manager if they have management skills. Trust account officers may also find opportunities in mutual fund marketing and portfolio management.

Education and Training

The position requires a four-year degree with courses in accounting, finance, and business management. Courses in the social sciences and English are also helpful as Trust Officers come into contact with a wide variety of people in their duties. The position requires detailed knowledge of banking laws and regulations, federal banking regulations governing administration of trusts, and the federal laws regulating investment advisors and managers of pension funds.

Experience, Skills, and Personality Traits

Most Trust Officers have had some experience in banking or financial services and have had experience handling financial assets. Important personal skills are excellent communication, analytical, and organizational skills, plus computer literacy with word processing and accounting spreadsheet programs.

Unions and Associations

Trust Account Officers may become members of the American Bankers Association and the National Association of Trust Audit and Compliance Professionals for business networking and career advancement opportunities. Certification programs available include the Certified Corporate Trust and Certified Trust Financial Adviser from the American Bankers Association.

Tips for Entry

1. Gain experience in banking working part time in a trust department or branch office while attending college
2. Attend local meetings of banking associations and investment groups to learn about job opportunities.
3. Contact the placement office at your college to arrange interviews with potential employers.

CALL CENTER SERVICE REPRESENTATIVE

CAREER PROFILE

Duties: Answers customer telephone inquiries; cross-sells banking products and services

Alternate Title(s): Telebanker, Telephone Banker

Salary Range: $14,378 to $58,344

Employment Prospects: Good

Advancement Prospects: Fair

Prerequisites:

Education or Training—High school diploma or equivalent

Experience—One to two years' telemarketing experience

Special Skills and Personality Traits—Strong interpersonal and telephone skills; good typing skills; ability to present telephone script in a cheerful, persuasive manner

CAREER LADDER

```
┌─────────────────────────────────────┐
│   Team Leader, Customer Service       │
└─────────────────────────────────────┘

┌─────────────────────────────────────┐
│   Senior Call Center Service          │
│         Representative                 │
└─────────────────────────────────────┘

┌─────────────────────────────────────┐
│   Call Center Service Representative  │
└─────────────────────────────────────┘
```

Position Description

Call Center Service Representatives market an array of financial products and services by contacting bank customers and prospects by telephone. Call Center Service Representatives usually follow a pre-formatted script in their contacts with customers and prospects. They normally work from lists of contact names, compiled from customer records, city directories, or telephone lists purchased from list brokers.

Call Center Service Representatives employed by financial institutions perform customer service functions in addition to marketing. They contact prospects by telephone from a list of names supplied by supervisor, read a short script, and gather information for leads. They attempt to validate interest in a particular product or service. They may open new accounts or refer callers to the appropriate banking department. They support field sales and financial services sales representatives and set up sales appointments for sales representatives.

Call Center Service Representatives are usually required to make a certain number of completed calls per day or work shift, and are trained to recognize cross-selling opportunities and recommend other banking products such as credit cards, ATM cards, or home banking to checking account customers. They may also provide telephone support for home banking customers needing assistance.

Representatives, also called telebankers, maintain records of telephone calls completed and use their judgment and reasoning skills to solve customer service problems, determine appropriate fee reversals, or refer callers to other bank employees. They collect information about service problems or customer complaints and refer customer disputes to the appropriate manager for resolution.

Call Center Service Representatives work in a telephone-calling center, usually working a 40-hour week. Most telebanking positions are shift work positions requiring work some evenings on a rotating basis and some weekends.

Salaries

Call Center Service Representatives receive an hourly rate or weekly salary. Annual basic earnings of telephone representatives in 2004 were between $14,378 and $58,344, according to America's Community Bankers, a banking association. Telephone service representatives usually receive, in addition to salary, company-paid health and life insurance, tuition reimbursement, childcare reimbursement, and participation in retirement plans. Telephone representatives working evenings often earn a higher hourly rate.

Employment Prospects

Employment opportunities for Call Center Service Representatives tend to rise or fall with consumer demand. When the economy is strong, companies hire more telemarketers. Financial institutions such as banks have employed telemarketers to supplement conventional sales channels such as offices and increase market share of deposit or loan accounts. Employment opportunities are probably greatest in financial institutions that have large numbers of credit card or checking account customers. Many Call Center Service Representatives start out as part-time employees working 20 to 30 hours a week, and move into full-time positions as they gain experience.

Outsourcing customer service functions to call centers overseas will have an impact on call center hiring in the United States. Outsourcing to lower-wage markets is affecting many industries to some extent as companies attempt to keep operating expenses under control. In the financial services industry, the activities most prone to outsourcing are those related to servicing high-volume, low-margin accounts such as residential mortgages, credit cards, or consumer loan payment processing.

While some call center positions are being outsourced to save money, not all service center jobs are going overseas. A 2004 survey of call center employees by Call Center Careers found that 53 percent of employees contacted said their jobs had not been outsourced. Another 16 percent said their jobs had been outsourced but remained in the United States. But about one-third said their jobs had in fact been outsourced overseas.

Advancement Prospects

Call Center Service Representatives can advance with experience to become a team leader, managing a group of six to seven telemarketers. Some advancement prospects will come about as people leave for other jobs outside banking. Individuals with leadership skills could get promoted to a managerial position such as call center manager or assistant manager.

Financial industry deregulation is beginning to change the job functions typically performed by Call Center Service Representatives. Commercial banks, for instance, can now sell mutual funds and annuities, both of which require special licenses, in addition to conventional banking services. With additional training, experienced Call Center Service Representatives might be able to advance into sales associate positions marketing investment products to retail customers. Improving job-related skills, though, is the most important factor contributing to career advancement in financial services telemarketing. Financial institutions often will sponsor the training necessary to advance into higher salaried positions.

Education and Training

This is an entry-level position. A high school degree or the equivalent is the minimum education requirement. Some college courses in business, marketing, and related courses are helpful. Skill improvement or learning new skills, such as learning how to troubleshoot basic computer problems and recommend solutions is important to advancement. After they are hired, Call Center Service Representatives go through a short-term on-the-job training program.

Experience, Skills, and Personality Traits

Call Center Service Representatives need to have a working knowledge of every product and service offered in the bank. Experience in sales, marketing, or customer service is helpful. Some knowledge of computers and account reporting software used in banks is also helpful. Employers prefer enthusiastic, goal-oriented, motivated people who are interested in helping customers find the product or service they want. Workers must have the ability to present a telephone script in a cheerful persuasive manner and an ability to follow directions given by supervisors.

Unions and Associations

There are no professional associations representing Call Center Service Representatives. They can participate in banking industry career development programs, such as classroom or correspondence courses from the American Institute of Banking. AIB courses are usually available through local or regional banking associations.

Tips for Entry

1. Courses in business math, communication, and English are a useful educational background for the position.
2. Most financial institutions hiring telemarketers find the people they need through ads placed in local newspapers or career Web sites.
3. A number of employment sites on the Internet have job postings for telemarketers and telephone support staff. Check sites like Call Center Careers (http://www.callcentercareers.com).

CALL CENTER MANAGER

CAREER PROFILE

Duties: Directs telephone marketing at banking call center; directs work scheduling; oversees staff recruitment and training

Alternate Title(s): Telebanking Manager

Salary Range: $38,384 to $60,035

Employment Prospects: Good

Advancement Prospects: Fair

Prerequisites:

Education or Training—Four-year undergraduate degree

Experience—Three to five years' experience, with emphasis in sales

Special Skills and Personality Traits—Strong communication and interpersonal skills; ability to lead and motivate staff; detailed knowledge of bank policies and account opening procedures

Special Requirements—State and general brokerage licenses may be required to sell insurance and investment products

CAREER LADDER

```
┌─────────────────────────────────┐
│       Marketing Manager         │
└─────────────────────────────────┘

┌─────────────────────────────────┐
│       Call Center Manager       │
└─────────────────────────────────┘

┌─────────────────────────────────┐
│  Telemarketing Representative   │
└─────────────────────────────────┘
```

Position Description

Telephone banking is replacing conventional "bricks and mortar" banking for many routine banking functions. Financial institutions are centralizing customer service and new accounts marketing in centrally located call centers. The Call Center Manager has responsibility for managing these centers and meeting sales goals. Duties include maintaining adequate staffing, coaching and training, and evaluation of job performance by internal call center employees. The Call Center Manager works with sales managers and product managers to establish team sales and referral goals for the call center. The service center may also act as a customer service center (a help desk) for PC banking or Internet banking customers who do their banking from home computers. Call center employees typically work a 40-hour week, but may work evenings and weekends during marketing campaigns. Long hours during peak periods are one of the downsides to working in a telebanking call center.

The Call Center Manager coordinates referrals from branch managers and customer service representatives. The manager identifies service problems and recommends solutions. He or she is responsible for routing of sales leads. The manager also interviews sales staff to get feedback on quality of sales and increase cross-selling opportunities, that is, selling additional products to customers using one or more bank services. Some banks have dedicated call centers for marketing of life and health insurance products or mutual funds. Additional licenses are required to market non-bank (products not protected by federal deposit insurance) financial services such as insurance and investment securities.

Salaries

Compensation for Call Center Managers is determined by level of responsibility, years of experience, and location. Call Center Managers are typically paid a salary plus performance bonus for meeting sales targets. Average compensation for Call Center Managers in financial institutions in 2004 varied from $38,384 to $60,035, according to a survey by America's Community Bankers.

Employment Prospects

Call center Managers require more diverse management skills than many other occupations, according to Incoming Calls Management Institute. Knowledge of customer behavior skills, human resources management, written and verbal communication skills, real-time management, forecasting, statistics, and information systems technology are all part of the environment.

Advancement Prospects

Call Center Managers can advance to positions in the credit department or bank product marketing. Alternatively, they can remain in the call center and accept positions of increasing responsibility in customer service and sales, such as marketing manager or product manager.

Education and Training

Normally, a four-year college degree is required for the position. Call center employees come from varied backgrounds, and many have academic backgrounds in the liberal arts and social sciences in addition to business and marketing. Most banks offer continuous training starting after employment.

Special Requirements

Licenses from the appropriate regulatory agencies may be preferred. Call Center Managers who approve sales of life or health insurance must obtain a license to sell insurance products from their state's insurance department. Those involved in sales of annuities or mutual funds will need a Series 6 license (for annuities) and Series 7 Registered Representative license from the National Association of Securities Dealers.

Experience, Skills, and Personality Traits

Call Center Managers need to have excellent interpersonal skills and motivational skills because managing people is an important part of the job. A detailed knowledge of banking policies and procedures for opening new accounts, and the ability to resolve service problems are prerequisites in this position.

Unions and Associations

Call Center Managers can become members of banking associations, including the American Bankers Association, American Institute of Banking (the education affiliate of the ABA), or the ABA Marketing Network, a division of the American Bankers Association.

Tips for Entry

1. Sales and marketing experience can help land a job managing a bank telebanking center.
2. Career fairs and association meetings can provide useful opportunities for networking.

BUSINESS DEVELOPMENT MANAGER

CAREER PROFILE

Duties: Responsible for soliciting and developing new business with locally owned and managed businesses; originates and structures commercial loans; reports to commercial lending manager

Alternate Title(s): Business Banking Officer, Business Development Officer, Corporate Development Officer, Business Banker

Salary Range: $63,850 to $113,000

Employment Prospects: Good

Advancement Prospects: Good

Prerequisites:

Education or Training—Bachelor's degree in business, finance, or related field

Experience—Three to five years' commercial lending experience; prior sales experience preferred

Special Skills and Personality Traits—Good communication, organizational, and negotiating skills; good interviewing and research skills; general understanding of financial institution policies and procedures

Special Requirements—Certification optional

CAREER LADDER

```
┌─────────────────────────────────┐
│  Manager, Business Development  │
└─────────────────────────────────┘

┌─────────────────────────────────┐
│  Business Development Manager   │
└─────────────────────────────────┘

┌─────────────────────────────────┐
│        Account Officer          │
└─────────────────────────────────┘
```

Position Description

Business Development Managers are responsible for marketing banking products to current and prospective business customers and high-net-worth individuals. They identify opportunities for marketing all the services offered by the bank, including business loans, cash management, pension management, foreign exchange, and interest rate exposure management. They perform administrative follow-up to gather information required for loan approvals or to resolve customer problems such as overdrawn checking accounts. They bring in appropriate specialists to discuss technical products with bank customers.

Duties performed will vary according to the size of banking institution, the number of business accounts serviced, and geographic location. Banks located in or near metropolitan population centers will offer a greater variety of banking products or services. In larger financial institutions, the relationship manager may also function as a consultant on pending mergers and acquisitions. Smaller financial institutions will have a narrower list of products. Business Development Manager in these banks will more likely carry the duties of commercial bank lenders.

The position requires extensive travel, and Business Development Manager normally service a specified number of customers in a region or territory. This position offers a unique opportunity to see the inner workings of many different companies in different industries. The Business Development Manager responsible for building a customer base through direct sales calls, and referrals from existing customers and from branch offices. He or she coordinates the bank's internal-credit analysis of pending loan applications.

Salaries

Business Development Managers are compensated with a combination of salary and incentive bonus awarded annually.

Salaries range from $63,850 to $113,000 in 2004, according to a survey by America's Community Bankers. Salaries are influenced by experience, level of education, and type of financial institution.

Employment Prospects

There is strong demand for salespeople in financial services. Banking relationship managers have prior financial services experience or have some experience selling financial products, and are promoted from other positions in banking. Business Development Managers come from varied backgrounds. Business Development Managers with experience in targeted industries, such as real estate development, or who have business contacts in these industries will be sought-after candidates. Individuals with demonstrated skills selling marketing annuities, mutual funds, and other investment services will also be in demand.

Advancement Prospects

Business Development Managers have several advancement opportunities. They may move up to become product managers and assume responsibility for growth and marketing of specific financial products, such as bank cards, cash management services, or trust banking services. Business Development Managers with lending experience could also move into credit administration or loan administration, and provide marketing support for the corporate loan department.

Education and Training

A four-year college degree is required. There is no specific academic training for a career in financial marketing. Employers look for individuals with general academic backgrounds, including courses in business, economics, and marketing. Courses in the social sciences and liberal arts also provide useful background. Employers provide extensive on-the-job training to qualified candidates.

Special Requirements

Career advancement may be aided by completing a certification program such as the Certified Lender-Business Banker awarded by the American Bankers Association's Institute of Certified Bankers.

Experience, Skills, and Personality Traits

Strong interpersonal skills and organizational skills are a priority in this position. Business Development Managers must be able to deal effectively with people. Effective marketers have an ability to communicate clearly with others in non-technical language, and to act as a financial consultant or adviser. They are self-starting individuals, able to work independently and work long hours to meet sates goals. A detailed knowledge of banking products and services is a necessary-component of the job.

Unions and Associations

Business Development Managers may join several banking associations, including American Bankers Association, Bank Marketing Association, and Risk Management Association (formerly Robert Morris Associates) for career development and networking opportunities.

Tips for Entry

1. Good business lenders know about business trends in the community. Join local community associations to build important contacts.
2. Banks look to hire experienced lenders who can bring new loan business to the bank.
3. State banking associations provide opportunities for networking and learning more about job opportunities.

MARKETING SPECIALIST, FINANCIAL SERVICES

CAREER PROFILE

Duties: Designs and prepares marketing campaigns and promotions; may specialize in one or two product lines

Alternate Title(s): Product Manager

Salary Range: $49,000 to $83,000 and up

Employment Prospects: Good

Advancement Prospects: Good

Prerequisites:

Education or Training—Four-year college degree with courses in business, finance, and marketing

Experience—Three to five years' financial services experience in sales or marketing

Special Skills and Personality Traits—Excellent written and verbal communication skills; ability to interpret market research data; detailed working knowledge of financial services products, customers, and market trends

CAREER LADDER

```
┌─────────────────────────────┐
│      Marketing Manager      │
└─────────────────────────────┘

┌─────────────────────────────┐
│     Marketing Specialist    │
└─────────────────────────────┘

┌─────────────────────────────┐
│      Marketing Analyst      │
└─────────────────────────────┘
```

Position Description

Financial institutions often promote their services by designing marketing activities around specific products or groups of products. Over the last 20 years or so, banks have used media advertising and promotional campaigns to try to build valuable brand images with key customer groups. A Marketing Specialist or product manager is responsible for the growth and profitability of one or more banking services, such as cash management, credit cards, or home mortgages. This individual is responsible for all marketing, promotion, sales, and customer service activities relating to that product.

Marketing Specialists conduct market surveys, arrange focus group studies, and make forecasts about the potential market for specific products or services. They analyze the cost of providing the service, set product prices, and make estimates about profitability. They promote the product by developing advertising copy, marketing brochures, and training procedures for the staff that will be engaged in selling the product. After the product has been introduced, they conduct follow-up research to determine how well the

product has been accepted and what modifications are necessary to reach sales goals.

A Marketing Specialist may perform tasks such as:

- evaluating competitor products and making pricing recommendations
- identifying the market potential for new products
- preparing sales brochures and displays to call public attention to the product
- assisting in sales staff training
- gathering comments from users for possible improvements

Marketing Specialists attend industry conferences and trade shows to gather competitive information about trends in their market, and are frequent speakers at industry conferences and seminars. Larger financial institutions usually have a separate Marketing Specialist or product manager for each line of products, under the direction of an overall marketing manager.

Marketing Specialists usually focus their attention on product design and development. They work closely with the financial services sales staff, but usually do not have a direct role in product sales.

Salaries

Salaries of financial services Marketing Specialists vary by employer, industry specialty, and geographic location. More specialized positions, which usually require more years of experience and more detailed product knowledge, tend to pay the highest salaries. Salaries are competitive with earnings of other bank marketing professionals. The middle 50 percent earned between $49,000 and $83,000 in 2004.

Employment Prospects

There is strong demand for financial professionals who can develop customized banking or financial products for the corporate market. These services include such areas as cash management, risk management, asset securitization, and investment banking. Much of this employment growth is occurring outside the traditional areas of banking—deposit gathering and lending.

Some people become Marketing Specialists by going through a bank management training program. Consumer bankers become product specialists by working their way up the organization, starting their careers in a branch banking office and advancing to the marketing department, In specialty areas, people with industry-specific knowledge are often hired from outside the bank. Many specialists hired from outside banking have prior work experience in the industries they will be contacting as product managers.

Advancement Prospects

Opportunities for advancement are good, but competition is strong. With experience, marketing specialists can advance to more senior positions, perhaps becoming marketing manager in their specialty and direct the activities of a marketing team. People with successful track records often move to a similar but higher-paying position in another bank or financial services firm. Others can become industry consultants, working in their specialty field.

Education and Training

Most people entering this field have a four-year degree in business, with a concentration in marketing. Courses in accounting, business management, and statistics are also helpful. An M.B.A. is a strong plus for the Marketing Specialist career track.

Experience, Skills, and Personality Traits

Several years experience in positions of increased responsibility is usually required to master the skills of financial services marketing. The important skills include a mastery of analytical tools, including statistics, public opinion polling, and other market research techniques. Excellent verbal and written communication skills are needed to be able to communicate marketing strategies to coworkers and senior management. The individual should be entrepreneurial or visionary in planning, and detail-oriented in putting a marketing plan into action.

Marketing Specialists in financial services need to have an in-depth understanding of their market, its history, and its service requirements. For example, product development specialists in corporate cash management services should be familiar with industry practices in cash collection, disbursement, and short-term investments. Specific requirements will vary by industry.

Unions and Associations

Financial services Marketing Specialists can become members of several professional associations, such as the Association for Financial Professionals or the ABA Marketing Network, a division of the American Bankers Association, for career advancement and networking opportunities.

Tips for Entry

1. While in college, learn about marketing by helping with promotional activities for social clubs, sports, or other student organizations.
2. College-level courses in marketing, communications, and media are especially helpful. Look carefully at case studies of marketing successes or failures for further insights.
3. As in other financial career paths, contact development through networking, internships, and summer employment can put you in touch with potential employers.

MARKETING MANAGER

CAREER PROFILE

Duties: Directing and coordinating marketing of financial services; may oversee marketing activities for a customer-specific product group

Alternate Title(s): Marketing Director, Marketing Officer

Salary Range: $46,650 to $79,681

Employment Prospects: Good

Advancement Prospects: Fair

Prerequisites:

Education or Training—Four-year college degree with courses in business administration and marketing; M.B.A. or graduate degree helpful

Experience—Five to eight years of financial industry knowledge and experience

Special Skills and Personality Traits—Excellent communication, organizational, and leadership skills; ability to interpret and analyze market research data; detailed working knowledge of banking products and services, as well as state and federal regulations dealing with financial product marketing

CAREER LADDER

```
┌─────────────────────────┐
│   Divisional Manager     │
└─────────────────────────┘

┌─────────────────────────┐
│   Marketing Manager      │
└─────────────────────────┘

┌─────────────────────────┐
│   Marketing Officer      │
└─────────────────────────┘
```

Position Description

The essence of marketing is finding the right balance between market demand and product offering. The major objective is attracting and retaining as many customers as possible for an organization. Marketing is taking on greater importance in banking, as commercial banks evolve into general financial services companies selling investment products and insurance in addition to traditional bank deposits and loans.

Despite the industry's trend toward greater diversification, deposits and loans are still the main source of bank profitability. Marketing Managers direct the planning of the annual marketing budget and maintain records of marketing expenses. They assist branch offices in developing strategies for acquiring new depositors and making new loans. They coordinate the development of media advertising and sales literature with advertising agencies or outside vendors. They are responsible for the release of new product announce-

ments through newsletters and special mailings. They act as advisors to financial institution departments on the content and design of marketing materials for internal or external distribution.

Marketing Managers consult with other banking officers and managers on a regular basis to develop sales goals for each branch office, banking region, and the entire organization. One of their primary tasks is directing employee training when new products are announced.

Marketing Managers also:

- assist in the development of telemarketing campaigns
- make recommendations to the division manager about budgetary needs of the marketing department
- edit and write advertising copy for use in promotions
- prepare general press releases for release to the news media
- coordinate special events such as branch openings

- promote the bank's presence in the community by participating in community functions
- review products and services of competing financial institutions and make suggestions about product changes to senior management

Marketing Managers report to a divisional manager, such as the head of retail banking. Larger financial institutions often have marketing specialists assigned to each business group; they manage product development for different product lines and coordinate sales activities with their sales staff. Marketing Managers usally work a 40-hour week, but often work longer hours during marketing campaigns.

Salaries

Salaries vary according to duties and experience. Annual salaries of bank Marketing Managers in 2004 were between $46,650 and $79,681 according to America's Community Bankers, a banking association. Marketing Managers of larger financial institutions in metropolitan areas earned higher salaries. The average salary, including commissions or bonuses was $70,472.

Employment Prospects

Employment opportunities should grow about as fast as in other occupations through 2014. There is very good demand for financial professionals who can develop products for the corporate market, such as cash management services, corporate finance, and mutual funds. Many people hired as Marketing Managers for mutual funds and investment products are hired from other investment firms.

Advancement Prospects

Advancement is to positions of increased responsibility, such as manager of consumer banking marketing or corporate banking. Because promotion opportunities in the same financial institution are often limited, Marketing Managers frequently advance their careers by taking similar but higher paying positions at competing financial institutions.

Education and Training

A four-year college degree is required, with courses in marketing and business administration. Courses in accounting or finance are helpful.

Experience, Skills, and Personality Traits

As banking becomes more segmented along product lines, individuals with brand management and product design experience will be increasingly in demand. Marketing Managers should have at least one year's experience in banking, one year in direct sales, or five years of marketing experience.

The marketing of financial products is highly regulated. Some working knowledge of state and federal regulations governing product promotion is very important. Individuals are expected to be familiar with consumer protection regulations dealing with disclosure of interest rates.

Unions and Associations

Marketing Managers can join the professional associations such as the American Bankers Association Marketing Network or the Consumer Bankers Association for career advancement and networking opportunities.

Tips for Entry

1. In college, try to get a broad business background in marketing, communications, and media courses.
2. Try placing yourself in the hands of the consumer. Ask yourself, "Would someone buy this product?"
3. Develop a curious mind. Build a file of case studies of marketing campaigns to learn what worked and what didn't work.
4. For insights into career networking and internships, check out Web sites of industry associations and major employers. The ABA Marketing Network's Web site (www.aba.com/MarketingNetwork) offers career information and links to resources for individuals interested in a career in bank marketing.
5. Attend local chapter meetings of the Bank Marketing Association to take advantage of networking opportunities with industry professionals.

OPERATIONS MANAGER

CAREER PROFILE

Duties: Oversees management of a bank's information systems department, including technical support, branch office networking, training, and database operations

Alternate Title(s): Branch Operations Specialist; Manager, Information Systems

Salary Range: $45,153 to $65,316

Employment Prospects: Good

Advancement Prospects: Fair

Prerequisites:

Education or Training—Four-year college degree in information systems or computer science; courses in business administration helpful

Experience—Three to five years' experience in positions of increased responsibility, preferably in financial services

Special Skills and Personality Traits—Ability to schedule tasks and supervise staff; technical problem-solving ability; good written and verbal communication skills; familiarity with relevant operating systems; working knowledge of bank computer systems, policies, and operating procedures

CAREER LADDER

```
┌─────────────────────────────────┐
│   Chief Information Officer      │
└─────────────────────────────────┘

┌─────────────────────────────────┐
│     Operations Manager          │
└─────────────────────────────────┘

┌─────────────────────────────────┐
│   Assistant Information          │
│   Systems Manager                │
└─────────────────────────────────┘
```

Position Description

The Operations Manager oversees all data processing activities supporting the deposit servicing and lending functions of a bank. The Operations Manager has responsibility for assuring that branch office computer systems are running smoothly and that customers receive proper credit for deposits to a checking or savings account. They direct and control management of branch office software and computer systems. Larger financial institutions usually have Operations Managers for each department.

The Operations Manager supervises branch level and back office data processing support, including support staff for checking, savings, retirement accounts, automated teller machine cards, traveler's checks, and savings bond interest coupons. The managers are responsible for balancing and maintenance of automated teller machines.

They administer branch banking self-audit programs, and assure compliance with federal and state bank regulatory agencies. They control and report branch losses, such as loss resulting from incidents such as clerical error or theft. The Operations Manager coordinates investigations following a reported loss with the bank's security officer, head of retail banking, and law enforcement agencies.

Other duties performed include:

* providing training for operations group employees
* maintaining current policies and procedures manuals
* issuing periodic status reports to branch office managers, senior managers, and bank directors
* participating in selecting and hiring of staff
* conducting staff meetings to review operational problems and changes to banking regulations affecting bank operations
* managing security procedures in branch offices
* handling customer questions and complaints regarding operational issues

Operational Managers work in an office setting, usually working a 40-hour week. They may work longer hours during a data processing conversion or upgrade to a new balance reporting/branch information system. The position reports to the Senior Operations Officer or Administrative Officer.

Salaries

Salaries of branch operating officers and operations specialists were comparable to other mid-level employees in banking. Annual salaries of branch operations officers were reported at between $45,153 and $65,316, according to a 2004 salary survey by America's Community Bankers. Salaries depend on the size of the organization and its information technology department, and the number of people supervised. The average annual salary, including commissions and bonuses, was $56,546.

Employment Prospects

There is fairly strong demand for Operations Managers with good technical skills, a familiarity with emerging areas in computer networking and excellent management skills. The best opportunities are often in smaller financial institutions and credit unions than big commercial banks. Individuals are usually promoted to this position from more junior-level positions, such as systems analyst, or they are hired from outside the bank.

Advancement Prospects

Advancement prospects to more senior positions in banking are fair, considering the large number of qualified candidates. For individuals with the right skills, advancement is usually to more senior level position in bank operations or general administration. An Operations Manager with some experience in lending operations could advance to become head of retail banking.

In larger financial institutions, promotion from Operations Manager to more senior positions is usually linked to completion of additional training or a post-graduate degree program such as master's in business administration. Money center banks and large regional banks often have a chief information officer (CIO), who has broad responsibility for bank investments in information technology. This position usually reports directly to the chief executive officer or senior management committee.

Education and Training

A four-year degree with courses in business management and information processing is generally required. A strong background in management and employee supervision is more important than detailed knowledge of computer operations. The Operations Manager must be familiar with programs, computer networks, and systems analysis, but the primary focus of the job is management.

Financial institutions usually provide extensive training in branch office operations management through in-house training programs, correspondence courses, or industry-sponsored training schools and seminars.

Experience, Skills, and Personality Traits

Some hands-on experience with computer systems is essential, usually at least three to five years experience in various phases of bank operations. Individuals need to be computer literate, and have a working knowledge of personal computer-based accounting and balance reporting systems. Individuals should have excellent oral and written communication skills and organizational skills. The most qualified candidates have a mastery of technical issues, an ability to supervise and motivate subordinates, and can communicate effectively with other managers. Some technical knowledge of banking operations in one or more operational areas, such as retail banking, mortgage processing, or branch networking, is essential in order to function in the position. Individuals should also be familiar with applicable federal or state regulations that require some level of operational support.

Unions and Associations

Operations Managers can participate in state chapter meetings of the American Bankers Association or the American Institute of Banking, the educational affiliate of the ABA, or the Bank Administration Institute for career advancement and networking opportunities. Attending regular professional group meetings to keep up with technical issues is an important part of career development.

Tips for Entry

1. Be sure to supplement college courses in computer science with courses in business-related topics such as accounting and business administration.
2. Work-study positions in your college computer center or internships with local financial institutions provide opportunities to supplement classroom instruction with practical real-world experience.
3. As in other bank-related positions, posting your résumé on Internet job banks is a good way to get in contact with employers.
4. A varied career background is important. After a few years as a systems administrator or technical services analyst, you are in a position to move up to a position with supervisory responsibility.

COMPLIANCE OFFICER

Duties: Develops, administers, and monitors internal programs to ensure compliance with applicable federal and state laws and regulations; issues guidelines for marketing of banking services to the public

Alternate Title(s): Compliance Manager, Risk and Compliance Officer

Salary Range: $42,025 to $67,660

Employment Prospects: Good

Advancement Prospects: Good

Prerequisites:

Education or Training—Bachelor's degree; postgraduate education a plus; law degree may be a requirement in some institutions

Experience—Two to four years' related experience

Special Skills and Personality Traits—Excellent written and verbal communication skills and organizational skills; excellent research skills, computer literacy with word processing and spreadsheet accounting programs; extensive knowledge of all financial institution policies and procedures; ability to read and interpret government regulations, trade journals, and legal documents. Must be able to respond to inquiries from regulatory agencies, courts, and outside consultants

Special Requirements—Professional certification or licensing is a plus

```
┌──────────────────────────────────┐
│     Senior Compliance Manager     │
└──────────────────────────────────┘

┌──────────────────────────────────┐
│        Compliance Manager         │
└──────────────────────────────────┘

┌──────────────────────────────────┐
│        Compliance Officer         │
└──────────────────────────────────┘
```

Position Description

The Compliance Officer is the administrative staffer responsible for overseeing compliance with federal and state laws and regulations governing the sale of financial products and services. The Compliance Officer is usually a member of the audit and/or legal staff. Specific job functions and duties will vary by institution. In general, the size of the bank and the number of staff members devoted to the compliance function will define the position and specific job requirements. Some banks have a committee approach to the compliance function, assigning parts of the job function to different staff members. The compliance manager in smaller institutions may have other responsibilities in addition to compliance. The Compliance Officer may also be responsible for inter-

nal audit or may serve as community reinvestment officer, and in this capacity assume responsibility for compliance with the Community Reinvestment Act (CRA), the federal law encouraging equal access to credit and fair lending in economically disadvantaged communities.

The position requires careful attention to detail and an ability to interpret legal opinions handed down by the courts regarding permissible activities of financial institutions. Federal antiterrorist laws, including the USA PATRIOT Act of 2001, impose additional duties on bank compliance officers, which stimulated the hiring of more compliance officers to handle the increased workload. The Patriot Act requires banks to report suspicious money transfers by a wide range of organizations, including suspected terrorist groups, and collect additional information about customers opening new accounts. The Compliance Officer is also responsible for reviewing advertising, promotional brochures, bank forms, and documents for compliance with banking regulations, such as interest rate disclosures required on consumer loan documents. In general, the Compliance Officer is responsible for identifying risks and internal control weaknesses, and proposing solutions to bank management.

Their duties include:

- administering banking programs to ensure compliance with federal and state laws and regulations; and communicating to all employees any changes in regulations affecting their conduct on the job
- reviewing and interpreting new and pending banking laws
- supervising the financial institution's records and retention program
- coordinating the financial institution's disaster recovery program
- scheduling compliance audits and reports results of these audits to the board of directors
- providing bank management with regular reports on the institution's compliance
- scheduling meetings with department managers to provide information on compliance changes affecting their departments
- supervising audit reviews by internal and external auditors
- recommending changes in bank policy to meet compliance regulations

Salaries

Salaries are determined by several factors, including years of experience, geographic location, and size of financial institution. Compliance Officers working full time in larger financial institutions, or who manage a compliance and audit department are paid higher compensation than Compliance Officers in smaller banks. Salaries ranged from $42,025 to $67,660, according to a salary survey by America's Community Bankers. The median salary earned by Compliance Officers was $53,040.

Employment Prospects

Average growth is expected through 2012. Additional job openings will arise from retirements and transfers to other occupations. Consolidation in the financial services industry over the next several years will diminish the market demand for Compliance Officers. At the same time, Compliance Officers who have specialty skills or backgrounds such as risk management or who have postgraduate education such as a law degree will be in somewhat greater demand.

Advancement Prospects

Compliance Officers have several advancement options. They can advance to more senior functions in the audit or legal departments, such as internal auditor or manager of the auditing department. A bank Compliance Officer, with experience and the necessary legal background (a law degree) may advance to the general counsel position—the top legal officer in their institution.

Education and Training

A bachelor's degree with courses in accounting, finance, and related fields is a minimum requirement for positions in bank auditing and compliance. Education and training requirement will vary by job function. For example, a Compliance Officer employed in a bank trust department will be expected to have knowledge of general trust law, federal regulations governing trust functions, and the Employee Retirement Income Security Act (ERISA).

Special Requirements

In addition to a college degree, professional certification or licensing is a plus in many institutions. A law degree may be a requirement in some banks.

Experience, Skills, and Personality Traits

Three to five years experience in financial services or banking is a requirement for Compliance Officers. Also desirable is a background in legal accounting, audit, or previous experience as a Compliance Officer. The successful candidate will have strong research and computer skills, and excellent communication and organizational skills. The Compliance Officer's job requires a detail-oriented individual, who can work under deadline pressure. Experience as a paralegal may also be an asset to a career in bank compliance.

Unions and Associations

As professional employees, Compliance Officers are not usually members of labor unions. They can become members of professional associations for career advancement and networking, such as the American Institute of Banking, the educational affiliate of the American Bankers Association. Certifications available to Compliance Officers include the ABA Certified Regulatory Compliance manager designation.

Tips for Entry

1. Attend courses sponsored by American Institute of Banking to learn about the fundamentals of bank compliance.
2. Most jobs in this field become available through promotion when incumbents leave for another job; networking with banking professionals can open the door to an interview.
3. Follow job leads in newspaper advertisements and career search sites on the Internet.

RESIDENTIAL MORTGAGE ORIGINATOR

CAREER PROFILE

Duties: Markets residential mortgage loans and related mortgage loans to financial institution customers; responsible for loan closing and preparation of loan documents; contacts appraisers, real estate brokers, and others for new business leads

Alternate Title(s): Home Mortgage Consultant, Residential Mortgage Specialist

Salary Range: $20,400 to $88,572 (excluding commissions)

Employment Prospects: Good

Advancement Prospects: Fair

Prerequisites:

Education or Training—Four-year degree with courses in business management, finance, or related courses

Experience—Two years in mortgage or consumer lending, or equivalent experience in related areas

Special Skills and Personality Traits—Excellent communication, organizational, and marketing skills; ability to work independently with minimal supervision; good computer skills; knowledge of state and federal laws relating to real estate closings

Special Requirements—General understanding of the various types of mortgage instruments, financial institution policies and procedures, and federal and state regulations concerning residential mortgages

CAREER LADDER

```
┌─────────────────────────────────────┐
│     Commissioned Loan Officer        │
└─────────────────────────────────────┘

┌─────────────────────────────────────┐
│        Senior Loan Officer           │
└─────────────────────────────────────┘

┌─────────────────────────────────────┐
│   Residential Mortgage Originator    │
└─────────────────────────────────────┘
```

Position Description

Residential Mortgage Originators work for commercial banks, credit unions, savings institutions, and mortgage companies. They work with realtors, property appraisers, attorneys, and bank business development officers to develop new business opportunities. Loan originators interview mortgage applicants and monitor the progress of the loan from the application to closing. They work closely with the bank's loan processors to ensure that new loans comply with the bank's underwriting guidelines. Mortgage originators interview customers applying for loans, analyze and screen preliminary loan requests, and package loans for review by senior loan officers or loan committees.

Mortgage originators solicit new loans from prospective borrowers, gather background financial information, help the borrower fill out mortgage loan applications, and submit loan applications for processing. They determine whether loan applicants meet the lender's credit criteria or loan standards. The loan originator may call the applicant to resolve discrepancies in the credit application, such as a credit report showing late payments.

Residential Mortgage Originators spend much of their time out of their office, working with laptop computers, cellular phones, and pagers to stay in contact with their offices and clients. Mortgage loan officers may work from their home, and they usually are assigned a geographic territory in which they work. They work closely with branch office managers and will frequently call on potential customers referred by a branch office in their region. Mortgage loan officers may work a 40-hour week, but they may work evenings and weekends, especially when there is a heavy volume of mortgage originations and loan refinancings.

Specific job functions include:

- interviewing loan applicants and explaining loan terms and conditions
- analyzing the applicant's financial status, credit history, and property to determine the feasibility of granting a loan
- ordering appraisals, credit reports, and reference checks.
- verifying the borrower's salary or requesting copies of tax returns if the borrower is self-employed
- preparing loan documentation in accordance with financial institution standards
- screening loan requests according to financial institution policies and types of loans offered
- providing status reports to bank management on residential loan production
- coordinating loan closings with buyers, sellers, and real estate agents
- counseling delinquent borrowers or referring delinquencies to the loan collection department
- resolving customer complaints

The residential mortgage field has numerous specialty positions that service market subsegments. Subprime mortgage originators process loan applications of applicants who have had past credit problems or have limited borrowing experience. (Subprime mortgage lending, the fastest-growing industry segment, accounted for one of every five mortgage loans originated in 2005.) Home renovation specialists process loan applications for home renovation financings; in a renovation loan the lender advances funds to renovate a property along with the funds necessary to purchase the mortgaged property. Funds are advanced based on the expected appraised value of the property after completion of the renovations.

Renovation loans can be any of several types; some lenders offer a construction-to-permanent loan—a single loan covering renovation construction and home purchase. The Federal Housing Administration's 203(k) loan program, which offers low-downpayment mortgage financing on owner-occupied homes, is another popular option. Reverse mortgage specialists originate loans to senior citizens in which the lender advances funds to the lender, providing income after retirement, in exchange for a lien on the borrower's property.

Salaries

Residential mortgage lenders earn much of their income from sales commissions. A number of salary arrangements are possible: a base salary plus commissions based on loan production volume. Newly hired loan officers receive a base salary plus a drawdown against future commissions. The base salary is gradually reduced as lenders become more experienced and their loan production increases. Commissioned mortgage lenders earned average commissions of $92,571 in 2004. Salaried mortgage loan officers earned annual salaries (excluding commissions) ranging from a low of $20,400 to $88,572.

Employment Prospects

Employment opportunities for commissioned mortgage lenders will grow about as fast as employment opportunities in general, according to the Bureau of Labor Statistics. The mortgage market is very sensitive to interest rates, which means job opportunities may shrink during periods when mortgage lending is declining. Employment opportunities in niche markets, such as subprime lending or renovation financing, may be better than in the market as a whole. Employment opportunities in renovation lending are closely tied to regional economic conditions. Regions where home values have appreciated but home buyers and home owners need financing to upgrade their homes may have greater demand for renovation loans—and home renovation lenders.

Advancement Prospects

Advancement opportunities for Residential Mortgage Originators depend on experience, as in other fields in bank lending. Mortgage lenders with successful track records—having met or exceeded production goals with average or lower-than-average loan losses—may advance to handle more complicated loan financings, such as construction loans or commercial mortgages. They can advance to become team leaders, overseeing a group of lenders plus supporting loan processors and clerical staff. Some opportunities will come about through turnover when other lenders move to positions with another financial institution or reach retirement age.

Education and Training

Most financial institutions seek candidates with at least a four-year college degree including courses in business, finance, and marketing. Also helpful are courses in the social sciences and the liberal arts. Financial institutions normally provide extensive on-the-job training to starting mortgage originators, supplemented with periodic seminars as new types of mortgage financing are introduced. The training requirements vary by financial institution and by the specific requirements of the position.

Special Requirements

The mortgage lending position requires a general understanding of the various types of mortgage instruments, financial institution policies and procedures, and federal and state regulations concerning residential mortgages. Industry certification is optional and is generally not a requirement to enter the field. Industry certifications include the Accredited Residential Underwriter and Certified Mortgage Banker designations from the Mortgage Bankers Association.

There are no special licensing requirements. Newly hired lenders go through a short training program in which they become familiar with mortgage underwriting guidelines of federal agencies such as Fannie Mae and Freddie Mac, which purchase loans from mortgage originators in the secondary mortgage market, or the Federal Housing Authority, an agency within the Department of Housing and Urban Development that insures mortgage loans. Most lenders have loan origination guidelines that match or exceed the federal agency guidelines.

Experience, Skills, and Personality Traits

Mortgage lenders should have at least two years experience, preferably in consumer lending or mortgages. Prior experience in mortgage lending or commission-paid financial sales is helpful, though not a requirement. As there is a high degree of customer contact, excellent communication skills, organizational skills, and marketing skills are important. Productive mortgage lenders must also have excellent people skills for interviewing prospective loan customers.

Getting a mortgage approved involves many separate steps, so attention to detail is important. Also important is an ability to work closely with builders, appraisers, and other professionals.

Unions and Associations

Mortgage lenders can become members of the Mortgage Bankers Association through their employer, which provides networking opportunities and skills improvement. The Mortgage Bankers Association sponsors seminars and distance learning courses for individuals involved in real estate lending.

Tips for Entry

1. Attending job fairs sponsored by state mortgage bankers associations is an effective way to get to know potential employers.
2. Check job opportunities at one of the many banking industry Web sites for available positions in your area.
3. While one to two years' experience is usually a requirement, lenders will sometimes hire individuals with no previous banking experience. Contact employers in your area directly or ask for referrals from friends or associates.

COMMERCIAL REAL ESTATE LOAN OFFICER

CAREER PROFILE

Duties: Develops and structures mortgage loans for office buildings, shopping centers, and other commercial properties; solicits new business opportunities; acts as a financial adviser to commercial loan clients

Alternate Title(s): Commercial Real Estate Lender

Salary Range: $69,502 to $102,120

Employment Prospects: Good

Advancement Prospects: Fair

Prerequisites:

Education or Training—Four-year college degree with courses in business, economics, or finance; M.B.A. degree a plus

Experience—Three to five years' commercial mortgage lending or loan underwriting

Special Skills and Personality Traits—Broad understanding of the commercial mortgage lending field and working knowledge of Microsoft Office Suite

Special Requirements—Real estate appraisal certification optional but not required

CAREER LADDER

```
┌─────────────────────────────┐
│   Commercial Real Estate    │
│        Loan Officer         │
└─────────────────────────────┘

┌─────────────────────────────┐
│   Team Leader, Commercial   │
│      Mortgage Lending       │
└─────────────────────────────┘

┌─────────────────────────────┐
│        Senior Lender        │
└─────────────────────────────┘
```

Position Description

Commercial Real Estate Loan Officers develop and structure mortgage loans for office buildings, shopping centers, hotels, and other commercial properties. They manage loan transactions from origination through credit analysis, loan documentation, loan committee review, and follow-up loan monitoring after the loan closing. They oversee and provide guidance for the bank's credit analysis staff and documentation assistants. They also act as financial advisors for commercial loan clients; commercial loan borrowers view their banker as a source of information or advice on deal structuring in addition to the mortgage financing. Commercial mortgage officers are sometimes known as investment bankers in the world of commercial banking because they originate loans on properties that are held for investment purposes by real estate developers or investor groups.

The job description of commercial bank loan officers has broadened in the last five years, partly because of intensified competition for bank deposits and other customer relationships. Commercial mortgage lenders wear multiple hats; they are responsible for cross-selling other bank products, such as deposit accounts, and generating other business relationships with their loan customers. The loan officer is responsible for individual loan production, loan quality, loan profitability, and compliance with loan terms as stated in the loan documentation and compliance with banking laws and regulations.

Origination of commercial mortgages is broken down by loan size: The commercial lender refers smaller loans to a credit analyst, who prepares an analysis and review of financial statements; larger loans—usually loans larger than $1 million—are referred to the bank's loan committee for final approval. Some travel is required, although mostly to visit clients in a defined regional territory. Commercial lenders entering the business typically spend the first five years of their careers building relationships with prospective borrowers.

Among their various duties, Commercial Real Estate Loan Officers perform the following tasks:

- analyze and prepare commercial loan and commercial real estate transactions
- prepare formal loan analysis presentations for approval
- assemble loan documents such as appraisals, financial statements, and borrower tax returns before loan closing
- oversee first-level administration of all loan accounts in their portfolio
- manage the borrower's relationship with the bank, analyzing client needs for other banking products
- conduct continuous reviews of the borrower's compliance with loan terms and covenants
- direct activities supporting the company's image in areas of responsibility
- comply with state or federal lending laws and internal policies and procedures

Salaries

Salaries are determined by experience and qualifications at the time of hire. A Commercial Real Estate Loan Officer's salary is usually a combination of base salary plus sales commissions and incentive bonuses for reaching performance goals. Salaries in 2004 ranged between $69,502 and $102,120, according to America's Community Bankers. Annual salaries, including commissions, averaged $207,462.

Employment Prospects

Commercial real estate lending has its ups and downs. Lenders are most in demand when the real estate market is booming and loan interest rates are low, as happened in 2001–05. When the real estate market bottomed in the early 1990s after several years of speculative development, many lenders pulled back from the market, reduced staffs, and retreated from the commercial loan market. The largest banks want experienced lenders, people who can bring in a loan portfolio or at least a list of potential clients who are likely to become borrowers.

While most financial institutions want experienced lenders, there are ways to break into the business by working in a related area and gaining experience. One way to gain experience is to work for a few years in loan workout, handling problem loans that either have some deficiencies in the loan file, such as missing information, or are delinquent. By learning at the back end of the loan cycle how to research the fundamental weaknesses in a loan that goes bad, loan officers learn what it takes to originate loans that perform as expected and remain high-quality loans.

Advancement Prospects

Advancement is a function of time and experience gained on the job. The more a lender learns, the faster he or she can grow into more senior positions with more responsibility. Learn how to do the more complex types of loans and advise less experienced lenders. An experienced lender can become a team leader, advising less seasoned lenders. A team leader may oversee three to five lenders and have loan approval authority in concert with the loan officers. Advancement to more senior positions in the bank such as senior lender or department head is also possible. Experienced lenders can move laterally into careers in commercial lending at life insurance companies or commercial finance companies that make commercial property loans.

Education and Training

A four-year degree in finance, accounting, or economics with a concentration in finance is generally a minimum requirement. Many financial institutions prefer hiring lenders with MBAs and at least three to five years' experience as commercial lenders or commercial loan underwriters. Financial recruiters seem to prefer candidates with M.B.A.s when contacting employers for referrals.

Special Requirements

Commercial Real Estate Loan Officers should have broad knowledge of commercial loan underwriting and familiarity with Microsoft Office Suite (Word, PowerPoint, and Access) software programs. No certification is necessary to enter the field. In the early 1990s, when the commercial real estate market was very soft, some commercial real estate lenders became licensed real estate appraisers as a career backstop. Since then, fewer lenders opt to maintain their appraisal licenses.

Experience, Skills, and Personality Traits

Problem-solving and organizational skills are highly important, along with leadership, initiative, and ability to forge professional relationships with real estate professionals and others. As in other banking positions where interaction with peer-level professionals and clients is important to success, individuals must have strong written and verbal communication skills. Knowledge of the commercial loan business and deal structuring is important, but most employers are looking for individuals who have some experience in financial sales, people who can manage the bank's entire relationship with its customers. Bank employers also look for individuals who have some knowledge of the local or regional loan market, or who have a file of prospective clients who may become borrowers at some point in the future.

Unions and Associations

Commercial lenders can participate in activities of their state banking associations or associations such as the Mortgage Bankers Association at the national level to keep up with trends in the field or take part in association-sponsored seminars to maintain their job skills.

Tips for Entry

1. As in other bank lender positions, internships provide a valuable introduction to learning the business and making contacts with potential employers. Most banks will review internships on a case-by-case basis. They like the free labor, and it is a valuable way for interns to learn the business firsthand and make contacts with potential employers.
2. Networking through business associations and non-profit organizations helps build visibility.
3. Contact recruiters. Many positions in high-growth fields such as mortgage lending are filled through recruiters and search firms.
4. It's all about sales; banks today are more comfortable hiring people who have a background in sales.
5. Banking industry Web sites are good sources of job leads, particularly for individuals who are willing to relocate.

ACCOUNTING AND CORPORATE FINANCE

ACCOUNTING CLERK

CAREER PROFILE

Duties: Maintains, balances, and reconciles accounting records; enters and verifies account transaction data; may record changes in loan balances, accounts payable, and accounts receivable

Alternate Title(s): Account Information Clerk

Salary Range: $24,250 to $30,750

Employment Prospects: Fair

Advancement Prospects: Good

Prerequisites:

Education or Training—High school diploma or equivalent, with a background in business math, business writing, and communication; on-the-job training usually available

Experience—Prior industry experience or work-study experience helpful though not generally required

Special Skills and Personality Traits—Ability to perform calculations with speed and accuracy; follow oral and written instructions; good communication skills, organizational skills, and typing skills

CAREER LADDER

```
┌─────────────────────────────┐
│       Office Manager         │
└─────────────────────────────┘

┌─────────────────────────────┐
│      Staff Accountant        │
└─────────────────────────────┘

┌─────────────────────────────┐
│      Accounting Clerk        │
└─────────────────────────────┘
```

Position Description

Accounting Clerks compute, classify, and record numerical data in order to develop and maintain financial records. They record accounting debits and credits, compare current and past financial reports, and monitor loans, accounts payable, and accounts receivable to insure that payments are up to date and properly recorded. The Accounting Clerk's job is an important one. The data compiled by Accounting Clerks enable an organization's management to interpret its financial performance and make business decisions. Maintaining accurate accounting records is an essential task in preparing quarterly reports to stockholders and filing income tax reports.

Accounting Clerks are employed in financial institutions, insurance companies, government agencies, and businesses. In large organizations bookkeepers and Accounting Clerks are usually classified by job responsibility, such as Accounting Clerk I or Accounting Clerk II. Their job classification determines their responsibilities; job duties and salaries increase with higher job classifications.

Duties performed by Accounting Clerks include the following:

- entering and verifying transaction data and computing changes to accounts
- posting operating expenses to appropriate accounts
- counting cash receipts, maintaining a cash book or control record
- filing and maintaining clerical records and reporting pertinent information to accounting, bookkeeping, or operational managers
- preparing and mailing bills, invoices, or statements
- recording salaries, taxes paid, and benefits
- preparing monthly bank reconciliations
- recording investment account activity

More advanced clerks may review invoices and statements, and prepare reports for management. Other responsibilities may include auditing financial reports for accuracy and compliance with departmental, corporate, or government procedures.

Accounting Clerks work in an office setting, usually 35 to 40 hours a week. The position requires minimal travel. This can be a good-career choice if you like working with numbers, have good organizational skills, and have an aptitude for problem solving.

Salaries

Salaries for Accounting Clerks can vary according to number of years experience and job responsibilities. Salaries in 2005 ranged between $24,250 and $30,750, according to Robert Half International Inc., a staffing services firm. Experienced Accounting Clerks with several years experience can earn annual salaries of $30,000 or more a year. In addition to salary, fulltime Accounting Clerks receive health insurance and paid vacation, and can participate in employer-sponsored retirement plans.

Employment Prospects

This is an entry-level position. Demand for Accounting Clerks is expected to grow at a slower pace than other service industry positions over the next several years. One factor limiting job growth is the increased use of computers in performing routine office functions. Larger organizations are centralizing accounting functions in business service centers and automating their transaction processing to reduce the need for manual data entry and information processing.

While overall job growth will be lower than in the recent past, there are numerous opportunities. Employee turnover will produce some job openings. Job growth is expected to be strongest in small, rapidly growing, organizations. Despite the trend toward reduced office staffing, a growing economy will stimulate growth in financial transactions, leading to increased demand for accounting services.

Advancement Prospects

Accounting Clerks workers can advance to positions of increased responsibility in the accounting department, such as setting up and managing financial databases. With training in employee supervision they can also become department heads and office managers. Individuals who have college degrees can also move up to higher profile management positions such as department head, auditor, or accounting manager.

Education and Training

High school graduates are preferred in Accounting Clerk positions. Some employers seek applicants who have completed two years of college and earned an associate's degree or have graduated from a post-high school business program. Employers look for individuals who have taken business, bookkeeping, or accounting courses in high school or local community colleges.

Some employers have extensive on-the-job training programs, such as work-study programs offered in cooperation with a local junior college or university. Work-study programs combine practical on-the-job experience and academic study in business and accounting courses. The participating academic institutions can also provide job placement services to help qualified individuals find employment.

Experience, Skills, and Personality Traits

Accounting Clerks are expected to have a working knowledge of personal computers, word processing, spreadsheet accounting programs, and other office equipment. Prior work experience or work-study experience is helpful, but is not generally a requirement. Accounting Clerks work unsupervised for long periods of time, and should be self-starting individuals, able to work independently. They need to have strong organizational abilities in order to concentrate on detailed work, and excellent interpersonal skills so they are able to communicate results of their work to others.

Unions and Associations

Accounting Clerks may become members of a labor union such as the Office and Professional Employees International Union. Public employees may belong to the American Federation of State, County, and Municipal Employees. Some Accounting Clerks may be represented by the same labor union representing manufacturing employees.

Tips for Entry

1. Get experience handling cash, learning about product pricing, or assisting customers; this can provide valuable insight into career opportunities in accounting.
2. Volunteer to help manage the books for a community organization while in school, or get involved in fundraising for a nonprofit organization.
3. Explore work-study programs or internships; these programs can help to develop important contacts after graduation leading eventually to full-time employment.
4. Investigate job opportunities by answering newspaper advertisements and applying directly to companies. State employment services can also provide job leads.
5. Interim employment or temporary assignments can lead to longer-term and even full-time employment. Temporary assignments are often arranged through employment agencies or search firms.

BUDGET ANALYST

CAREER PROFILE

Duties: Examines budget estimates for completeness, accuracy, and compliance with procedures and regulations; monitors accounting reports to identify over-spending; may assist in design of budget control systems

Alternate Title(s): Budget Accountant, Budget Consultant

Salary Range: $35,000 to $87,500

Employment Prospects: Good

Advancement Prospects: Good

Prerequisites:

Education or Training—Four-year degree with courses in accounting or finance

Experience—One to two years' experience in accounting or in a financial environment

Special Skills and Personality Traits—Excellent analytical and organizational skills; good interpersonal skills; good computer skills; ability to meet deadlines; detailed knowledge of accounting principles, capital budgeting, and project planning

CAREER LADDER

```
┌─────────────────────────────┐
│     Senior Budget Analyst   │
└─────────────────────────────┘

┌─────────────────────────────┐
│       Budget Analyst        │
└─────────────────────────────┘

┌─────────────────────────────┐
│   Entry-Level Budget Analyst│
└─────────────────────────────┘
```

Position Description

Allocating limited financial resources among various projects can be a challenging task in any organization. Budget Analysts have a primary role in the development, analysis, and execution of budgets. Budgets are financial plans used to estimate future spending requirements and allocate capital and operating resources. The analysis of spending patterns and planning for future operations are an integral part of the decision-making process in most corporations, non-profit organizations, and government agencies. About one-third of Budget Analysts work in federal or state government agencies.

Budget Analysts in private industry look for ways to improve efficiency and increase profitability. They provide advice and technical assistance in the preparation of annual budgets. At the beginning of the budget cycle, managers and department heads submit proposed operating and financial plans to Budget Analysts for review. In the evaluation process the Budget Analyst compiles all the relevant data and makes cash flow projections about proposed budgets, taking into consideration the organization's assets, its outstanding short-term and long-term debt, and other liabilities.

Their duties include:

- examining budget estimates for completeness, accuracy, and compliance with procedures and regulations
- examining requests for budget revisions, recommended approval or denial, and related correspondence
- analyzing monthly department budgeting and accounting reports to maintain controls over expenditures
- providing technical assistance to senior management in the preparation of budgets
- informing managers of the status and availability of funds in different budget accounts
- monitoring financial reports to verify that allocated funds have been spent as specified
- working on financial reporting, budget forecasting, and cost accounting issues
- supporting special projects

The Budget Analyst's duties have broadened in the last several years, as organizations used budgeting controls to manage corporate restructurings and downsizings. In addition to their normal responsibilities, Budget Analysts may measure organizational performance and assess the budget impact of various programs and policies.

Budget Analysts usually work a 40-hour week in an office setting. They may work longer hours during the initial drafting of budgets, and during mid-year and year-end budget reviews.

Salaries

Salaries of Budget Analysts are determined by experience, education, and type of employer. Budget Analysts with one to three years' experience earned from $41,500 to $52,500 in large companies (companies with sales of $250 million or more) and from $35,000 to $45,750 in small companies (sales under $25 million). More experienced Budget Analysts earned between $65,750 and $87,500 in large companies and between $51,500 and $66,750 in small companies, according to Robert Half International Inc. In addition to salary, Budget Analysts receive typical corporate benefits, including paid vacations, insurance, employee savings, and pension plans.

Employment Prospects

The employment outlook is competitive due to the large number of qualified applicants. While the number of budget analyst positions will grow about as fast as average for all positions through 2014, employment growth will be driven by the need for good financial analysis in both the public and private sectors. For this reason, layoffs of budget analysts are less likely to occur than for people in other occupations. Budget analysts are less subject to corporate downsizings because of the importance of he financial analysis performed by budget analysts.

Advancement Prospects

Starting Budget Analysts work under close supervision, working as a member of a budget team. As they become more proficient in their work, they may be promoted to intermediate-level positions within one to two years, and then to more senior positions with increased responsibility. Advancing to a higher level can lead to a supervisory position. Due to their importance and high visibility, senior Budget Analysts can advance to management positions in various parts of the organization.

Education and Training

A four-year degree with courses in accounting, finance, business adminstration, or public administration is pre-

ferred. Some employers have a preference for candidates with academic backgrounds in business-related courses or candidates with a master's degree, because business courses emphasize quantitative analytical skills. Financial industry experience or experience preparing budgets may sometimes be used as a substitute for formal academic training.

Entry-level analysts may receive some formal training when they begin their careers. Most learn the key job-related skills by working through a full budget cycle, becoming familiar with all of the steps involved in the budgeting process.

Experience, Skills, and Personality Traits

Because the Budget Analyst's job involves manipulating numbers, analysts should have strong analytical skills, and a working knowledge of statistics and accounting. Individuals should have one to three years experience working in a financial environment, or equivalent academic background. Having a working knowledge of electronic spreadsheet, database, and graphics software is also important in this position. Budget Analysts must also be able to work under strict time constraints and meet budget deadlines. Strong oral and written communication skills are essential in being able to prepare and present budget proposals to decision makers. Budget Analysts should have a detailed working knowledge of generally accepted accounting principles (GAAP), capital budgeting, and project planning.

Unions and Associations

As professional employees, Budget Analysts can become members of industry associations such as the American Accounting Association or the Financial Executives Institute, for networking opportunities and career advancement. Some of these are listed in Appendix III.

Tips for Entry

1. Get a solid background in financial accounting, economics, or a related discipline while in college.
2. Explore career opportunities through summer employment or college-sponsored internship programs.
3. Keep abreast of news in the field by reading trade magazines or visiting company and trade association Web sites.
4. As companies specialize their services, they will look increasingly for individuals with expertise in their field. Consider taking a double major in college to improve your chances of gaining an interview.

AUDITOR

CAREER PROFILE

Duties: Reviews an organization's financial statements for accuracy and completeness; reports results of auditing review to senior management; makes recommendations for improvements in internal controls and risk management

Alternate Title(s): Internal Auditor

Salary Range: $35,500 to $92,250; median salary is $35,700

Employment Prospects: Very good

Advancement Prospects: Excellent

Prerequisites:

Education or Training—Four-year degree in accounting or internal auditing; industry certification or graduate degree helpful for advancement

Experience—Several years of increasing responsibility as a junior auditor or member of an audit team

Special Skills and Personality Traits—Ability to compare and interpret facts and figures; good problem solving skills; excellent communication skills; ability to manage subordinates; high standards of personal integrity

Special Requirements—Professional certification required for advancement

CAREER LADDER

```
┌─────────────────────────────────┐
│  Director of Internal Auditing  │
└─────────────────────────────────┘

┌─────────────────────────────────┐
│            Auditor              │
└─────────────────────────────────┘

┌─────────────────────────────────┐
│         Junior Auditor          │
└─────────────────────────────────┘
```

Position Description

As organizations grow in complexity, their information management needs must also change. Auditors have responsibility for the integrity and reliability of business information. Auditors review an organization's accounting processes and verify the accuracy and completeness of financial results reported to senior management by business units. Auditors are the first line of defense in controlling an organization's exposure to accounting manipulation and financial fraud. They help implement policies which assure the integrity of the organization's accounting statements. Changing market demand has given Auditors additional responsibilities, including serving as consultants to senior management on risk management and protecting the assets of the organization through improved risk controls and information reporting. Computers are rapidly changing the nature of work for Auditors. Auditors must be technically "savvy," and have a working knowledge of computer networks and the Internet. A growing number of Auditors have extensive computer skills and specialize in correcting problems with software or developing software to meet specialized data requirements.

In organizations with an internal auditing staff, Auditors review business practices for compliance with established security controls, including corporate policies, federal and state laws, and regulations. Auditors examine and evaluate financial and informational systems, management procedures, and internal controls, and ensure that records are accurate and controls are adequate. In smaller firms the auditing function may be "outsourced" to a public accounting firm that provides auditing services to corporate clients.

Duties of internal Auditors include:

- collecting data or information from all relevant sources
- analyzing data and information with the aid of computer spreadsheets and other analytical tools
- processing and tabulating information for reporting purposes
- interpreting the value of financial information to others
- providing consultation and advice to management and other groups
- communicating information to management, coworkers, or others
- monitoring financial reporting policies and procedures, and making appropriate recommendations to management
- evaluating financial information for adherence to generally accepted accounting standards to verify the accuracy of information as reported
- reporting to management about audit results
- analyzing financial statements and other records and using accepted accounting procedures to determine financial condition
- inspecting account books and accounting systems for effectiveness and use of accounting procedures to record transactions

Recently, the internal Auditor's role has been redefined in many corporations—a move intended to ensure that Auditors are really independent of corporate policy in carrying out their duties. Internal auditors today are likely to report to an audit committee rather than to corporate management. Several years ago, more than 90 percent of internal auditors reported to the chief financial officer, according to the Internal Auditors Association, an industry trade group. The percentage of auditors reporting directly to the CFO declined to 40 to 50 percent in 2005.

The well-publicized corporate accounting scandals of several years ago led to the passage of the Sarbanes-Oxley Act of 2002 and tighter controls over the reporting of a company's financial condition to investors and the public. Sarbanes-Oxley gave new duties to internal auditors, including the following:

- consulting on internal controls—the systems designed to prevent manipulation of financial information
- consulting on internal controls in relation to enterprise risk management
- assisting the organization in identifying, evaluating, and implementing risk and control assessments
- recommending controls to assess related risks
- assisting with design systems of internal control
- drafting procedures for systems of internal control
- assisting with maintenance of internal controls repository
- conducting effectiveness testing on behalf of management
- taking the role of lead project manager for all or part of the efforts in compliance with Section 404 of Sarbanes-

Oxley, which requires public companies to attest to the effectiveness of their internal accounting controls
- providing training or information on internal control identification and assessment
- detecting financial statement fraud

Salaries

Salaries will vary according size of firm, location, level of experience, and professional credentials. Salaries tend to increase with experience and responsibility. Auditors with at least one professional designation earn the highest salaries. Average salaries for entry-level internal Auditors at small companies (up to $25 million in sales) ranged from $35,500 to $42,250 in 2006, according to a salary survey by Robert Half International. Information technology Auditors had the highest base salary, with average starting salaries of $67,000 to $92,250. Internal Auditors with experience handling reporting and internal controls rules created by the Sarbanes-Oxley Act can earn anywhere from $90,000 to $130,000.

Employment Prospects

The job market for Auditors is very good. This means there will be more employment opportunities for auditors through at least 2012, and strongest demand for new Auditors comes from the big accounting firms and large public corporations. With the increased demand from larger companies, small to midsized firms are reporting difficulty attracting qualified people for auditing positions. In addition, the role of accountants and Auditors is changing, and this may spur more job growth.

Advancement Prospects

There is much competition for auditing and accounting-related jobs in prestigious firms. Top accounting firms pay the highest starting salaries and offer the best advancement opportunities. There is a high degree of mobility within the accounting professions. Practitioners often shift into management accounting or internal auditing from public accounting. In the corporate world Auditors often start as auditor trainees or junior auditors. As they rise through the organization they may advance to manager of internal auditing or budget director.

Education and Training

Auditors normally have a four-year college degree with courses in accounting, finance, information systems, and computer networking. Some colleges have academic programs in internal auditing. Alternatively, a four-year degree in business administration or a liberal arts degree with business courses may be acceptable for entry-level jobs. Industry certification is recommended for advancement in the field. An M.B.A. degree is helpful for advancement into management positions. Industry certification is generally required for advancement in the auditing profession.

Special Requirements

Industry certifications include Certified Internal Auditor (CIA), Certification in Control Self-Assessment (CCSA), and Certified Internal Systems Auditor (CISA).

Experience, Skills, and Personality Traits

Internal Auditors usually have several years' experience in performing audit projects of increasing complexity. Auditors should have an aptitude for mathematics and be able to analyze, compare, and interpret facts and figures quickly. Clear communication skills in reporting results of their work to management are very important. Auditors must also have good people management skills and have high standards of integrity.

Unions and Associations

As professional employees, Auditors may become members of professional organizations such as the Financial Executives Institute or the Institute of Internal Auditors and join special interest discussion groups devoted to auditing issues. Auditors can also earn specialized auditing designations, awarded by the Bank Administration Institute and the National Association of Certified Fraud Examiners.

Tips for Entry

1. Get a solid background in accounting, economics, and finance with additional courses in computer networking at a college or university offering an internal auditing program.
2. Gain practical knowledge of auditing opportunities through summer internship programs sponsored by a college or industry association.
3. If you can get an entry-level job as a junior auditor, volunteer to help with planning or analysis. Document your achievements and get recommendations that will be useful in applying for higher level jobs.
4. Complete a certification program in auditing to increase your advancement opportunities.
5. See The Institute of Internal Auditor's Web site (http://www.theiia.org) for additional information on a career in auditing.

FORENSIC ACCOUNTANT

CAREER PROFILE

Duties: Investigates financial misconduct by inspecting records, collecting evidence, and interviewing; may act as expert witness in civil and criminal litigation

Alternate Title(s): Forensic Examiner, Investigative Accountant

Salary Range: $57,750 to $92,000

Employment Prospects: Good

Advancement Prospects: Good

Prerequisites:

Education or Training—Four-year degree with courses in accounting or finance

Experience—Two or more years' experience in investigative work or a related field

Special Skills and Personality Traits—Excellent analytical skills and communication skills; Certified Public Accountant (CPA) license; industry certification

Special Requirements—Industry certifications completion, several exams toward certification

CAREER LADDER

```
┌─────────────────────────────┐
│  Partner, Accounting Firm   │
└─────────────────────────────┘

┌─────────────────────────────┐
│    Forensic Accountant      │
└─────────────────────────────┘

┌─────────────────────────────┐
│     Staff Accountant        │
└─────────────────────────────┘
```

Position Description

Forensic Accountants work for accounting firms or independently as freelance consultants. They investigate incidents of suspected financial misconduct or white-collar crime, and help prepare evidence that may be used in civil or criminal trials, utilizing auditing and accounting investigative skills.

Forensic accounting is often referred to as "investigative accounting." The term forensic refers to legal proceedings or argumentation presented in a court of law. Forensic Accountants are trained to analyze and verify financial records. They prepare reports that may be used in evidence at a trial, and may be called as expert witnesses, an independent authority, to testify at a trial.

Forensic Accountants analyze, interpret, and summarize complex financial statements and business-related issues in a manner which is both understandable and properly supported by evidence. Accountants coordinate fraud investigations with outside investigators, attorneys, and criminal prosecutors. They review suspect files referred by insurance underwriters and report cases of suspected insurance fraud

to government agencies and the courts. If a company files an insurance claim after suffering a fire, the insurance company may hire a Forensic Accountant to verify that a company's reported loss was as great as the amount claimed.

During an investigation, Forensic Accountants are often involved in:

- investigating and analyzing financial statements
- developing computerized models to assist in the presentation of financial evidence
- assisting in legal proceedings, such as testifying in court and preparing visual aids
- assisting in the recovery of assets
- coordinating activities with private investigators, forensic document examiners, consulting engineers, and other experts

Besides working on business-related investigations, Forensic Accountants often work on criminal cases. They may be retained by the United States District Attorney's Office, the courts, or regional and local police forces.

Forensic Accountants work in an office setting, using computers and telephones. Some travel is required, usually to gather information and present evidence at trials. Forensic Accountants work long hours under tight schedules, especially on litigation about to go to trial. This can be a good career choice if you are analytical, can work under deadline pressure, and have good problem-solving ability.

Salaries

Forensic Accountants earn salaries comparable with those earned by other accountants. Forensic accountants working in large companies earned between $68,000 and $92,000 in 2005, according to Robert Half International Inc. Accountants employed at small companies earned salaries ranging from $57,750 to $69,000. Experienced Forensic Accountants have the opportunity to earn more than other accountants because accounting firms typically charge more for litigation support services.

Compensation in addition to salary typically includes paid vacations, health insurance, participation in employer-sponsored retirement plans, and reimbursement for use of their own vehicle for company business.

Employment Prospects

Employment opportunities for Forensic Accountants are expected to grow at a faster rate than other accounting occupations over the next several years. Contributing to this increased demand are the anticipated growth in computer-related crime and cyber attacks on the Internet. Forensic Accountants and investigators often have the specialized training in evidence gathering and analysis necessary to combat computer-related crime in the legal system.

Advancement Prospects

As they gain experience in investigative work, Forensic Accountants have the opportunity to work on more complex cases or advance to a management position. They may have the opportunity to manage a litigation support department, supervise a team of investigators, or become an accounting firm partner. Many will advance their careers by starting up their own consulting practices, charging higher hourly rates for their services.

Education and Training

A four-year degree with a concentration in business and finance, with a minor in accounting, is a standard requirement for entry. Individuals interested in becoming a Forensic Accountant should take additional college courses qualifying them for a certified public accountant (CPA) license. Most states require CPAs to have completed 150 credit hours, or the equivalent of a master's degree, and pass a qualifying exam. Forensic Accountants also take courses

toward industry certification and maintain their competency by attending continuing education courses.

Special Requirements

Forensic Accountants must have a certified public accountant license, and have completed some exams toward an industry certification, such as Certified Fraud Examiner. Industry certifications available include the Forensic Examiner Diplomate from the College of Forensic Examiners and Certified Fraud Examiner, from the Association of Certified Fraud Examiners.

Experience, Skills, and Personality Traits

Forensic Accountants begin their careers as accountants and learn forensic techniques through experience. Forensic Accountants have all the skills of traditional accountants and auditors. They need to have a clear understanding of the accounting practices employed in each business they investigate. An examiner has to take into consideration all the factors that could affect sales, including cost of goods sold and seasonal fluctuations in sales. Generally, two or more years' experience in accounting is the minimum period before an accountant can take the qualifying CPA examination.

Besides having business knowledge, Forensic Accountants need to have an inquiring mind, a problem-solving ability, and excellent written and verbal communication skills. Because they may be called as expert witnesses at a trial, an important job-related skill is the ability to communicate financial information-clearly and concisely in a courtroom setting.

Unions and Associations

Forensic Accountants can become members of several professional associations for continuing education and networking opportunities. Among these are the American Society of Professional Examiners, the Forensic Accountants Society of North America, and the National Association of Certified Fraud Examiners.

Tips for Entry

1. While attending college, explore internships with accounting firms or law firms to gain practical experience and make industry contacts.
2. Attend local chapter meetings of the Association of Certified Fraud Examiners to learn about career opportunities from industry practitioners.
3. College placement offices can help arrange on-campus interviews with accounting firms. Informational interviews with on-campus recruiters are an excellent way to learn about different careers.
4. Take writing or communication courses or join a college debating society to polish important communication skills.

MANAGEMENT ACCOUNTANT

CAREER PROFILE

Duties: Coordinates and reviews financial records; prepares reports based on financial records; prepares other reports as required by management

Alternate Title(s): Corporate Accountant, Staff Accountant

Salary Range: $62,000 to $114,000

Employment Prospects: Good

Advancement Prospects: Good

Prerequisites:

Education or Training—Four-year college degree with emphasis in accounting

Experience—One to two years' accounting experience

Special Skills and Personality Traits—Excellent analytical skills; excellent communication skills

Special Requirements—Professional licensing or certification recommended

CAREER LADDER

```
┌─────────────────────────────┐
│     Accounting Manager      │
└─────────────────────────────┘

┌─────────────────────────────┐
│   Management Accountant     │
└─────────────────────────────┘

┌─────────────────────────────┐
│      Cost Accountant        │
└─────────────────────────────┘
```

Position Description

Management Accountants record and analyze financial information in the companies where they work. They analyze and interpret financial information that executives need to make sound business decisions. They also prepare financial reports for nonmanagement groups including stock-holders, creditors, regulatory agencies, and tax authorities. Within accounting departments, they may work in areas including financial analysis, planning and budgeting, and cost accounting.

Computers are rapidly changing the nature of work for Management Accountants. A growing number of accountants have extensive computer skills. Some accountants use their computer skills to correct software problems or develop software to meet unique data requirements. With the aid of these software packages, accountants summarize and organize transactions in standard formats for easy retrieval and analysis. These accounting packages greatly reduce the amount of tedious manual work associated with data entry and record-keeping. Desktop computers connected to a host network and laptop computers equipped with modems enable accountants be more mobile and extract large amounts of data from large mainframe computers.

In a politically volatile world, new concepts in risk management are gradually reshaping the accounting profes-

sion. Enterprise-wide risk management, a holistic approach to identifying business opportunities while minimizing the risks, is becoming accepted practice in more corporations and accounting firms. New federal laws such as the Sarbanes-Oxley Act of 2002 impose greater requirements for disclosure of internal management controls on financial reporting.

Duties performed include:

- preparing financial operating statements and posting journal entries to the general ledger
- providing general support to other areas of the accounting bookkeeping department
- researching and preparing management reports
- evaluating subsidiary journals for errors and omissions and entering corrected data into the general ledger
- reviewing the monthly balance sheet and profit and loss (P&L) statement
- preparing state tax reports
- reconciling daily cash flow statements to monthly bank statements
- reconciling payroll and cash disbursement accounts
- reviewing accounts payable aging and vendor statements to identify payment problems
- performing other duties assigned by accounting supervisor

Management Accountants are usually part of executive teams involved in strategic planning or new product development. Most Accountants employed by corporations work a standard 40-hour week. This can be a good career choice if you are analytical, have good problem-solving ability, and like working in an office setting.

Salaries

Salaries of Management Accountants vary according to years of experience, size of employer, and geographic region. Management Accountants earned total compensation, including salaries and bonuses, ranging from $65,000 annually to $134,000 in 2005, according to the Institute of Management Accountants. The average base salary in 2004 was $86,319 for accountants with one to five years' experience and $76,609 for those with six to 10 years' experience as Management Accountants.

Accountants with advanced degrees and professional certifications such as Certified Management Accountant usually earn higher salaries than individuals without post-graduate degrees or professional certification. Geographic region also influences employee salaries. Management Accountants working in the Northeast, Mid-Atlantic, and West Coast had the highest average salaries, compared to the Midwest and Southern United States.

Employment Prospects

Employment of accountants is expected to grow faster than average for all occupations through 2014. The changing role of accountants and auditors in the wake of recent financial scandals will spur job growth and people who earn professional recognition through certification or licensure will have the most promising job prospects. Applicants with a master's degree in accounting or a master's degree in business administration with a concentration in accounting will also have an advantage. Employment prospects in management accounting may not be as promising as those in public accounting that is working at a public accounting firm rather than a corporation but there will be ample opportunities for qualified candidates.

Advancement Prospects

Management Accountants usually start their careers as cost accountants, junior internal auditors, or trainees for other accounting positions. With experience, they can advance to accounting manager, chief cost accountant, budget director, or manager of internal auditing. Many senior corporate executives, including controllers, financial vice presidents, and chief financial officers, have backgrounds in accounting or finance. There is a large degree of mobility in the accounting profession. Accounting professionals often shift into auditing or management accounting from public accounting, or from management accounting into auditing. It is less common, though, for Management Accountants employed in corporations to move into public accounting at a major accounting firm. Academic credentials beyond college can provide the additional credentials necessary to move into a consulting career in accounting. A master's degree can be the entry into a new position or a new career path.

Education and Training

A four-year degree with an emphasis in accounting or a related field is required for the position. Beginning accounting positions usually require 24 credits in accounting or an equivalent combination in education and experience. Courses in business economics, computer science, and finance are helpful. Also helpful are courses in communication and public speaking. Some employers prefer applicants with a post-graduate degree in accounting or a master's degree in business administration with an emphasis in accounting.

New employees usually receive additional training in key job-related skills soon after they are hired. Many accountants specialize their careers in certain areas of accounting, and take continuing education courses to become eligible for advancement and promotion.

Special Requirements

Professional certification, while not required for Management Accountants, can attest to professional competence in the accounting field. Applicants for the Certified Management Accounting (CMA) credential from the Institute of Management Accountants must pass a four-part examination, agree to meet continuing education requirements, and have worked at least two years in management accounting.

Experience, Skills, and Personality Traits

Individuals planning a career in accounting should have an aptitude for mathematics, and be able to analyze and compare figures quickly. A working knowledge of accounting principles, procedures, and information reporting systems is necessary for accountants. They must be able to communicate results of their work, orally and in writing, to senior management, company directors, and others. They should have a high sense of integrity because readers of financial statements rely on the accuracy of information presented in an accounting report.

Unions and Associations

Staff accountants can become members of professional associations, including the American Accounting Association, the American Institute of Certified Public Accountants, or the Institute of Management Accountants. Eligible certifications are the Certified Public Accountant (CPA) from the American Institute of Certified Public Accountants, the Certified Management Accountant (CMA) from the Institute of Management Accountants, or the Accredited Business Accountant from the National Society of Accountants.

Tips for Entry

1. Previous experience in accounting or auditing can open doors to a career in accounting. Many colleges offer summer employment and part-time internships, which are useful in acquiring practical knowledge and industry contacts.

2. Look into employment opportunities posted on professional association Web sites such as the Institute of Management Accountants' Career Center (http://www.imanet.org).

3. While in college try to get some practical experience working as an officer for a student organization where money management is involved.

4. Take courses in computer science and communication to build up job-related skills.

5. After landing your first job, take courses for professional certification such as Certified Management Accountant to improve your advancement opportunities.

6. Some state Certified Public Accountant societies sponsor internships for accounting majors or offer scholarships. Check their Web sites for more information.

TAX ACCOUNTANT

CAREER PROFILE

Duties: Prepares federal, state, and local tax returns; provides administrative support

Alternate Title(s): Tax Adviser

Salary Range: $62,500 to $83,250

Employment Prospects: Good

Advancement Prospects: Fair

Prerequisites:

Education or Training—Four-year degree with courses in accounting or finance; graduate degree or industry certification preferable

Experience—Two to five years' general taxation experience

Special Skills and Personality Traits—Computer literacy, spreadsheet and analysis skills; excellent communication skills; knowledge of corporate tax laws and tax preparation software

Special Requirements—Professional certification optional, but recommended

CAREER LADDER

```
┌─────────────────────────────┐
│   Senior Tax Accountant     │
└─────────────────────────────┘

┌─────────────────────────────┐
│      Tax Accountant         │
└─────────────────────────────┘

┌─────────────────────────────┐
│       Tax Analyst           │
└─────────────────────────────┘
```

Position Description

Tax Accountants prepare tax returns for an organization. They use their knowledge of the U.S. Internal Revenue Code and state laws to guide the organization's tax policy and manage strategy on tax-related issues. They recommend compliance strategy on all tax reporting requirements, while attempting to minimize tax liability. They prepare special tax reports and represent the organization at tax hearings.

Tax Accountants use their knowledge of the tax code and research on the effects of taxes on corporate earnings to recommend changes in accounting practices to reduce an organization's tax liability. Tax accounting is one of the most difficult fields in accounting to enter as a career. Taxation is a complex and constantly changing field, and for this reason, those choosing to make tax work their career often specialize their work in one particular area, such as corporate tax, property tax, or sales and use taxes. Some Tax Accountants are independent practitioners who handle the tax needs of highly compensated individuals and owners of privately owned businesses. They offer professional guidance on a range of issues, from estate planning and charitable giving to evaluating qualified retirement plans and compensation planning.

Their duties include the following:

- directing the preparation of all tax records as required by municipal, state, and federal tax authorities
- preparing federal and state estimated quarterly tax returns
- preparing tax depreciation calculations
- determining taxable income for business units
- providing tax information reports to other corporate departments for budgeting and forecasting
- researching tax-related issues and managing tax compliance
- ensuring maintenance of proper tax records
- reconciling tax discrepancies and resolving errors
- advising senior management or any changes or proposed changes in tax law

- assisting other tax group members on special assignments and projects
- supervising clerical staff

Tax Accountants make extensive use of computers and office automation that help manage the filing of tax returns and minimize the handling of paperwork. Automated tax accounting software makes it possible to process tax returns for multiple jurisdictions in a nearly paperless environment until final versions are printed. Tax Accountants work under tight schedules and they must be able to prioritize their work to meet accounting reporting deadlines. They work in an office setting with minimal travel requirements. They typically work a 40-hour week, but often work longer hours when preparing quarterly tax reports and annual tax returns.

Salaries

Salaries of Tax Accountants are determined by years of experience and organization size. Salaries of tax managers in corporations with $25 million to $250 million in sales were between $62,500 and $83,250 in 2005, according to Robert Half International, a staffing services firm.

Employment Prospects

Employment opportunities for accountants, including Tax Accountants, are expected to grow about as fast at the average for all occupations through 2012, according to the U.S. Labor Department. Some vacancies will occur from the need to replace accountants who retire or transfer to other occupations. The changing role of accountants and auditors will also stimulate job growth. Job opportunities are best for management accountants who can advise on business strategy in addition to performing their normal accounting duties. Many candidates enter the field as tax analysts, and work primarily on tax research issues, researching recently enacted or proposed tax code revisions. Accountants who have had previous experience as tax auditors for government agencies may find their tax experience helpful in moving over to the private sector.

Advancement Prospects

Advancement opportunities are fair, but the competition is heavy. With experience, Tax Accountants can move up to positions of increased responsibility, such as tax manager. Successful tax managers in large organizations can move into middle management positions at their parent company's headquarters. Experienced tax managers can also advance their careers by moving into consulting, either in a solo practice or by joining an accounting firm providing tax management services to corporate clients and wealthy individuals.

Education and Training

A four-year degree with an emphasis in accounting or a related field is required for the position. Some employers prefer candidates with a master's in business administration and a Certified Public Accounting license.

Special Requirements

Professional certification, while not required for Tax Accountants, can attest to professional competence in the accounting field. Certification can help independent Tax Accountants build a client base of companies relying on their services. Certification requires several years of independent study and completion of a final exam. Candidates for the Accreditation Council for Accounting and Taxation's Accredited Tax Adviser designation must complete 90 hours of continuing education and pass a qualifying exam. The Accreditation Council offers a more general designation, Accredited Business Accountant/Accredited Business Adviser. This designation tests an individual's proficiency in financial accounting, managerial accounting, business law and ethics, and taxation. Available certifications include the Certified Member of the Institute (CMI), offered by the Institute for Professionals in Taxation to qualifying tax professionals in property tax and sales tax management, and the Accredited Tax Preparer and Accredited Tax Adviser designations from the Accreditation Council for Accounting and Taxation.

Experience, Skills, and Personality Traits

Individuals planning a career in accounting should have an aptitude for mathematics and be able to analyze and compare figures quickly. A working knowledge of financial spreadsheets and database systems is a prerequisite. Candidates need to have excellent written and interpersonal communication skills, a working knowledge of accounting, and have the ability to work independently. They must be able to communicate results of their work fairly and accurately to clients, government agencies, and others. They should have a high sense of integrity because readers of tax reports rely on the accuracy of information presented in statements they prepare.

Unions and Associations

Tax Accountants can become members of the Institute for Professionals in Taxation for networking and career advancement opportunities. The association sponsors educational programs and seminars and it also maintains a Web site job bank.

Tips for Entry

1. Take review courses in accounting sponsored by state affiliates of the National Society of Accounting (affiliated with the Accreditation Council for Accountancy and Taxation) in preparation for ACAT professional exams.

2. Develop new skills to remain competitive; employers look for candidates with strong technology, project management, and interpersonal skills.

3. State accounting associations or CPA societies can help arrange internships for accounting majors; some may also offer scholarships.

4. Check out current job opportunities on industry Web sites such as the Institute for Professionals in Taxation Web site (http://www.ipt.org), or career Web sites such as http://www.accountingjobs.com and post your résumé with an online jobs clearinghouse.

5. Stay current with industry trends by reading accounting trade magazines and browsing accounting Web sites; the American Institute of Certified Public Accountants has numerous free educational publications on the accounting profession.

TAX PREPARER

CAREER PROFILE

Duties: Prepares tax returns for small business owners and individuals; may represent clients in tax appeals

Alternate Title(s): None

Salary Range: $15,000 to $50,000 and up

Employment Prospects: Very good

Advancement Prospects: Good

Prerequisites:

Education or Training—High school degree or equivalent with moderate on-the-job training

Experience—Some accounting experience helpful though not required

Special Skills and Personality Traits—Excellent math skills, good computer skills, good interpersonal skills

Special Requirements—Licensing required in some states

CAREER LADDER

```
┌─────────────────────────────┐
│       Group Manager         │
└─────────────────────────────┘

┌─────────────────────────────┐
│       Office Manager        │
└─────────────────────────────┘

┌─────────────────────────────┐
│        Tax Preparer         │
└─────────────────────────────┘
```

Position Description

Tax Preparers are on the front lines in the daily battle to help taxpayers deal with complicated tax laws and regulations. Tax Preparers review an individual's or a business's financial records, past returns, and income statements; compute the taxes owed, and fill out the forms needed to complete each tax return. They interview clients to collect the information needed to fill out applicable state or federal tax returns. If they do not have all the answers. Tax Preparers must be willing to research tax bulletins and tax law handbooks. Tax Preparers have to be good at organizing, bookkeeping, and using a computer to calculate taxes owed, and they must perform all these tasks on deadline. Finally, they must have the patience to work with clients whose financial records are in disarray or who may be ignorant of many tax rules.

Specific tasks performed include the following:

- reviewing client financial records and past tax forms to make an initial estimate of taxes owed
- interviewing clients to get additional information about income, deductible expenses, and allowances
- consulting tax handbooks and bulletins to determine procedures for preparing unusual returns

- calculating the fee for preparing each return according to the complexity and the amount of time needed to prepare it
- reviewing completed tax returns to detect errors

Tax Preparers who are enrolled agents, a designation awarded by the Internal Revenue Service after candidates pass a two-day exam, also represent their clients at IRS tax audits, examinations, and appeals. As federally authorized tax practitioners, licensed by the U.S. Treasury Department, enrolled agents can represent clients before IRS administrative proceedings in all 50 states. Many Tax Preparers do tax work part time, working seasonally from January through mid-April, and hold down other jobs in a related field for the rest of the year. Individuals who become enrolled agents often enter this field as a second career, after having careers in accounting or a related profession in which they already have an established client base.

Salaries

Tax Preparers may be self-employed, or they may be employees of a small accounting firm or a large company specializing in tax preparation. Tax Preparers' earnings vary according to experience and the number of hours worked in a calendar year, which means there is a wide range in compensation. Annual earnings can range from about $15,000 for part-time Tax Preparers working through the four-month tax season to an average of $50,000 for those working throughout the year. Tax Preparers working in a large tax preparation firm earn an hourly rate plus commissions based on collected fees and sales of related products. Enrolled agents, because of their specialized knowledge of tax laws, have earnings comparable to those of public accountants and auditors ($49,890 to $66,900 annually), according to the U.S. Bureau of Labor Statistics. In complex tax cases an enrolled agent can earn more than a certified public accountant (CPA) performing similar work.

Employment Prospects

Most Tax Preparers get their jobs by applying directly to the firm where they want to work. In a large chain or franchise operation, new employees begin as trainees and after a few months progress to become tax return checkers and eventually full-fledged preparers. There are two tracks to becoming an enrolled agent. An individual can become an enrolled agent if he or she demonstrates special competence in tax matters by taking a written, two-day examination, covering all aspects of the U.S. Tax Code, and passing a background check. A second entry path allows individuals with five years of experience at the Internal Revenue Service to become an enrolled agent, bypassing the written exam. Because of the specialized knowledge required to become an enrolled agent and the requirements to maintain a license, there are only about 40,000 practicing enrolled agents.

The Bureau of Labor Statistics predicts that there will be plenty of job opportunities through 2012. Plans to streamline the tax code are put forward almost every year, but taxes seem to become more complicated. Consumers and business owners will continue to need help filling out their tax forms.

Advancement Prospects

Advancement in this field is determined by reputation and the individual's skill at building a successful practice. Some eventually open their own businesses. Some Tax Preparers advance to more senior positions, gaining competence through continuing education. They may advance to managing a small office or a group of Tax Preparers in a large firm. Franchise opportunities are also available from the large multistate tax preparation firms for those interested in running their own business. The majority of enrolled agents are sole practitioners, although some have one or two employ-

ees. As the firm grows and more clients are added, the agent may hire additional employees to share the workload.

Education and Training

At the entry level, a high school degree or equivalent is a standard requirement, although some college or business accounting courses are helpful. In most states Tax Preparers learn their trade through proprietary schools associated with large tax preparation firms. Tax Preparers are encouraged to update their knowledge and skills by taking continuing education courses, which strongly influence compensation levels and advancement opportunities.

Special Requirements

There are no federal certification requirements for Tax Preparers, and only two states, California and Oregon, require Tax Preparers who are not already attorneys or certified public accountants to be certified. Enrolled agents are certified by the Internal Revenue Service and are required to complete about 30 hours in continuing professional education every year to maintain their professional certification.

Experience, Skills, and Personality Traits

Collecting, evaluating, and analyzing information are important skills for Tax Preparers. They must be adept at spotting errors in computations and written information. Because Tax Preparers spend much of their time collecting information from taxpayers, strong interviewing skills and communication skills are also important, as are good computer skills.

Unions and Associations

Many enrolled agents are members of the National Association of Enrolled Agents, a trade association with more than 11,000 members established to advance the interests of enrolled agents and their clients.

Tips for Entry

1. Look for community college or four-year college programs in accounting or taxation.
2. Check job banks and other online search engines for employment opportunities.
3. Learn more about enrolled agent positions from the National Association of Enrolled Agents.
4. Check into certification programs from the Accreditation Council for Accountancy and Taxation.

INVESTOR RELATIONS OFFICER

CAREER PROFILE

Duties: Distributes financial information to investors and the public; issues press releases about corporate events; organizes teleconferences and meetings with financial analysts

Alternate Title(s): Investor Relations Manager

Salary Range: $99,000 to $143,000

Employment Prospects: Good

Advancement Prospects: Excellent

Prerequisites:

Education or Training—Undergraduate degree, with courses in finance, economics, and journalism

Experience—Two to five years' experience

Special Skills and Personality Traits—Excellent verbal and written communication skills; ability to explain business strategy to financial analysts and Journalists; good organizational skills

Special Requirements—Chartered Financial Analyst (CFA) certification helpful for advancement

CAREER LADDER

```
┌─────────────────────────────────┐
│        Financial Analyst        │
└─────────────────────────────────┘

┌─────────────────────────────────┐
│   Investor Relations Officer    │
└─────────────────────────────────┘

┌─────────────────────────────────┐
│ Junior Investor Relations Officer │
└─────────────────────────────────┘
```

Position Description

Investor Relations Officers distribute information on financial events, such as corporate earnings and acquisitions, to the investing public and help develop corporate strategy. The IR professional today is one of the most influential individuals in the corporation.

The Investor Relations Officer issues press releases to explain significant events and organize meetings or teleconferences with investors and financial analysts. Investor Relations Officers also are responsible for preparation of the company annual report, organizing the annual meeting with shareholders and meetings with financial analysts who follow the company's performance. Investor Relations Officers have frequent contact with senior company executives.

Events of the last 10 years have redefined and broadened the job functions of the Investor Relations Officer. Besides communicating with investors and key constituencies (shareholders, financial analysts, strategic business partners, and even employees), IR professionals are assuming a leadership role in managing risk, shareholder activism issues,

and the more visible involvement of regulatory agencies such as the Securities and Exchange Commission in enforcing compliance with state and federal securities laws.

The investor relations position may be a staff position or a function performed by a public relations firm specializing in financial public relations. Large corporations, or companies with sales above $500 million, usually have a designated Investor Relations Officer. This is a challenging job, and a good position if you are analytical, have an ability to grasp the essentials of financial reporting, and like working with investors and the financial press. Investor Relations Officers consult on a regular basis with financial analysts and investment portfolio managers. They assist corporate management in devising appropriate investment banking strategies.

Investor Relations Officers need to stay current with changes in financial regulations, which affect the disclosure of sensitive financial information. An example is the Securities and Exchange Commission's Regulation FD (Fair Disclosure), which requires companies to disclose information that can materially affect their stock price to all interested parties—securities analysts who follow the company's financial performance, investors, and the public—at the same time. Regulation FD was an attempt to prevent disclosure to selected investors who may own large positions in a company's stock.

Salaries
The median salary of an Investor Relations Officer in the United States was $117,499 in 2006. The middle 50 percent had compensation ranging from $99,426 to $143,074, according to a survey by Salary.com. As in other positions in finance, total compensation can vary dramatically by factors such as company size, industry, credentials, and years of experience. Investor Relations Officers at companies in regions with a high cost of living, such as New York City, Chicago, or Los Angeles, earn proportionately more than those working outside the major metropolitan areas.

Employment Prospects
There is good demand for experienced Investor Relations Officers. Employment opportunities for investor relations professionals are expected to grow about as fast as average through 2014 as public companies increase their efforts to provide guidance to shareholders, investors, and the public at large as to future earnings and business growth. The rise of the activist shareholder in the last few years, in particular the hedge funds, will also have some impact on investor relations hiring. People come to investor relations from various backgrounds, including public relations, accounting finance, and corporate law. Those entering the field for the first time may benefit from college level courses in finance or postgraduate certificate programs in investor relations.

Advancement Prospects
Investor relations professionals have several career advancement options. They can advance to a financial analyst position in the corporate finance department, move into line management, and manage a corporate operating group or business unit, or they can move into marketing and sales. IR professionals with the right credentials have the potential to move up into senior management, potentially to the CEO position. Another option is moving into an investor relations consulting firm specializing in financial public relations.

Education and Training
An undergraduate degree is required. Most investor relations professionals have college backgrounds in finance or economics, with courses in business, business law, or communication. A background in the liberal arts is helpful because IR managers deal with a wide variety of people in the course of their jobs. Some universities offer an investor relations certification program for individuals interested in moving into investor relations from another career such as law, finance, or communications, or for IR practitioners interested in improving their on-the-job skills. These certification programs are endorsed by the National Investor Relations Institute.

Special Requirements
The Chartered Financial Analyst designation, while not required, can help an Investor Relations Officer become a more effective counselor, and can open the door to more senior positions.

Experience, Skills, and Personality Traits
Investor Relations Officers entering the field generally have at least three to five years experience in financial public relations or have previously worked in the corporate finance department. Key skills required for the position include strong verbal and written communication, strong analytical skills, and computer spreadsheet literacy. It is also helpful to have a knack for problem solving and to be able to present management with different scenarios for handling a particular situation.

The investor relations position requires a broad view of corporate structure, a general understanding of financial markets, public relations, developed communication skills, and a comprehensive understanding of federal and state laws and regulations relating to securities. Also important are well-developed skills in strategic planning and operations management.

Unions and Associations
Investor Relations Officers can become members of the National Investor Relations Institute for networking opportunities and career advancement. NIRI has local chapters in most states.

Tips for Entry
1. Attend local or regional meetings of the National Investor Relations Institute to learn more about job opportunities.
2. Management recruiters are another source of job leads; recruiters can also help negotiate salary and benefits.
3. Build a file of key job skills, such as negotiating or communicating, on your home computer and chart your progress over time.
4. Periodically check the National Investor Relations Institute Web site (http://www.niri.org) for career management tips and publications available in the NIRI bookstore.

FINANCIAL ANALYST

CAREER PROFILE

Duties: Assesses the economic performance of companies or markets; determines prospects for growth or appreciation in value; makes investment recommendations

Alternate Title(s): Securities Analyst

Salary Range: $35,000 to $150,000 plus

Employment Prospects: Good

Advancement Prospects: Good

Prerequisites:

Education or Training—Undergraduate degree plus some postgraduate education; M.B.A. desirable

Experience—Two to three years experience

Special Skills and Personality Traits—Excellent written and verbal communication skills; good organizational skills and a high degree of judgment; able to work independently and develop ideas in a concise framework; excellent research skills; thorough knowledge of investment analysis and economic principles

Special Requirements—Chartered Financial Analyst designation required for advancement

CAREER LADDER

```
┌─────────────────────────────────────┐
│   Director of Research Department    │
└─────────────────────────────────────┘

┌─────────────────────────────────────┐
│          Financial Analyst           │
└─────────────────────────────────────┘

┌─────────────────────────────────────┐
│          Research Assistant          │
└─────────────────────────────────────┘
```

Position Description

Financial Analysts are the largest group of professionals working in the brokerage and investment management businesses. Analysts are employed in a wide range of industries, including Wall Street brokerage firms, corporations, regional securities firms, banks, insurance companies, mutual funds, and private foundations.

Securities analysts review companies and industries to determine the suitability for investment, as determined from investment guidelines or investment policy. They consider and evaluate alternative economic scenarios, and their impact on portfolio holdings. They gather the necessary information for preparing investment reports and recommendations, and make presentations to senior officers and to investment committees. They prepare statistics measuring investment results, and determine the value of holding alternative types of investments.

Most analysts specialize their research in a particular industry, such as pharmaceuticals, computers and semiconductors, or telecommunications. Within the securities industry, there is also a distinction between "sell side" analysts, who work for investment banks and "buy side" analysts, who work for investors in securities such as mutual funds and pension fund investors.

The Securities and Exchange Regulation FD (short for "fair disclosure") and federal legislation enacted in 2002, the Sarbanes-Oxley Act, impose new regulations on the way financial information is released to the public and to the financial analyst community. The new regulations are meant to ensure that financial information affecting a company's stock price reaches all interested groups at the same time. The securities industry research settlement of 2003, spearheaded by New York attorney general Eliot Spitzer, provides an incentive for brokerage firms to use independent third-party research when promoting stocks to investors. The stock research agreement, set initially for a five-year period, is expected to stimulate demand for independent research, but its impact on hiring by independent research providers is less clear. The independent stock research business is divided between a handful of large companies that are largely fully staffed and a large number of very small boutique research firms that have limited staffing.

Salaries

Salaries in the securities industry tend to vary quite a bit and are influenced by a number of factors, such as the type of firm, the amount of securities it underwrites, and the qualifications of the applicant. Salaries of Financial Analyst vary according to experience and credentials when hired. Analysts with one to three years' experience earned from $35,000 to $47,750 in small companies and from $41,500 to $52,500 in large companies in 2005, according to Robert Half International. Senior analysts in small companies had salary ranges from $42,250 to $54,750; salaries ranged from $53,000 to $68,250 for those employed in companies with sales above $250 million. Job candidates with M.B.A. degrees usually get higher starting salaries than candidates without an M.B.A. Some securities firms offer starting analysts lower salaries than the top brokerage firms. You have to weigh the tradeoff of taking a lower salary against the potential job experience, which may qualify you for a higher paying position elsewhere.

These salary figures do not include annual performance bonus, which may be up to two-thirds of base salary. Salaries paid by regional brokerage firms are generally less than those paid by the top Wall Street investment banks, sometimes called "Bulge Bracket" firms because they are active in all major financial markets serviced by the securities industry.

Employment Prospects

Entry-level positions in securities research are getting harder to find for college graduates with no industry experience. Much of the first-pass stock research formerly done by entry-level analysts is now done offshore in Asian financial centers by research analysts who are paid much lower salaries. However, Financial Analysts with previous experience in a covered industry are much sought after.

Advancement Prospects

Experienced Financial Analysts may also find opportunities at independent investment research firms. The 2003 global financial analyst research settlement, in which the major Wall Street banks agreed to buy investment research from unaffiliated independent companies for at least five years, has led to an increase in the amount of research purchased from the independent firms, if not an increase in employment at some of the larger independents. About 100 to 150 independent research firms are the major suppliers of independent investment research.

Education and Training

An undergraduate degree in finance or a related field is an essential requirement. Analysts should have a general understanding of economics and statistics, and have computer literacy in financial spreadsheet programs. Many Financial Analysts have post-graduate degrees such as an M.B.A. degree. Many employers have limited training budgets or have eliminated on-the-job training altogether; they want starting analysts who can begin work immediately and contribute to productivity.

Special Requirements

Graduate degrees or professional certification are considered a necessity for advancement. The Chartered Financial Analyst (CFA) designation, awarded by the Association for Investment Management and Research, is one of the fastest growing professional credentials in the world. More than 60,000 investment professionals have earned the CFA designation.

Experience, Skills, and Personality Traits

The Financial Analyst position requires excellent verbal and written communication skills. Also helpful is an ability to work with numbers and spreadsheet programs. Employers look for people who can work independently, can thrive under pressure, and work long hours, often 50 to 70 hours a week in major investment banks.

Unions and Associations

Financial Analysts may join several professional organizations for networking and following the latest industry trends. Some of the major associations are Association for Investment Management and Research, the National Investor Relations Institute, and the Securities Industry Association.

Tips for Entry

1. Do your homework before the job interview; give potential employers a fully researched investment idea demonstrating your capability during the interview. Go to local or regional meetings of Securities Analysts to learn more about the job market.
2. Visit securities industry Web sites to pick up helpful job tips; the New York State Society of Securities Analysts (http://www.nyssa.org) has plenty of useful information.
3. While still in college look into internship programs at companies hiring large numbers of Analysts, such as securities firms or mutual fund companies.

CREDIT ANALYST, FINANCE

CAREER PROFILE

Duties: Analyze current credit data and financial statements of businesses and individuals to determine the degree of risk in extending credit or lending money; prepare reports to management for use in making credit decisions

Alternate Title(s): Credit Associate

Salary Range: $36,750 to $45,750

Employment Prospects: Good

Advancement Prospects: Good

Prerequisites:

Education or Training—Four-year degree with an emphasis in finance and accounting; two-year degree acceptable with related work experience

Experience—Two to five years of experience; background in credit or banking preferred

Special Skills and Personality Traits—Must be able to verify information, gather and analyze data, use judgment in making recommendations; excellent managerial and communication skills; extensive knowledge of financial institution policies and procedures; knowledge of PCs and spreadsheet accounting programs; knowledge of credit scoring (loan scoring) computer programs may be required in some jobs

CAREER LADDER

```
┌─────────────────────────────┐
│   Chief Credit Executive    │
└─────────────────────────────┘

┌─────────────────────────────┐
│       Credit Analyst        │
└─────────────────────────────┘

┌─────────────────────────────┐
│       Credit Trainee        │
└─────────────────────────────┘
```

Position Description

Anyone who has applied for a bank loan or mortgage has come into contact, directly or indirectly, with a Credit Analyst. Credit Analysts are crucial to the success of banks and other financial institutions in which business growth is tied closely to making new loans. Analysts evaluate the financial condition of businesses and individuals. Their decisions help guide the process of approving loans. Commercial and business analysts evaluate credit risks in loans to businesses, while consumer Credit Analysts review personal loans.

Credit Analysts review the borrower's loan documentation, obtain credit references, and check the borrower's credit rating with a credit bureau. The amount of background work required depends on the type of loan and the amount requested. An auto loan requires much less documentation and background checking than a $500,000 revolving line of credit.

Salaries

Salaries of Credit Analysts are determined by several factors, including the individual's experience, education, and the size of the organization. Large banks and corporations tend to pay higher salaries than smaller ones. Salaries tend to increase with the number of years' service. Credit Analysts in firms with sales of $250 million or more earned salaries ranging from 36,750 to $45,750 in 2005, according to Robert Half International Inc. Individuals with a Certified Public Accountant or Certified Credit Executive designation, and those with advanced degrees, earned salaries up to 10 percent higher than these figures.

Employment Prospects

Employment opportunities for credit analysts are expected to grow more slowly than average, according to the U.S. Bureau of Labor Statistics. Among the reasons for this slower-than-average job growth are greater use of technology in evaluating and scoring loan applications and job consolidation in some industries, resulting in fewer employment opportunities for college graduates.

On the other hand, newer scoring methodologies for evaluating consumer and business credit are constantly being introduced to the market. As these become available and accepted by key user groups, they may stimulate employment opportunities for professionals seeking to further their career and college graduates entering the field for the first time.

Advancement Prospects

Advancement for Credit Analysts is generally to a supervisory position. Experienced Credit Analysts can expect to move up to credit manager after three to five years, and ultimately to the position of chief credit executive. With each promotion Credit Analysts take on increased responsibility, such as training newly hired analysts and coordinating the credit department with other internal operations. Advancement may be linked to completion of credit certification programs offered by the National Association of Credit Management. Because advancement opportunities may be limited, Credit Analysts may leave the company for a better-paying job at another firm.

Education and Training

Individuals starting as entry-level Credit Analysts usually have college degrees. Credit Analysts take college courses in accounting, business management, economics, and statistics. Some analysts go on to earn an M.B.A. degree or a master's in another field.

Experience, Skills, and Personality Traits

An aptitude for mathematics and problem solving is a job requirement. Because they work with numbers all day, Credit Analysts must be skilled in organizing, analyzing, and reporting data.

Computer literacy, especially in managing spreadsheet and database programs is an essential part of the job. Some employers also want Analysts who have experience with enterprise resource planning (ERP) systems, which link together various parts of the organization for reporting and analysis. Industry certification may also be a requirement in some positions.

Unions and Associations

Credit Analysts may belong to professional associations for networking and career advancement, such as the National Association of Credit Management. The National Association of Credit Management has a three-step industry certification program: Credit Business Associate, Credit Business Fellow, and Certified Credit Executive.

Tips for Entry

1. The National Association of Credit Management offers useful information and interviews with people in the field on its career Web site (http://www.creditworthy.com).
2. Learn about the credit management business through part-time employment as a bank clerk or customer service representative.
3. Get involved in student organizations. Experience handling money as an organization's treasurer can be a very useful experience.
4. College internships are another way of breaking into the industry and making valuable contacts that can be useful during a job search.

RISK MANAGER

CAREER PROFILE

Duties: Develops and implements strategies to identify potential losses; works with brokers, insurance companies, and consulting firms to implement risk control and risk finance programs

Alternate Title(s): Risk and Insurance Manager

Salary Range: $73,000 to $103,000 plus

Employment Prospects: Good

Advancement Prospects: Good

Prerequisites:

Education or Training—Four-year degree with courses in business, risk management and insurance, finance, accounting, and law; an M.B.A. degree may be required in some situations

Experience—Five to seven years' experience in risk management or insurance

Special Skills and Personality Traits—Excellent communication skills and organizational skills; strong analytical and problem-solving skills

Special Requirements—Industry certification such as Associate in Risk Management required by many organizations

CAREER LADDER

```
┌─────────────────────────────┐
│     Chief Risk Officer      │
└─────────────────────────────┘

┌─────────────────────────────┐
│        Risk Manager         │
└─────────────────────────────┘

┌─────────────────────────────┐
│        Risk Analyst         │
└─────────────────────────────┘
```

Position Description

The Risk Manager is responsible for risk control strategies in an organization. Risk Managers work in corporations, insurance companies, and government agencies. There are two basic elements in risk management: risk controls such as insurance policies to control the severity of losses; and risk finance programs that set aside funds for events not covered by risk controls.

The Risk Manager's job is to assess the probability of loss if the business opens a new plant, and its exposure to risk from normal business activities. Risk control strategies can range from risk avoidance and risk transfer to an insurance company to risk retention. Some business risks are managed through a captive insurance subsidiary. If a project is accepted, Risk Managers may seek to transfer that risk to a third party, such as a property and casualty insurance company.

Risk Managers are also important participants in managing the global risks affecting a business, and devising strategies to manage these risks. A recent evolution in risk management is enterprise-wide risk management, in which the company takes a holistic view of all financial and nonfinancial risks to the business. Risk Managers spend much of their time on an office setting, but are required to travel on a regular basis to production departments.

Many firms will hire Risk Managers from investment banks because investment banking firms have developed risk financing techniques that combine commercial insurance and the capital markets. This process allows businesses to obtain commercial insurance for previously uninsurable business risks, such as risk of catastrophic loss from hurricanes or earthquakes.

Salaries

Salaries earned by Risk Managers have increased dramatically in recent years, largely because of increased demand for risk managers working in hedge funds and other specialized investment managers. The median salary for a risk management supervisor in 2005 was $90,123, according to Salary.com. The middle 50 percent earned compensation from $73,000 to $103,000. More-senior positions in large firms command higher salaries. Total compensation for a vice president of risk management at a hedge fund is between $248,000 and $303,000, according to Risk Talent Associates, a search firm. Cash bonuses and performance bonuses can boost earnings significantly, as much as 50 to 70 percent for hedge fund Risk Managers.

Employment Prospects

Demand for experienced Risk Managers is expected to increase over the next several years in the investment management field. Risk Managers with experience in compliance reporting will be increasingly in demand as large hedge funds adapt to changes in financial regulations. Starting in 2006, large hedge funds began registering as investment advisors with the Securities and Exchange Commission. Risk management and financial compliance have begun to merge as investment firms come to understand the risks of noncompliance with financial regulations.

Advancement Prospects

Risk Managers can advance to positions of increased responsibility, ultimately advancing to the position of Chief Risk Officer. Risk Managers can also work in related fields, such as human resources or employee benefits management. Some leave the corporate world to become risk management consultants for major accounting firms or management consulting firms.

Education and Training

The risk management position requires a broad background in business management and finance. Some universities have academic programs in risk management and insurance. Courses in accounting, finance, business law, engineering, management, and political science are also helpful.

Special Requirements

Many organizations require an industry certification in risk management, such as the Associate in Risk Management, conferred by the Risk and Insurance Management Society. RIMS has recently introduced a second-level certification, the Fellow in Risk Management program. Also available is the Canadian Risk Management designation from the Canadian Risk Management Society.

A detailed knowledge of insurance fundamentals and risk financing is also important to the job, as is a knowledge of employee health and product safety, fire prevention, and environmental protection.

Experience, Skills, and Personality Traits

Regardless of industry segment, risk professionals need a balance of skills: a technical understanding of the financial markets, a strong knowledge of trading regulations, some previous experience with financial regulatory agencies (such as prior work experience), and outstanding business and communication skills.

Unions and Associations

Risk management professionals can join the Risk and Insurance Management Society, the Public Risk Management Association, and other organizations for networking and career advancement opportunities.

Tips for Entry

1. College placement officers can help arrange job interviews with prospective employers.
2. Attend industry meetings sponsored by the Risk Insurance Managers Society to learn about new developments in the field.
3. Get a broad academic background and learn how business works; managing risk is an integral part of the business world.
4. The Spencer Educational Foundation, affiliated with the Risk and Insurance Management Society, offers academic scholarships to academically outstanding students pursuing careers in risk management and insurance.

BILLING CLERK

CAREER PROFILE

Duties: Prepares statements and invoices; keeps record of payments collected

Alternate Title(s): Billing Specialist

Salary Range: $26,000 to $33,750

Employment Prospects: Good

Advancement Prospects: Fair

Prerequisites:

Education or Training—High school diploma or equivalent

Experience—General office or clerical experience; some experience with office computers helpful

Special Skills and Personality Traits—General literacy; good attention to detail and ability to perform repetitive work; problem-solving ability; working knowledge of office computer systems or billing terminology required in some organizations

CAREER LADDER

```
┌─────────────────────────────────┐
│  Supervisor, Accounts Receivable │
└─────────────────────────────────┘

┌─────────────────────────────────┐
│        Billing Manager          │
└─────────────────────────────────┘

┌─────────────────────────────────┐
│         Billing Clerk           │
└─────────────────────────────────┘
```

Position Description

Billing Clerks prepare statements, invoices, and bills of lading (contracts issued to a shipper), and maintain records of payments collected. Billing Clerks review purchase orders, sales tickets, and other records to calculate the total amount a customer owes. They compute the billable amount using calculators or office computers.

In some organizations, such as accounting firms, law firms, or consulting firms, Billing Clerks calculate client fees. They keep records of the work performed for a client, the number of billable hours, and the total dollar amount payable. Billing Clerks in trucking companies use rate books to calculate freight charges due. After collecting billing information, clerks prepare customer statements, bills, or invoices. They may prepare a simple statement or a detailed invoice with billing codes for each line item. After billing information has been entered on computers, billing machine operators print the bills, which are then mailed to customers.

Electronic invoicing is replacing paper invoices in a growing number of organizations, resulting in faster collection of customer payments and a reduction in postage and mailing expenses. These paperless billing systems are redefining the duties of Billing Clerks. Billing Clerks using such a system can calculate charges due and prepare bills in one step. They also have time for more important tasks, such as checking errors in customer statements or payments received from customers. Before bills are mailed or transmitted electronically, Billing Clerks check them once again for accuracy.

Billing Clerks also:

- telephone customers about their accounts
- adjust customer records for early payment discounts
- trouble-shoot payment records for problems such as incorrect billing or discounts taken in error
- maintain records of invoices by customer account or product line

Billing Clerks are supervised by a billing manager. In small organizations they often work alone; larger organizations usually have groups of Billing Clerks working together. Billing Clerks usually work a 40-hour week, but may work overtime to meet deadlines.

Salaries

Salaries vary according to experience, size of employer, and geographic region. Billing Clerks earned between $26,000 and $31,500 in 2005 if employed at small companies and between $27,000 and $33,750 at large companies, according to Robert Half International Inc. Full-time Billing Clerks receive, in addition to salary, company benefits such as life and health insurance, sick leave, and participation in employer-sponsored retirement plans.

Employment Prospects

Employment opportunities for Billing Clerks should grow about as fast as opportunities for all jobs. Innovations such as corporate purchasing cards, which are payment cards that function much like credit cards, and the growing use by corporations of electronic payment networks could influence the number of jobs created over the next several years.

Declining job growth is forecast for billing machine operators, the result of office automation in processing accounts receivable. Billing Clerks will perform the duties formerly done by billing machine operators. Despite the lack of employment growth, many job openings will occur as workers transfer to other occupations. The turnover rate in this occupation is relatively high.

Advancement Prospects

With experience, Billing Clerks can advance to more senior positions such as billing manager or supervisor in the accounts receivable/billing department. Billing Clerks who have an associate's degree or higher can advance to positions requiring some education in accounting or business management, such as accounting clerk.

Education and Training

Billing Clerk is an entry-level position in the corporate world. Applicants need to have a high school diploma or the equivalent. Courses in bookkeeping, math, typing, and word processing are helpful. Some Billing Clerks are college graduates who take entry-level positions in order to get into a company. Once hired, Billing Clerks receive on-the-job training in computer systems and billing procedures.

Experience, Skills, and Personality Traits

Employers prefer individuals who have some computer experience and general office experience. They look for people who have good math skills, are detail oriented, and can perform repetitive work for long periods. Good fact checking and problem-solving skills are very useful in this position.

Some employers require candidates to have a working knowledge of office computer systems or billing terminology. Health maintenance organizations, for instance, look for people who are familiar with medical terminology and insurance claims processing.

Unions and Associations

Some Billing Clerks may be members of the Office and Professional Employees International Union or other labor unions and pay union dues.

Tips for Entry

1. Taking courses in commonly used PC programs such as word processing and spreadsheet programs can be very useful; skill improvement is key to advancement in this career path.
2. Look for employment opportunities in local newspapers and attend job fairs; contact employers directly.

PURCHASING MANAGER

CAREER PROFILE

Duties: Buys goods and services for an organization; supervises buyers and purchasing agents

Alternate Title(s): Purchasing Coordinator

Salary Range: $38,000 to $57,500

Employment Prospects: Good

Advancement Prospects: Fair

Prerequisites:

Education or Training—Four-year college degree

Experience—Two to five years' experience

Special Skills and Personality Traits—Strong communication skills, negotiating skills and computer skills; working knowledge of supply chain management

Special Requirements—Industry certification helpful for advancement

CAREER LADDER

```
┌─────────────────────────────┐
│    Purchasing Supervisor    │
└─────────────────────────────┘

┌─────────────────────────────┐
│     Purchasing Manager      │
└─────────────────────────────┘

┌─────────────────────────────┐
│      Purchasing Agent       │
└─────────────────────────────┘
```

Position Description

Purchasing Managers seek to obtain high-quality merchandise at the lowest purchase cost. They determine which commodities or services are best, choose the suppliers, negotiate an acceptable price, and award contracts ensuring delivery at the appropriate time. They also supervise buyers and purchasing agents.

Purchasing Managers study sales records and inventory records of current stock, identify foreign and domestic suppliers, and keep abreast of market trends affecting both supply or demand for materials for which they are responsible. Before contacting vendors, Purchasing Managers consult numerous sources of information, including industry catalogs, trade periodicals, directories, trade journals, and Internet sites. They also keep track of economic information relating to their product line. They use computers to keep track of market conditions, price trends, and watch the futures market to follow changes in commodity prices.

They research the reputation and history of suppliers. They attend industry trade shows and conferences, and visit suppliers' plants to gather information and discuss business or technical issues influencing the purchase decision. After reviewing a supplier's prices, availability, quality, and delivery, bids are solicited. Contracts are awarded and orders placed with the winning bidders. Specific duties and responsibilities often vary by industry and employer. In many industries the Purchasing Manager has the same duties as a buyer or purchasing agent.

In large industrial organizations, a distinction is often drawn between the work of a buyer or a purchasing agent and that of a Purchasing Manager. Purchasing agents and buyers often focus on routine purchasing tasks. They often specialize by commodity or group of related commodities, such as metals or petroleum products. Purchasing Managers usually handle the more complex decisions, often supervising a group of purchasing agents. Purchasing Managers handle the deals that are too large, or too complicated, for purchasing agents.

Purchasing Managers also:

• prepare purchasing guidelines and notify purchasing agents of changes to guidelines
• prepare market analysis reports
• review purchasing orders for compliance with company policy
• coordinate purchasing activities with other departments
• arrange for disposal of surplus inventory

Changing business practices have altered the traditional roles of Purchasing Managers. Many businesses have long-term supply contracts with selected vendors, which has several advantages from the buyer's viewpoint. Manufacturers can reduce their overhead costs by dealing exclusively with one or two vendors; larger volume orders often qualify for volume purchase discounts. A major responsibility for Purchasing Managers is working out delivery problems with the supplier because the success of the relationship affects the buying firm's performance.

Purchasing Managers often work more than 40 hours a week, including evenings and weekends. Seasonal buying patterns in key market segments can influence the amount of hours worked. For example, Purchasing Managers who work in retailing are very busy during the winter holidays.

Salaries

Earnings vary with industry, experience, and level of responsibility. Salaries of Purchasing Managers ranged from $38,000 to $48,750 in small companies and from $42,250 to $57,500 in large companies with sales over $250 million a year in 2005, according to Robert Half International Inc. Purchasing Managers receive the same benefits as their coworkers, including paid vacations, life and health insurance, and employer-sponsored pension plans.

Employment Prospects

Employment opportunities for Purchasing Managers and agents are expected to grow at a slower rate than other occupations through 2014. There are several causes for the decline: jobs being eliminated by industry mergers; the increased use of corporate purchase cards, which function like credit cards, for routine purchases such as office supplies; and the growing use of business-to-business commerce over the Internet, reducing the number of entry-level jobs because much of the work can now be done by computers.

Advancement Prospects

Advancement is usually to positions of increased responsibility, such as purchasing supervisor, or in companies with several operating divisions, to director of corporate purchasing. Some Purchasing Managers advance their careers by changing jobs or industries. Many positions will become available as current employees switch jobs or reach retirement age. Individuals who have a master's degree in finance or a related area or who have extensive experience with computer systems have the best opportunities to advance into upper management.

Education and Training

A four-year degree with courses in accounting or finance is required. Courses in computer science and network management are recommended because much of the Purchasing Manager's job involves managing computer networks, or the employees who manage a network.

Educational requirements vary by industry. Major retailers, such as department stores, look for people with general business backgrounds, while engineering companies want people with some technical education in their background.

Special Requirements

Industry certification is optional. Certification is rarely required for employment or advancement, but it conveys professional competence and experience. Available certifications are Accredited Purchasing Practitioner, for entrylevel Purchasing Managers, and Certified Purchasing Manager, both from the National Association of Purchasing Management, and the Certified Purchasing Professional from the American Purchasing Society.

Experience, Skills, and Personality Traits

Prior experience as a buyer, purchasing agent, or assistant purchasing manager is recommended. Individuals should be familiar with wholesaling and retailing practices in the industry where they are seeking employment. Strong communication skills, negotiating skills, and computer skills are very important in this position. Problem-solving skills and an ability to work with numbers, using common spreadsheet accounting programs, is helpful. A willingness to assume a leadership role in planning projects, and get others involved, are good personality traits. Supply chain management has gone through some major changes in the last decade. Individuals who want to make a career in this field should be familiar with current systems technology, in both theoretical and practical applications.

Unions and Associations

Purchasing Managers can join the Institute for Supply Management, or the American Purchasing Society for professional development and networking opportunities. Among other member services ISM has an online career center, accessible on its Web site, http://www.ism.org, and sponsors online courses. The APM also has a job bank accessible on its Web site, http://www.americanpurchasing.com.

Tips for Entry

1. Suggestions for other financial positions are applicable here, too. Networking and contact development are important in making the right career choice, starting in college.
2. Job shadowing (spending a day or two with a practitioner) and internships are effective ways to get practical experience while still in college.
3. Check Internet job sites and professional associations for job leads and job finding tips.

CASH MANAGER

CAREER PROFILE

Duties: Manages an organization's daily cash balance; executes funds movement transactions; invests surplus funds in short-term investments and arranges short-term financing when necessary

Alternate Title(s): None

Salary Range: $45,000 to $75,000

Employment Prospects: Good

Advancement Prospects: Excellent

Prerequisites:

Education or Training—Four-year degree with courses in accounting or finance; M.B.A. degree preferred for senior positions

Experience—Three to five years' experience in treasury operations with increasing levels of responsibility

Special Skills and Personality Traits—Proficiency in financial spreadsheet systems; detailed understanding of money market investments and corporate banking services

Special Requirements—Certification in cash management (Certified Treasury Professional) a plus

CAREER LADDER

```
┌─────────────────────────────┐
│        Treasurer            │
└─────────────────────────────┘

┌─────────────────────────────┐
│       Cash Manager          │
└─────────────────────────────┘

┌─────────────────────────────┐
│   Assistant Cash Manager    │
└─────────────────────────────┘
```

Position Description

The Cash Manager is responsible for maintaining and controlling the daily cash balances of an organization. The Cash Manager must get the best use from available cash coming in from customer payments, while minimizing external borrowing costs. Business organizations and even nonprofit agencies owe their success in the marketplace to their ability to finance ongoing projects, by marshalling their cash reserves or by obtaining short-term financing.

In a large company, the Cash Manager helps manage foreign currency risk and relationships with national and international banks. An understanding of the business cycle and the organization's cash cycle is essential in projecting the firm's daily cash surplus or cash deficit. The Cash Manager is responsible for investing surplus funds in short-term marketable securities or, in the case of a deficit, arranging necessary short-term financing through trade credit, bank lines of credit, commercial paper issuance or from other

sources. The Cash Manager usually reports to the corporate treasurer, but may report to an assistant treasurer or vice president of finance in larger corporations.

Duties of the Cash Manager include:

- managing account balances in cash management servicing banks, including compensating balances, lockbox arrangements, and cash transfers
- managing daily disbursement of funds to trade creditors
- managing domestic and international cash flows
- monitoring daily positions and hedging activity
- managing investment of short-term cash and cash flow and interest rate forecasting
- supervising activities of clerical employees

In a mid-sized corporation the position of Cash Manager is often combined with other treasury functions. The Cash Manager may also serve as corporate treasurer or controller. Larger corporations (sales above $500 million) have a treasury department with more defined job responsibilities, and have a financial professional serving in each treasury position.

Salaries

Salaries of corporate Cash Managers vary according to company size, geographic location, and complexity of the job. Cash Managers employed by U.S. companies earned an average annual base salary of $61,500 and bonus of $6,800, in 2005, according to the Association for Financial Professionals. Although salary increases are smaller than they were 10 years ago, average weekly salaries of corporate treasury professionals increased by about 3.6 percent in 2004, which is in line with pay increases for all professional workers, AFP says. The middle 50 percent had earnings between $45,000 and $75,000 annually, including bonuses and other investor compensation. In addition to salary, Cash Managers may receive a signing bonus, an annual performance bonus tied to company profitability, and a retention bonus. Cash Managers working in the northeastern U.S. received the highest salaries, and those employed in the Midwest received the lowest average salary and bonus.

Employment Prospects

There is a shortage of professional labor in corporate finance. Employment for financial managers is expected to grow about as fast as the industry average through 2014. The need for skilled financial managers will increase due to the demands of global trade, the proliferation of complex financial instruments, and changing federal and state regulations. Competition for managerial positions is strong, which means the number of applicants for Cash Manager positions will probably exceed the number of job openings. However, many opportunities exist for skilled, resourceful financial managers who keep abreast of the latest financial instruments and regulations, and those who have experience in more than one industry. Developing a specialty expertise in a rapidly growing industry, such as healthcare, may be helpful in securing a job.

Advancement Prospects

Cash Managers advance by moving into positions of increased responsibility. After three to five years they may advance to assistant treasurer or treasurer. Cash Managers with leadership skills may become chief financial officer. Job turnover in this position is relatively high. Nearly half of corporate finance officers have been involved in a merger or acquisition (often leading to a reduction in treasury staff) within the last five years. Many Cash Managers leave their company for similar positions in other organizations following a merger.

Education and Training

A four-year degree with courses in accounting, finance, or another related field is a requirement for the position. A postgraduate degree such as an M.B.A. is usually a requirement for advancement to more senior positions in corporate treasury.

Special Requirements

Industry certification is often required for entry to the position. Individuals who have industry certification (Certified Treasury Professional) have a competitive edge over other job applicants. The Association for Financial Professionals confers the Certified Treasury Professional designation on those who pass an examination and have at least two years relevant experience.

Experience, Skills, and Personality Traits

Prior experience in corporate finance is a requirement for the position. Also required is a broad understanding of cash management products and services, short-term money market investments, and corporate banking services. Cash Managers need to have excellent communication skills, strong negotiating skills, good organizational skills, and have computer literacy with spreadsheet accounting programs.

Unions and Associations

Cash Managers can become members of professional associations such as the Association for Financial Professionals and the Financial Executives Institute for networking and professional development.

Tips for Entry

1. Attend industry events and seminars to keep up with the field and explore networking opportunities.
2. Improve your negotiating and interpersonal skills to land a job with a top company.
3. College internship programs are often a door opener to job opportunities after graduation.
4. Check industry Web sites such as Association for Financial Professional's site for job leads (http://www.AFPonline.org).

TREASURER

CAREER PROFILE

Duties: Directs financial planning, funds procurement, and investing; develops treasury department strategic goals, objectives, and budgets; manages cash forecasting and budgeting; prepares financial reports for management

Alternate Title(s): Treasury Manager, Director of Treasury

Salary Range: $84,000 to $347,000

Employment Prospects: Good

Advancement Prospects: Good

Prerequisites:

Education or Training—Four-year degree; M.B.A. or equivalent graduate degree often required

Experience—Five to 10 years' experience with increasing responsibility; analytical ability to read and analyze financial statements; working knowledge of customer service activities, including billing and collections; knowledge of cash management systems and investments, risk management and enterprise resource planning (ERP) systems

Special Skills and Personality Traits—Excellent communication and problem-solving abilities; excellent organizational skills and interpersonal skills

Special Requirements—Industry certification usually a requirement in larger corporations

CAREER LADDER

```
┌─────────────────────────────┐
│   Chief Financial Officer    │
└─────────────────────────────┘

┌─────────────────────────────┐
│          Treasurer           │
└─────────────────────────────┘

┌─────────────────────────────┐
│      Assistant Treasurer     │
└─────────────────────────────┘
```

Position Description

Treasurers direct an organization's financial goals, objectives, and budgets. They manage the investment of funds and manage associated risks, supervise cash management activities, execute capital raising strategies to support the organization's growth. Specific job functions will vary according to the size of organization and structure. Fortune 500 companies typically have a Treasurer, cash manager, and controller, all of whom report to the chief financial officer.

In addition to general duties, Treasurers and other financial officers perform tasks unique to their organization or industry, and must understand special tax laws and regulations affecting their industry. For example, financial officers of multinational companies must be familiar with the local banking systems in countries where they do business, as well as foreign exchange hedging and currency management techniques. Health care financial managers must be conversant with issues surrounding health care financing and federal funding programs such as Medicare and Medicaid.

Improvements in data collection and analysis have had the effect of expanding the role of corporate Treasurer. In many large organizations the Treasurer functions as an adviser to business unit managers on matters as diverse as business risk management and customer service. With greater demands on their skills, finance managers work longer hours, often up to 50 to 60 hours per week. They are also required to attend meetings of finance and economic associations, and they may travel frequently to visit subsidiary firms or meet customers.

Their duties include:

* managing the organization's borrowings, liquidity portfolio, and investments
* developing and maintaining the organization's financial institution and investment broker relationships
* developing financial management policies for portfolio investing, borrowing, and related policies; recommends these policies to the CFO
* directing special projects related to financial decisions
* supervising treasury analysts and other personnel assigned to the department

The overall responsibilities of corporate Treasurers have broadened in recent years, and they often include review or oversight of nonfinancial activities that are thought to have some strategic value to the organization. Increasingly, the Treasurer is getting involved as an adviser in risk identification and risk control/risk mitigation efforts, mergers and acquisitions, and shareholder relations. This is a senior management position, requiring a combination of analytical skill and the ability to manage and motivate others to achieve organizational goals.

Salaries

Annual compensation for Treasurers can vary by industry group, location, size of the organization, and other factors. Large organizations often pay more than smaller ones. Financial managers in private industry receive, in addition to annual base salary, compensation in the form of performance bonuses and deferred compensation in the form of employee stock options. Salaries of corporate Treasurers are determined by company size, industry experience, and other factors such as industry credentials. Corporate Treasurers in firms with sales up to $50 million a year earned between $84,000 and $110,000 in 2005, while those employed by companies with sales over $250 million earned between $244,000 and $347,000, according to Robert Half International Inc. These figures include employee bonus and incentive pay. People with industry certifications can expect to earn 5 to 10 percent above the average annual compensation.

Employment Prospects

The employment outlook for Treasurers is good for those individuals with the right skills. Recent industry surveys have found a very strong occupational outlook for treasury professionals. Mergers, acquisitions, and corporate downsizings will continue to adversely affect employment opportunities, but overall growth of the economy and the need for senior level financial expertise will more than offset the job losses to corporate restructuring and downsizing. Due to the important work treasury departments perform, the treasury recruitment market is more resistant to economic downturn than most other areas in corporate finance.

Advancement Prospects

As the senior ranking treasury department manager, the Treasurer is in line to move higher in the ranks, possibly becoming chief financial officer or chief executive officer.

An alternative is moving to a treasury position with a larger company, usually accompanied by an increase in total compensation. Another advancement option is moving to a treasury position with a nonprofit agency or a government agency.

Treasurers leaving their positions for new opportunities elsewhere do so for two reasons: 1) their job is too limited in scope and responsibility and fails to live up to their expectations; 2) their current employer offers insufficient opportunity for promotion and advancement within the firm.

Education and Training

A four-year degree, with courses in finance, business management, and accounting is a requirement. Many employers look for individuals with a master's degree and additional industry certification such as a Certified Public Accounting (CPA) designation. Also important is having a strong analytical background, preferably in finance or risk management. These programs develop the analytical skills necessary to perform the job, and provide a background in the latest financial analysis methods, which are extensively used in corporate treasury.

Special Requirements

Corporate Treasurers are expected to earn an industry certification by a professional trade association and maintain their status by earning continuing education credits awarded at industry-sanctioned events and seminars. The Certified Treasury Professional (CTP) given by the Association for Financial Professionals is the professional designation for corporate treasurers. Larger companies, those with annual sales above $500 million, often require the CTP designation as a condition of employment.

Experience, Skills, and Personality Traits

Candidates for financial management positions need a broad range of skills, including strong analyical skills and problem-solving skills. Interpersonal skills are increasingly important because success in the job is tied to an ability to motivate people. They must be creative thinkers and problem solvers. Those involved in international finance may find fluency in a second language helpful in their jobs.

Experience in a particular industry can be more important than formal education. Financial institutions generally recruit financial managers with prior experience in banking. A background in treasury management is also useful in pursuing a career in nonfinancial companies, because corporations are now using many of the credit risk and interest rate risk management tools pioneered by financial institutions.

A solid background in computer-based accounting and financial control systems is a general requirement in corporate finance today. Individuals are expected to have a working knowledge of treasury workstations, balance reporting and investment systems, and quantitative risk analysis methods such as Value at Risk. Also becoming important in the field is some knowledge of enterprise resource planning (ERP) systems, which combine accounting data such as sales and financial data in an integrated network.

Unions and Associations

Treasurers can become members of several professional organizations, including the Association for Financial Professionals, the Financial Executives Institute, and the National Association of Corporate Treasurers for networking and career advancement opportunities.

Tips for Entry

1. Be entrepreneurial. Get to know other parts of the organization. During an interview, suggest ways treasury can help business managers meet their goals.

2. Short-term or interim assignments can be a door opener to a longer relationship; the same is true for college internships.

3. During the job interview, ask questions about job specifics; many organizations don't have a fully written job description for the position.

4. If your interest is working internationally, foreign language fluency can be an asset.

5. Accounting and finance professionals with strong information technology experience will see increased demand for their skills.

6. Include recent accomplishments in your job résumé, such as projects managed and goals accomplished.

CONTROLLER

CAREER PROFILE

Duties: Prepares financial reports summarizing an organization's financial position; maintains and monitors accounting records; prepares financial reports of income and condition to regulatory agencies; coordinates activities of internal and external auditors; responsible for day-to-day finance and accounting procedures

Alternate Title(s): Divisional Controller, Financial Controller

Salary Range: $61,250 to $147,250

Employment Prospects: Good

Advancement Prospects: Good

Prerequisites:

Education and Training—Four-year degree in accounting, business, or finance. An M.B.A. degree is desirable in larger firms. Certified Public Accountant (CPA) designation usually required

Experience—Several years of increasing responsibility in budgeting, financial planning, and cost accounting; senior-level positions require at least eight years' experience

Special Skills and Personality Traits—Strong analytical, interpersonal, and organizational skills; ability to lead projects; excellent communication skills; detailed working knowledge of manual and automated accounting systems

Special Requirements—CPA certification often required in larger organization

CAREER LADDER

```
┌─────────────────────────────────────┐
│  Treasurer or Vice President Finance │
└─────────────────────────────────────┘

┌─────────────────────────────────────┐
│             Controller              │
└─────────────────────────────────────┘

┌─────────────────────────────────────┐
│         Assistant Controller         │
└─────────────────────────────────────┘
```

Position Description

The financial Controller holds a key position in large, complex organizations. The Controller manages the organization's financial records, its accounting practices, as well as its borrowing relationships with outside financial institutions and relations with the financial community in general. The Controller is responsible for preparation of short-term and long-term budgets, such as sales forecasts and expense budgets, accounts receivable, and capital investing. The Controller prepares accounting reports for senior management and external reports to government regulatory agencies. The Controller manages day-to-day funds disbursements, including the company's payroll, and coordinates activities of internal and external auditors.

Controllers are the main budget planners in corporations, and may function at the division or business-unit level, or be responsible for overall budgeting and expense-related disbursements for an entire corporation. In large corporations, the Controller has a high-profile job, reporting directly to the chief financial officer and the corporate finance committee.

At the corporate level, the Controller's duties include:

- ensuring the timely and accurate processing of accounting and financial reports to management and audit staff
- assuring adequate protection of business assets through internal controls, auditing, and insurance coverage
- forecasting short-term and long-term cash requirements
- executing cash disbursements
- managing accounts payable and accounts receivable and cost accounting functions
- managing corporate income tax compliance
- maintaining internal accounting controls

- supervising the activities of business unit Controllers and corporate treasury
- developing annual operating budgets and monitoring the achievement of these plans
- coordinating the activities of outside auditors to ensure that each audit performed by the auditing firm is performed in a timely and cost-efficient manner
- contributing to senior management decisions on special projects, acquisitions, reorganizations, and long-range planning activities

The Controller's job requires extensive accounting experience. Holders of the position often come from big accounting firms, or have previously been employed by accounting firms. In large organizations the corporate Controller is responsible for day-to-day financial and accounting functions. In addition to coordinating financial reporting, the Controller manages professional development of subordinate managers. In a small organization, the Controller may have responsibility for all financial and budgeting controls in the firm.

Salaries

Salaries tend to increase with size of the organization, years of experience, responsibilities, and geographic location. Fortune 500 corporations and multinational corporations pay the highest salaries for corporate Controllers, while middle-market companies pay more moderate salaries. Controller salaries ranged from $61,250 in small firms to $147,250 in companies with sales over $250 million, according to a 2005 survey by Robert Half International. Typically, corporate Controllers are compensated with a combination of salary and performance bonus plus stock options.

Employment Prospects

Employment prospects for corporate Controllers should remain favorable through 2014. Businesses have a continual need to refresh their professional ranks with people who are able to handle increasingly complex financial transactions, assess global risks, and generate financial reports as required by internal or external users of information. As in other managerial occupations, jobseekers will face competition because the number of qualified jobseekers can exceed the positions available at any time. Competition is most intense in the largest corporations, which have active college-campus recruiting programs. Many businesses have raised salaries to significantly higher levels to recruit the most qualified applicants.

Advancement Prospects

Controllers have excellent prospects for advancing to more senior positions, moving from divisional Controller to corporate Controller. Other options include advancing to chief financial officer or taking a similar position in a different company, perhaps a smaller company offering better opportunities for advancement. Some Controllers change careers, becoming consultants with a large accounting firm or an independent consultant.

Education and Training

A four-year degree in accounting, finance, or a related course of study is a minimum requirement for employment. An M.B.A. degree is recommended for entry to Fortune 500 corporations.

Special Requirement

Industry certification in accounting, notably the Certified Public Accountant (CPA) certification, is often a requirement in larger organizations, and in nearly all organizations a CPA designation is necessary for advancement.

Experience, Skills, and Personality Traits

Controllers usually have several years experience performing complex tasks, such as leading cost management projects, and team leadership skills are preferred. Also important is an aptitude for abstract reasoning, and excellent interpersonal skills and communication skills.

Well-developed financial analysis skills and management skills are also important. Advancing in the field generally requires having a proven ability to recruit, train, and motivate employees to meet revenue and sales goals.

Accounting systems in large organizations are highly automated operations. The Controller's position requires having a working knowledge of both manual and automated accounting systems, and a detailed knowledge of micocomputer-based accounting and financial management software.

Unions and Associations

As professional employees, Controllers can belong to professional associations, such as the Financial Executives Institute (FEI) and join special interest groups devoted to networking issues.

Tips for Entry

1. Join professional organizations for networking and career advancement opportunities.
2. Managing money for nonprofit or college organizations can provide useful experience.
3. Attend job fairs and check out career Web sites for job leads and to learn more about job requirements.
4. Internships and summer employment arranged through a university can lead to job opportunities in finance or accounting opening the door to a career in finance.
5. Interim assignments are another option if you have some industry experience; these can lead to a longer term employment offer.

CHIEF FINANCIAL OFFICER

CAREER PROFILE

Duties: Directs finance and accounting functions, preparation of financial reports and investment activities of an organization

Alternate Title(s): CFO

Salary Range: $84,500 to $347,000 and up

Employment Prospects: Fair

Advancement Prospects: Poor

Prerequisites:

Education or Training—Four-year degree with emphasis in accounting and finance; M.B.A. often preferred

Experience—Four to 10 years' or more experience in corporate finance with increasing levels of responsibility

Special Skills and Personality Traits—Visionary or strategic thinking; strong leadership skills and interpersonal skills; ability to delegate responsibility

Special Requirements—Professional certification such as Certified Public Accountant (CPA) designation

CAREER LADDER

```
┌─────────────────────────────┐
│   Chief Operating Officer    │
└─────────────────────────────┘

┌─────────────────────────────┐
│   Chief Financial Officer    │
└─────────────────────────────┘

┌─────────────────────────────┐
│         Treasurer            │
└─────────────────────────────┘
```

Position Description

The Chief Financial Officer is the top financial officer of an organization, usually a public corporation. They direct all accounting and financial functions, preparation of financial and fiscal reports, and investment activities. They formulate, through subordinate officers, financial plans, policies, and relations with key outside organizations, including lending institutions, shareholders, and the financial community. The CFO is normally a senior officer, reporting directly to the president, chief operating officer, or chief executive officer.

In carrying out their duties, the CFO's function is principally as the financial architect of their organization. He or she works closely with senior executives to provide financial support for the achieving strategic goals. The CFO directs the financial activities of the accounting group, ensuring the integrity of financial data, providing timely and accurate analysis and management reports, and ensuring adequate accounting controls.

As a high-level executive the CFO must know how to delegate responsibility to subordinates, allowing trusted managers to take charge of various accounting, treasury reporting, and other functions. The CFO must be able to present budget and planning proposals to the CEO (chief executive officer), the highest corporate executive, or to the board of directors.

Strategic planning and visionary skills are becoming more important in what is becoming a global economy. Corporations are starting to run their business activities with an integrated or enterprise-wide approach to management, examining the cumulative impact of various business functions on corporate earnings, market share, and so on. Increasingly, it is the CFO's responsibility to bring together the corporate treasurer, controller, risk manager, and other senior officers, to try to develop creative solutions to business problems.

Salaries

As high-profile officers, Chief Financial Officers are generously compensated for their efforts. Typically, CFOs receive a combination of salary, annual bonus tied to company performance, and stock options. Signing bonuses have become common, especially for experienced CFOs. A smaller number of companies offer retention bonuses to keep valued employees on staff.

Actual compensation earned by CFOs varies according to a wide number of factors, including company size, industry, geographic location, and professional experience. CFOs of public companies earned between $84,500 and $347,000 in 2005, according to Robert Half International Inc. Chief financial officers in companies with sales above $500 million had the highest total compensation (ranging from $244,000 to $347,000). These figures assume that there is a corporate controller reporting to the CFO.

CFOs of commercial banks earned average salaries (excluding bonuses) significantly less than corporate CFOs—a median salary of $97,759 in 2003, says America's Community Bankers, a banking association.

Employment Prospects

There is nationwide competition for experienced CFOs, although the number of openings available at any given time is likely to be small. Competition for the choicest assignments, such as CFO for a Fortune 100 company, can be especially intense. Vacancies in top companies are often filled by executive search firms.

An individual who has created an impressive record as a manager may be in a position to move up to a CFO position being created for the first time, but there are no guarantees. For instance, a corporate treasurer could move up to become CFO, filling a job vacancy, as long as they are well-rounded individuals experienced in computer systems and strategic planning in addition to corporate treasury functions.

Advancement Prospects

As the top financial officer, the CFO already occupies a senior-level position. Further advancement to chief operating officer or chief executive officer is possible, but in practice difficult to achieve. Many CFOs advance their careers by leaving their companies to take similar positions at other firms.

Education and Training

The foundation for a Chief Financial Officer is a strong undergraduate and graduate background, usually with a high grade point average. A four-year degree with an emphasis in accounting and finance or related courses is the minimum academic criteria, and many employers look for candidates with an M.B.A. degree or a postgraduate degree in finance. Courses in information technology and database management are also helpful.

Special Requirements

Professional certification is generally a standard requirement. Most CFOs have achieved at least one certification, and often several, from recognized professional groups. Perhaps the most common is the Certified Public Accountant (CPA) designation.

Available certifications include the Certified Public Accountant designation, from the American Accounting Association.

Experience, Skills, and Personality Traits

Most employers want to interview individuals with a strong track record and four to 10 years or more experience in a variety of corporate finance positions. Strong written and interpersonal communication are essential to the job; CFOs spend much of their time making presentations to senior executives, financial analysts, and the board of directors.

In recent years, the skill requirements of CFOs have stiffened up; employers want people who can help develop strategy and function as a business partner to the CEO in addition to performing their financial duties.

Strong communication and interpersonal skills are important for CFOs, as are financial expertise and a strong sense of personal integrity and professional ethics.

Unions and Associations

As financial professionals, CFOs can become members of business associations such as the Association for Financial Professionals or the Financial Executives Institute for professional networking and career advancement.

Tips for Entry

1. The suggestions given earlier for the treasurer position apply here also, but to a greater degree. Individuals who demonstrate entrepreneurial flair or who add value by getting projects done on schedule will always be in demand.
2. As in other finance positions, contacts and connections are always useful, particularly when approaching a company for the first time. Executive recruiters can also help with initial contacts leading to an interview.
3. The Internet is an excellent source of information about positions at all levels. Use the Internet to do research on prospective employers and keep up with trends, especially if you are considering changing industries.

INSURANCE

ACCOUNT EXECUTIVE, INSURANCE

CAREER PROFILE

Duties: Responsible for acquiring new accounts for insurance agency or brokerage; services existing accounts

Alternate Title(s): Account Manager

Salary Range: $50,000 to $90,000

Employment Prospects: Good

Advancement Prospects: Good

Prerequisites:

Education or Training—Bachelor's degree

Experience—Three to five years' experience with emphasis in sales; prior insurance experience required

Special Skills and Personality Traits—Strong communication and interpersonal skills; ability to lead and motivate staff; ability to analyze problems of insurance clients and recommend solutions; has strong verbal, interpersonal, and written communication skills

Special Requirements—Insurance license may be required in some states

CAREER LADDER

```
┌─────────────────────────────┐
│        Sales Agent          │
└─────────────────────────────┘

┌─────────────────────────────┐
│     Account Executive       │
└─────────────────────────────┘

┌─────────────────────────────┐
│    Marketing Assistant      │
└─────────────────────────────┘
```

Position Description

Account Executives are employed by insurance brokers and agencies to prospect for new business and maintain the relationship between the office and its clients. Account managers promote current and future products to their clients, and monitor the client's insurance and risk management needs. They recommend insurance coverage appropriate for the client's needs and consult with technical specialists when necessary. Another job function is coordinating enrollment activities, internal document control in the office, and database management. In essence, the account executive tracks the insurance clients and makes sure that clients are properly serviced.

Account Executives have job functions very similar to those of insurance brokers and agents (insurance *producers* in industry jargon), but have less on-the-job experience than agents or brokers. The Account Executive may assume the broker or agent's duties when the broker is out of the office.

Account Executives also:

- obtain information from agency clients needed to write proposals for insurance coverage

- generate new sales leads by attending community and association meetings and making direct sales calls, referring leads on eligible prospects to the agency sales manager
- deliver proposals for insurance coverage to agency prospects and clients, close the sale, and deliver policies.
- review periodically insurance coverage for agency clients and make recommendations regarding changes in coverage
- prepare and maintain insurance risk ratings and procedures manuals
- assist in collection of insurance premiums on new and assigned clients
- maintain agency sales reports
- attend agency sales and training sessions as required

Account Executives usually work a 40-hour week in an office setting. They perform much of their client service work with telephones, fax machines, and office computers. Account Executives may make day or evening sales or service calls to agency clients when the servicing agent is unavailable, and they often attend evening business meetings to develop sales leads. This is a good career choice if you like helping people meet their financial goals and can handle a variety of assignments.

Salaries

Starting salaries for insurance Account Executives range from $50,000 to $90,000 depending on experience, academic training, and geographic location. Account executives receive generous fringe benefits, including paid life and health insurance, paid vacations, and can participate in employer-sponsored retirement plans.

Employment Prospects

Employment prospects for insurance Account Executives should grow about as fast as opportunities for all other occupations through 2014. Hiring of Account Executives will be driven by the insurance industry's need to fill sales and marketing positions in fast-growing markets and also by the replacement of employees exiting the industry or reaching retirement age. The increasing number and variety of investment products sold by insurance companies, such as retirement planning, long-term health insurance, and variable annuity investments, will fuel much of this growth in employment over the next decade. Opportunities for sales agents starting their careers should be better in smaller insurance companies or insurance brokerages that pay lower salaries than larger firms but generally have more employment opportunities at any time.

Advancement Prospects

Account Executives may be promoted to broker or agent in their insurance agency. With experience, they can become full-fledged sales agents or brokers, usually after two to three years.

Education and Training

A four-year college degree in business or finance is required. Agencies generally provide their own on-the-job training to qualified candidates with prior training in insurance automation systems.

Special Requirements

State insurance licenses may be required in some states, Account executives selling property, and consulting insurance would need to obtain the appropriate license from their state's insurance department.

Experience, Skills, and Personality Traits

The ability to manage people is important. Account development skills are required, and so is the ability to successfully generate, maintain, and build sales over a period of time. Bargaining and negotiating skills are used when it comes to setting a price and building support within the agency. Account Executives should have strong verbal, interpersonal, and written communication skills. Also important is an ability to analyze complex insurance issues in order to deal with client needs.

Unions and Associations

Account Executives can join insurance associations such as the National Association of Independent Agents or the Council of Insurance Agents and Brokers for networking and other opportunities.

Tips for Entry

1. Attend meetings of industry associations to learn more about the business.
2. Networking skills are important in developing job leads.
3. Check out industry Web sites for job leads in your region.
4. Web sites such as Insurance Job Zone (http://www.insurancejobzone.com) can provide additional job levels.

CUSTOMER SERVICE REPRESENTATIVE, INSURANCE

CAREER PROFILE

Duties: Responsible for handling incoming telephone calls from customers and field insurance representatives

Alternate Title(s): None

Salary Range: $28,000 to $45,000

Employment Prospects: Good

Advancement Prospects: Good

Prerequisites:

Education or Training—Associate degree in general business

Experience—Two years' experience in a call center

Special Skills and Personality Traits—Excellent communication and organizational skills; good listening skills; problem-solving skills; ability to work with minimal supervision

Special Requirements—State insurance license required in many states

CAREER LADDER

```
┌─────────────────────────────────┐
│   Customer Service Supervisor   │
└─────────────────────────────────┘

┌─────────────────────────────────┐
│ Customer Service Representative │
└─────────────────────────────────┘

┌─────────────────────────────────┐
│    Administrative Assistant     │
└─────────────────────────────────┘
```

Position Description

A Customer Service Representative in the insurance industry wears many hats, but generally is the person who deals directly with customers. The Customers Service Representative also works closely with agents, brokers, claims adjusters, and underwriters to make sure the customer's interests are being served. Some of the job responsibilities include educating customers about insurance coverage, changes in policies and policy requirements, processing new accounts, and handling complaints. Customer Service Representatives are expected to be familiar with details of insurance policies and how to calculate premium billing. Knowing how to read a policy and where to get assistance in responding to inquiries about policy coverage is critical in maintaining good relations with customers.

Customer Service Representatives do a lot more than handle phone calls from insurance customers. They write insurance policies, counsel insurance customers on insurance bills and policy coverages, and process billing adjustments for overcharges. Customers do not want to be over- or underinsured;

they look to the CSR for answers to questions and advice on how much insurance coverage is sufficient. Service representatives explain changes in policy coverage, billing, and claims processing. Some customers visit their insurance company's field office to have their policies reviewed in person.

In an insurance agency the CSR may also be responsible for managing the customer claims filing process, including acting as a liaison between the customer and the agency. The CSR also represents the agency in dealings with insurance companies. Agency CSRs are responsible for many reports, such as maintaining policy expiration lists, initiating policy renewals, maintaining timely and accurate billings, and keeping the customer accounts receivable file current. In large insurance companies, CSRs may handle customer queries about a wide range of financial services products, including annuities, mutual funds, and insurance products.

Salaries

Customer Service Representatives earn an annual salary plus bonus and paid overtime. Salaries can range from $28,000 to $45,000 annually. Insurance service representatives typically work a 40-hour week.

Employment Prospects

There is steady demand for insurance Customer Service Representatives. Some CSRs enter the filed as trainees or are promoted from administrative assistant positions. In agencies the CSR job is often considered considered an entry-level position, which may lead to more responsible positions with experience. Most CSRs enter the field through promotion from other entry-level positions such as complaint analyst or administrative assistant.

Advancement Prospects

In insurance agencies the CSR job may lead to a position in sales. In larger insurance organizations there are more options for advancement. Customer Service Representatives can become service managers or customer service supervisors and take on the responsibility for a group of Customer Service Representatives, or they can advance to become team leaders and handle training for both newly hired and veteran CSRs.

Education and Training

A high school degree or equivalent is preferred. Insurance agencies provide the on-the-job training to new CSRs and periodic refresher courses in new policies and procedures. Insurance companies invest heavily in employee training to keep their Customer Service Representatives abreast of changes in the field; training is done off-site at company-sponsored seminars, and some training is computer-based. Customer Service Representatives have to be good listeners and develop the ability to focus on customer needs without becoming emotionally involved. Empathy, flexibility, and an ability to stay focused are essential personality traits.

Special Requirements

Many states require insurance Customer Service Representatives to obtain state licenses. The licensing is offered by the state insurance department, and is contingent on successful completion of examinations and a certain number of hours of continuing education within a certain time period.

Certifications for CSRs include the following: Accredited Customer Service Representative (ACSR) from the Independent Insurance Agents of America, the Certified Insurance Service Representative designation from the Society of CISR, and the Associate in Customer Service (ACS) designation from the Life Office Management Association.

Experience, Skills, and Personality Traits

Generally, two to three years' experience in an insurance agency call center is sufficient to qualify for a position as Customer Service Representative. CSRs should have excellent telephone skills, adequate math and computational skills, and very good organizational skills.

Unions and Associations

As professional employees Customer Service Representatives can belong to professional associations, such as the Insurance Institute of America.

Tips for Entry

1. Insurance agencies are always looking for qualified Customer Service Representatives. Applying directly to an agency or insurance company is the easiest way to get an interview.
2. Insurance associations can be helpful in identifying prospective employers and job leads.
3. Check out current job opportunities in newspaper ads and insurance industry Web sites.

FIELD REPRESENTATIVE, INSURANCE

CAREER PROFILE

Duties: Responsible for growth and development of insurance agency sales force; helping sales agents meet their sales goals; representatives spend much of their time traveling

Alternate Title(s): Field Sales Manager

Salary Range: $40,000 to $70,000

Employment Prospects: Good

Advancement Prospects: Good

Prerequisites:

Education or Training—Bachelor's degree with courses in accounting or finance

Experience—Three to five years' insurance industry experience, preferably in a sales capacity

Special Skills and Personality Traits—Excellent communication and organizational skills; ability to recruit, select, and train insurance sales agents highly desirable; knowledge of contract administration and training is helpful

Special Requirements—Membership in the Million Dollar Round Table optional; designation of CLU or ChFC may be required in some jobs

CAREER LADDER

```
┌─────────────────────────────┐
│   District Sales Manager    │
└─────────────────────────────┘


┌─────────────────────────────┐
│    Field Representative     │
└─────────────────────────────┘


┌─────────────────────────────┐
│        Sales Agent          │
└─────────────────────────────┘
```

Position Description

Field Representatives are the link between insurance agents who sell the policies and insurance companies which write the policies. Field Representatives must be good listeners and good communicators. Reps are salaried employees who function as district managers for life insurance and property and casualty insurance companies.

The field sales manager is responsible for the growth and development of a proactive sales force. Recruitment, selection, and training of sales agents is a focal point of this job.

Field Representatives also:

- make regular sales calls to independent agents and brokers promoting their line of insurance
- review insurance policies in effect to ensure that applications are accurate and complete
- submit updated information concerning policyholders in their territory to the insurance company's home office

- help local agents review client insurance policies to determine whether clients are sufficiently insured against losses
- conduct training workshops and seminars on sales and sales methods to help increase the amount of insurance sold in their region
- explain the insurance company's procedures for underwriting new policies and new types of insurance
- provide educational information for distribution to policyholders
- supervise, select, and train district office (field office) staff

Field Representatives spend much of their working time, often more than 50–60% a year, making sales calls to insurance agencies in their sales territory that handle their company's line of insurance. An ability and willingness to work on the road is an important facet of the job. This can be a good-career choice if you are interested in a sales or marketing career and like helping others achieve their own career goals.

Salaries

Starting salaries are in the $28,000 to $40,000 range, depending on experience and academic background. Sales representative can also earn annual incentive bonuses based on performance. Experienced Field Representatives can earn from $50,000 to $70,000, including bonuses or other incentive compensation.

Employment Prospects

Employment prospects are good, because insurance companies will need field managers to recruit and motivate agents. About half of insurance policies are written directly by insurance companies and half by agents who represent one or more insurance companies. The sales manager's job is acting as a liaison between the insurance company and the field agents. The insurance industry trend toward direct sales and doing more business over the Internet may reduce the need for field agents and representatives in certain lines of insurance. Insurance is a complex field, however, and most insurers will continue to rely on their Field Managers to maintain contact with local insurance agents.

Advancement Prospects

A Field Representative job often leads to more senior positions in management. Many insurance company senior executives began their careers as Field Representatives, learning the details of insurance sales and marketing. For instance, an experienced Field Representative could become a district sale manager and eventually a corporate-level manager of agency-directed sales.

Education and Training

A four-year college degree with courses in sales, finance, or marketing is usually a requirement for the position. A background in the liberal arts is also good academic preparation because Field Representatives must be able to establish good rapport with sales agents and others who work for their company.

Special Requirements

State insurance licensing is usually required. Industry designations such as the Chartered Life Underwriter (CLU) or Chartered Financial Consultant (ChFC) are helpful, though not mandatory. Life insurance Field Representatives may want to join the Million Dollar Round Table, an organization of top producing insurance sales agents.

Experience, Skills, and Personality Traits

Prior insurance industry experience is usually preferred. Field Representatives should have excellent communication and organizational skills, since they function as district sales managers for insurance companies. Strong organizational and motivational skills are desirable talents for building a sales force. Some knowledge of insurance industry sales management and training methods is very helpful.

Unions and Associations

Insurance industry trade associations such as the American Insurance Association provide useful networking and professional development opportunities.

Tips for Entry

1. A background in liberal arts with some business courses can be a great preparation for this position.
2. Insurance industry certification such as Chartered Financial Consultant can improve your chances of getting hired.
3. Check out insurance industry Web sites for the latest opportunities.

AGENT/BROKER, PROPERTY AND CASUALTY INSURANCE

CAREER PROFILE

Duties: Sells property insurance to individuals and businesses; recommends types and amounts of coverage based on analysis of client circumstances; may collect premiums from policyholders and keep record of payment

Alternate Title(s): Fire, Casualty, Marine Insurance Agent, Broker

Salary Range: $30,000 to $100,000 and up

Employment Prospects: Good

Advancement Prospects: Good

Prerequisites:

Education or Training—Associate's degree plus related work experience; on-the-job sales training provided by employers

Experience—Two years' experience in insurance or financial services sales experience

Special Skills and Personality Traits—Must be highly self-motivated, able to work independently, and like helping people meet their financial objectives

Special Requirements—Must have state license to sell insurance; industry certification required for advancement in the field

CAREER LADDER

```
┌─────────────────────────────────┐
│   Insurance District Manager     │
└─────────────────────────────────┘

┌─────────────────────────────────┐
│   Insurance Sales Manager        │
└─────────────────────────────────┘

┌─────────────────────────────────┐
│   Insurance Sales Agent          │
└─────────────────────────────────┘
```

Position Description

Property and casualty insurance Agents (known in the industry as insurance *producers*) sell insurance policies protecting individuals and businesses against losses from physical damage. They represent the insurance company in negotiating and servicing insurance contracts. There are two broad categories of insurance Agents. Agents can be independent contractors representing one or more insurance companies or employees of an insurance company. Independent Agents usually pay for their own auto and travel expenses, and also pay clerical staff salaries and agency costs out of income if they own and operate their own agency.

Insurance Brokers are independent businesspeople who perform the same services as sales Agents, but they have authority to obtain insurance from many different insurance companies. Brokers represent the insurance buyer in negotiating insurance coverage, and they function as the policyholder's licensed, legal representative. They try to place insurance at the best rate and terms. An insurance brokerage operates somewhat like a branch office of an insurance company, except that it is independently owned and managed. An insurance Broker can quote insurance coverage, issue policies on behalf of insurance underwriters, collect premiums, and process claims.

The property/casualty agent's objective for the first two years is to build a client base, a list of prospects that will eventually become business. Companies want their Agents to function as field underwriters and write profitable business with low rates of loss.

Job titles and responsibilities of insurance sales Agents are determined by their relationship with the insurance company they represent. A general Agent is an insurance company's representative in a given territory, and is paid on a commission basis. General Agents may appoint independent local Agents as needed. An independent Agent represents insurance companies under contract, and also is paid by commissions. Insurance Agents employed by an insurance company (called direct writers) are salaried employees and are not responsible for their own expenses. Many insurance Agents are multi-line Agents, selling both life and casualty insurance. A growing number of insurance Agents provide clients with a broad range of services, including financial planning and estate planning. Some may have licenses to sell annuities and mutual funds.

Insurance sales people perform similar functions, regardless of their client relationship. They advise clients on insurance needs, maintain records, and help policyholders settle insurance claims. Property insurance Agents issue a "binder" providing temporary coverage between signing of the policy application and policy issuance. Brokers do not issue binders as they do not directly represent the insurance company.

Insurance Agents and Brokers spend most of their time out of the office, traveling locally to meet clients and prospects. They usually work more than 40 hours a week, including evenings and some weekends. An insurance Agent's initial success after entering the field is contingent upon his or her ability to seek out new clients from personal contacts and referrals from other insurance producers. Difficulty in developing a sufficient number of clients drives many Agents from the field within the first two years of employment. This can be a good career choice if you like working with people and selling.

Duties include:

- obtaining data about client needs and resources, and reviewing current coverage
- ordering or issuing new policies
- collecting premiums from policyholders
- assisting clients in reports of losses and claims settlement
- explaining changes in insurance coverage
- discussing the advantages or disadvantages of various policies
- contacting the insurance underwriter and submitting forms to obtain binder coverage
- establishing client's method of payment
- explaining bookkeeping requirements for clients providing group insurance plans
- resolving client problems relating to insurance claims

Salaries

Demand for insurance Agents should increase in pace with population growth. Insurance Agent earnings vary according to the method of compensation, geographic location, the insurance company represented, and the amount of insurance sold. Independent Agents normally receive commission payments based on the volume of business produced,

whereas Agents who represent one insurance company exclusively may be paid by salary, a salary plus bonus, or a salary plus commission. Insurance brokers are compensated through commissions paid on total sales volume. Commissions can depend on the type and amount of insurance sold, and whether the policy was a new policy or a renewal.

Newly hired Agents typically receive a starting base salary in the high $20,000 range and earn commissions on sales generated. Experienced Agents receive a higher starting salary in the high $30,000s to $40,000. The base salary is reduced on a yearly basis after the first two years to a nominal base salary. Agents earn incentive bonuses based on sales performance and reported losses (insurance claims) filed by clients for whom they write policies. Agents with five or more years experience can earn annual salaries of $80,000 to $100,000 or more. Agents can earn annual bonuses based on how well their new business performs and enter sales contests to win money, prizes, or vacation trips. Agent commissions can be 12 to 15 percent of the premium charged to the customer on first-year premiums on auto insurance. Independent brokers receive higher commissions but receive no base salary.

Employment Prospects

Employment opportunities for property/casualty insurance Agents and Brokers will grow about as fast as opportunities in all occupations through 2014, according to the U.S. Bureau of Labor Statistics. Job growth in this field is influenced by increased competition from direct-writing insurance companies that sell insurance policies directly to the public, consolidation of independent insurance brokerage firms into larger, more competitive sales organizations, and new products developed by insurance underwriting companies. Insurance brokerages and agencies are actively recruiting entry-level employees who have impressive academic records or some experience selling financial products.

Advancement Prospects

There are several advancement options. Advancement is usually through promotion to positions of increasing management responsibility. Sales Agents with no prior experience are hired as sales trainees and given an on-the-job orientation. Insurance Agents who show ability and leadership may be promoted to sales manager in a regional office. However, Agents with strong client bases may prefer to remain in sales because of the higher pay opportunities for sales professionals.

Education and Training

A high school diploma is a minimum education requirement. Insurance sales Agents must have strong verbal and written communication skills, and a high degree of self-confidence. Also important are an ability to work independently without supervision and a strong desire to help people meet their financial goals. While a college degree is not required to enter the field, many U.S. colleges offer degree programs in insurance. If college courses are taken, some courses in accounting, economics, business law, and insurance are recommended.

Special Requirements

All states require insurance Agents and Brokers to be licensed in the state where they do business. Agents must pass a written examination covering the fundamentals of property and casualty insurance and state insurance laws. Most insurance companies sponsor study courses for state licensing exams. Additional licensing is required for the sale of mutual funds and annuities. Career advancement in insurance is tied to studying to increase skills and keeping up with industry trends. Courses may be sponsored by insurance companies or by industry trade associations.

Certification programs available to insurance sales Agents may include the Accredited Adviser in Insurance from the Insurance Institute of America, and the Chartered Property Casualty Underwriter (CPCU) from the American Institute for Property and Liability Underwriters.

Experience, Skills, and Personality Traits

Skills important in the insurance industry include an understanding of general business and marketing principles, sensitivity and compassion in listening to others, and an ability to explain complex subjects in simple terms. An ability to work long hours and handle rejection are personality traits of successful insurance salespeople. They must have the ability to gain the respect and confidence of customers and clients.

Unions and Associations

As professional employees, insurance sales Agents typically do not belong to labor unions. They may become members of professional associations, such as the Independent Insurance Agents of America and the National Association of Professional Insurance Agents.

Tips for Entry

1. College training may help get an understanding of the technical aspects of insurance. Many colleges and universities have courses in insurance; some offer bachelor's degrees in insurance.
2. Sales experience helps; if you have sales experience in another industry, it can help launch a career selling insurance.
3. Contact associations such as Professional Insurance Agents of America for job tips and contacts with potential employers.
4. Consider alternative career paths by starting your career with the insurance subsidiary of a commercial bank. Banks are entering the insurance field through banking deregulation and are becoming more active marketers of insurance products.
5. Improve your networking skills to build a successful career in insurance sales.
6. Participate in social, church, and community groups to build your network and maintain visibility with prospects.
7. Summer employment in the insurance industry and college work-study programs are helpful in building personal contacts.
8. College recruiting is an important source of job leads; big insurance companies frequently recruit through on-campus interviews.
9. Learn about an insurance career by visiting the in VEST career education Web site (www.InVESTprogram.org), sponsored by the Independent Insurance Agents of America.

INSURANCE AGENT/BROKER, LIFE

CAREER PROFILE

Duties: Sells insurance providing life insurance and retirement income to new and existing clients; maintains contact with clients to review and update coverage

Alternate Title(s): Life Insurance Adviser, Life Underwriter

Salary Range: $29,980 to $66,160

Employment Prospects: Fair

Advancement Prospects: Good

Prerequisites:

Education or Training—High school diploma; some employers prefer candidates with two-year or four-year college degrees

Experience—Prior sales or financial services marketing experience helpful

Special Skills and Personality Traits—Excellent communication skills and interpersonal skills; strong self-discipline and organizational skills

Special Requirements—Pass written licensing examination

CAREER LADDER

```
┌─────────────────────────────┐
│   Insurance Sales Manager    │
└─────────────────────────────┘

┌─────────────────────────────┐
│    Insurance Agent/Broker    │
└─────────────────────────────┘

┌─────────────────────────────┐
│    Insurance Sales Trainee   │
└─────────────────────────────┘
```

Position Description

Life Insurance Agents and Brokers sell life insurance, variable annuities, and related insurance products to new and existing clients. Life Insurance Agents work as field representatives for companies they represent and have a contractual agreement with these companies. Some Agents are called life underwriters because their duties may include estimating insurance risk in policies they write. Life Insurance Brokers represent the buyer and their role is obtaining insurance policies offering the best rates and coverage for their clients. Some Brokers obtain other insurance coverage (auto, health, or other insurance) usually provided in a comprehensive policy at a reduced premium rate.

Life Insurance Agents provide their client prospects with a variety of insurance options, such as term insurance (death benefit only), or ordinary life insurance based on client needs and ability to pay. They write comprehensive plans for business owners, such as key man life insurance and group health insurance. Some Agents specialize in occupational groups, such as small business owners or physicians, to build up a stable client base and a source of repeat business.

Life Insurance Agents work as self-employed professionals, and are not employees of insurance companies. Because they must generate their own sales leads, active client prospecting is part of the life insurance Agent's job. Life Insurance Agents selling to individuals are highly disciplined and they rely on personal intuition to identify prospects and solicit sales. An Agent's clientele is built up gradually over a long period of time. Twenty to 30 personal contacts per week may yield eight to 12 interviews and zero to three new sales.

Specific duties include:

- obtaining information on client needs
- issuing or underwriting new policies
- assisting clients or beneficiaries in filing claims
- resolving client problems regarding insurance claims
- explaining changes in insurance or suggesting changes in insurance beneficiaries
- reviewing client financial status
- developing a comprehensive plan for death benefits, retirement income needs, or college education expenses

• arranging for client's physical exams and obtaining completed insurance application

Life Insurance Agents spend much of their work week visiting clients and prospects, as many as three or four nights a week, and often spend part of their weekends completing insurance company forms and doing paperwork. This can be a good career choice if you enjoy helping people meet financial goals and like selling.

Salaries

Annual earnings of Life Insurance Agents vary widely. New Agents starting their careers earn an average of $21,000, according to the U.S. Department of Labor. Beginning Agents receive a moderate salary as they build their client base. This salary is gradually reduced, and after a year or two is replaced by a drawing account—a fixed dollar amount advanced against anticipated commissions. The median annual earning of salaried insurance sales agents was $41,720 in 2004, according to the U.S. Bureau of Labor Statistics. The middle 50 percent earned between $29,980 and $66,160. Many independent life insurance brokers are paid by commission only. The amount of the commission depends on the type and amount of insurance sold and whether the sale is a new transaction or a renewal. Salaried agents may be paid in one of three ways: salary only, salary plus commission, or salary plus bonus. Brokers and agents may also receive bonuses or incentive compensation for meeting sales goals.

Employment Prospects

There is fair to moderate employment growth in life insurance sales. Projected growth in the U.S. population, the heavy turnover among new Agents and retirements by Agents in the field, will contribute to the hiring of new Agents. At the same time, changes in the way insurance companies market insurance will impose limits on future employment opportunities. Many of the largest insurance companies are increasing their use of direct mail and telephone sales, supplementing direct sales by field Agents. Future demand for life insurance sales agents or brokers depends on sales of insurance and other financial products. The Bureau of Labor Statistics expects employment of insurance agents to grow more slowly than all occupations through 2014, although there will be opportunities for college graduates with sales ability, strong communication skills, and some knowledge of financial products. Bilingual agents will also be in demand for their ability to service a wider group of potential customers. Over the next decade, most job openings will result from the need to replace agents who leave the field or retire.

Advancement Prospects

Life Insurance Agents can advance to positions of increased responsibility, handling a larger client base. They can also move into sales management and help train new Agents, eventually becoming assistant managers or branch managers in their office. Some Agents may advance their careers by specializing in one type of insurance, such as group health and life insurance.

Continuing education is an essential aspect of career advancement in life insurance. Many states require continuing education to maintain licensing. Professional associations offer numerous certification programs, all requiring continuing education on a regular basis. Membership in associations, while voluntary, helps to maintain client trust.

Education and Training

Life Insurance Agents and Brokers come from varied backgrounds. A high school diploma is the minimum education requirement, and many employers prefer hiring individuals with an associate's degree or at least some college courses. Four-year degree programs with a major in insurance have become more common in recent years. At least 60 U.S. colleges offer insurance degree programs.

College-level courses in English, law, sociology, other liberal arts courses, and some business courses are helpful in pursuing a career in insurance. Life insurance representatives receive extensive formal training, starting with preparation classes to help new Agents prepare for state licensing exams. More advanced training, usually tied to specific insurance products, is offered as needed. Many life Insurance Agents are choosing to obtain the proper licenses to sell other financial products and financial planning services in addition to life insurance. Agents earning a passing grade on the Series 6 exam administered by the National Association of Securities Dealers can sell mutual funds; a Series 7 license—the main NASD securities license—qualifies the agent as a general sales representative. A Certified Financial Planner (CFP) designation from the Certified Financial Planner Board of Standards or a Chartered Financial Consultant credential issued by The American College demonstrates competency in personal financial planning. Both have continuing education requirements to maintain certification.

Special Requirements

Life Insurance Agents are required to pass a written licensing exam and obtain a license in each state where they sell life insurance. The licensing exam, administered by state insurance departments, tests their knowledge of insurance fundamentals and state insurance laws. In most states new Agents may be able to sell insurance under a temporary certificate while preparing for the written examination. Information on licensing requirements can be obtained by contacting state insurance departments, or downloaded from their Web site.

Agents that sell securities, such as annuities or mutual funds, must obtain a separate securities license. In addition, most life insurance companies require prospective Agents to pass an aptitude test developed by the insurance company or by LIMRA International, an industry-sponsored research organization (formerly the Life Insurance Marketing and Research Association) at the time they are hired.

There are several certification programs available, including: Accredited Adviser in Insurance, from the Insurance Institute of America; Diploma in Life Insurance or Health Insurance, awarded by the Life Underwriters Training Council; Chartered Life Underwriter, from the American College of Bryn Mawr; and Certified Professional Insurance Agent, from the Certified Professional Insurance Agents Society.

Experience, Skills, and Personality Traits

The job-related skills important to a career in insurance sales are the skills often acquired from experience. Many employers look for individuals who have some post-college work experience in marketing or sales. Prior sales or financial services marketing experience is helpful in a career in insurance sales. Sales Agents must have excellent communication skills and be self-disciplined individuals able to work long hours. They must be able to describe insurance coverage in clear, unambiguous language, and answer questions about coverage and objections to coverage.

Personality traits such as personal empathy, interest in others, and a willingness to help clients meet financial goals are important in launching a life insurance sales career. Successful Agents possess these qualities to one degree or another. Life Insurance Agents should also have a personal belief in the value of insurance.

Unions and Associations

Life Insurance Agents and Brokers can become members of professional associations such as the National Association of Insurance and Financial Advisers or the National Association of Life Underwriters for networking opportunities and career advancement programs.

Tips for Entry

1. Learn about requirements for a career in life insurance through part-time or summer employment in an insurance agency.
2. Look into student-agency programs sponsored by insurance companies to get practical experience in the field while attending college.
3. College-level courses in insurance can provide insight into the insurance industry's history and current opportunities.
4. Sales experience helps. If you have sales experience in another industry or have a Series 7 securities license, that experience can help launch a career selling insurance.
5. Become active in local community, business, and church-related groups to become known in the community and build a file of personal contacts.

CLAIMS REPRESENTATIVE

CAREER PROFILE

Duties: Takes information from insurance clients reporting a loss; maintains files on active claims; reports to claims adjuster

Alternate Title(s): Claims Clerk

Salary Range: $18,000 to $45,100

Employment Prospects: Good

Advancement Prospects: Good

Prerequisites:

Education or Training—High school education or equivalent

Experience—Some insurance industry experience is required.

Special Skills and Personality Traits—Excellent telephone skills and filing skills; adequate math and computing skills; knowledge of insurance claims processing and customer service procedures; pass the selection process

CAREER LADDER

```
┌─────────────────────────────┐
│      Claims Adjuster        │
└─────────────────────────────┘

┌─────────────────────────────┐
│   Claims Representative     │
└─────────────────────────────┘

┌─────────────────────────────┐
│ Claims Representative Trainee│
└─────────────────────────────┘
```

Position Description

Insurance companies need Claims Representatives to process policyholder claims, check the legitimacy of these claims, and help customers understand any reason their claim has been adjusted. There is plenty of personal contact, the work is interesting, and there are opportunities for advancement. Claims Representatives process incoming telephone calls from insurance clients; in this position they handle many of the day-to-day functions of the industry, such as taking information about new claims. Claims Representatives can work in an insurance agency or an insurance company.

Claims Representatives take information over the phone from insurance clients reporting a loss. They may also receive this information from insurance agents or brokers. After gathering enough information to report a claim, the Representative transfers the claims data to the appropriate insurance company via telephone, fax, or computer. The Claims Representative enters claims-related information into the agency's computer system or filing system to maintain an accurate, up-to-date, record of claims for use by other agency employees. Information gathered by the Claims Representative is reviewed by the claims adjuster. Claims Representatives may issue agency checks to the insured after a claim has been settled.

Salaries

Beginning Claims Representatives can earn starting salaries of $15,000 to $18,000, with potential salaries as high as $45,100 after several years service and annual cost-of-living increases in compensation.

Employment Prospects

The recent growth in insurance claims filed under all types of personal and business insurance should provide adequate demand for skilled Claims Representatives. Employment opportunities for Claims Representatives will grow about as fast as average through 2014. This is a trainable job. Newly hired Claims Representatives go through a period of on-the-job training before being assigned a position. Applicants with some computer literacy or some previous experience working in an insurance office are the most qualified candidates.

Most insurance companies are trying to reduce their claims staff in an effort to hold down costs. Large companies rely on customer service representatives in call centers and are installing new software to reduce the amount of time it takes to handle a claim.

Advancement Prospects

Claims Representatives can advance to become claims adjusters after several years of experience, or can move into other clerical positions in the agency.

Education and Training

Most insurance agencies and insurance companies require a high school education or equivalent degree. Claims Representatives receive on-the-job training after hiring and periodic training in new products and insurance industry procedures. Some additional training in standard office computer software or insurance company procedures may be helpful for those entering the field as new employees.

Experience, Skills, and Personality Traits

Most agencies want applicants with some claims processing experience, at least one to two years experience. High school graduates with excellent clerical and telephone skills are acceptable candidates. Applicants must be familiar with insurance industry claims processing procedures. Much of this can, however, be acquired through a period of on-the-job training.

Unions and Associations

Claims Representatives are not normally members of labor unions. They can become members of insurance associations, such as the National Insurance Claims Association.

Tips for Entry

1. Apply directly to the insurance agency or insurance company.
2. Part-time work while attending high school or college can provide valuable experience and job leads later on.

INSURANCE CLAIMS ADJUSTER

CAREER PROFILE

Duties: Authorizes, denies, or settles routine property and casualty insurance claims; determines whether insurance claims are covered by the client's policy, confirms payment, and when necessary investigates the circumstances surrounding a claim

Alternate Title(s): Claims Investigator

Salary Range: $33,900 to $57,410

Employment Prospects: Good

Advancement Prospects: Good

Prerequisites:

    Education or Training—Associates' degree or higher; four-year degree required by many employers

    Experience—Two to four years' experience processing insurance claims; general understanding of business law, insurance contracts, and the technical aspects of claims processing

    Special Skills and Personality Traits—Excellent communication skills and negotiating skills

    Special Requirements—Certification optional

CAREER LADDER

```
┌─────────────────────────────────┐
│   Senior Insurance Adjuster     │
└─────────────────────────────────┘

┌─────────────────────────────────┐
│   Insurance Claims Adjuster     │
└─────────────────────────────────┘

┌─────────────────────────────────┐
│        Insurance Clerk          │
└─────────────────────────────────┘
```

Position Description

Insurance Claims Adjusters are directly involved with people who have experienced a loss. The adjuster acts on behalf of the insurance company or the insured in settlement of a claim, negotiating differences in value. Their work leads to agreement between the parties about the amount of the loss and the insurance company's liability for that loss. An adjuster may be a salaried employee of an insurance company or a person independently engaged by the insurer. Specialist adjusters spend their time investigating complex claims.

Working conditions can vary tremendously, since adjusters often rush to the scenes of disasters such as fires or hurricanes; some adjusters (in-house adjusters) stay in their office and review claims reported to the insurance company. Their duties include:

- interviewing the claimant and witnesses
- confirming insurance coverage for the claims received
- interviewing medical specialists

- taking recorded statements to document accident facts
- consulting police and hospital records
- inspecting property damage to determine the insurance company's liability
- determining whether claims adjusters have followed proper policies and procedures in settling claims
- negotiating settlements and assuring proactive conclusion of claims

Some Insurance Claims Adjusters find employment as self-employed public adjusters, which means they are independent contractors and are not paid a salary by an insurance company. Public adjusters earn a percentage of the claim paid out by the insurance company. They may perform other duties, such as taking inventory, hiring appraisers and engineers, and negotiating with insurance companies over the extent of coverage and the cost of repairs. Public adjusters say that their knowledge of the insurance industry can cut through red tape, as when the insurance company disputes part of the policyholder's claim or when handling complicated claims, and can help consumers or businesses get back on their feet more quickly.

Salaries

Earnings of Insurance Claims Adjusters and representatives vary widely, depending on the type of work performed, job responsibilities, and the degree of difficulty in performing job tasks. Salaries ranged from $33,900 to $57,410 in 2004. The median annual earnings for insurance adjusters and investigators was $44,220. Adjusters may receive additional benefits including use of a company car during working hours. Claims adjusters who are insurance company employees receive additional benefits as part of their job. Adjusters often are supplied with a laptop computer, cellular telephone, and company car or are reimbursed for the use of their own car for business purposes.

Employment Prospects

Employment opportunities for Insurance Claims Adjusters are expected to grow about as fast as average over the next 10 years. College graduates have the best opportunities to enter the field. Some job openings will result from attrition, or replacement, of workers who move to other occupations or reach retirement age.

Advancement Prospects

Claims Adjusters start out as trainee adjusters. New employees are educated through a combination of on-the-job training, classroom instruction, and field work. Advancement from this position is to senior claims adjuster, and then claims supervisor. A claims manager is one level above supervisors and is responsible for managing the claims department, hiring, and supervising.

Education and Training

An associate's degree is a minimum requirement for the position. Many employers look for candidates with a business or technical degree with an emphasis in insurance. Courses in accounting, banking, finance, business law, and economics are helpful. Those planning a career in technical claims adjusting should also take courses in their field of concentration, such as engineering, biology, or medical science. A well-rounded education should also include liberal arts and social science courses.

Special Requirements

Professional designations include the Associate in Claims designation offered by the Insurance Institute of America, the Certified Insurance Representative designation, and the Associate, Life and Health Claims from the Life Office Managers Association.

Experience, Skills, and Personality Traits

The position requires individuals who possess good judgment and an ability to interpret factual information. Also important are a sincere interest in people and an ability to work under pressure. Word processing skills and database management skills are also important.

A broad background in various kinds of damages or losses is essential for this position. This background information is usually gathered through on-the-job training. Also important for advancement is an in-depth understanding of insurance and the technical aspects of processing claims.

Unions and Associations

As professional employees, Claims Adjusters are not usually members of labor unions. Claims Adjusters may become members of professional associations, including the International Claims Association and the Society of Certified Insurance Service Representatives.

Tips for Entry

1. Try to find employment with an insurance company that works with independent agencies and provides agency training.
2. Networking is key to finding a job as an adjuster; insurance companies are always looking to hire qualified individuals.
3. Career Web sites can provide additional job leads in your area.
4. Contact state insurance departments for a list of insurance companies in your state and contact employers directly to learn about job opportunities.

INSURANCE CLAIMS EXAMINER

CAREER PROFILE	CAREER LADDER

Duties: Processes group medical and dental claims for the benefits division of an insurance agency or insurance company; approves routine claims

Alternate Title(s): Claims Adjuster, Insurance Investigator

Salary Range: $28,000 to $69,000

Employment Prospects: Good

Advancement Prospects: Good

Prerequisites:

Education or Training—Four-year degree with courses in business management or liberal arts

Experience—One to three years' experience in claims management; general understanding of claims processing procedures in life and health insurance

Special Skills and Personality Traits—Excellent communication and interpersonal skills; excellent organizational and analytical skills. Word processing and other computer skills helpful

```
┌─────────────────────────────┐
│     Insurance Examiner      │
└─────────────────────────────┘

┌─────────────────────────────┐
│     Insurance Adjuster      │
└─────────────────────────────┘

┌─────────────────────────────┐
│  Insurance Processing Clerk │
└─────────────────────────────┘
```

Position Description

Insurance Claims Examiners decide whether life, health, or disability insurance claims are covered by a client's policy, confirm payment and when necessary, investigate the circumstances surrounding a claim. Claims examiners who work for property and casualty insurers or for independent adjusting firms plan and schedule the work required to process claims and determine the amount the insurance company will pay toward that claim. Claims examiners employed by life and health insurance companies check claims filed for completeness and accuracy, and investigate questionable claims or claims exceeding a certain amount.

Insurance Claims Examiners review the causes of a death, particularly in the case of an accident, since most life insurance companies pay additional benefits for accidental death. They review new applications for life insurance to make sure applicants have no serious illnesses that would prevent them from qualifying for insurance. They review claims for disability insurance by employees filing workers' compensation claims for jobrelated injuries. In the course of their work, Insurance Claims Examiners consult with other professionals. They talk to accountants, architects, construc-

tion workers, engineers, lawyers, and physicians for expert evaluations of a claim. When a policyholder's claim is contested or when an examiner suspects fraudulent or criminal activity the examiner refers claims to investigators and may also testify in court proceedings.

Duties performed include:

- interviewing the claimant and witnesses
- interviewing medical specialists
- consulting police and hospital records
- inspecting property damage to determine the insurance company's liability
- determining whether claims adjusters have followed proper policies and procedures in settling claims
- reporting overpayments or underpayments
- referring claims requiring litigation to legal counsel

Salaries

In 2005, most claims examiners had salaries in the $28,000 to $69,000 range, according to the Bureau of Labor Statistics. Earnings vary according to experience, location, and level of responsibility. The median annual expected salary for a senior claims examiner in 2006 was $44,266, according to a survey by Salary.com. The middle 50 percent earned from $38,944 to $51,431 annually.

Employment Prospects

The employment outlook for Insurance Claims Examiners is fairly good over the next several years, although expected job growth will be about average compared to all other occupations, the Bureau of Labor Statistics reports. College graduates entering the field may find plenty of opportunities, especially in the faster-growing parts of the country. Although insurance companies have tried to hold down costs by restricting job growth, experienced examiners will always be in demand. Because of the high level of contact with policyholders and other professionals, an insurance examiner's job cannot be automated or shipped overseas. College graduates who have taken some business courses or high school graduates with some experience in the field will find this a challenging and interesting career.

Advancement Prospects

Advancement in this field is generally to positions of increased responsibility, such as claims supervisor or claims department manager. Advancement prospects are good, depending on qualifications and experience. As examiners demonstrate competence, they are assigned higher and more difficult claims. With experience, a claims examiner could be promoted to a managerial position in the home office.

With on-the-job experience and coursework in insurance, claims representatives can advance to senior and supervisory positions. Qualified examiners may also move laterally into positions in insurance underwriting and management. Some experienced examiners also choose to start their own businesses. They become independent examiners working as contract employees of insurance companies and receive a portion of claims paid out.

Education and Training

A high school degree is acceptable in the field, but many employers prefer a college education with courses in business or the liberal arts. Many claims examiners qualify for this type of work on the basis of prior experience. While no specific college major is preferred, courses in insurance or business management would be helpful. Most insurance companies provide extentive on-the-job training.

In most states there are no specific educational or licensing requirements for Insurance Claims Examiners. Most insurance companies prefer to hire college graduates. An advanced degree is helpful for individuals who wish to specialize in certain types of medical or life insurance claims. Some companies now require that claims representatives take written aptitude tests for communication, analytical, or math skills. Professional associations sponsor continuing education courses and issue certifications that may be helpful for advancement in this career.

Continuing education is important in this field because new federal and state laws and court decisions affect how insurance claims are handled and who is covered by insurance policies. Claims examiners working on life or health claims must also stay up to date with new medical procedures and prescription drugs.

Experience, Skills, and Personality Traits

Claims examiners should have excellent interpersonal skills and organizational skills, which is helpful in analyzing complex group health insurance claims. Also useful are good word processing and other computer skills. A general understanding of claims processing procedures is important, and generally a requirement for the position. No specific industry designation is required for entry to the field.

Unions and Associations

Claims examiners can become members of insurance associations such as the American Association of Health Plans or the Health Insurance Association of America for networking and career development opportunities.

Tips for Entry

1. A background as a claims representative can lead to a position as claims examiner.
2. Insurance associations can provide networking opportunities.
3. Check insurance Web sites for up-to-date information on trends and job leads.

INSURANCE FRAUD INVESTIGATOR

CAREER PROFILE

Duties: Investigates possible cases of insurance fraud; makes recommendations to insurance company attorney

Alternate Title(s): Claims Investigator, Field Investigator

Salary Range: $30,000 to $58,000

Employment Prospects: Good

Advancement Prospects: Good

Prerequisites:

Education or Training—Four-year degree with courses in business and finance

Experience—One to three years' experience investigating insurance claims; experience in law enforcement helpful

Special Skills and Personality Traits—Excellent interviewing skills and report-writing skills; strong analytical skills; working knowledge of insurance industry data collection techniques relating to investigations

Special Requirements—Industry certification recommended for advancement

CAREER LADDER

```
┌─────────────────────────────────┐
│   Senior Fraud Investigator     │
└─────────────────────────────────┘

┌─────────────────────────────────┐
│  Insurance Fraud Investigator   │
└─────────────────────────────────┘

┌─────────────────────────────────┐
│      Investigator Trainee       │
└─────────────────────────────────┘
```

Position Description

Insurance Fraud Investigators work for investigation firms, insurance companies, or independently as freelance insurance consultants. They investigate possible cases of insurance fraud such as claims fraud or arson for profit. They collect evidence and recommend to unit managers appropriate deterrence measures to prevent or minimize the probability of fraudulent claims. They report results of their investigations to staff attorneys, who may pursue legal actions to recover losses incurred as a result of suspicious claims. Fraud investigators use video surveillance, check backgrounds and personal references, financial statements, and accident scene reports to uncover fraudulent insurance claims.

Specific job responsibilities may include:

- providing telephone or written guidance to line managers on investigations in progress
- reviewing information collected from field investigations and recommending additional steps to secure necessary background information
- conducting field investigations and initiating appropriate surveillance activities
- functioning as company liaison with civil authorities, insurance company investigators employed by other insurance companies, and insurance information bureaus
- managing an investigation in progress until the case has been closed
- providing updated reports on progress of investigations and recommendations for further actions
- assisting in presenting fraud detection programs to field employees and headquarters staff
- participating in interviewing of new candidates for the fraud investigation unit
- representing the fraud investigation unit at industry conferences and educational seminars
- assisting in providing training to claims adjusters and other employees involved in claims processing

Insurance Fraud Investigators work closely with insurance claims processors, underwriters, law enforcement agencies, and state insurance departments. Results of their investigative work are reported to state department of insurance fraud bureaus and to the National Insurance Crime Bureau, which is an industry clearinghouse for information about insurance claims fraud.

Insurance Fraud Investigators work long hours, under very disciplined working conditions. Investigators typically set their own schedules and work irregular hours. They frequently work evenings and weekends to interview witnesses or claimants when they are available. Because fraud investigators may be called to investigate high-profile cases, they must present a positive public image for the company. They also are available to assist line managers by answering questions involving insurance claims where insurance fraud is suspected, and provide training in detection methods for other insurance company employees.

Salaries

Salaries of Insurance Fraud Investigators are comparable to salaries of other insurance industry employees involved in investigative work and claims analysis. Annual salaries of Insurance Fraud Investigators in 2006 were between $30,000 and $58,000, according to industry sources. More experienced investigators earn higher salaries if they have special skills, such as investigating computer crime where insurance is involved. Additional benefits typically include paid health and life insurance, participation in company-sponsored retirement plans, use of a company car or reimbursement for use of their own vehicle for company business.

Employment Prospects

Employment opportunities for Insurance Fraud Investigators should grow slightly faster than opportunities for other insurance industry jobs over the next several years. Factors influencing this increased market demand are growing recognition of the importance of early detection in dealing with white collar crime and insurance fraud. The increased use of scientific investigative techniques in gathering evidence leading to potential criminal prosecutions is also contributing to job growth in the field.

Advancement Prospects

Experienced Insurance Fraud Investigators can advance to more senior positions in fraud investigations, taking on more complex cases and managing a team of fraud examiners. Fraud investigators can eventually advance to become departmental manager in an insurance company's special investigative unit. Some may advance their careers by taking positions with a state insurance department fraud prevention bureau.

Education and Training

There is no specific college major recommended as best preparation for a career as an Insurance Fraud Investigator. Several colleges offer full-time programs leading to an insurance major. College courses in business, economics, and finance are helpful, although a degree in almost any field is adequate. Most large insurance companies have their own training programs in which new employees learn the basic job-related skills.

Special Requirements

Industry certification, such as Certified Professional Insurance Investigator from the Investigative Resources Global Investigations Training Institute, can be helpful in career advancement.

Experience, Skills, and Personality Traits

Insurance Fraud Investigators must possess excellent interviewing skills and report writing skills in gathering and reporting information. Analytical thinking and problem solving is very important in this field, and investigators must have the ability to approach problems creatively, with a minimum of supervision, and recommend a solution. Computer skills are also important, and investigators should have basic knowledge of word processing and spreadsheet accounting programs. Prior experience in law enforcement or crimimal investigations for an insurance company is also desirable. Some working knowledge of data collection and analysis relating to insurance industry investigations would be helpful.

Unions and Associations

Insurance Fraud Investigators can become members of professional associations for professional support, networking, and career advancement. These include the National Association of Professional Insurance Investigators, the International Association of Arson Investigators, and the Investigative Resources Global Investigations Training Unit.

Tips for Entry

1. Contact a professional association specializing in your area of interest to learn more about the academic and other requirements for a career in that field.
2. Arrange interviews with on-campus recruiters from insurance companies through your college's career placement office.
3. Check out current job openings posted on industry Web sites such as the National Insurance Crime Bureau's Web site (http://www.nicb.org).

ACTUARY

CAREER PROFILE

Duties: Makes estimates or forecasts about the probability of future events, using mathematical and statistical calculations. Compiles appropriate pricing for insurance policies

Alternate Title(s): None

Salary Range: $54,770 to $107,650

Employment Prospects: Good

Advancement Prospects: Excellent

Prerequisites:

Education or Training—Four-year degree with courses in accounting, mathematics, and statistics

Experience—Three to five years' experience for certified actuaries; qualified college graduates may enter the field as starting actuaries

Special Skills and Personality Traits—Well-rounded analytical skills and organizational skills in solving problems; excellent communication skills in presenting recommendations to non-actuaries

Special Requirements—Advancement in the field requires years of rigorous study to become professionally certified actuaries; life insurance actuaries must attain the Fellow of the Society of Actuaries (FSA) designation to become fully accredited; actuaries working in property and casualty insurance must attain the Casualty Actuarial Society (CAS) designation

CAREER LADDER

```
┌─────────────────────────────┐
│   Fellowship-Level Actuary   │
└─────────────────────────────┘

┌─────────────────────────────┐
│      Associate Actuary       │
└─────────────────────────────┘

┌─────────────────────────────┐
│     Entry-Level Actuary      │
└─────────────────────────────┘
```

Position Description

Actuaries are the financial architects of the insurance industry. Actuaries calculate the financial risk an insurance company takes when it writes an auto insurance or life insurance policy. Actuaries spend their time calculating probabilities of loss from sickness or injury, property loss from fire, hurricane, or other natural disaster, or the death of the insured in the case of life insurance. An Actuary's calculations, or estimates of future expected losses, determine insurance premium rates, or the cost of insurance paid by the policyholder. The work is demanding; insurance rates must be competitive but high enough to cover all possible claims and expenses.

About two-thirds of Actuaries work for insurance companies; the rest are employed by consulting firms and rating agencies that gather information for smaller insurance companies. About 90 percent of insurance company Actuaries work for life insurance companies; others are employed by various property and casualty insurers. Some Actuaries work in government, and help manage the Social Security program and Medicare programs. The role of the Actuary has recently been broadened in some insurance companies, where staff Actuaries perform managerial and marketing functions as part of their duties. An actuarial career can be a good choice if you like working with numbers.

Corporations today try to look at the connections among the many risks facing the organization instead of calculating the impact of each risk separately. This holistic approach to risk management, known informally as enterprise risk management because it emphasizes risk analysis across the entire organization, is changing the work performed by Actuaries. ERM is the process of identifying, evaluating, and managing the full range of risks borne by an enterprise. In 2005 the Society of Actuaries added a new professional certification in enterprise risk management, intended to provide opportunities for Actuaries to compete for positions in the broader financial services market, such as bank and brokerage firms, in addition to positions in the insurance industry.

Salaries

Earnings are determined by where an Actuary works and the number of actuarial exams passed. Annual starting salaries for Actuaries, excluding any signing bonuses, averaged $52,741 in 2005, according to the National Association of Colleges and Employers. The national median salary is about $75,000. The middle 50 percent earned between $54,770 and $107,650 according to the Bureau of Labor Statistics. Actuaries who work in consulting can earn higher salaries than those who work in either government or business. Actuaries can expect regular pay increases as they gain experience and pass exams. Salaries over $100,000 are common for full members of the Society of Actuaries. Insurance companies and consulting firms give merit increases as Actuaries gain experience and pass examinations. Some companies also offer bonuses to Actuaries who earn a professional designation.

Employment Prospects

Getting a job as an Actuary usually requires some experience as well as college coursework. Life insurance companies and consulting firms offer summer or part-time work to college students interested in getting some on-the-job experience. The best job prospects for entering actuaries will be for candidates who have passed at least one or two of the initial actuarial exams.

Overall employment opportunities in this field will grow about as fast as average through 2014, according to the Bureau of Labor Statistics. Employment opportunities are very good for those who pass the qualifying exams, which limit the number of qualified candidates entering the field.

New Actuaries entering the field may find more employment opportunities at consulting firms that provide actuarial services to the insurance industry than at insurance companies. Companies that do not find it cost effective to perform their own actuarial studies are increasingly hiring consulting firms to analyze the various risks. A small minority of Actuaries are employed by security and commodity brokers or by government agencies.

Advancement Prospects

Entry-level Actuaries often rotate among different jobs to learn about different phases of insurance work, such as mar-

keting, underwriting, and product development. Actuaries generally advance after passing several exams and joining the Casualty Actuarial Society or the Society of Actuaries. As they pass their exams, Actuaries earn more and are eligible for promotion to positions with higher levels of responsibility. Up to nine exams are required to become accredited as a fellow Actuary, the highest designation in this field.

Because people with actuarial skills are valuable in other industries that deal with risk, some advancement opportunities can be found in related industries, such as banking, information services, and accounting. Medicare reforms effective in 2006—the addition of prescription drug benefits to Medicare recipients—and the increased regulation of managed health care will create new opportunities for Actuaries.

Education and Training

Individuals entering the actuarial profession usually have college degrees in mathematics, statistics, and actuarial science. Some colleges offer four-year programs in actuarial science. Additional courses in business, social science, and the humanities are recommended to ensure a well-rounded education.

Special Requirements

Professional certification is required for advancement in the field. Many employers provide incentives and support for starting Actuaries, such as providing time during working hours to study for exams and raises upon passing exams. Professional certifications are recognized throughout the industry and are required for those who certify insurance company financial statements. The Society of Actuaries, a professional association, has two certifications: "Associate of the Society of Actuaries," for individuals who have an understanding of the basic mathematics used by Actuaries, and "Fellow of the Society of Actuaries" for actuaries with demonstrated in-depth knowledge of techniques in a specific practice area.

Experience, Skills, and Personality Traits

An Actuary must have good mathematical skills and an ability to perform abstract reasoning. Useful personality traits are an analytical mind and a problem-solving capability. Actuaries must be able to explain their process and results to non-actuaries. Successful Actuaries are strategic thinkers and excellent communicators.

Unions and Associations

Actuaries can belong to several professional associations for networking and professional advancement, including the American Academy of Actuaries, American Society of Pension Actuaries, Casualty Actuarial Society, Conference of Consulting Actuaries, and the Society of Actuaries.

Tips for Entry

1. Life experience counts. Round out your résumé with campus activities and volunteer work while attending college. Be sure to list communication and organizational skills, and jobs demonstrating your leadership.
2. Gain industry experience in an internship, part-time employment, or summer employment. Initiate contact with companies where you would like to work and ask about internship opportunities.
3. Research a company on the Internet or at a library before an interview and ask at least one or two solid questions to let the interviewer know you have done your homework.
4. Graduate early if possible. Off-cycle college graduates sometimes get a jump on job opportunities.
5. Additional information about an actuarial career can be found on the Internet at http://www.beanactuary.com, a careers Web site sponsored by the Casualty Actuarial Society and the Society of Actuaries.

INSURANCE POLICY RATER

CAREER PROFILE

Duties: Calculates amount of premium to be charged for various types of insurance; may analyze insurance bills to determine premium activity or claims activity; provide statistical analysis of insurance/claims activity

Alternate Title(s): Underwriting Technician, Underwriting Assistant

Salary Range: $30,000 to $55,000

Employment Prospects: Good

Advancement Prospects: Fair

Prerequisites:

    Education or Training—Bachelor's degree, with courses in insurance or mathematics

    Experience—One to two years' experience; prior insurance experience desirable

    Special Skills and Personality Traits—Excellent computer skills, including spreadsheet and database programs; aptitude for calculating mathematical problems

    Special Requirements—Industry certification may be required for entry into the field, or for advancement

CAREER LADDER

```
┌─────────────────────────────┐
│    Insurance Underwriter     │
└─────────────────────────────┘

┌─────────────────────────────┐
│        Senior Rater          │
└─────────────────────────────┘

┌─────────────────────────────┐
│    Insurance Policy Rater    │
└─────────────────────────────┘
```

Position Description

An Insurance Policy Rater calculates insurance premiums on new and renewing insurance policies, using a rating manual or computer software. (A rate is the cost for a given unit of insurance, on which premiums are based.) The rate is based on specific coverages, items, and qualifications (the fine print in insurance policies). Raters select the premium rate based on the type of policy and amount of coverage, using standard insurance risk factors such as the use and age of an automobile, where the car is parked, your age, and driving history. Insurance premiums determined by the policy rater are then passed to an insurance underwriter, who approves the policy.

There are many types of Insurance Policy Raters. Tasks for each are similar although specific job duties vary according to the type of insurance coverage being rated and the person or entity covered. A commercial lines rater classifies, rates, and determines the premiums for new policies and renewal policies, and special endorsements (extra items covered by insurance) to a policy.

Insurance Policy Raters may also calculate commissions payable to the agent or broker producing the business. They also update the rating manuals and manage policies and procedures relating to insurance coverage; consult with underwriters in reviewing information provided by insured clients for accuracy; changes in coverage, classification, and compliance with underwriting guidelines; and compile statistical reports.

Salaries

Salaries for Insurance Policy Raters are comparable to salaries earned by mid-level insurance employees, generally ranging from $20,000 for newly hired raters to $55,000 or more for senior raters with five to 10 years' or more experience. Insurance Policy Raters receive generous insurance company fringe benefits, such as paid life and health insurance, annual performance bonuses, and can participate in employer-sponsored retirement plans.

Employment Prospects

Demand for Insurance Policy Raters will be less strong over the next several years than in other areas of insurance, such as claims processing. While there is steady demand for this position, many of the functions performed by Insurance Policy Raters in casualty insurance and life insurance companies will be done by computer as insurance companies automate routine functions to reduce operating expenses. Demand may be strongest in companies underwriting the more exotic lines of insurance, such as alternative risk transfer insurance and insurance-linked financial derivatives (for example, weather insurance), which are less easy to automate.

Advancement Prospects

Advancement in this position is to insurance jobs with increased responsibility, such as senior policy Rater. Senior Raters also have management responsibility for Insurance Policy Raters working in an insurance specialty group. Because policy Raters work closely with insurance underwriters, another advancement option is moving into a career in underwriting.

Education and Training

An undergraduate degree is usually required, with coursework in business, computer science, insurance, or mathematics, with a strong concentration in liberal arts, speech, communications, and social science. There is no specific academic preparation for Insurance Policy Raters, but a solid foundation in mathematics is considered essential

Special Requirements

Professional certifications are useful for advancement in the field, especially for those considering a move into underwriting. Among these are the Chartered Property Casualty Underwriter (CPCU) designation from the American Institute of the CPCU, Associate in Underwriting designation from the Insurance Institute of America, and the Fellowship in Life Underwriting from the Life Underwriting Training Council. Some employers may require job candidates to have a General Insurance or Associate in Insurance designation.

Experience, Skills, and Personality Traits

Prior experience in insurance claims processing, policy rating, or underwriting is helpful in understanding this position. The main skills required are good judgment, ability to deal with responsibility, an aptitude for numbers, computer literacy with spreadsheet programs, and an ability to analyze data and weigh both sides of an issue. Good communication skills are also important, as there is a high level of contact with insurance sales agents, brokers, and underwriters. This is a good position for someone who is well-organized and a steady worker.

Unions and Associations

Insurance Policy Raters may join processional associations for networking opportunities and to improve job skills by attending industry sponsored seminars. These associations include the American Insurance Association and the Casualty Actuarial Society.

Tips for Entry

1. Get a good academic background in computer science and math.
2. Do Web searches under the search term "underwriting technician."
3. The job function of Insurance Policy Rater is being automated by computerized financial and accounting systems. Those who upgrade their computer skills in the newer technologies will have an advantage over others entering the field.
4. Attend local or regional meetings of insurance associations for networking opportunities.

INSURANCE UNDERWRITER

CAREER PROFILE

Duties: Determines whether to accept or reject applications for insurance coverage; determines the insurance premium a client should pay given the amount of risk involved

Alternate Title(s): None

Salary Range: $40,000 and up

Employment Prospects: Good

Advancement Prospects: Good

Prerequisites:

Education or Training—Four-year college degree

Experience—Three to five years' insurance industry experience

Special Skills and Personality Traits—Good judgment and a strong sense of business; ability to explain results of your work to others in the industry; excellent computer skills with spreadsheet and database management programs

Special Requirements—Certification required for advancement

CAREER LADDER

```
┌─────────────────────────────┐
│  Senior Underwriter or      │
│  Underwriting Manager       │
└─────────────────────────────┘

┌─────────────────────────────┐
│  Underwriter                │
└─────────────────────────────┘

┌─────────────────────────────┐
│  Junior Underwriter         │
└─────────────────────────────┘
```

Position Description

An underwriter determines the acceptability of insurance risks, based on the insurance company's guidelines and marketing strategy. The Underwriter reviews an agent's application submitted on behalf of a client, evaluates the information given, asks for additional information if necessary, and determines a price. In addition, the Underwriter determines that the risk is properly classified and evaluates the company's risk portfolio to determine that it is performing correctly. Underwriters determine the cost of insurance (the insurance premium) by analyzing the claims experience of the policyholder and the "book rates" as computed by an insurance actuary.

Underwriting is moving away from assessment of individual risk toward portfolio analysis, or looking at the entire book of business in a given town or geographic area and determining what works and what needs to be fixed to bring actual experience in line with company guidelines. This in turn has an impact on insurance rates and pricing of individual insurance policies. Underwriting is ultimately responsible for the growth and profitability of the insurance company.

Their duties include:

- reviewing applications for insurance and comparing applications to loss experience and actuarial studies to determine if the applicant is an acceptable risk
- evaluating future loss potential, e.g., catastrophic loss
- insuring adequate pricing of insurable risks
- preparing insurance quotation for insurance agents
- assisting agents in responding to questions about the proposed coverage and rates
- recommending declining an application if the proposed insurance cannot be underwritten as an acceptable rate or does not meet underwriting guidelines

There are many different types of underwriters. A corporate underwriter works from the insurer's home office and evaluates a portfolio of business based on known probabilities and statistics, and an evaluation of the human element. A field underwriter accepts, declines, or modifies applications for personal lines coverage submitted by insurance agents or brokers. A commercial lines underwriter does the same for commercial lines coverage. A specialist commercial lines Underwriter has a job outside the normal underwriter career path, and must have extensive experience in certain technical fields. A fidelity and surety bond underwriter analyzes situations that could lead to accidental loss and the obligations to be guaranteed by fidelity or surety bonds.

Salaries

Insurance underwriter salaries vary according to experience, employer type, and geographic location. Life insurance underwriters earn higher salaries than-casualty underwriters, and underwriters in the northeastern United States tend to get the highest salaries. Annual salaries average from about $40,000 for starting underwriters to $50,000 or more.

Employment Prospects

Insurance Underwriters come from varied backgrounds. Many have previous experience working in insurance, working in marketing, sales, or collections. Many begin their insurance careers as policy raters. Underwriters generally start as junior or entry-level underwriters, in which on-the-job training is provided.

Advancement Prospects

The career path from entry-level underwriter is usually to underwriter, then to senior underwriter with increasing levels of responsibility at each step. Underwriters can advance to personal (or commercial lines) underwriting supervisor, and then to underwriting manager. A fidelity and surety underwriter is generally promoted to senior fidelity and surety underwriter.

Experienced Insurance Underwriters can move anywhere in the organization. They can advance to a more senior position in the insurance company home office. The typical career ladder starts out at the entry level, the underwriter then move up to portfolio underwriter, writing policies for a specific line of business. Additional advancement can lead to a position as an underwriting manager for a group of underwriters and up to senior management–level positions such as vice president overseeing a specific industry group or business line.

Education and Training

A four-year liberal arts or business college degree is required. Generally, any college major with courses providing opportunities for working and dealing with people would be helpful. Concentration in a technical area, such as specialty lines underwriting, would require taking courses in that field.

Any college courses stressing analytical work, such as business mathematics, statistics, or actuarial science, are helpful preparation for a career in underwriting.

Special Requirements

Professional designation is required for advancement. Several designations are available, depending on the Underwriter's career path. These are: Chartered Property Casualty Underwriter designation from the American Institute for CPCU, Associate in Underwriting (AU) from the Insurance Institute of America, Chartered Life Underwriter from the Society of CLU, and the Fellowship in the Life Underwriting from the Life Underwriting Training Council. Many health Insurance Underwriters have earned the Certified Employee Benefits Specialist designation.

Experience, Skills, and Personality Traits

Generally, underwriters must have an interest in working with people, an ability to act responsibly, and excellent communication skills. Also important is an ability to learn quickly and analyze data and weigh both sides of often complex issues.

Also important is an ability to work with data-mining tools, which turn mountains of raw data into useful information, and the Microsoft Excel spreadsheet program. Problem-solving skills are important for insurance underwriters, as are good research skills. Underwriters devote much of their time to examining various state or federal laws and regulations and trying to figure out what was originally intended when a law was written and whether the company is compliant with state insurance regulations. Excellent communication skills come in very handy for trying to sell a new proposal to senior management.

Unions and Associations

Insurance Underwriters may belong to several national associations, including the Society of CLU (Chartered Life Underwriters) and the Insurance Institute of America for career advancement and network opportunities.

Tips for Entry

1. A well-rounded academic background in the liberal arts with some business courses is an important first step in learning how business works. Attend local or regional meetings or national underwriting societies for networking with insurance professionals and learning more about underwriting as a career.
2. Get information on specific job opportunities from insurance Web sites such as the Insurance Career Center (http://www.insurance.about.com).
3. College internship programs at insurance companies can open doors, allowing you to establish contacts with potential employers.
4. Take advantage of college-sponsored or employer-sponsored career fairs to learn about new opportunities.

BENEFITS ADMINISTRATOR

CAREER PROFILE

Duties: Administers corporate health insurance, life insurance, and disability insurance; supervises claims for medical plans; negotiates contracts with health-care providers

Alternate Title(s): Benefits Manager, 401(k) Administrator

Salary Range: $49,970 to $89,340

Employment Prospects: Good

Advancement Prospects: Good

Prerequisites:

    Education or Training—Bachelor's degree in business, insurance, or accounting

    Experience—Several years' experience in claims analysis and management

    Special Skills and Personality Traits—Excellent communication and interviewing skills; excellent organizational skills; knowledge of claims processing and filing; knowledge of employee welfare and benefits administration, general medical and workers' compensation claims processing, and legal issues

    Special Requirements—Certification Optional

CAREER LADDER

```
Benefits Manager
```

```
Benefits Administrator
```

```
Benefits Analyst
```

Position Description

Benefits Administrators help design and implement employee health and life insurance programs for employers. They manage third-party insurance programs, purchased from life insurance companies, health maintenance organizations, and other healthcare providers. Benefits Administrators supervise the handling and submission of health insurance, workers' compensation, and general liability claims filed by employees. They also function as an intermediary or liaison between the employer, health insurers, and healthcare providers.

Administrators are involved in day-to-day management of insurance programs to ensure adequate coverage for employees. They are also responsible for negotiating policy renewals with health-care insurers.

Benefits Administrators responsible for employee health benefits coordinate plan management with third party administrators and insurance companies, and they handle retiree billing and death benefits.

Managers of 401(k) plans notify employees of plan diversification options, process rollovers from other qualified retirement plans, and plan distributions to employees. They handle hardship withdrawals from a company-sponsored plan and 401(k) loans, and they locate recipients of unclaimed benefits and dividend checks.

Retirement planning administrators perform retirement calculations, process inquiries from retirees about their benefits, and coordinate payment of retiree benefits. They also prepare quarterly statements and annual statements of account balances required by federal law.

Other duties performed include the following:

- preparing benefits cost analyses
- recording benefit plan changes to management
- notifying employees of benefit plan changes
- directing clerical support functions, such as updating records and processing insurance claims
- providing training for new employees

Benefits Administrators typically work a 40- to 50-hour workweek in an office setting. This position reports to the director of human resources.

Salaries
Benefits Administrators earned salaries between $49,970 and $89,340 annually in 2004. Benefits in addition to salary usually include paid life and health insurance, paid vacations and sick leave, and participation in employer-sponsored retirement plans.

Employment Prospects
Employment opportunities should grow at a rate faster than overall job opportunities over the next several years. More employers are offering company-funded health and welfare programs to attract qualified employees. Also contributing to job growth is the widespread popularity of defined contribution pension plans such as 401(k) plans, which are funded through payroll deduction programs, usually with matching employer contributions up to a certain dollar amount of salary.

Advancement Prospects
With experience, Benefits Administrators can advance to more senior positions with increased management responsibility. They might advance to higher positions in human resources management, eventually becoming manager of human resources. Advancement to higher salaried positions is often linked to continuous improvement of job-related skills and industry certification.

Education and Training
A four-year college degree is recommended, with courses in accounting, human resources management, business administration, or insurance. Courses in spreadsheet accounting, database management, and other popular computer programs are helpful. Employer-sponsored training is available from a number of sources, including the Institute for

Insurance Education and Research, which sponsors training programs in benefits management.

Special Requirements
Certifications available to Benefits Administrators include the Certified Employee Benefits Specialist, cosponsored by the International Foundation of Employee Benefit Plans and the Wharton School of the University of Pennsylvania.

Experience, Skills, and Personality Traits
Prior experience in benefits administration or claims administration is considered essential. Experience as a service provider with an insurance company is helpful. Benefits Administrators should have excellent communication and interviewing skills, and good organizational, analytical, and interpersonal skills. The position requires a working knowledge of corporate welfare benefits and legal issues facing corporate benefits plans. Administrators of pension plans and 401(k) plans should have knowledge of investment principles and financial markets, and investment options available to program participants.

Unions and Associations
Benefits Administrators can join several industry associations for networking and career advancement opportunities, including the American Association of Professional Group Insurance Administrators, the Health Insurance Association of America, the American Payroll Association, and the 401k Association.

Tips for Entry
1. Take college-level courses in finance, business management, and law for a useful academic background.
2. Internship programs can provide a practical understanding of industry practices and build contacts with potential employers.
3. Take courses toward completion of Certified Employee Benefits Specialist certification.

LOSS CONTROL SPECIALIST

CAREER PROFILE

Duties: Responsible for developing and implementing safety programs and minimizing accidents; evaluating work environments; identifying hazards and making recommendations for eliminating potential risks

Alternate Title(s): Loss Control Consultant, Loss Control Representative

Salary Range: $50,000 to $85,000

Employment Prospects: Good

Advancement Prospects: Good

Prerequisites:

    Education or Training—Four-year degree with courses in engineering or science

    Experience—Experience analyzing commercial and industrial sites for fire hazards, environmental risks, and other risks

    Special Skills and Personality Traits—Strong oral and written communication skills; organizational and analytical skills; computer competence in word processing, spreadsheets, and database systems; knowledge of federal and state laws and regulations governing workplace safety, such as OSHA (Occupational Safety & Health Administration), workers' compensation, and Americans with Disabilities Act.

    Special Requirements—Certification in safety management generally required for advancement

CAREER LADDER

```
┌─────────────────────────────────┐
│    Risk and Insurance Manager    │
└─────────────────────────────────┘

┌─────────────────────────────────┐
│     Loss Control Specialist      │
└─────────────────────────────────┘

┌─────────────────────────────────┐
│     Loss Control Assistant       │
└─────────────────────────────────┘
```

Position Description

The job of the Loss Control Specialist is to protect America's workforce, the general public, and the environment from injury or illness. Loss Control Specialists work with business executives of large industrial firms, public institutions, and city planners to identify and correct potentially harmful situations. The job requires technical knowledge and management ability developed through years of education and practical experience. Loss Control Specialists help insured organizations or those who are seeking insurance coverage to identify risks and reduce the possibility of accidents, fires, and other losses. The position usually requires a great deal of travel.

The safety professional has the responsibility for studying materials, structures, building and safety codes, and operations/procedures to find the best way to use resources to control hazards that might cause accidental injuries, fires, explosions, or other potentially loss-producing events. Loss Control Specialists analyze fire and safety inspection reports to determine the best risk prevention strategy and the ideal cost. They gather and compile data necessary for the renewal of liability insurance, executive risk, and property insurance policies. They gather information necessary to develop insurance budgets, review contracts requiring certificate of insurance from property and casualty insurance carriers. They conduct surveys and investigate risk exposures and accidents and make recommendations to assist insured clients maintain loss-control programs. This is a good career choice if you are analytical and have an interest in engineering.

Duties of Loss Control Specialists include:

- conducting workers' compensation analysis prior to filing a claim and following-up audits
- consulting with employers and employer safety committees regarding safety procedures and OSHA walk-through audit
- conducting onsite safety and property inspections
- meeting with safety committee management (required by federal law)

Salaries

Salaries range from $50,000 to $85,000 for Loss Control Specialists. Compensation varies according to employer, years of education, and experience.

Employment Prospects

The largest employers of safety professionals are manufacturing, insurance, construction insurance, consulting firms, and the government. This is a very broad field and there are ample opportunities for individuals to specialize in a particular facet of the business, such as air pollution controls or groundwater environmental hazards. Job prospects in this field should grow at a rate faster than the overall economy through 2014.

Advancement Prospects

There are many opportunities for advancement in the insurance industry. Some Loss Control Specialists move into jobs in private industry or with government agencies.

Education and Training

A four-year college degree is generally required, with an emphasis in engineering, science, safety management, industrial management, or a related area. Demonstrated ability to interpret workers' compensation laws and understand industrial health and occupational health programs is important.

Special Requirements

Some additional training or certification is generally required, such as the Certified Safety Professional or Professional Engineer designation.

Experience, Skills, and Personality Traits

Generally two to four years' experience is required. Previous safety training experience is required for advancement to more senior positions. Individuals considering a career in this field should be detail-oriented and have excellent analytical and research skills. Excellent communication skills are also important in this job. The safety management position requires detailed knowledge of federal and state laws and regulations governing workplace safety and workers' compensation.

Unions and Associations

Loss Control Specialists usually belong to one or more associations, such as the American Society of Safety Engineers or the Risk Insurance Management Society.

Tips for Entry

1. Some universities have programs in safety management endorsed by the American Society of Safety Engineers.
2. Read trade journals newsgroups and Web sites relating to workplace safety issues.
3. Professional associations may also provide job leads through networking at association events and job listings on their Web sites.

COST CONTAINMENT SPECIALIST

CAREER PROFILE

Duties: Works with insurance sales staff and clients to design individual and group health-care plans or employee benefit plans; consults with employers on strategies to manage the cost of health insurance

Alternate Title(s): Private Health-Care Cost Manager

Salary Range: $35,000 to $55,000

Employment Prospects: Good

Advancement Prospects: Fair

Prerequisites:

Education or Training—Four-year degree; graduate degree in healthcare administration helpful

Experience—Two to five years experience in health-care counseling

Special Skills and Personality Traits—Good interviewing skills and interpersonal skills; attention to detail; problem-solving ability; detailed working knowledge of healthcare networks such as health maintenance organizations and employer-funded benefit plans

Special Requirements—Certification optional

CAREER LADDER

```
┌─────────────────────────────────┐
│   Cost Containment Supervisor   │
└─────────────────────────────────┘

┌─────────────────────────────────┐
│   Cost Containment Specialist   │
└─────────────────────────────────┘

┌─────────────────────────────────┐
│        Staff Assistant          │
└─────────────────────────────────┘
```

Position Description

Employee health insurance is the largest single expense to employers after wages and salaries. A medical Cost Containment Specialist is a consultant who helps employers manage their group health insurance plans and looks for ways to reduce health insurance costs wherever possible. These health insurance specialists contact hospitals, health maintenance organizations, and physicians to negotiate for healthcare services at the best competitive rate, usually at some discount for group coverage. They use their knowledge of managed care networks to arrange multiyear contracts for their clients.

They help employers design employee education and wellness programs. They make cost-management recommendations, such as making prescription drugs available through company-owned pharmacies. They recommend and help implement cost containment measures, such as employee counseling, random drug testing, and voluntary prescreening for cancer and other life-threatening illnesses.

Cost Containment Specialists are employed by health-care consulting firms, independent insurance agencies, and insurance companies. They do much of their work on a contractual basis with individual employers. Medical consultants can help an employer manage their insurance program in-house, or they can provide cost management services working as independent contractors.

With the rapid growth of computer technology in health-care management, much of the process can be done by computer once an employee health-care management plan is set up. Cost Containment Specialists generally work from an office but spend much of their time traveling to hospitals and other healthcare providers.

Medical Cost Containment Specialists work in an office environment, usually working a 40-hour week. They spend about 20 to 30 percent of their time traveling to employers and coordinating employee meetings.

Salaries

Salaries for insurance Cost Containment Specialists range from $35,000 to $55,000. People who have more experience in the field or an advanced degree can earn higher salaries. They may also receive incentive bonuses based on individual and company performance and employer-paid benefits such as life insurance, health insurance, and retirement plans.

Employment Prospects

Market demand for insurance professionals skilled in healthcare claims management has been strong and is expected to continue through 2014, according to the U.S. Department of Labor. Some insurance agencies have a Cost Containment Specialist on staff, but most insurance agencies (and most employers) hire independent consultants who work with them on a project or retainer basis.

Advancement Prospects

Medical Cost Containment Specialists usually begin their careers as account executives that market insurance management services to employers or call on health-care providers. With experience, they can advance to positions of increased responsibility, managing a group of insurance claims specialists. Another alternative is taking a position with a large employer or independent insurance agency and acting as an in-house consultant on health-care cost management.

Education and Training

An undergraduate degree is required for this position. Courses in business administration and health-care management are helpful. Some employers prefer hiring individuals with master's degrees in health administration. More than 60 U.S. colleges have accredited programs leading to a master's degree in health services administration. An M.B.A. degree is also helpful.

Special Requirements

Available industry certifications include the Certified Employee Benefits Specialist designation co-sponsored by the International Foundation of Employee Benefit Plans and the Wharton School of the University of Pennsylvania.

Experience, Skills, and Personality Traits

Experience in managed care contracting with physicians and other health services providers is required. Strong analytical, negotiating, and communication skills are very important. Consultants also need to be good problem solvers, and have an ability to conceptualize solutions to complex situations.

A thorough knowledge of health-care contracting and managed care pricing is a requirement for the position. Also important is an understanding of cost containment and healthcare cost management and insurance reimbursement policies.

Unions and Associations

As professional employees, Cost Containment Specialists may join associations such as the Health Insurance Association of America for networking and career advancement opportunities.

Tips for Entry

1. While in college contact insurance companies and consulting firms and arrange an exploratory interview to learn more about healthcare consulting as a career.
2. You can contact employers by doing a Web search using the search terms "medical management" or "health-care cost managers."

DATA ENTRY CLERK, INSURANCE

CAREER PROFILE

Duties: Updating customer records; verifing accuracy of data

Alternate Title(s): Data Entry Processor

Salary Range: $21,920 to $27,655

Employment Prospects: Fair

Advancement Prospects: Fair

Prerequisites:

Education or Training—High school diploma or equivalent; computer training helpful

Experience—General office or clerical experience; working knowledge of insurance company recordkeeping and forms

Special Skills and Personality Traits—General literacy; fast, accurate, typing ability; ability to perform repetitious work and meet production deadlines

CAREER LADDER

```
┌─────────────────────────────┐
│   Senior Data Entry Clerk    │
└─────────────────────────────┘

┌─────────────────────────────┐
│      Data Entry Clerk        │
└─────────────────────────────┘

┌─────────────────────────────┐
│      Data Entry Trainee      │
└─────────────────────────────┘
```

Position Description

Insurance Data Entry Clerks use computers or a special purpose data entry device to type in policy data, updating insurance company records. They enter names of new policyholders, changes in beneficiary, or life changes such as marriage, death, or the birth of a child.

Data Entry Clerks must be fast, accurate typists and have an ability to work at a consistent, steady pace. Duties performed vary according to experience and job responsibility. Some Data Entry Clerks process new accounts; others handle insurance claims. Entry-level Data Entry Clerks perform routine functions such as adding names of policyholders.

More experienced workers use their judgment skills to correct errors or solve problems. If someone tries to enroll in an insurance plan for which they don't qualify or submits incomplete information on an application for insurance, Data Entry Clerks have the responsibility to spot these errors and try to fix them before they are added to company records.

Data Entry Clerks may also:

- compare data entered on the keyboard with source documents
- examine letters from policyholders or agents and others to determine what policy changes to make

- compute insurance refunds and send policy cancellation letters
- notify the insurance agent and the account department of the cancellation
- calculate insurance premiums and commissions on individual policies
- check computations of premiums due

Insurance Data Entry Clerks usually work a 40-hour week under an office manager's supervision, but may work overtime during peak periods. They usually work in metropolitan areas or at the insurance company's home office.

Salaries

Entry-level Data Entry Clerks earn minimum wages, between $21,920 and $27,655 nationally. Experienced data entry processors can earn much higher salaries, up to $40,000 or more. Some employers offer performance bonuses in addition to salary.

Employment Prospects

Employment opportunities for Data Entry Clerks should grow about as fast as opportunities for all occupations over the next several years. One reason for the slow growth outlook is that many routine data entry functions can now be done by computer. But because insurance policies have complex documentation and are constantly being updated, there should be steady demand for experienced Data Entry Clerks.

Advancement Prospects

With experience, Data Entry Clerks can move into positions of increased responsibility. Advancement is usually to a supervisory position, such as senior Data Entry Clerk or office manager.

Education and Training

This is a trainable position. Most employers require a high school diploma or the equivalent. Some employers prefer people with computer training at a vocational school or junior college. Successful data entry operators have a high level of computer literacy.

Experience, Skills, and Personality Traits

Employers are interested in people with some clerical experience and familiarity with office machines. Many will train

people with good typing skills, usually a minimum of 150 to 170 keystrokes a minute. They look for people who can perform repetitive work for long periods of time and maintain peak efficiency.

Some knowledge of insurance-related terminology and insurance documents is required to achieve competency in the position, and is a prerequisite to advancement.

Unions and Associations

Data Entry Clerks can belong to clerical worker unions, such as the Office and Professional Employees International Union.

Tips for Entry

1. Take courses in word processing and other computer software. Skill improvement is a necessary step toward advancement in this field.
2. Employers usually hire Data Entry Clerks through help wanted advertising and job fairs.

INVESTMENT BANKING
AND SECURITIES

BROKERAGE CLERK

<table>
<tr><td>CAREER PROFILE</td><td>CAREER LADDER</td></tr>
</table>

CAREER PROFILE

Duties: Records purchases and sales of securities in investment firms; provides administrative support for stockbrokers

Alternate Title(s): Sales Assistant

Salary Range: $28,000 to $45,000

Employment Prospects: Good

Advancement Prospects: Fair

Prerequisites:

Education or Training—Four-year degree

Experience—One to three years' sales or marketing experience

Special Skills and Personality Traits—Excellent organizational, interpersonal, and communication skills

Special Requirements—Brokerage licenses required to trade securities

CAREER LADDER

```
┌─────────────────────────────┐
│      Securities Broker      │
└─────────────────────────────┘

┌─────────────────────────────┐
│      Trading Assistant      │
└─────────────────────────────┘

┌─────────────────────────────┐
│       Brokerage Clerk       │
└─────────────────────────────┘
```

Position Description

Brokerage Clerks provide administrative support for securities firms. They work in securities firms, discount brokerage firms, commercial banks or savings associations that have brokerage divisions. The position has two main duties: sending out records of financial transactions; and performing administrative functions supporting the purchase or sale of investments.

Brokerage Clerk job titles depend on the type of work they perform. Purchase-and-sale clerks, who typically work in brokerage branch offices assisting retail stockbrokers, match orders to buy with orders to sell. Dividend clerks make sure that stock or cash dividends are paid on time. Transfer clerks carry out customer requests for changes to security registration. They also check stock certificates to make sure that banking regulations are followed. Margin clerks post accounts and watch activity in customers' accounts. Their job is to make sure that customers trading from a margin account stay within the rules of stock purchases.

Brokerage Clerks assisting stockbrokers must be knowledgeable about investment products so they can communicate clearly with clients. They may contact customers, take orders over the phone, and inform clients of changes in their accounts. They may assist two brokers, performing back-up clerical support. As part of their duties, brokerage assistants take telephone calls from clients and process the paperwork for opening and closing accounts. They verify the details of stock certificates such as the owner's names and transaction dates to insure the accuracy of brokerage transactions and comply with government regulations.

Brokerage Clerks who have a brokerage license, a Series 7 General Registered Representative license, can make recommendations to clients at the instruction of a broker. The National Association of Securities Dealers administers the Series 7 license. Branch office Brokerage Clerks also:

- compute federal and state transfer taxes and brokerage commission rates
- post transaction data on accounting ledgers
- verify stock transactions
- accept and deliver securities
- keep records of daily transactions by brokerage clients

Brokerage assistants work in an office setting, usually in metropolitan areas, and spend much of their time on the telephone or watching computer screens. They usually work an eight-hour day, 40 hours a week, but may work overtime when trading volume of stocks and bonds is unusually high.

Salaries

Salaries of Brokerage Clerks vary by region. Highest salaries are earned in metropolitan areas, especially in the New York City region. The level of required technical expertise or experience can also affect earnings. Annual salaries of Brokerage Clerks in 2004 were between $28,000 and $45,000, according to the U.S. Labor Department. In addition to salary, full-time Brokerage Clerks receive paid health and life insurance, paid sick leave, vacations, and participation in employer-sponsored retirement plans.

Employment Prospects

Employment opportunities for Brokerage Clerks should grow faster than average through 2012. Some Brokerage Clerks are college graduates. Many graduates take entry-level positions to get into a company or to get into the finance and accounting field.

The employment outlook for this position is fairly competitive. The job is interesting and challenging and can eventually lead to a much higher-paying career as a securities broker. Employment opportunities are difficult to predict because the number of available positions is tied to the ups and downs of the economy and the stock market. When the market is rising, so does investment activity, resulting in an increase in hiring by brokerage firms. However, some openings will result from the need to replace workers who transfer to other occupations or stop working.

Advancement Prospects

Brokerage Clerks have several advancement options. They can move to positions of increased responsibility in a brokerage branch office, such as senior Brokerage Clerk. Some advancement opportunities into related clerical or support occupations are possible with years of experience and a college degree. Brokerage Clerks who have securities licenses can become stockbrokers and manage investment portfolios for clients.

Education and Training

Most Brokerage Clerk jobs are entry-level positions. Individuals should have at least a high school diploma or the equivalent. A growing number of securities firms require a four-year college degree with courses in business, finance, or the liberal arts. Courses in business math, business writing, and word processing are helpful. Once hired, Broker-

age Clerks are trained on the job. New employees usually receive training from a supervisor. Some formal classroom training may be necessary, such as training in computer systems and securities processing. Brokerage firms provide continuing training to maintain job-related skills.

Special Requirements

A securities industry license is required for Brokerage Clerks who make investment recommendations. People who make recommendations to clients must obtain a Series 7 General Securities Registered Representative license and a Series 63 Uniform Securities License.

Experience, Skills, and Personality Traits

Some experience in financial service sales or marketing or prior experience in an office is helpful, though not a strict requirement. Knowledge of word processing and financial spreadsheet programs is very helpful. More important than prior industry experience are a pleasant and professional telephone manner, a personal interest in the securities markets and the world of investing, and a desire to succeed in the securities industry. Brokerage Clerks must be detail-oriented and be comfortable working with numbers. They must also be trustworthy because they frequently deal with confidential information.

Unions and Associations

Brokerage Clerks can participate in meetings of the Security Traders Association or the Securities Industry Association for career development or networking opportunities.

Tips for Entry

1. Some college courses in economics or finance are helpful, although a degree in economics is not necessary for the position.
2. Most securities clerks and Brokerage Clerks find employment by applying directly to the bank, savings and loan, or securities firm looking to fill positions.
3. Some financial institutions offer summer employment or internship programs, which are helpful in getting practical experience and making contacts with industry executives.
4. Temporary employment agencies and state employment agencies are other sources of job leads in this field.
5. Learn about investing and money management by joining an investment club or attend local chapter meetings of the American Association of Individual Investors.

FLOOR BROKER

CAREER PROFILE

Duties: Executes trades for clients on the floor of a securities exchange

Alternate Title(s): Market Maker, Trader

Salary Range: $40,750 to $131,000

Employment Prospects: Good

Advancement Prospects: Fair

Prerequisites:

Education or Training—Four-year college degree

Experience—One to three years' experience

Special Skills and Personality Traits—Good communication skills, computer skills, and organizational skills; strong desire to succeed

Special Requirements—Must meet state licensing requirements, pass state exam, and receive securities license

CAREER LADDER

```
┌─────────────────────────────┐
│     Head of Floor Trading   │
└─────────────────────────────┘

┌─────────────────────────────┐
│        Floor Broker         │
└─────────────────────────────┘

┌─────────────────────────────┐
│       Brokerage Clerk       │
└─────────────────────────────┘
```

Position Description

When investors buy or sell shares of stock trading on a stock exchange, their instructions are given to Floor Brokers on the trading floor of the exchange. Floor Brokers are employees of a member firm who execute orders, as agents, for clients of their firm. Virtually all stock trades by individual investors in exchange-listed stocks are eligible for trading through a Floor Broker. These Floor Brokers should not be confused with *floor traders,* who trade securities as principal for their own account, rather than as a broker acting on behalf of their clients.

In a typical floor trade, brokerage sales representatives relay their client's instructions through the firm's computers to the floor of a securities exchange, such as the New York Stock Exchange. At the exchange the Floor Broker proceeds to the exchange trading post where that stock is traded and negotiates the bid/ask price with other Floor Brokers, attempting to get the best price for the client. The broker executes the trade at the best competitive price available and writes a floor ticket summarizing details of the trade and forwards the purchase price to the sales representative. If a security is not traded on the exchange floor, as in the case of bonds or over-the-counter stocks, the Broker sends the order to the brokerage firm's trading department.

Upon completion of the trade the member firm's client is notified through his registered representative back at the firm. The trade is then entered into the three-day securities clearance and settlement cycle, an electronic matching of buy and sell orders, and is posted to the client's account.

The New York Stock Exchange, the largest securities exchange in the United States, has the largest number of Floor Brokers and traders—a total of 1,336—and it accounts for more than one-half the average daily dollar volume of securities traded in U.S. markets. The steady rise in trading volume occurring away from the floor of the New York Stock Exchange is pushing the exchange to become more innovative and a bigger user of electronic trading for at least some orders, imitating its biggest rival, the NASDAQ over-the-counter market.

In 1999 the NYSE announced plans to introduce an Internet-based order book, allowing exchange members for the first time to directly execute trades of 1,000 shares or less without having to go through a Floor Broker. The New York Stock Exchange's move to make exchange-based trading more accessible to its member firms follows the Securities and Exchange Commission's decision to permit electronic communication networks to apply to become exchanges.

Electronic trading for small lot orders will, over time, alter the traditional role of Floor Brokers, although its impact may take years to measure.

Floor Brokers typically work a 35- to 40-hour week.

Salaries

Earnings of securities brokers depend in large part on the amount of brokerage commissions generated from the sale or purchase of securities. Commission earnings are sensitive to economic cycles and trading volume, and are likely to be lower when there is a slump in the stock market. Broker compensation in addition to salary usually includes an annual bonus, which is based on the profitability of the firm and brokerage-trading group. Full-time salaried employees also receive paid vacations and health insurance, and can participate in employer-sponsored pension plans.

Floor Broker salaries are also influenced by firm location. Earnings in 2005 excluding incentive bonuses ranged between $101,000 and $170,000 annually.

Employment Prospects

Most Floor Brokers begin their careers as brokerage clerks or are hired as brokerage trainees. Employment opportunities for brokers should grow about the same as opportunities in all industries though 2014, according to the U.S. Labor Department. Job growth will be influenced to a large degree by the increasing flow of investments into the securities markets as people seek higher rates of return from stocks, mutual funds, and other investments. Some job openings will occur as people leave the industry for other work or reach retirement age.

Advancement Prospects

Floor Brokers can advance to become a sales representative or stockbroker. With experience a Floor Broker could become head Floor Broker for his or her firm, and manage exchange trading handled through all brokers working on the exchange floor. Most brokers who do not go into management advance their careers by increasing the number and size of accounts they handle. Advancement into a managerial position away from the exchange floor increasingly requires a master's degree.

Education and Training

A four-year college degree is generally the minimum academic requirement. Though not essential to the job, most applicants have college degrees. College studies provide good background and help applicants understand economic trends and conditions.

Most brokerage firms provide some training for new employees, either a formal training program with classroom instruction or informal on-the-job training. Brokers must go through continuing education every three years to retain their securities brokerage license, the Series 7 Registered Representative license. Classes focus on regulatory updates and new investment products.

Special Requirements

Securities and commodities sales workers must obtain state licenses and pass an exam. A background check and a personal bond may be required in some cases. Floor Brokers must receive a Series 7 license, indicating a passing score on the General Securities Registered Representative Exam administered by the National Association of Securities Dealers.

Experience, Skills, and Personality Traits

Floor Brokers spend their working day negotiating pricing details and trying to get the best price for their firm and their clients. They need to have good communication and negotiating skills, and an ability to perform calculations quickly. This can be a stressful occupation, requiring self-confidence and a strong desire to succeed. Usually, one to three years' experience in securities trading or processing is required for entry-level Floor Brokers.

Unions and Associations

Floor Brokers can become members of the Security Traders Association or Securities Industry Association for career advancement and networking opportunities.

Tips for Entry

1. Sales experience is very helpful. Brokerage firms look for individuals who have prior experience selling, preferably on a commission-paid basis.
2. Check want ads and Internet job postings and apply directly to the hiring firm.
3. As with other financial positions, contacts and networking are often the essential first steps to landing a position. Summer employment or internships can be very helpful.
4. Take preparation courses for the Series 7 Registered Representative Exam as soon as you are eligible. Most firms give you one to two years to pass the exam.

COMMODITIES BROKER

CAREER PROFILE

Duties: Acts as agent for customers and traders in purchasing or selling commodities; acts on behalf of others in acting as market maker

Alternate Title(s): Futures Broker

Salary Range: $50,000 to $170,000

Employment Prospects: Good

Advancement Prospects: Excellent

Prerequisites:

Education or Training—No formal education required; college degree preferred; on-the-job training provided by futures exchanges

Experience—One to three years' experience on a commodity or futures exchange, or a futures trading firm

Special Skills and Personality Traits—Strong communication skills and selling skills; ability to exercise independent judgment and act quickly in a pressured environment

Special Requirements—Most pass the National Commodities Futures Examination (Series 3 Exam)

CAREER LADDER

```
┌─────────────────────────────────────┐
│   Commodity Trading Adviser          │
│   or Senior Commodities Broker       │
└─────────────────────────────────────┘

┌─────────────────────────────────────┐
│        Commodities Broker            │
└─────────────────────────────────────┘

┌─────────────────────────────────────┐
│          Floor Broker                │
└─────────────────────────────────────┘
```

Position Description

Commodities Brokers are the middlemen in the commodity futures markets. They solicit or accept orders from businesses and individuals to trade futures and options contracts on a commodities exchange and are paid a fee, or commission. (A futures contract is an agreement to deliver a specified commodity at a designated date, time, and place.) Brokers usually concentrate on a specific product, such as coffee, wheat, or hog bellies. Commodities Brokers work at a brokerage house, on the floor of a commodities exchange, or independently.

Commodities Brokers buy and sell standardized commodity contracts to manage price risk or gamble on price movements. Buyers of commodity futures contracts, a widely traded contract, want to minimize price fluctuations in commodities or raw materials, while commodity sellers try to lock in a price for their products. Commodities Brokers often specialize by financial instrument, such as futures options, options on futures, or commodity swaps, rather than by industry. Trading activity on U.S. commodity exchanges set records in 2005, led by a surge in trading of crude oil futures, natural gas futures, and other energy-related contracts.

Commodities Brokers spend much of their time soliciting prospective clients and opening managed futures accounts, which are managed by a professional commodity trading adviser (CTA). Starting brokers open broker-assisted accounts for individual investors who want advice managing their accounts. They do not have daily contact with the customer and do not make trading recommendations, which will be done by a more senior broker. More-experienced investors have self-directed accounts and do their own trading with a minimum of advice from their brokers. Work hours of commodity brokers are flexible. They usually work a 40–50-hour week, but work schedules will vary. Brokers will start their day in mid-morning some weeks and at other times will work into the evening hours contacting clients at home.

Duties performed can include the following:

• executing trades
• collecting and summarizing research from the research desk

- marking positions to market, adjusting for daily price changes
- maintaining daily reports on positions and trading desk profit and loss
- checking that trade and settlement details are correct
- reconciling trade breaks or failed trades
- supporting more experienced traders with on-the-spot market analysis

Salaries

Commodities Brokers with a Series 3 commodity trading license can earn about $50,000 per year. Brokers who are working toward their license will earn less. Starting brokers receive a commission on each trade made by retail customers through broker-assisted staff. Experienced Commodities Brokers can have earnings from $101,776 to $170,000, according to Salary.com. Median floor broker salary in 2005 was $132,000. Compensation increases as the number of accounts managed increases.

Employment Prospects

Commodity trading companies are known for giving new hires a lot of responsibility right away. Some come in from the trading floor, and others come from outside the industry. Individuals can get into trading directly from college with no industry experience. Entry-level traders spend their first several months in supporting roles helping more experienced traders—as a trader assistant, for instance.

Another trend driving employment in the futures industry is the number of new contracts being created. New commodity contracts stimulates demand for Commodity Brokers. This trend is expected to grow in step with the move toward globalization and the trend toward broker specialization. New types of futures contracts are continuously being offered on the commodities exchanges, creating new employment opportunities for commodities brokers.

Advancement Prospects

Brokers typically advance by working up to more responsible positions and a larger group of clients. A Broker who executes trades may advance to become a full service broker. A Broker can also advance to become a money manager or commodity trading adviser (CTA) and make investment decisions for clients.

Commodities Brokers can move into other areas of the firm, such as marketing or management. Some brokers want to remain traders, advancing their careers by building up their client base. Other advancement opportunities can be found in investment management. Fast-growing hedge funds have been augmenting their trading departments; more than 400 hedge funds had energy-trading strategies in 2005, according to *Forbes* magazine.

Education and Training

There are no formal education requirements to become a Commodities Broker, and some very successful brokers have entered the field with only a high school education. In today's market, however, most people hired have a college degree with a major in business, economics, mathematics, or a related field.

Experience, Skills, and Personality Traits

Commodities Brokers must have quick reflexes and an ability to think on their feet. They need to have a thorough understanding of financial markets and money management, and a keen interest in anything from international news to the weather that can influence commodity prices. Successful brokers are risk takers, willing to make decisions quickly and deal with the occasional failures that are part of the job. One to three years experience on a commodities or futures exchange, or with a futures trading firm, is helpful.

Strong communication and sales skills are essentials in this career. Commodities traders must have a good work ethic and be willing to put in the time necessary to open new accounts. Brokers should have excellent telephone sales skills and be comfortable talking to people. Sales talents learned in previous experience will come into play in this career. It is also important to have an interest in the world of finance and a desire to communicate that interest to prospective clients.

Special Requirements

Before becoming a Commodities Broker, you must pass the National Commodities Futures Examination (the Series 3 Exam), the licensing exam for futures brokers. The test covers marketing and trading knowledge, and industry rules and regulations. The test is administered by the National Association of Securities Dealers. Floor brokers are not required to take the exam, but receive intensive training at the exchange.

Unions and Associations

As professional employees Commodities Broken can belong to professional associations such as the National Futures Association, the Futures Industry Association, or the Commodity Floor Brokers and Traders Association for business networking and career management.

Tips for Entry

1. Visit one of the commodity futures exchanges and observe Commodities Brokers in action on the trading floor. All of the exchanges offer free guided tours.
2. Read industry publications and learn what trading advisors say about their industry and their jobs; contact the Center for Futures Education (http://www.thectr.com), which publishes a 24-page booklet that

discusses the National Commodities Futures Exam and how to become a Commodities Broker.

3. Do your own research. Select a commodity and follow it, using trading simulation software from one of the exchanges.

4. For hands-on experience, consider a summer job as a runner at a commodities exchange. Runners relay buy or sell orders from the exchange phone clerks to the Brokers in the trading pit, and to and from members on the exchange floor.

BRANCH OFFICE ADMINISTRATOR, BROKERAGE

CAREER PROFILE

Duties: Directs and coordinates buying and selling of securities from a brokerage office; manages sales and administrative support staff

Alternate Title(s): Branch Manager

Salary Range: $50,000 to $90,000

Employment Prospects: Good

Advancement Prospects: Fair

Prerequisites:

    Education or Training—Four-year college degree

    Experience—Three to five years' experience in financial services branch administration

    Special Skills and Personality Traits—Strong communication, organizational skills, and interpersonal skills

    Special Requirements—Securities licenses required

CAREER LADDER

```
┌─────────────────────────────────┐
│    Field Supervision Director     │
└─────────────────────────────────┘

┌─────────────────────────────────┐
│    Branch Office Administrator    │
└─────────────────────────────────┘

┌─────────────────────────────────┐
│ Junior Branch Office Administrator│
└─────────────────────────────────┘
```

Position Description

Branch Office Administrators supervise brokerage office activities supporting the purchase or sale of investment products for clients of the firm. They interview and hire investment representatives (securities brokers), and supervise administrative support workers and office receptionists.

Branch Office Administrators have three primary duties: servicing customers, providing marketing support for brokers, and performing administrative tasks related to customer accounts. They answer the telephone, greet office visitors, respond to customer inquiries, and investigate service problems or customer complaints.

Administrators provide marketing support for the office's investment representatives. This includes mailing marketing literature and surveys to customers, making presentations at investment seminars, and making follow-up calls to customers.

The Branch Office Administrator is responsible for all administrative functions related to customer accounts and trading activity, and other tasks related to the daily operation of the branch office. This includes planning and preparing for daily activities, processing customer deposits, and transfers of securities. They implement plans to assure compliance with rules set by the brokerage firm and by regulatory agencies. They establish and maintain internal controls to control margin accounts, short sales, and options to reduce clerical errors and client complaints.

Branch Office Administrators may also:

- direct in-service training programs
- review records of daily transactions
- analyze operations to determine profitability of gross sales and identify areas of improvement
- conduct staff meetings to discuss changes in policy
- prepare activity reports for evaluation by management

Junior branch office managers assist the Branch Office Administrator in carrying out administrative functions within the branch. They work with the Branch Office Administrator to develop new systems that will help the branch run more efficiently and assist in supervising administrative and clerical staff workers in the branch office.

Salaries

Salaries can vary according to type of firm and region. Branch Office Administrators outside of the New York City area earn salaries of $50,000 to $90,000 or more. Those employed in New York City may earn a considerably higher salary. Benefits in addition to salary usually include paid health and life insurance, annual performance bonuses based on firm profitability, and employer-sponsored retirement plans.

Employment Prospects

Employment prospects for Branch Office Administrators should be about average over the next several years. Opportunities are closely linked to the number of new offices planned by discount brokers and full-service brokers and continued investor interest in the stock market. Some openings will come about from employee turnover or retirements.

Online trading of securities, conducted over the Internet without using a broker, could some day become a factor in the securities industry, but its impact on employment may not be fully known for a while. Most investors look to investment professionals for advice, often by visiting a branch office.

Advancement Prospects

Advancement is generally to a position with increased responsibility, such as managing a larger branch office. Another option is advancing to positions in field supervision and overseeing the activities of branch offices in a region. Some managers will advance their careers by moving into higher paying positions at competing firms.

Education and Training

A four-year college degree is required for the position. Courses in accounting, business administration, and finance are helpful.

Special Requirements

Securities licenses are required for this position, usually a Series 7 General Securities Registered Representative license, a Series 8 Branch Office Manager license, and a Series 63 Uniform Securities license.

Experience, Skills, and Personality Traits

Several years' experience in branch administration or financial services marketing is usually required. Branch Office Administrators assist customers with financial planning and selecting investments, so they need to have excellent communication skills and a detailed knowledge of the investment products offered by their firm. Strong organizational skills are also important in implementing business strategy. Strong senses of ethics and personal integrity are important personality traits.

Unions and Associations

Branch Office Managers can become members of the Securities Industry Association for professional development at association-sponsored seminars and networking opportunities.

Tips for Entry

1. College courses in business administration, law, and accounting are helpful.
2. Learn about the stock market and real estate market by joining an investment club.
3. Follow business news by reading the business section of news magazines and newspapers and trade publications such as *Registered Representative* magazine.

SECURITIES BROKER

CAREER PROFILE

Duties: Handles clearing orders to buy and sell securities; assists clients in managing their overall financial situation

Alternate Title(s): Account Executive, Financial Adviser, Financial Consultant

Salary Range: $49,000 to $131,000 and up

Employment Prospects: Good

Advancement Prospects: Good

Prerequisites:

Education or Training—Four-year college degree with courses in finance or liberal arts degree with courses in business, economics, and marketing; on-the-job training

Experience—Three to five years' experience in business or the financial services industry, or recent college graduates with courses in business and finance

Special Skills and Personality Traits—Good communication skills and interpersonal skills; ability to work under stressful working conditions; strong desire to succeed

Special Requirements—Must pass federal and state licensing exams and background check; professional certifications helpful for advancement

CAREER LADDER

```
┌─────────────────────────────────┐
│   Branch Office Administrator    │
└─────────────────────────────────┘

┌─────────────────────────────────┐
│        Securities Broker         │
└─────────────────────────────────┘

┌─────────────────────────────────┐
│          Broker Trainee          │
└─────────────────────────────────┘
```

Position Description

Securities Brokers sell financial products and services to consumers, business owners, and organizations using their knowledge of securities and investment plans, market conditions and regulations, and client financial needs. The majority of brokers work in branch offices of major brokerage firms, providing personalized financial consultation in addition to securities trading. Those employed by discount brokerage firms, which trade securities at discounted brokerage commissions, but provide limited financial advice, may work in regional call centers, taking customer telephone orders. Brokers spend much of their time giving clients financial advice rather than selling securities, and many brokers prefer calling themselves financial advisers or financial consultants, rather than brokers.

Most securities sales representatives work in offices under stressful conditions. For beginning brokers, the most important part of the job is finding clients and building a customer base. Starting representatives spend much of their time contacting potential clients, relying on telephone solicitation to individuals on brokerage firm lists or names of individuals who have done business with the firm in the past. Many beginning brokers leave the occupation because they are unable to build a sufficient client base. Once established, brokers have strong attachment to their occupation because of high earnings potential and continuing training provided by brokerage firms.

Brokers explain market terms and trading practices, offer financial advice on purchase or sale of securities, and create an individual client portfolio which may consist of stocks, bonds, mutual funds, certificates of deposit, annuities, and other investments. Brokers provide information about the advantages and disadvantages of an investment based on client goals and the latest price quotes and information on corporations and issuers of securities. Most service the investment needs of individual investors, but brokers may also work with corporate clients, pension plans, and state and local government agencies. Most brokers typically work a standard 40-hour workweek, and may arrange client consultations evenings and weekends. New brokers spend their time learning the firm's products and qualifying for examinations.

New Securities and Exchange Commission rules require stockbrokers to abide by certain ground rules when advising their clients If they are clearly providing advisory services, they are duty bound to act in a customer's best interest; if they are acting as brokers—as a salesperson—they must be clear about that role. If acting as a financial planner, the broker must register with the SEC as an investment adviser, which means they have a fiduciary duty to the client.

Their duties include:

- identifying potential clients using mailing lists, personal contacts, and advertising
- interviewing clients to determine their financial goals, assets available for investment, and interest in investing in securities
- providing clients with information and advice on purchases or sales of securities
- completing sales order tickets, submitting completed tickets for transaction processing
- meeting with clients on a regular basis to review account performance and financial goals
- developing and implementing financial plans
- selling securities (stocks, bonds, annuities, mutual funds), certificates of deposit, insurance, and other financial products

Salaries

Brokerage salespeople are usually compensated with a salary and bonus, or a percentage of assets managed. Salaries tend to increase with the number of individual accounts managed. Most brokerage firms pay starting brokers with a "draw against commission," or a minimum salary based on commissions they can be expected to earn. The salary gradually decreases as brokers gain experience and begin building a client base, and is replaced with commissions. Discount brokers are usually paid through a salary, supplemented with a performance bonus tied to the profitability of their office. Median annual earnings were $69,000 in 2004, according to the U.S. Bureau of Labor Statistics.

Employment Prospects

Demand for Securities Brokers should be about average through 2014. Recent growth in personal disposable income will stimulate demand for financial professionals to help people achieve better investment returns to meet financial goals. Employment in the brokerage industry will be adversely affected by a decline in the economy or the stock market. However, the wide variety of investment choices available and the growth of self-directed retirement plans will stimulate demand for brokers. The growth of Internet sales of investment products will reduce the need for brokers for routine transactions, but people will continue to seek the advice of professionals for investment advice.

Advancement Prospects

Securities Brokers with at least three years' experience can advance in several ways. Brokers can develop a specialty practice servicing corporate retirement and 401(k) plans, working as part of a team of investment professionals. Brokers with excellent interpersonal skills can advance into management positions, such as managing a brokerage branch office. Additional responsibilities also qualify a broker for higher salary and performance bonus compensation.

Experience, Skills, and Personality Traits

Securities Brokers usually have prior experience in the securities industry, such as assisting other brokers or working in investment research. Some have had sales or marketing experience in banking, insurance, or other industries. Recent college graduates with degrees in business, finance, or related fields but no securities industry experience start out as broker trainees. Securities Brokers need strong verbal and written communication skills, good interpersonal skills in working with clients, and an ability to work long hours under often stressful working conditions. Successful brokers have a good aptitude for numbers, a strong desire to succeed, and a keen interest in investing.

Education and Training

A four-year college degree with courses in business, finance, or marketing is normally required. Most brokerage firms provide extensive on-the-job training, up to two years in bigger firms, and continuing training to maintain skills.

While there is no uniform accreditation to become a financial adviser, stockbrokers can earn any of several professional certifications as they build their client base. As brokerage firms compete more actively for wealthy investors, they have begun to encourage their stockbrokers to earn the Chartered Financial Planner (CFP) designation. The CFP designation, widely recognized by consumers, is commonly held by independent financial planners.

Brokers starting out may want to earn the AAMS (Accredited Asset Managed Specialist) designation from the College of Financial Planning to get a general understanding of financial planning concepts before deciding to pursue the CFP designation, which takes more time. To get the CFP title, candidates must have at least three years of work experience, complete a financial planning curriculum at an accredited college or university, and pass a two-day exam. CFP holders must also complete 30 hours of continuing education every two years to maintain their certification.

Special Requirements

Beginning brokers must pass the licensing requirements, which include a passing grade in the General Securities, Registered Representative Examination given by the National Association of Securities Dealers (NASD). Brokers successfully completing this exam receive a Series 7 brokerage license from the NASD. Brokers are expected to take additional examinations within two years of employment to sell insurance and commodities, and continuing courses sponsored by their firm to maintain proficiency. Available industry certifications include: Certified Financial Planner (CFP), Certified Fund Specialist (CFS), Chartered Financial Consultant (ChFC), Chartered Mutual Fund Counselor (CMFC), and Registered Investment Adviser (RIA).

Securities Brokers who give advice about investing in securities are required to become registered investment advisors. If they manage $25 million or more in client assets, they must register with the Securities and Exchange Commission; if the amount managed is under $25 million, they register with the securities agency in the state where they have their principal place of business. Some investment advisers employ investment adviser representatives, people who handle most of the client work.

Unions and Associations

As professional employees, brokers do not usually belong to labor unions. They can belong to professional organizations including the Securities Industry Association (SIA).

Tips for Entry

1. Get a solid background in business courses at a college or university to gain understanding of investment management and business practices.
2. Employment opportunities may be greater in smaller brokerage firms or commercial banks, recently deregulated to sell investment securities in branch offices, than in bigger firms.
3. To build a client base, give lectures on investments at libraries and social clubs, or teach an adult education course on personal investing.
4. Take advantage of campus mentoring programs. Some Wall Street brokerage firms send executives to college campuses to mentor students who are undecided about their college majors.
5. Brokers starting their careers may go through some lean months while building a client base. Build up a personal financial reserve to get you through the first year or two as the initial base salary is reduced.

SALES TRADER

CAREER PROFILE

Duties: Submits buy and sell orders of stocks and bonds; recommends purchase, retention, or sale of specific securities; notifies customers following trading execution

Alternate Title(s): Financial Trader

Salary Range: $50,000 to $125,000+

Employment Prospects: Good

Advancement Prospects: Good

Prerequisites:

Education or Training—Four-year degree; M.B.A. degree or graduate degree often required for advancement

Experience—One to two years' securities industry experience in trading or sales

Special Skills and Personality Traits—Excellent communication and analytical skills; good computer skills and communication skills.

Special Requirements—Must pass the registered representative exam (Series 7); pass the selection process and obtain state licensing

CAREER LADDER

```
┌─────────────────────────────┐
│      Senior Trader          │
└─────────────────────────────┘

┌─────────────────────────────┐
│      Sales Trader           │
└─────────────────────────────┘

┌─────────────────────────────┐
│     Trading Assistant       │
└─────────────────────────────┘
```

Position Description

Investors use securities Sales Traders to buy and sell shares of stock, bonds, mutual funds, and other financial products distributed through the securities markets. Sales Traders work in brokerage firms, mutual fund companies, commercial banks, and insurance companies. They have access to "quote boards" or computer terminals that provide continually updated information on prices of securities. Established traders usually work a 40-hour week. Starting traders, who are seeking customers, may work much longer hours in order to build a client base. When sales activity increases, due to changes in trading volume in the market, the announcement of key economic data by the government, or sudden changes in the economy, the pace of trading activity may increase significantly. This can be a good career choice if you like working with numbers and can work well under pressure.

Typical duties performed by Sales Traders include:

• relaying buy and sell orders through their firm's office to the floor of a securities exchange

• supplying the latest price quotations on securities
• supplying information on the activities and financial positions of corporations issuing securities

Sales Traders assist their firm in rounding up buyers for small blocks of securities, often functioning as a go between or liaison between the block traders, who handle large volume trades, and the brokerage firm's institutional salesmen who distribute securities to pension funds and other big investors. Sales Traders initiate phone calls to clients, keep abreast of changes in the markets, and pitch investment ideas and offer market commentary. Sales Traders try to present the "big picture" in pitching investment ideas to clients, and usually have less information about clients than the sales force. When questions arise they refer clients to a research analyst for further consultation and recommendations.

Some trader positions are very specialized, requiring more extensive industry experience or a combination of experience and on-the-job training. Block traders work on the trading floor of brokerage firms and keep their eyes on four or more computer monitors. Block traders deal in active, mature markets such as stocks, commercial paper, government bonds, and corporate bonds. These markets are characterized by a high volume of buy and sell orders daily. Block traders come from different backgrounds; some are M.B.A. graduates, some have worked their way up from trainee or entry-level positions. Block traders are hired for their strong work ethic, street smarts, and willingness to work long hours in the high-pressure environment of a trading room.

Other traders specialize in selling more exotic products, or what Wall Street calls "structured finance." These structured finance products constitute a fast-growing business and are essentially hybrid securities. Examples are mortgage-backed securities and asset-backed securities (essentially pools of bonds backed by some form of debt, such as mortgages or credit card receivables). Low-volume, more complex instruments such as interest rate swaps are customized to meet unique situations, and are traded much less frequently. Trading in these securities requires more specialized knowledge of securities and markets, and more upfront work prior to executing each trade.

Salaries

Most firms pay Sales Traders a fixed salary plus an annual incentive bonus pegged to the profits generated by the trading group. Traders starting as trading assistants move into full-fledged trading positions after two to three years. At this time firms begin to judge traders on their profit contribution to the firm. When the trading group does well, everyone in the group benefits.

Salaries vary regionally and by type of firm, from a low of $50,000 to $125,000 and up. The highest salaries are earned by sales traders working in the New York City metropolitan area, ranging from $150,000 to $225,000. Equity traders who execute trades but do not make sales pitches can earn salaries from $80,000 to $140,000. Annual compensation, including annual bonus, can exceed $1 million for experienced traders. In the years when trading volume is low, and fewer commissions dollars are generated, traders receive a smaller bonus.

Employment Prospects

There are good employment opportunities for securities Sales Traders. Growth in trading activity in the financial markets and the addition of after-hours trading will create opportunities for experienced traders and probably for trading assistants moving into trading positions. Most traders begin their careers as trading assistants. Some firms hire recent college graduates into these assistant trading positions, with the prospect of becoming full-time traders. Trading assistants perform many of the duties of traders, such as relaying messages from the floor of the stock exchange and contacting customers.

Advancement Prospects

Traders start their careers as trading assistants and go through an extensive on-the-job training program. Advancement is linked to a trader's ability to generate trading activity. Successful traders are adept at building a "book of business" with clients who do a lot of trading with that firm. Advancement could be to head trader in a trading group. Some traders in the equity markets move to specialist firms, and become market makers in the stocks of specific companies, or they move into other positions in financial services such as research analyst or financial planner.

Education and Training

A four-year degree is the minimum level of education for most trader positions. Traders come from various academic backgrounds, including liberal arts. A degree in business or economics is helpful. Some firms, notably the "numbers crunching" firms that use quantitative models as the basis for trading strategy, look to hire individuals with postgraduate degrees or an M.B.A. degree.

Most employers provide on-the-job training to help securities traders meet the requirements for registration. In most firms the training period generally takes about four months. Trainees in large firms generally receive classroom instruction in securities analysis and the finer points of selling securities, and go through a training period lasting up to two years. In smaller firms, Sales Traders generally receive training provided by outside firms specializing in securities industry training. Many trainees take correspondence courses in preparation for the securities examination.

Special Requirements

Sales Traders must complete the requirements for a Series 7 General Registered Representative Exam and the Series 63 Investment Adviser Exam if they make investment recommendations to clients. Traders must also obtain a license from state regulators in the state where they do business.

Experience, Skills, and Personality Traits

Being a successful trader requires a combination of skills. Individuals should have excellent computational skills and an ability to calculate numbers very quickly. Sales Traders need to have a grasp of market forces such as earnings, management, and economic trends that drive stock prices. On the fixed-income side, traders need to have excellent mathematical and quantitative skills. Intangible skills are also very important; mainly a trader's "instinct" about the market, and an ability to make rapid decisions with little information to go on, and an ability to assess investor sentiment.

Unions and Associations

Sales Traders can become members of several trade associations for career advancement, skills improvement, and networking opportunities. Among these are the Bond Market Association and the Security Traders Association.

Tips for Entry

1. College placement offices are helpful for individuals seeking entry-level positions.

2. Contact state bankers' associations for a list of brokerage firms licensed in your state or contact firms directly to inquire about job openings.

3. Read newspapers and magazines that report on trends in financial investments and new financial products offered to the public.

4. Study different companies and watch their share prices every day.

5. Join an investment club to learn more about the world of investing, or create a model portfolio of stocks from different companies and track their performance over time.

INVESTMENT BANKER

CAREER PROFILE

Duties: Raises capital for corporations and municipalities through sale (initial public offering) of new securities to the public; acts as a general financial adviser for clients

Alternate Title(s): Associate, Managing Director

Salary Range: $60,000 to $130,000 and up

Employment Prospects: Good

Advancement Prospects: Good

Prerequisites:

Education or Training—Four-year degree with emphasis in finance, business, and accounting; post-graduate degree or M.B.A. often required for advancement

Experience—Three to five years' experience in a financial environment or equivalent academic background

Special Skills and Personality Traits—Excellent written and interpersonal communication skills; excellent analytical and research skills; creativity, problem-solving ability, and sales ability

Special Requirements—Chartered Financial Analyst (CFA) certification required for client advisory or investment research positions

CAREER LADDER

```
┌─────────────────────────────────────┐
│ Vice President, Investment Banking   │
└─────────────────────────────────────┘

┌─────────────────────────────────────┐
│ Associate, Investment Banking        │
└─────────────────────────────────────┘

┌─────────────────────────────────────┐
│ Entry-Level Research Analyst         │
└─────────────────────────────────────┘
```

Position Description

Investment banking is one of the most visible and demanding careers in corporate finance. The big investment banks on Wall Street recruit the most talented graduates of U.S. colleges and business schools, and pay some of the highest salaries. Investment Bankers perform dozens of specialized services, but the most important of these are corporate finance and trading. In corporate finance the Investment Banker assists corporations or state and local governments in raising capital through the sale of a stock or bond offering to the investing public.

Following a successful public offering, investment banks attempt to maintain investor interest in securities sold to the public by actively trading securities they underwrite, or bring to market. Full-service investment banks have brokerage divisions that buy and sell stocks, bonds, and other financial instruments for retail investors and big institutional investors such as public pension funds. They also engage in proprietary trading with the firm's own capital whenever they see an opportunity to make a profit.

Investment banking firms are usually broken out by company size for comparison and industry ranking purposes. The big full-service investment banks have the largest number of employees and are the most active participants in securities underwriting and trading. These banks are informally known as *bulge bracket* firms because they share the largest participation in a public underwriting of securities. Smaller investment banks have a regional market focus or are specialty firms active in certain market niches. Some of these specialty firms are oriented toward bond trading or equity trading, while others specialize in offering merger and acquisition (M&A) advisory services to corporate clients.

Investment Bankers hired after college graduation usually begin their careers as investment analysts or research analysts, working as junior members of an investment banking team. The work performed by starting Investment Bankers can vary drastically from one department to another. They may be assigned to work in corporate finance, equity trading, or mergers and acquisitions.

Individuals starting a career in corporate finance spend much of their time writing "pitchbooks" promoting the investment bank's research and underwriting capabilities, often in connection with a client company's initial public offering, or IPO. Analysts working in investment banking will learn the fundamentals of financial analysis during their first two years on the job.

Their duties typically include:

- performing market research and analysis supporting capital market transactions
- identifying potential risks and opportunities
- preparing detailed models of financial projections, debt ratings, and company valuations
- preparing financial statements, cash flow projections, and performance projections
- assisting in corporate due diligence reviews, a formal review of financial statements and internal records of companies involved in a transaction

Depending on their career path, a starting Investment Banker may also begin a career as an equity trader or bond trader, or as a salesperson pitching a recently underwritten stock offering to clients. Duties of traders and salespeople are different from those of investment analysts. Individuals in trading and sales have a high degree of customer contact. Their duties emphasize monitoring trading screens to keep up with financial markets and their ability to anticipate, and service, customer needs.

Starting Investment Bankers working in corporate finance or investment research put in long hours, up to 80 hours a week, including weekends. The sales and trading side of an investment bank is much less hierarchical than the corporate finance side, and the workweek doesn't demand quite so many hours. Investment banking can be a good career choice if you are analytical, can make decisions quickly, and like working in a fast-paced environment.

Salaries

Salaries for Investment Bankers depend on their academic background, what they do, and who they work for. Entry-level bankers with a college degree and limited work experience can earn anywhere from $25,000 to $60,000. Associate-level positions for individuals with a master's degree or financial analysts with two to four years work experience pay salaries from $60,000 to $130,000, including a signing bonus. New York City firms tend to pay more than firms in other regions due to the higher cost of living in the New York metropolitan area.

Investment Banker salaries tend to rise steeply with experience as newly hired bankers move up the promotion ladder, reaching about $200,000, excluding the annual incentive bonus, after five years. Year-end bonuses, which are tied to job performance and firm profitability, can range anywhere from 20 to 50 percent of base salary to 100 percent of base salary. This is an opportunity to earn a seven-figure income.

Employment Prospects

Individuals typically enter investment banking in one of three ways: getting hired directly from college, moving up from an analyst position, or transferring from management, accounting, or legal departments. Investment banking can be a difficult field to break into, largely because the applicant pool is so large and investment banks tend to be very selective. The top investment banks receive several thousand résumés a year; they hire only a few dozen M.B.A. graduates and even fewer college graduates.

Investment banking is a business that reinvents itself every several years. In the years following the market collapse of 2000–02, Wall Street investment banks began emphasizing trading of financial derivatives and exotic financial instruments while downplaying advisory services for corporate clients. Many of these advisory services are now performed by boutique companies formed by investment bankers previously affiliated with one of the major Wall Street firms.

Employment in securities industry firms is highly cyclical. Employment began falling in the wake of the financial market meltdown starting in 2000, hitting bottom in 2003. Three years later, as this is being written, securities industry employment has not fully recovered the jobs lost since 2000. Employment growth in this cyclical industry is not spread evenly across the board, so it pays to contact a large number of firms when job hunting. Many of the largest firms have a practice of filling open positions early in the year after tallying their gains and losses for the previous year.

Advancement Prospects

Investment banking is a meritocracy; firms put a premium on job performance and meeting sales goals. Advancement is through moving into positions of increased responsibility. Analyst-level Investment Bankers who successfully complete a two-year training program can become associates. Associates generally take on more client contact as they become more acquainted with project finance, advancing to vice president in three to four years, eventually becoming a managing director.

Aside from promotion to a management-level position, there are other advancement opportunities. Research analysts who cover fast-growing industries wield considerable clout and the competition among firms for top analysts can be intense. Equity traders who develop an expertise for gauging risk and pricing securities can move into very senior positions due to their knowledge of markets and money. Some bankers move into private client servicing, providing financial advice to wealthy individuals.

Education and Training
A four-year degree with an emphasis in accounting, finance, economics, or related courses is a general requirement for entry, although post-graduate degrees are becoming increasingly common. Whether they work in corporate finance, investment research, or another department, newly hired bankers often go through a training program of up to two years. Future advancement depends on successful completion of that program. Investment banks encourage their associates to advance their skills through post-graduate education. Many have tuition reimbursement programs for associates entering an M.B.A. program.

Special Requirements
A Chartered Financial Analyst (CFA) designation available from the Association for Investment Research and Management is necessary for advancement in positions in investment research or client servicing.

Experience, Skills and Personality Traits
Success in investment banking requires a combination of strong interpersonal skills, excellent communication skills, and analytical skills. Most jobs in investment banking involve some working knowledge of advanced mathematics and economic modeling, and an ability to make decisions quickly under deadline pressure. Also important are good computer skills and a working knowledge of spreadsheet modeling. A sales ability is useful for individuals in corporate finance and trading.

Unions and Associations
Investment Bankers can become members of associations such as the Securities Industry Association or the Security Traders Association for career networking and skills improvement through association-sponsored seminars.

Tips for Entry
1. November and December are good months to send your résumé to an investment bank. Most new hires are made in January or February.
2. Be persistent. Getting a job with an investment bank is a numbers game, so try to contact as many people as you can.
3. Pick the first firm you work for carefully. Investment banks put a premium on employee loyalty and try to fill job vacancies through promotion. Your chances of getting hired are reduced if you change jobs frequently.
4. Read up on industry trends in trade magazines such as *Institutional Investor* or *Investment Dealers Digest.*
5. When interviewing, go for the position that is most interesting, not the job with the highest signing bonus. Quality of work is very important, especially if you want to get into a top M.B.A. school after a few years with a Wall Street firm.

PERFORMANCE ANALYST

CAREER PROFILE

Duties: Calculates rates of return on investment portfolios and identifies the sources of investment performance; prepares performance presentations for investors

Alternate Title(s): Investment Performance Analyst

Salary Range: $35,000 to $100,000 and up

Employment Prospects: Very good

Advancement Prospects: Good

Prerequisites:

Education or Training—Four-year degree

Experience—One to three years of experience in an investment firm is helpful, though not required

Special Skills and Personality Traits—Strong mathematics aptitude, college courses in algebra and statistics

CAREER LADDER

```
┌─────────────────────────────┐
│     Performance Analyst      │
└─────────────────────────────┘

┌─────────────────────────────┐
│  Senior Performance Analyst  │
└─────────────────────────────┘

┌─────────────────────────────┐
│     Department Manager       │
└─────────────────────────────┘
```

Position Description

As investors search out the best opportunities around the world, the financial markets are becoming more global in nature. With the growth of international investing came a need for investment professionals to calculate apples-to-apples comparisons of investment performance across markets, which in turn makes it easier for investment managers to communicate with their clients about past performance and future investment strategies. Clients of a registered investment advisory firm want to see investment results presented in a variety of different ways.

The Performance Analyst ensures that investment results are accurately calculated and reported every month or every quarter. Increasingly, these opportunities are being found in developing markets in Eastern Europe, Asia, and South America. U.S.-listed stocks accounted for only 28 percent of the world's stock market in 2006. More than half the world's largest companies are located outside the United States.

The analyst prepares attribution analysis reports, statistical reports, and other reports for marketing as needed. The Performance Analyst works closely with investment portfolio managers and investment writers to effectively communicate results to retail and institutional investors and investment committees. The analyst is in daily contact with product managers, portfolio managers, fund accountants, internal and external auditors, and others to get the latest financial performance data. If employed in a financial institution, the Performance Analyst may also be a member of the bank's internal risk management team.

Performance Analysts do more than calculate return on investment. They calculate the amount of risk the investment manager is taking and determine whether the manager is adequately compensated. They calculate performance attribution reports. Performance attribution is the process of identifying the source of investment return, or investment performance, and then comparing that return to a benchmark index.

Specific duties include the following:

- preparing portfolio and benchmark reports
- maintaining and updating performance databases
- preparing shareholder reports to mutual fund investors and reports to the mutual fund board of directors
- answering daily requests for performance data from various internal and external groups
- maintaining relationships with data vendors supplying relevant investment or market data

Salaries

Performance Analysts entering the field typically earn salaries starting around $35,000 and rising to $75,000, depending on experience and qualifications. The average annual compensation is around $80,000, according to the Spaulding Group, a financial training organization based in New Jersey. A department manager, someone who has responsibility for a financial research department, can earn $200,000 and as much as $500,000, depending on his or her responsibilities and the market breadth of the company.

Employment Prospects

There is high demand for Performance Analysts, although this is still a niche market. There was sufficient demand that the CFA Institute started a new credentialing program for performance professionals, the Certified Global Investment Performance Standard (CGIPS). Market demand for better performance measurement is being driven partially by the availability of sophisticated analytical techniques for measurement of investment performance and the growing acceptance of the Global Investment Performance Standard, formally introduced in November 2005 by the CFA Institute.

The major employers are investment management firms, investment consulting firms, custodial banks, and independent performance verification firms that review investment managers for compliance with the GIPS standard. Many of the public accounting firms have verification practices.

Advancement Prospects

There are two advancement tracks for Performance Analysts. First, they can move up to manage teams of analysts and eventually manage an investment research department. Second, because performance measurement is so important to investment management, a Performance Analyst can move into other parts of an investment firm, such as marketing or portfolio management.

Education and Training

This is a trainable job. Individuals with a four-year college degree can enter the field directly from college. A degree in finance is a strong selling point, though not essential. The most important academic requirement is a strong mathematical aptitude and college courses in advanced algebra. Also helpful is some general knowledge of value-at-risk methodologies, portfolio stress testing, statistics, and correlation analysis. Most investment firms sponsor continuing education programs in which newly hired analysts can learn how to measure investment returns, earning continuing education credits while taking courses.

Experience, Skills, and Personality Traits

Strong verbal and written communication skills as well as presentation skills are important in this position. Performance Analysts need to be able to communicate complicated things clearly. Performance Analysts often handle various assignments simultaneously, an ability to handle multiple tasks is an important trait. Performance Analysts are detail-oriented, self-motivated individuals who exhibit a flair for creativity. Also important are solid analytical skills developed from academic training and a self-starting personality—the ability to work independently with minimal supervision. Some knowledge of financial data vendors and working knowledge of Microsoft Office Suite and desktop PC programs such as Adobe Acrobat are helpful. Finally, analysts should have a strong interest in financial markets and the marketing aspects of money management.

The most important requirement is a solid understanding of the mathematical measurement tools typically used in evaluating investment returns. The world of investing is driven to a large extent by computer-based measurement tools. A good mathematics background is the foundation to a career as a Performance Analyst.

Unions and Associations

Performance Analysts can become members of the CGIPS Association, an affiliate of the CFA Institute for career advancement and networking opportunities. The CGIPS Association sponsors a certification program for Performance Analysts. The designation is awarded to those who pass their course requirements and have at least two years of experience in a performance-related position.

Tips for Entry

1. Develop mathematical skills through college-level courses.
2. While in college, take a course in investment management to learn about portfolio theory and performance measurement.
3. Contact your college placement office to learn about campus visits by hiring firms.
4. Learn as much about investments as possible: how people invest, how trades are done. You need a solid understanding of the whole picture to work in this area. Learn what goes on elsewhere in the investment industry.

OPERATIONS SPECIALIST, SECURITIES

CAREER PROFILE

Duties: Performs daily portfolio accounting activities, trade processing and settlements, and account reconciliation

Alternate Title(s): Client Operations Specialist, Operations Associate

Salary Range: $40,000 to $65,000

Employment Prospects: Good

Advancement Prospects: Good

Prerequisites:

Education or Training—Four-year degree in business or accounting

Experience—Two to five years in banking, brokerage, or investment management

Special Skills and Personality Traits—Working knowledge of office PC software, strong organizational and analytical skills

Special Requirements—Securities license required in some positions

CAREER LADDER

```
┌─────────────────────────────────┐
│      Operations Specialist       │
└─────────────────────────────────┘

┌─────────────────────────────────┐
│       Operations Manager         │
└─────────────────────────────────┘

┌─────────────────────────────────┐
│    Group Manager, Operations     │
└─────────────────────────────────┘
```

Position Description

All organizations require effectively and timely administrative support to function efficiently. In the securities and investment industry, the Operations Specialist provides administrative support to client servicing. While this is not a trading position, the Operations Specialist supports daily trading activities by providing assistance in record keeping and account reconciliation.

The Operations Specialist is the primary contact for all client-servicing activities including trade executions, providing mutual fund or account information, and answering client inquiries. The Operations Specialist opens new accounts, makes changes to existing accounts, and resolves exception items. The specialist also reviews transactions for completeness, accuracy, and compliance with company policies and with regulations issued by the National Association of Securities Dealers and the Securities and Exchange Commission. The Operations Specialist may also be asked to contribute ideas on how to better meet client needs, improve departmental workflows, and develop standardized solutions to client servicing issues. Specialists also participate in regularly scheduled training sessions to improve skills in every aspect of trade processing and client servicing.

Operations Specialists who service hedge fund clients or institutional investors may become involved in trade support for sophisticated trading strategies involving arbitrage trading, swap agreements, commodities, and foreign exchange trading.

Specific job functions for office and administrative support employees will vary according to the firm and its client base. Operational support specialists often serve as a liaison between the trading desk and the technical support staff. As administrative support workers, they help ensure that trade instructions from clients are being processed in an orderly fashion and are meeting established quality standards.

Duties performed may include the following:

- working with traders to ensure appropriate valuations of securities and trading positions
- ensuring that trades are accurately recorded in the central database

- analyzing confirmation details to ensure that trade details are forwarded to traders and trade counterparties
- working with data administration staff to ensure that trades are executed in compliance with company policy and industry regulations
- participating in quality control audits

Salaries

Operations Specialists' earnings are directly related to education, experience, and industry. Salaries for most specialist positions are negotiable based on background and experience. Specialist positions at hedge funds and firms serving institutional clients such as pension funds, endowments, and foundations pay the highest compensation. Earnings, which may include incentive bonuses or performance bonuses, can vary by industry. Specialists at insurance companies and depository financial institutions had median annual earnings of $49,600 and $37,000, respectively, in 2004. The middle 50 percent earned between $65,000 and $93,000 in 2005, according to the Securities Industry Association. Securities firms located in New York City usually offer higher compensation packages.

Employment Prospects

While this is a competitive field there are entry-level opportunities for qualified individuals. Those with relevant work experience at a securities firm a hedge fund or in retail banking are mostly likely to be considered. For some positions, it may be sufficient simply to have an understanding of some of the products marketed, whereas other positions will require actual work experience of one to five years. Candidates with the requisite job-related skills or educational background may also be considered. After a period of supervision during the first few months in the position, individuals entering the field will be asked to work unsupervised for large parts of the day. Employment in some firms may also be contingent on attainment of securities industry licenses such as the Series 6, Series 7, or Series 63 license from the National Association of Securities Dealers.

Advancement Prospects

Operations Specialists advance by moving into positions of increased responsibility. Those who successfully demonstrate an ability to achieve their objectives and meet their deadlines can advance to more senior positions, in which they manage a group of operational support workers as a team leader. Advancement to more senior positions is usually contingent on achieving some recognized financial industry credentials such as a Chartered Financial Analyst (CFA) or Certified Public Accountant (CPA) designation.

Education and Training

A four-year college degree is usually required for entry-level positions. College-level courses should have an emphasis in accounting, business, or finance. An alternative path is a high-school degree or graduate equivalent degree with four or five years of work-related experience. Most job-related skills can be acquired through a period of supervised training over a period of several months after being hired.

Special Requirements

Some firms may require applicants to obtain a Series 7 (General Brokerage License) or Series 63 license from the National Association of Securities Dealers or to obtain licenses within the first year of employment.

Experience, Skills, and Personality Traits

At least one to two years in financial industry customer service experience is a minimum requirement for the position. A working knowledge of common PC-based software such as the Microsoft Office suite or similar programs is a prerequisite. Operations Specialists spend much of their day in regular contact with customers, so they need to have excellent verbal and written communication skills and an ability to work with other customer service employees as part of a team. Problem-solving skills and excellent organizational skills are an important attribute.

Unions and Associations

Professional associations such as the Securities Industry Association offer a forum for educational advancement and networking with industry peers.

Tips for Entry

1. Internet job banks and bulletin boards have regular listings Operations Specialist positions.
2. Mutual fund companies frequently list employment opportunities on their Web sites.
3. As with other securities industry positions, networking through professional associations can provide job leads.

RATINGS AGENCY ANALYST

CAREER PROFILE

Duties: Evaluates credit risk of corporations and government entities selling debt securities; issues credit ratings

Alternate Title(s): Ratings Analyst

Salary Range: $47,410 to $82,730

Employment Prospects: Good

Advancement Prospects: Fair

Prerequisites:

Education or Training—Four-year degree; graduate degree preferred for some positions

Experience—One to three years' experience in securities analysis

Special Skills and Personality Traits—Strong written and verbal skills; working knowledge of spreadsheet accounting programs and financial databases

Special Requirements—Chartered Financial Analyst (CFA) designation helpful for advancement

CAREER LADDER

```
┌─────────────────────────────┐
│    Senior Ratings Analyst    │
└─────────────────────────────┘

┌─────────────────────────────┐
│    Ratings Agency Analyst    │
└─────────────────────────────┘

┌─────────────────────────────┐
│      Research Assistant      │
└─────────────────────────────┘
```

Position Description

Ratings Agency Analysts evaluate the credit risk of debt securities issued by corporations and government entities and issue credit ratings. Some agencies also evaluate and assign ratings to equity securities. Ratings agencies evaluate corporations, government agencies, financial services companies, foreign governments, and structured finance securities such as asset-backed and mortgage-backed securities. Mutual fund managers, pension funds, and other investors rely on ratings agency data to make investment decisions on which securities to buy as portfolio holdings and which ones they want to sell.

Ratings analysts contact the debt security issuers to obtain and clarify financial information. Ratings analysts have frequent contact with senior managers of the companies and issuers they rate, debt and equity securities underwriters, investors, and the news media. They have access to inside information that enables them to compare business strategies of companies in the same industry.

Ratings analysts work with financial models that attempt to forecast default probability under different economic and interest rate scenarios. They write research reports on individual corporations and industry sectors. In conducting their research, they may attend management and due diligence meetings of debt issues. They present the recommendations from their research to ratings committee meetings and publish results of their work in agency publications. Ratings committee meetings often take several weeks of preparation. During the committee meeting, the presenting Analyst makes a rating recommendation. After an open discussion a vote is taken and the recommendation is approved or rejected.

Ratings analysts work a 40-hour week, using computers and electronic databases to collect information. Analysts also attend industry conferences to learn about emerging trends and periodically visit companies they rate to review management strategy and talk to senior officers of the firms.

Salaries

Ratings Agency Analysts receive an annual salary. Salaries for ratings analysts are somewhat lower than salaries earned by financial analysts in investment banks. As a group, financial analysts earned between $47,410 and $82,730 in 2004, according to the U.S. Department of Labor's Bureau of Labor Statistics. Ratings analysts receive other benefits, including health insurance, life insurance, and paid vacations, and can participate in employer-sponsored retirement plans.

Employment Prospects

A person joining a ratings agency directly from college usually starts out as an assistant analyst helping a team of ratings analysts prepare company and industry reports. Individuals with at least one year of graduate school or an M.B.A. degree begin as associate analysts. Standard & Poor's Corporation rates more than $2 trillion of securities and employs more than 800 analysts. Moody's Investor Service rates $5 trillion of securities and employs more than 500 Analysts.

Much of the growth in ratings agency employment over the last 10 years has been in rating newer kinds of financial instruments, such as structured finance products—mortgage-backed and asset-backed securities.

Advancement Prospects

Ratings Agency Analysts have several advancement options. With experience, they can move up to more senior positions in the firm, such as manager of a ratings group covering an industry sector. They might also move into financial analyst or risk analyst positions with Wall Street investment banks. Another option would be taking a position with a rated bank or corporation and assisting the firm in preparing financial information for distribution to ratings agencies.

Education and Training

Most Ratings Agency Analysts have a four-year degree and have completed at least one year of graduate studies. Rating agency associates (an entry-level position) often have an M.B.A. degree or a graduate degree in economics, finance, or public policy.

Special Requirements

A Chartered Financial Analyst (CFA) designation, signifying professional competence in security analysis, is useful for advancement in the field, though is not a job requirement for starting Analysts.

Experience, Skills, and Personality Traits

Employers generally look for individuals with one to three years' experience in securities analysis, investment banking, or a combination of experience and a strong academic background. Ratings analysts must have strong written and verbal communication skills, excellent analytical skills. Some experience in financial modeling and financial databases is also helpful. Analysts need to be able to work effectively with other members of a research team. Ratings Analysts have to be good listeners and have good public speaking skills because they often publish their work and speak at industry conferences. A strong intellectual curiosity and an interest in research are good personality traits.

Unions and Associations

There are no professional associations for ratings analysts. Ratings analysts can participate in state chapter meetings of the Society for Securities Analysts, and frequently attend industry conferences as guest speakers.

Tips for Entry

1. College courses in finance, economics, and financial statement analysis are useful.
2. Read up on structured finance products in industry publications like Standard & Poor's *CreditWeek* to get familiar with current ratings agency trends.
3. Check newspaper classified ads and apply directly to firms.
4. Summer employment opportunities are another way to gain practical experience; contact rating agencies directly.
5. Informational interviews with Ratings analysts are an excellent way to learn more about the field; contact an agency and ask to speak to an analyst covering an industry of interest to you.

RISK ANALYST

CAREER PROFILE

Duties: Analyzes trading and investment portfolios for potential losses; evaluates risk controls under different interest rate and market scenarios; recommends risk mitigation strategies

Alternate Title(s): Risk Management Analyst

Salary Range: $50,000 to $100,000 and up

Employment Prospects: Good

Advancement Prospects: Excellent

Prerequisites:

　Education or Training—Four-year degree with courses in economics, finance, and statistics; postgraduate degree required for some positions

　Experience—Two to four years' experience in credit analysis or investment research

　Special Skills and Personality Traits—Excellent computational and problem-solving skills; excellent communication skills and computer skills; working knowledge of statistical models and methodologies used in risk analysis

　Special Requirements—CFA designation required for advancement in the field.

CAREER LADDER

```
┌─────────────────────────────────┐
│   Partner of Managing Director   │
└─────────────────────────────────┘

┌─────────────────────────────────┐
│          Risk Analyst            │
└─────────────────────────────────┘

┌─────────────────────────────────┐
│       Risk Analyst Trainee       │
└─────────────────────────────────┘
```

Position Description

In the world of Wall Street finance, risk is a double-edged sword. Many of the services Wall Street investment banks provide clients with are extensions of credit, in effect a loan. Risk Analysts weigh the probability of making a profit for the firm versus suffering a loss on a transaction. They evaluate credit risk to the firm under different interest rate and market scenarios and make recommendations to senior management and the firm's trading staff and investment bankers on strategies to minimize losses.

Wall Street credit is an extension of the securities business. When clients borrow money from a Wall Street firm, they are expected to repay the loan. Repayment terms depend on the transaction type, which can be anything from direct loans to foreign exchange purchases (or sales) and interest rate swaps. Investment banks measure risk in terms of exposure to a specific market sector—stocks, bonds, commercial paper,

foreign exchange, and so on. If the customer on the other side of a transaction cannot perform in the way they have agreed to, the investment bank has a risk it must deal with.

Risk Analysts work in an office setting, generally 40 to 50 hours a week, and have frequent contact with traders, investment bankers, and the compliance departments in their firms. Many positions in this field have job titles and duties that are unique to the position held. Included here are job titles such as derivatives risk analyst, market risk analyst, and portfolio risk analyst. In international banking, country Risk Analysts assign risk ratings for emerging market countries and advise senior management on credit risk strategy. This position may require periodic travel to the regions covered to visit key officials and local offices. Risk Analysts employed by credit ratings agencies evaluate credit risk of debt instruments, municipal and corporate debt, and commercial paper. They assign risk ratings indicating the issuer's ability to make debt service payments to bond holders.

Duties performed may include:

- developing and evaluating risk management methodologies
- assigning credit risk ratings for debt issuers
- providing financial reporting and risk analytics
- evaluating and testing pricing models

The Risk Analyst position is a relatively new, though highly visible, Wall Street career path. Risk analysts rose to positions of influence since 2000 as Wall Street firms sought ways to control the downside risks resulting from the explosion of new financial products coming to the markets, many created for specific customer needs.

Salaries

Salaries for Risk Analysts are comparable to other analyst positions in Wall Street firms. College graduates with no experience can earn $50,000 to $75,000 a year, depending on background and academic qualifications. After five years salaries can exceed $100,000. Analysts also receive an annual incentive bonus, which is determined from their job performance, their group's performance, and the profitability of the firm.

Salaries earned by Risk Analysts have been rising over the last several years in recognition of their contribution to investment bank profitability. Wall Street firms are starting to pay risk managers the same salaries as the investment bankers who generate new business and bring in clients for the firm.

Employment Prospects

There is good demand for Risk Analysts. Investment banks hire both recent college graduates for trainee positions and experienced analysts with specific skills. College graduates with no experience begin their analyst careers as analyst trainees. Experienced analysts with specific skills have a wide range of career opportunities in the field.

As in most Wall Street careers, employment prospects are related to job growth in the securities industry. However, investment firms continue to recruit Risk Analysts regardless of industry or financial market trends to replace analysts changing jobs or leaving the industry. When Wall Street is booming, there is strong demand for Risk Analysts. When Wall Street is retracting, people who manage risks of all sorts are very much in demand.

Advancement Prospects

Risk analysis is a highly specialized field. Advancement for new analysts is from analyst trainee to Risk Analyst after completion of a two-year training program. If they are hired

after two years they will specialize in analysis of certain types of financial instruments. Analyst trainees can also move into securities trading, working on the trading floor, or become an investment research analyst. Analysts could eventually move to management positions such as partner or managing director. Based on the level of expertise, there are many advancement opportunities.

Education and Training

A four-year college degree with courses in economics, finance, and statistics is required. Some more specialized positions may require an M.B.A. degree or a post-graduate degree in quantitative research. In general, the position requires strong mathematics and quantitative skills. One must have understanding of credit, knowing how to structure financial products and disassemble them into component parts and have some understanding of the risks involved in using them. Investment banking firms usually provide up to two years training in financial analysis for newly hired analysts with no industry experience. A working knowledge of scenario testing and evaluation methodology, usually gained from academic study, is important. Some analysts have advanced degrees, including Ph.d. degrees, but this is generally not a requirement for entry-level positions.

Special Requirements

A Chartered Financial Analyst (CFA) certification from the Association for Investment Management and Research is a near universal requirement for success as a Risk Analyst, and for advancement to more senior positions.

Experience, Skills, and Personality Traits

To be successful in this position, individuals have to be intellectually curious. This kind of work is a lot like doing puzzles. You have to like puzzles, taking things apart, and putting them back together. Good analytical skills, research skills, and written communication skills are important in the position, as is some working knowledge of the financial markets.

Unions and Associations

Risk Analysts may become members of the Capital Markets Credit Analysts Society and the Association for Investment Management and Research for networking and career advancement.

Tips for Entry

1. While in college, focus your studies on mathematics, accounting, and English, and take classes in financial statement analysis.

2. Internships are very helpful in building initial contacts, as well as learning about the work performed and business jargon.
3. Attend industry association meetings to learn about hiring trends and expand your list of employer contacts.
4. Join an investment club in college or manage your own stock portfolio to learn something about risk.
5. Read the *Wall Street Journal* and other financial papers to keep up with industry developments.
6. Check financial Web sites specializing in risk management or financial derivatives, such as Erisk (http://www.erisk.com) or Numa Web (http://www.numa.com) to explore employment opportunities.

SUPERVISORY ANALYST

CAREER PROFILE

Duties: Reviews and approves financial analyst research reports and other documents distributed to the public; examines analyst reports for compliance with firm and industry standards

Alternative Title(s): None

Salary Range: $100,000 to $150,000

Employment Prospects: Excellent

Advancement Prospects: Good

Prerequisites:

Education or Training—Four-year degree with emphasis in business and finance; financial journalism courses helpful

Experience—Securities industry experience and at least one year related background

Special Skills and Personality Traits—Excellent interpersonal skills and analytical skills; ability to work under tight deadlines; word processing and spreadsheet skills

Special Requirements—Must be sponsored by employer; must pass the New York Stock Exchange Series 16 exam; Chartered Financial Analyst (CFA) certification may be required for advancement

CAREER LADDER

```
┌─────────────────────────────────┐
│   Manager, Research Department   │
└─────────────────────────────────┘

┌─────────────────────────────────┐
│       Supervisory Analyst        │
└─────────────────────────────────┘

┌─────────────────────────────────┐
│         Financial Analyst        │
└─────────────────────────────────┘
```

Position Description

When investment banks recommend a company's stock to investors, they have to be certain that information presented in analyst research reports is accurate and complies with company guidelines and securities industry standards. That's the job of the Supervisory Analyst. The Supervisory Analyst reviews research reports prepared by securities analysts, such as stock purchase recommendations or industry reports. Securities research reports must be reviewed by the legal department and by a Supervisory Analyst before being released to the public. The legal department examines research reports for compliance with federal and state securities laws regarding disclosure of information. They will also look for potential conflicts of interest if the firm is already doing business with a company mentioned in an analyst's report.

The Supervisory Analyst looks at a research report to see whether there is any potentially misleading information such as promissory language about future stock per-

formance. They want to make sure that the analyst writing the report has been careful to make clear the information presented is his or her opinion about the companies discussed in the report. Supervisory Analysts do a lot of hedging and softening up of research reports to avoid making unwarranted claims or sweeping generalizations about a company or industry. Supervisory Analysts are also arbiters of good taste. They try to make certain that research reports have a tone and content consistent with securities industry guidelines, and contain appropriate language when discussing companies, keeping in mind that the average reader is entitled to a balanced report about the company, its current financial condition, and its prospects for future growth.

The Supervisory Analyst's job is a demanding one. Most analysts work 40- to 50-hour weeks, and some analysts work evenings and weekends. With the recent growth of the securities markets, the securities industry has become a 24-hour seven days a week business.

U.S.-based investment banks also review research reports for their overseas branches. Starting SAs may begin their employment on the night shift, approving analyst reports issued from branches in Hong Kong and Tokyo.

Salaries

Compensation packages for Supervisory Analysts are competitive with Wall Street salaries earned by securities analysts. Supervisory Analysts can earn base salaries ranging from $100,000 to $150,000, plus an annual bonus of 60 percent to 100 percent of base salary.

Employment Prospects

There is a worldwide shortage of Supervisory Analysts. The Supervisory Analyst position was almost unknown as recently as the mid-1990s. The growing volume of new securities issued in the worldwide securities markets, particularly in the developing countries in Asia, has spurred demand for Supervisory Analysts. As the rest of the world begins to conform to U.S. standards for securities registration (enabling companies to sell securities directly to U.S. investors), the issuing companies come under the jurisdiction of the New York Stock Exchange. Research reports on these companies must be reviewed by a Supervisory Analyst.

Most Supervisory Analysts enter the field after several years experience as securities analysts. In addition, there are fair to good entry prospects for financial journalists with experience editing investment research, qualifying them as candidates for a supervisory analyst position.

Advancement Prospects

A Supervisory Analyst can advance to a more senior position, such as associate director of equity research or research director for a brokerage firm or investment bank. Supervisory Analysts who want to shape the way research is done in their firm and presented to the world can advance to managerial positions and manage a group of research analysts plus support staff.

Education and Training

A four-year degree with courses in business, economics, or finance is generally recommended, although it is not a requirement. Some Supervisory Analysts have more varied academic backgrounds, such as a degree in journalism, and

receive training comparable to the training provided starting investment research analysts.

Special Requirements

Individuals seeking to become Supervisory Analysts are sponsored by their firm for the Series 16 Exam given by the New York Stock Exchange. A passing grade on the Series 16 Exam is a general requirement to become a Supervisory Analyst. Financial analysts who have the Chartered Financial Analyst (CFA) certification have completed the equivalent of the financial part of the Series 16 Exam, and need only take the regulatory part of the NYSE exam.

Experience, Skills, and Personality Traits

Supervisory Analysts should have excellent interpersonal and analytical skills, plus good computer literacy with spreadsheet programs and financial analytics. Because their duties focus on editing financial reports, excellent written communication skills are also very important.

Unions and Associations

Supervisory Analysts may become members of the CFA Institute. They may also become members of state societies of securities analysts affiliated with CFA Institute for networking and professional advancement opportunities.

Tips for Entry

1. Networking is the key to getting an interview. The Supervisory Analyst position is still relatively unknown outside the securities industry. Try contacting a major Wall Street firm, ask to talk to a Supervisory Analyst, and ask about the nature of the work and current employment opportunities.
2. Some executive search firms specialize in placing Supervisory Analysts; check the classified ads in major financial newspapers.
3. Spend some time as a junior analyst in a Wall Street firm and learn the business from the security analysts' side of the business.
4. Financial journalists with experience editing investment research may also qualify for Supervisory Analyst positions; if their sponsoring employer can make a persuasive argument to the New York Stock Exchange.

COMPLIANCE EXAMINER, BROKERAGE

CAREER PROFILE

Duties: Ensures that brokerage employees adhere to industry policies and regulations; supervises proprietary and customer trading to ensure compliance with securities industry regulations and company policy or guidelines on trading activities; also coordinates supervision with licensing authorities.

Alternate Title(s): Compliance Analyst; Compliance Officer

Salary Range: $36,000 to $47,500

Employment Prospects: Good

Advancement Prospects: Good

Prerequisites:

Education or Training—Bachelor's degree with courses in finance or a related field.

Experience—Two to three years' securities industry experience

Special Skills and Personality Traits—Excellent oral and written communication skills, analytical skills, and knowledge of financial markets

Special Requirements—Pass securities industry licenses and state licensing exams

CAREER LADDER

```
┌─────────────────────────────────┐
│     Director of Compliance      │
└─────────────────────────────────┘

┌─────────────────────────────────┐
│      Compliance Examiner        │
└─────────────────────────────────┘

┌─────────────────────────────────┐
│   Junior Compliance Examiner    │
└─────────────────────────────────┘
```

Position Description

Compliance Examiners are the watchdogs in the brokerage industry. They monitor securities trading activities by the brokerage firm itself (proprietary trading) and customer trading. Compliance review is a self-management process involving a combination of branch office audits, home office surveillance of trading activity, and counseling or training of brokers and account officers.

Examiners typically work unsupervised and they may work independently or as part of an audit team. Their primary duty is determining whether trading activity is in compliance with rules and regulations of the Securities and Exchange Commission, the National Association of Securities Dealers, state regulators, and the firm itself. Compliance Examiners review market activity for potential compliance and legal violations such as suspicious trading patterns (market manipulation and insider trading), and they monitor unusual security movements and trading at retail branch offices, such as unusually high

trading in low-priced or speculative stocks. They also respond to inquiries from federal and state regulatory authorities.

Their duties include:

- reviewing employee sales or purchases of securities for possible violations of insider trading prohibitions
- reviewing questionable credit reports and obtaining documentation necessary to investigate customer accounts for potential irregularities
- reviewing customer statements for evidence of churning, or excessive trading by a broker or financial adviser
- reviewing legal documents such as court orders, powers of attorney, and trusts
- answering head office inquiries and queries from brokerage branch offices regarding compliance rules and company policy
- answering questions from branch supervision managers regarding account restrictions and trade approvals

- coordinating compliance audits and policies with other departments

Senior-level Compliance Examiners have additional responsibilities, such as offering guidance on adherence to state "blue sky" securities registration laws and licensing issues, and analyzing the impact of new laws and regulations on policies, operating systems, and reporting procedures. They study new federal and state laws and regulations to determine whether advertising and promotional materials meet the disclosure and customer protection standards set by regulatory agencies. They may determine actions necessary to get regulatory approval to sell securities products and services, such as mutual funds.

Compliance Examiners work in an office setting, usually working 40 hours a week. They spend much of their time visiting branch offices, frequently up to 50 percent of their working time. This can be a good career choice if you are analytical, have good attention to detail, and have good problem-solving abilities.

Salaries

Salaries are determined by several factors, including years of experience, geographic location, and size of financial institution. Compliance managers working as full-time Compliance officers in a larger firm, or those who manage a compliance and audit department are paid higher compensation than compliance managers in smaller firms. Junior Compliance Examiners employed by firms outside New York City earned salaries ranging from $36,000 to $47,500 in 2000, according to the Securities Industry Association. Salaries in New York City may be higher. Senior-level Compliance Examiners can earn up to $75,000 or more.

Employment Prospects

Currently, chances of finding work in this occupation are good, since employment opportunities and earnings are both well above average. Job prospects in the brokerage industry are closely related to growth in the overall economy and the growth of financial assets managed by brokerage firms. Over the next five years the number of job openings is expected to be matched by the number of qualified managers or recent college graduates. Some applicants may move into this position via promotion from other compliance or audit positions.

Advancement Prospects

Advancement could be to a more senior audit and compliance position, such as managing a team of compliance officers. Another option would be moving into a compliance position with responsibility for disciplinary action for possible violations of securities regulations and company policies. Some Compliance Examiners with experience in disciplinary action could become enforcement/investigative officers with the National Association of Securities Dealers.

Education and Training

A four-year college degree with courses in accounting, economics, and finance is a minimum requirement. An advanced degree such as an M.B.A. or law degree is often required for advancement to more senior positions. Brokerage firms provide their own in-house training programs to maintain product knowledge and stay current with new industry regulations.

Special Requirements

Applicants are generally required to have passed the exams for at least two or three securities licenses, including the Series 7 General Brokerage License and the Series 63 Uniform Securities State Law Examination administered by the National Association of Securities Dealers. If the Compliance Examiner has responsibility for oversight of insurance sales, a state insurance license would also be a requirement.

Experience, Skills, and Personality Traits

Two to three years' experience in financial services is a requirement for Compliance Examiners. Also desirable is some previous experience, usually two to three years, in the securities industry. The successful candidate will have strong research and computer skills, excellent communication, organizational, and problem-solving skills. The Compliance Examiner's job requires a detail-oriented individual, who can work under deadline pressure.

Unions and Associations

Securities industry Compliance Examiners can become members of the Securities Industry Association, through sponsorship of their employer, for networking and career advancement opportunities.

Tips for Entry

1. Employment opportunities may be greater at regional brokerage firms specializing in retail customers and commercial banks entering the brokerage business for the first time than bigger, more established brokerage firms.
2. Get a solid background in securities law and finance through college courses in these subjects.
3. Take study courses in preparation for brokerage industry exams required for the position.

MONEY MANAGEMENT

CREDIT COUNSELOR

CAREER PROFILE

Duties: Counsels consumers with debt problems; arranges debt repayment

Alternate Title(s): Consumer Credit Counselor, Debt Counselor

Salary Range: $20,000 to $35,000

Employment Prospects: Excellent

Advancement Prospects: Good

Prerequisites:

Education or Training—Associate's degree

Experience—One to two years' customer service experience preferred

Special Skills and Personality Traits—Excellent communication skills; good computer skills; good math and organizational skills

Special Requirements—Insurance bonding required

CAREER LADDER

Group Manager

Credit Counselor

Credit Counselor Trainee

Position Description

Financial problems can happen to anyone, regardless of income. Credit Counselors help people who have problems paying their bills make repayment arrangements with creditors, while avoiding personal bankruptcy. Credit Counseling services provide assistance on several levels: advising consumers seeking financial relief on their available options, setting up debt repayment plans with creditors, and providing financial education to help clients manage their finances and stay out of debt.

Consumer Credit counseling owes its growth to the widespread availability of easy credit in the 1980s and '90s and the associated dramatic increase in credit delinquencies and consumer bankruptcies. During the 1990s consumer bankruptcy petitions nearly doubled, reaching about 1.3 million bankruptcy petitions filed in 2000. Credit counseling agencies assist consumers in finding solutions to their financial situation regardless of the cause—too much debt, the sudden loss of a job, unexpected expenses, or a combination. About 500 consumer credit counseling agencies currently operate in the United States; each state has one or more of these counseling services. Some of the largest counseling

organizations have multi-branch networks and operate in several states.

Credit Counselors work in an office setting, fielding inbound telephone calls from consumers seeking financial relief. Some callers are referred to an agency by their bank or another creditor. Counselors listen to the caller, attempt to offer a solution, or refer the caller to another agency or to an attorney.

If the caller is employed or has income from other sources, the counselor will suggest setting up a debt management plan. (Enrollment is free to the consumer. Credit counseling agencies are funded by the credit industry.) The counselor arranges a follow-up appointment, either an in-person office visit or a telephone consultation, to set up a repayment plan. If there is no reasonable possibility of repayment the counselor will suggest that the caller consider filing a bankruptcy petition in federal bankruptcy court. When a debt repayment plan is established, the counseling agency assumes responsibility for paying their clients' monthly bills and makes payments to creditors from a trustee account. Funds equal to the outstanding bills are deducted from the client's checking account.

The Credit Counselor will negotiate with creditors for extended repayment of current bills and petition creditors for interest rate relief, a reduction in the interest rate, on outstanding bills. Credit Counselors maintain telephone contact with their clients periodically, usually once a month, through the debt repayment period. Consumers entering a debt repayment plan usually can expect to repay their bills in full and become debt free over a 4½ to five-year period. The actual debt management period is, however, determined by the total debt outstanding and number of creditors.

Consumer Credit Counselors also:

- send creditors a monthly statement of bills paid on behalf of a client
- assist clients in correcting errors in credit reports
- provide other credit-related counseling and financial education as needed

Credit Counselors usually work a 40-hour week. Counselors perform much of their work by telephone, and have little face-to-face contact with clients. They handle a caseload of about 50 to 60 new clients a month, or about 600 clients over the course of a year. This can be a good career choice if you have good interpersonal skills and like helping people achieve their financial goals.

Salaries

Credit Counselors earn salaries from $20,000 to $35,000 a year. Credit counseling agencies are nonprofit organizations, so the opportunities to earn higher salaries are limited. Credit Counselors employed in most agencies receive paid medical insurance, health insurance, and vacation time in addition to salary.

Employment Prospects

For the qualified individual, someone who has a genuine interest in helping others and meets the education qualifications, employment opportunities are rated excellent. Credit counseling has grown as an industry over the last 20 years, increasing the total number of available positions. Job vacancies may also be created when credit counseling agencies open additional branch offices or current employees leave for other occupations. Demand for Credit Counselors is sensitive to changes in the economy. An increase in unemployment filings by debt-laden consumers seeking to regain financial stability would provide additional stimulus for hiring Credit Counselors.

Amendments to the federal bankruptcy code that became effective in 2005 require financial counseling and education for all individuals before they file a Chapter 7 or Chapter 13 bankruptcy petition from a nonprofit credit counseling agency. Pre-filing counseling sessions, required six months prior to filing, are meant to help consumers understand the potential advantages and disadvantages of filing a bankruptcy petition for discharge of debts before they do so. Individual debtors must also complete a course on personal financial management before their debts are discharged by a bankruptcy court.

Advancement Prospects

Most agencies prefer to promote from within the agency. Individuals who show leadership potential are easily promoted after a few years experience. They can advance to become a queue leader or group leader, managing the workflow for a group of Credit Counselors and assuming responsibility for their performance. Eventually, they could become an assistant office manager or office manager.

Education and Training

Most credit counseling agencies prefer individuals who have at least an associate's degree. New employees receive thorough training in office procedures and office skills, such as telephone skills and filing paperwork.

Special Requirements

Consumer Credit Counselors must obtain a surety bond from an insurance bonding firm. A surety bond, similar to insurance, provides protection against liability claims relating to performance of their duties. The National Foundation for Consumer Credit offers a counselor certification program, the Certified Consumer Credit Counselor.

Experience, Skills, and Personality Traits

Prior experience in credit counseling is not required because counseling is a trainable field. Counselors need to have excellent communication skills and listening ability, and take an empathetic view toward their clients. They should have basic math skills and be computer literate to the extent they can read a screen and follow instructions. Prior experience in customer service, whether face-to-face or by telephone, is helpful. Personal experience is also very helpful. Some of the best Credit Counselors are people who have themselves gone through credit counseling at some point in their lives.

Unions and Associations

There are no professional associations that represent consumer Credit Counselors. The National Foundation for Consumer Credit and the Association of Independent Consumer Credit Counseling Agencies set voluntary guidelines for professional conduct. Consumer counseling agency owners can affiliate with these organizations for professional guidance and member support.

Tips for Entry

1. Get a good background in math and communication courses while attending high school or college.
2. Check newspaper advertisements for position openings and apply directly to a credit counseling agency in your area.
3. College placement offices and state employment agencies are other good sources of job leads.
4. Some consumer credit counseling agencies sponsor internship programs for individuals interested in getting practical experience and learning about career opportunities in credit counseling.

FINANCIAL PLANNER

CAREER PROFILE

Duties: Designs and implements investment plans according to client needs, using their knowledge of tax and investment strategies and investment products. Meets regularly with clients to review financial performance

Alternate Title(s): Financial Adviser, Wealth Adviser

Salary Range: $30,000 to $60,000 and up

Employment Prospects: Good

Advancement Prospects: Good

Prerequisites:

Education or Training—Four-year college degree with courses in accounting, finance, law, or general business; industry certification helpful

Experience—Several years in financial services industry, preferably in marketing or sales; college graduates with strong interpersonal skills also accepted

Special Skills and Personality Traits—Problem solving and analysis; ability to understand complex financial concepts; strong interpersonal skills and communication skills; general understanding of financial products and how business works

Special Requirements—Pass state licensing examinations to sell financial products

CAREER LADDER

```
┌─────────────────────────────┐
│ Regional Manager/Field Leader │
└─────────────────────────────┘

┌─────────────────────────────┐
│      Senior Adviser          │
└─────────────────────────────┘

┌─────────────────────────────┐
│   Financial Planner/Adviser  │
└─────────────────────────────┘
```

Position Description

Financial Planners assist individuals, families, and businesses in formulating strategies to help them meet their short-term and long-term financial goals. Financial Planners use their knowledge of tax laws and investments, securities, and insurance to develop and implement financial plans. The ability to work well with numbers and people is a characteristic of a successful Financial Planner.

Planners will work with clients to devise the best mix of financial assets (stocks, bonds, and other investments), a process known as asset allocation, meeting the client's objective. Financial Planners meet with clients to understand their needs, identify financial goals, and make recommendations for reaching those goals through implementation of a financial plan. After gathering data from the client, and identifying problems or obstacles, a written plan recom-

mending specific actions is presented to the client. The planner normally meets with clients one to four times a year, depending on the complexity of the relationship, to review plan performance and revise the plan as needed. Planners may work with as many as 200 to 300 clients. Client meetings take about five hours of preparation time and about 1½ hours to review plan performance and financial goals.

Financial planning may include the following:

- goal assessment
- investment strategy and asset allocation
- saving for college
- retirement planning
- tax planning
- insurance planning
- charitable gift and estate planning

There are an estimated 300,000 Financial Planners working in the United States today. Most planners are independent practitioners, working in one-to-two person practices, although a growing number work in major financial services firms. Financial Planners cite the highly competitive nature of the business and the need to generate new business from client referrals, as potential deterrents to setting up a solo practice.

Over the last 10 years, financial planning has evolved into full-fledged asset management business. Planning firms today give their clients financial advice on how to meet their financial goals, but they manage client investments as well. Many clients come to a Financial Planner initially seeking investment management and then to have a financial plan written for some specific future goal, such as paying college expenses or planning their retirement. The Financial Planner is paid a percentage of the assets under management (typically ranging from 1.0 percent to 1.5 percent) as compensation for selecting the best mix of investments (stocks, bonds, and cash), distributing assets to various money managers (usually no-load mutual funds), and rebalancing the portfolio periodically to the client's original objective. Additional services such as an annual financial review can be charged at an hourly rate or a flat fee.

Financial Planners come from a variety of backgrounds: attorneys, accountants, and other professionals, and securities industry financial sales. The job requires self-discipline, an entrepreneurial orientation and a desire to actively market to locate prospective clients.

Salaries

Financial Planner salaries depend on the planner's position in the firm and the firm structure. Earnings may vary dramatically depending on whether the planner is employed by an independent financial planning firm, a solo practitioner, or a junior member in a larger firm. Starting salaries are usually in the $30,000 to $50,000 range, depending on the area of the country and the planner's previous experience. A planner who brings in a roster of clients when initially hired can earn a substantially higher starting salary, $50,000 or more, which reflects his or her contribution to firm revenues. An experienced independent Financial Planner can earn about $100,000 per year in total earnings after five to 10 years.

Employment Prospects

Financial planning is one of the fastest growing jobs in financial services. The entry of the baby boomer generation into middle age and the explosion of investment choices contribute to demand for Financial Planners. According to industry estimates, about 60 million Americans will need some type of financial planning services by 2020, about five times the 15 million currently serviced by planners.

Advancement Prospects

Financial Planners advance by managing more clients. Planners employed by a brokerage or securities firm who have strong interpersonal skills may be selected for a management training program after 12 to 18 months on the job. Financial Planners advance to more senior, better-paying positions by managing more clients and by gaining experience as Financial Planners. While many firms have their own career ladder, the usual progression is from entry-level associate to associate adviser (or wealth adviser) to senior adviser. In a progressive firm, one that is increasing its account relationships, a planner can advance to become a team leader, managing a group of Financial Planers, and eventually become a minority partner in the firm, a process that may take nine to 12 years. Planners are expected to acquire all the licenses and certifications or senior adviser, managing a group of Financial Planners. Having a Certified Financial Planner designation (awarded by the Certified Financial Planner Board of Standards, Inc., Denver) is generally a requirement to moving up to more senior positions.

Education and Training

Financial Planners normally have a four-year college degree in business, accounting, finance, or related courses. Some colleges offer degree programs with an emphasis in financial planning. College-level courses in financial planning usually cover investments, taxes, financial planning, estate planning, general accounting, and computer science for business. Most securities firms employing Financial Planners have extensive on-the-job training programs for beginners. After joining a firm, the beginning planner studies for licensing exams and learns the requirements of the job. Many firms look for individuals who are in the process of acquiring their investment advisers licenses (Series 65 or Series 66) or who expect to have their licenses within a year of joining a financial planning firm.

Special Requirements

Licensing requirements to become a Financial Planner include the following: Series 7 General Brokerage license, Series 65 Investment Adviser license, and state license to sell life accident, health, disability insurance, long-term coverage, and variable annuity products.

Industry certifications include: Chartered Financial Consultant (ChFC), issued by the American College in Bryn Mawr, Pennsylvania, and Certified Financial Planner (CFP) Certification. The latter requires completing a comprehensive course of study at a college or university offering a financial planning curriculum, and passing a comprehensive examination. Both certification programs have a continuing education component.

Experience, Skills, and Personality Traits

Beginning planners usually have three to five years' experience in financial services. Successful planners have had previous experience with long-term investment planning, insurance planning, estate planning, and retirement planning. Planners should have a strong work ethic, excellent communication skills, and a willingness to help people meet their financial goals.

Unions and Associations

Financial Planners can belong to professional associations, such as the Financial Planning Association or the Registered Financial Planners Institute, and join special interest groups devoted to industry issues. Some of these associations have state chapters.

Tips for Entry

1. Get a solid background in investment fundamentals in college courses and understand general business and economic trends.

2. Participate in extracurricular activities while attending college; this tells an employer you are a "people person" and interested in helping others.

3. Many financial planning firms look to hire individuals who attended a college or university that also sponsors a Certified Financial Planner (CFP) program. While attending one of these colleges, you can also do your academic pre-work for the two-day CFP exam. Some colleges, also offer four-year degree programs in financial planning.

4. While in college, look for internship opportunities to gain on-the-job experience and get to know industry professionals who can help advance your career.

5. Check the Financial Planning Association's online job board (www.fpanet.org) for a list of current job openings.

6. Attend local chapter meetings of a financial planning organization to learn more about industry practices and job opportunities.

RETIREMENT PLANNING SPECIALIST

<table>
<tr><td>

CAREER PROFILE

Duties: Develops marketing strategies for retirement account plans; oversees training of customer service representatives; reports to investment products director

Alternate Title(s): IRA Specialist, Requirement Adviser

Salary Range: $47,000 to $82,000

Employment Prospects: Good

Advancement Prospects: Fair

Prerequisites:

Education or Training—Four-year degree in business, finance, or related field

Experience—Three to five years' experience in banking or financial services

Special Skills and Personality Traits—Excellent verbal and written communication skills; excellent organizational and managerial skills. Must be self-starter and have sales aptitude; thorough knowledge of employer- sponsored benefit plans, including 401(k) plans and KEOGH plans; an understanding of the sales process

Special Requirements—Some states require licenses

</td><td>

CAREER LADDER

```
┌─────────────────────────────────────────┐
│   Director, Corporate Retirement Plans    │
└─────────────────────────────────────────┘

┌─────────────────────────────────────────┐
│      Retirement Planning Specialist       │
└─────────────────────────────────────────┘

┌─────────────────────────────────────────┐
│          IRA Accounts Officer             │
└─────────────────────────────────────────┘
```

</td></tr>
</table>

Position Description

Retirement Planning Specialists help employers establish and manage retirement plans for employees. They are employed by insurance companies, financial institutions such as banks, and pension consulting firms. Much of their work involves setting up and helping employers administer tax-qualified defined contribution plans, which enable employees to contribute funds on a pre-tax basis toward retirement savings.

Employee contributions are pooled together and invested in mutual funds or other qualifying investments. Corporate employees make contributions to 401(k) plans; teachers and hospital employees have 403(b) plans; public employees have 457 plans. (The names refer to different sections of the U.S. tax code.) Plan participants decide how to invest their retirement savings and bear the risk of any investments.

Retirement Planning Specialists have both administrative and employee education duties. When they perform administrative functions, they are responsible for the sale and service of retirement plans offered by insurance companies and other financial institutions.

Retirement Planning Specialists review current retirement plans and make appropriate recommendations. They may also provide sales support for telemarketing calls to brokers. They create new files for new customers. They assist in designing and developing marketing plans for retirement and other tax-deferred savings plans. They conduct research on retirement plans offered by competitors. They report on related industry products, pricing, and product features. They assist in the development of departmental goals, budgets, and writing marketing plans. Financial education duties include informing and educating employees about their investment options. They interpret and explain retirement savings plans to current and potential clients.

Retirement Planning Specialists usually work a 40-hour week, but may work longer hours during an enrollment period, when nonparticipating employees are eligible to sign up and become participants in a company-sponsored retirement plan.

Salaries

Salaries of Retirement Planning Specialists vary by qualifications and experience. Salaries in 2004 ranged between $47,000 and $82,000, according to the Bureau of Labor Statistics. People working in financial institutions such as banks earned from $27,288 to $46,500, according to America's Community Bankers, a banking association.

Employment Prospects

Employment opportunities for Retirement Planning Specialists should grow about as fast as all other occupations through 2014, according to the U.S. Department of Labor. Employment opportunities depend on such things as future growth in the total number of corporate retirement plans and increased rates of employee participation. Retirement planning is a very competitive field, and much of the growth in company participation has already occurred, except in the very smallest companies.

Advancement Prospects

Retirement Planning Specialists could advance to positions of increased responsibility, such as retirement planning manager or director of corporate retirement plans. Some advancement opportunities may come about as current employees change jobs or reach retirement age.

Education and Training

A four-year college degree with an emphasis in business administration, finance, or a related field is required. Courses in marketing, financial planning, or similar courses are helpful.

Special Requirements

State licenses may be required in some states.

Available certifications include the Certified Funds Specialist from the Institute for Business and Finance and the Certified Retirement Counselor from the International Foundation for Retirement Education and the Certified IRA Services Professional from the American Bankers Association.

Experience, Skills, and Personality Traits

This is a marketing position, so individuals should have excellent oral and written communication skills and strong organizational skills. Presenting program details at employee meetings is an important part of the job, so good public speaking skills are helpful. Some experience in financial services marketing is usually required, normally three to five years. A sales aptitude is a useful personality trait. Extensive knowledge of retirement services products, state regulations, and federal regulations is required. Knowledge of tax issues and portfolio design and financial planning is helpful.

Unions and Associations

Refinement Planning Specialists can become members of several professional associations for career advancement and networking, including the American Bankers Association, the National Association of Insurance and Financial Advisers, and the Institute for Business and Finance.

Tips for Entry

1. College courses in business, economics, and financial planning are a useful academic background for a career in this field.
2. Check Internet sites such as http://www.jobsinthe money.com for industry news and job leads.

MUTUAL FUND WHOLESALER

CAREER PROFILE

Duties: Promotes the sale of mutual funds and annuities

Alternate Title(s): Regional Wholesaler

Salary Range: $65,000 to $98,000 and up

Employment Prospects: Good

Advancement Prospects: Fair

Prerequisites:

    Education or Training—Four-year degree or equivalent work experience

    Experience—One to three years' experience in securities or mutual fund sales; fingerprinting and background check may be conducted

    Special Skills and Personality Traits—Excellent presentation skills and public speaking skills; knowledge of investment products

    Special Requirements—Obtain securities licenses

CAREER LADDER

```
┌─────────────────────────────────┐
│   Manager, Wholesale Marketing  │
└─────────────────────────────────┘

┌─────────────────────────────────┐
│     Mutual Fund Wholesaler      │
└─────────────────────────────────┘

┌─────────────────────────────────┐
│      Associate Wholesaler       │
└─────────────────────────────────┘
```

Position Description

With more than 8,500 stock and bond mutual funds competing for investors' attention, Mutual Fund Wholesalers are an important link between mutual fund companies and retail investors. Fund companies employ wholesalers to distribute funds bearing their name to brokerage firms, banks, and financial advisers who sell or recommend funds to investors.

There are two basic types of Mutual Fund Wholesalers: internal wholesalers and external wholesalers. Internal wholesalers work with the fund company's national sales manager and regional wholesalers to create a sales strategy for specific regions of the United States. They utilize their knowledge of mutual fund products to develop sales ideas and telemarketing campaigns to develop new relationships and increase sales. External wholesalers make sales calls on corporations and investment advisory firms to promote awareness and increase fund sales to mutual fund investors and company-sponsored retirement plans.

Some mutual fund companies have teams of internal wholesalers who work closely with regional wholesalers. The internal wholesalers make telephone calls, assist in developing marketing strategy, and perform back office support, giving the firm's regional wholesalers more time to spend courting the big name customers.

Internal Wholesalers perform a number of important functions:

- assisting in the development of sales and marketing strategies
- serving as a liaison to brokers who sell the distributor's funds and fund investors
- responding to telephone inquiries on portfolio management and fund performance
- identifying client needs and coordinating efforts to meet those needs
- conducting sales training seminars
- developing annual sales plan and budgets
- making sales presentations at company-sponsored seminars and special events

Internal Mutual Fund Wholesalers work in an office setting, working 35 to 40 hours a week. Their job is divided between telephone calling and in-person sales calls. Regional wholesalers have a sales territory and travel up 50 percent to 60 percent of their working time.

While growth in mutual funds under management is the goal of wholesalers in the money management industry and the primary driver of wholesaler compensation, many firms consider asset retention and profitability to be equally important. Toward that goal, a "hybrid" model for the wholesaler position is becoming more common. The hybrid model combines internal and external sales activities with sales activities directed from the fund distributor's home office.

Salaries

The salaries of Mutual Fund Wholesalers vary greatly depending on how their compensation is structured. Wholesalers can receive a base salary plus commissions earned on sales, a salary plus an annual performance bonus, or they can receive a draw (an advance against future commissions) rather than a salary. Newly hired Wholesalers may receive a guaranteed salary for the first year of employment followed by a draw against commissions in subsequent years.

Wholesalers employed by the larger companies, those with managed assets of $100 billion or more, receive the highest average incomes. Annual earnings of wholesalers employed by the big mutual fund groups are typically one-third higher than earnings of wholesalers working for fund companies with assets under $10 billion.

External wholesalers are the most highly compensated members of the sales team. Base compensation for external wholesalers varied from $65,000 to $98,000, according to a 2005 survey. Base salary for hybrid wholesalers, who have both internal and external sales functions, was between $54,000 and $65,000. Incentive compensation determined by the amount of gross sales generated added $100,000 to $125,000 for external wholesalers and $80,000 to $100,000 for hybrid wholesalers. Top-performing external wholesalers can earn up to $500,000 or more annually in total compensation—base salary plus incentive compensation.

Employment Prospects

Mutual fund distributors employ several or more Mutual Fund Wholesalers to represent their funds to brokerage firms, banks, and investment advisers. The bigger fund companies have the widest array of funds and dominate the managed fund industry in total assets under management. These companies have the largest number of wholesalers and the largest distribution networks, but competition for choice positions with the top fund groups can be intense. This is not an entry-level position.

Advancement Prospects

An internal Mutual Fund Wholesaler can advance to external wholesaler and become responsible for developing relationships with the broker-dealer community and developing new sales opportunities. Internal wholesalers can become external wholesalers after a few years experience. Some wholesalers choose to remain as wholesalers because they can earn high salaries without taking on management responsibilities.

Education and Training

Most applicants for Mutual Fund Wholesaler jobs have four-year college degrees. A college degree with courses in business, marketing, and the liberal arts gives useful academic preparation, though a degree is not required for the position. Employers often give equal weighting to individual talent and sales or marketing experience. Periodic on-the-job training is offered to maintain product knowledge and stay current with industry practices.

Special Requirements

As distributors of publicly offered investment products, Mutual Fund Wholesalers must be registered with the National Association of Securities Dealers and obtain state securities licenses. A minimum requirement is a passing score on the Series 6 Mutual Fund and Variable Annuity Exam and the Series 7 General Securities Registered Representative Exam. Both exams are administered by the National Association of Securities Dealers. Wholesalers must also be licensed by state securities regulators in each state where they do business. Fingerprinting and background checks may also be required.

Experience, Skills, and Personality Traits

Experience in a sales or marketing position, usually one to three years, is usually required. Some employers have a preference for hiring individuals who have worked as financial advisers or stockbrokers. Mutual Fund Wholesalers spend much of their time making presentations to customer groups or potential customers and making telephone sales pitches. Excellent presentation and public speaking skills, and strong organizational skills are important. Mutual Fund Wholesalers should also be familiar with investment performance of stock and bond mutual funds they represent, and other pertinent details such as the fund manager's investment style.

Unions and Associations

Mutual Fund Wholesalers can participate in activities of professional associations, including the Investment Company

Institute and the Securities Industry Association for career advancement and networking opportunities.

Tips for Entry

1. Take study courses in preparation for the Series 6 mutual fund and annuity sales, Series 7 general securities representative, and state securities licensing exams. Several independent training organizations offer both classroom and correspondence courses for these exams.

2. Prior experience as a financial adviser or stockbroker can provide useful background and insights into the distribution channels for mutual funds and annuities.

3. Presentation skills are important in this position. Consider taking a Dale Carnegie course or join a Toastmasters club to polish public speaking skills.

INVESTMENT CONSULTANT

CAREER PROFILE

Duties: Provides investment advisory services for institutional investors and high-net-worth individuals

Alternate Title(s): Asset Management Consultant

Salary Range: $50,000 to $150,000 and up

Employment Prospects: Good

Advancement Prospects: Excellent

Prerequisites:

Education or Training—Four-year degree with courses in finance and accounting; M.B.A. degree preferred

Experience—At least three years' experience with increasing responsibility

Special Skills and Personality Traits—Strong analytical skills and research skills, strong understanding of investment theory and current industry practices; in-depth knowledge of financial markets

Special Requirements—Chartered Financial Analyst (CFA) certification; investment adviser license (Series 63)

CAREER LADDER

```
Managing Director, Investment
Consulting

Investment Consultant

Associate or Analyst
```

Position Description

Investment Consultants help their clients navigate the complex world of investing. Proliferating investment choices and the stunning growth of financial assets in the last decade have created a bull market for investment advisers. The primary job of an Investment Consultant is building strong relationships with clients and investment portfolio managers and advising clients on investment strategy.

Investment Consultants work with pension funds, endowments, foundations, other institutional investors, and high net worth individuals in designing and implementing investment plans. They advise clients to write appropriate investment policy guidelines, including permissible investments, selecting the appropriate mix of investments meeting their needs, tolerance for risk, and investment guidelines. They select investment managers meeting the client's guidelines. They monitor the results of investment performance, and report on investment performance every quarter and meet with clients at least once a year to review investment strategy and make adjustments as required (such as portfolio rebalancing to the original allocation).

The most significant reporting responsibility of an Investment Consultant is preparation of quarterly executive summaries of investment performance and a comprehensive annual report. A typical quarterly report discusses significant contributors to investment performance. The report discloses major purchases and sales of securities during the reporting period and it compares investment performance of the client fund against industry benchmarks such as the Standard & Poor's 500 for equity funds or the Lehman Government-Corporate Index for bond fund managers.

The job requires a significant amount of travel, as much as 50 percent of the year, and a high level of personal interaction with clients. This is a good career choice if you are detail-oriented and have strong analytical and interpersonal skills.

Salaries

Investment Consultants are paid an annual salary based on qualifications and experience. Salaries for starting consultants usually start at around $50,000, rising to $150,000 or more for consultants with three to five years experience. Total compensation includes an annual incentive bonus for new clients brought in and achievement of annual business development goals. An Investment Consultant's annual compensation increases portionately with the size of their client base.

Employment Prospects

There is a steady demand for Investment Consultants. Employment opportunities are influenced to a large extent by the asset growth of defined contribution retirement plans such as 401(k) plans, traditional corporate pension plans, private foundations, and investments of wealthy individuals. Investment consulting firms are continually adding staff to keep pace with demand for investment advisory services. They're always looking for good people. Newly hired consultants start out as an associate or investment analyst and work their way up to become a client manager, partner, or managing director in their firm.

Advancement Prospects

Investment Consultants have excellent opportunities for advancement. Career advancement is, however, linked to personal productivity and the ability to generate new business for the firm. To advance in the consulting business, associate consultants must demonstrate an ability to build a defined practice, or a group of clients they service on a regular basis. The career goal of a consultant starting out is to become a client manager within five years. Having a defined practice makes the consultant more valuable to their employer. Consultants with a defined practice can also move to another firm, usually for a hefty increase in salary.

Education and Training

A four-year degree in finance, economics, or a related field is generally a requirement. Investment Consultants need a solid academic foundation in investment theory, economics, and the standard analytical tools used in measuring investment performance. Some employers have a preference for hiring candidates with an M.B.A. degree or a master's degree, if only to reduce the pool of qualified applicants. In many firms, though, a post-graduate degree is less important than having the right industry certification—a Chartered Financial Analyst designation.

Special Requirements

Investment Consultants must be licensed professionals, passing the Series 63 Investment Adviser exam given by the National Association of Securities Dealers. Another requirement is the Chartered Financial Analyst (CFA) cer-

tification, a three-part exam taken over three years by the Association for Investment Management and Research. Starting consultants should have completed at least one part of the CFA exam or have taken courses toward completion of the exam. The Certified Investment Analyst Certification is available from the Investment Managers Consultants Association.

Experience, Skills, and Personality Traits

Investment Consultants have to be good with numbers. They spend much of their time communicating hard-to-grasp concepts such as modern portfolio theory to diverse audiences. Consultants need to have excellent speaking and writing skills, and a degree of patience in listening to others. Also useful are good teaching skills, which come in handy when trying to explain before a group why the market was up or down in a particular quarter and how that market shift affected client portfolios.

Five years or more experience as an investment analyst, preferably working with investment professionals, is a general requirement. Prior experience may include investment performance analysis, market analysis, and research. For individuals starting out, the employer wants to know if the applicant has demonstrated the ability to work with people and numbers, perhaps as an intern in an accounting firm or an investment bank.

Unions and Associations

Investment Consultants can become members of the Investment Management Consultants Association (IMCA) to pursue personal networking opportunities and career advancement at IMCA-sponsored seminars.

Tips for Entry

1. While in college take courses in investment theory and portfolio management to get a head start on the Chartered Financial Analyst exam.
2. Follow industry trends in trade publications such as *Pensions & Investments Age* or *Plan Sponsor.*
3. Some of the best opportunities for individuals entering the consulting field are working with nonprofit organizations and family office managers, which have been underserved market segments.
4. To learn more about the field and whether you will like it, contact a large insurance company or brokerage firm and ask to talk to an investment consultant.
5. While in college, join an investment club and learn firsthand the world of investing.

PORTFOLIO MANAGER

CAREER PROFILE

Duties: Invests money for corporate and public pension funds, mutual funds, endowments and charitable foundations, and individuals; selects acceptable investments according to client's investment objectives and risk tolerance, or investment policy guidelines if the client is an institutional investor

Alternate Title(s): Fund Manager, Money Manager

Salary Range: $185,000 to $2 million

Employment Prospects: Good

Advancement Prospects: Excellent

Prerequisites:

Education or Training—Bachelor's degree, M.B.A. preferred; CFA designation required for advancement

Experience—Several years' experience with increasing responsibility

Special Skills and Personality Traits—Strong analytical skills, interpersonal skills, self-motivation, understanding of investment principles, including asset allocation and modern portfolio theory; in-depth knowledge of financial markets

Special Requirements—CFA designation; fluency in foreign language may be required for managers of global and international portfolios

CAREER LADDER

```
┌─────────────────────────────────┐
│   Co-manager or Lead Manager     │
└─────────────────────────────────┘

┌─────────────────────────────────┐
│       Portfolio Manager          │
└─────────────────────────────────┘

┌─────────────────────────────────┐
│       Financial Analyst          │
└─────────────────────────────────┘
```

Position Description

Portfolio Managers work for a money management firm or pension fund and select investments which meet the goals of a group of investors. The work requires patience, discipline, and an understanding of financial markets and companies. Managers have different approaches to securities selection. Some have a bargain hunting approach, selecting out-of-favor securities (value investing). Others pick securities they think will go higher in price (growth style investing). There are many different styles and approaches to investing. The Investment Company Institute says there are more than 20 different types of mutual funds, ranging from growth-oriented funds to precious metals funds.

Portfolio Managers develop and implement investment strategy, using a combination of investment analysis techniques. Most Portfolio Managers begin their career as members of a team of investment analysts and analyze certain market segments, such as semiconductor manufacturers or computer software firms.

Portfolio Managers typically work long hours, are goal-oriented, have excellent analytical skills, good communication skills, and a strong desire to succeed. Managers who advance in their careers are self-motivated individuals who have leadership ability but also can work independently. Fund managers also travel frequently, visiting companies they follow to learn firsthand about changes in business strategy or management.

Gathering information is a key part of the manager's job. Money managers spend hours every day on the phone with top managers of companies they own (or plan to own), their competitors and suppliers. They also talk on a regular basis with securities analysts and brokers in the major brokerage firms in an attempt to build a consensus view about the real value of a company to identify investment opportunities.

Portfolio Managers make the buy and sell decisions on the investments managed by an investment advisory firm. Investment managers make decisions within the guidelines of the investment firm's investment policy. They may also be limited in their decision making by portfolio restrictions put on accounts they manage by their clients, such as no defense industry stocks. Money managers get to face the challenges of investing. If you like the excitement of selecting investments and can deal with the uncertainty of waiting for the payoff, this field can be a rewarding career.

Salaries

Salaries vary by geographic region, experience, level of responsibility, type of investment portfolio managed, and employer. Fund managers with several years' experience are highly compensated. Salaries can range from the low $30,000 range for newly hired managers to $100,000 and up. Fund managers with five years' experience earned salaries from a low of $185,000 to a high of $2 million, according to a survey by Buck Consultants. Investment manager compensation may be pegged to portfolio performance, although incentive compensation is more common in the institutional fund management industry than it is in the mutual fund industry.

Equity managers usually receive higher salaries than bond fund managers. International and global fund managers are paid higher salaries because of the more specialized knowledge required to manage international portfolios. The investment management field is highly competitive, and investment management firms place great importance on manager performance. Being in the top quartile of manager rankings can earn you a substantial annual bonus.

Employment Prospects

The Portfolio Manager field can be difficult to break into, but there are good opportunities in mutual fund companies, hedge funds, and similar fund management companies serving individual investors and defined contribution 401(k) and similar plans. Less growth is expected in traditional pension plans because plan sponsors have shown a preference for employee-directed pension plans.

Because it is hard to break into the field of portfolio management, it is advisable to think carefully about strategy. You have to bring something to the table that others cannot deliver. This can be superior knowledge of specific markets or previous job experience. Working for a bank trust department, public pension fund, or mutual fund company can be a good way to break in the field. Most Portfolio Managers begin their careers as securities analysts who follow specific companies and report their investment research to a Portfolio Manager or portfolio management team.

Advancement Prospects

Hard work pays off in the money management industry. Managers whose investment picks perform well are rewarded with regular salary increases and annual performance bonuses. Investment professionals who make poor decisions for their investors or shareholders tend to have fairly short careers.

Investment managers tend to advance in their career by moving into jobs with increasing levels of responsibility. Managers who show an aptitude for stock selection are promoted to higher-profile positions, and they take on the responsibility for managing larger portfolios. Managers with leadership potential may advance into positions of co-manager or lead manager of a mutual fund, directing the activities of a group of investment managers. Fund managers in the very competitive mutual fund industry also advance their careers by changing jobs and moving to another mutual fund company, usually with an increase in salary and responsibility.

Education and Training

A four-year undergraduate degree is required. Portfolio Managers come to the field from a variety of academic backgrounds, but most have had courses in business management, economics, finance, and related fields. Managers specializing in a particular industry may have a post-graduate degree. International Portfolio Managers should have foreign-language skills.

Special Requirements

An industry designation, Chartered Financial Analyst (CFA), awarded by the Association for Investment Management and Research, is generally required for advancement in the field.

Experience, Skills, and Personality Traits

Portfolio Managers need good math and analytical skills. Individuals who can make good decisions under pressure or who can analyze large amounts of data and quickly reach two or three major conclusions will do well in this industry. Those who have a bias toward action and who are passionate about their careers will do well.

Unions and Associations

Portfolio Managers can become members of professional associations such as the CFA Institute or the Investment

Company Institute (ICI) for networking and career advancement opportunities.

Tips for Entry

1. Bank trust departments, insurance companies, and state and local pension funds offer the best opportunities to break into the field.
2. Join an investment club and get hands-on experience managing money.
3. Get a good foundation in taxable bonds and fixed-income securities; managing equities can be more exciting, but there are just as many opportunities in fixed-income securities.
4. Take courses in investment theory and portfolio management to get a head start on the CFA credentials examination sponsored by the CFA Institute.

FINANCIAL REPORTING MANAGER

CAREER PROFILE

Duties: Manages external reporting to the Securities and Exchange Commission; stays current with accounting rules and financial regulations; evaluates the impact of current and proposed regulations on business activities

Alternate Title(s): External Reporting Manager; Manager, Financial Reporting Compliance; Corporate Reporting Manager

Salary Range: $66,800 to $100,000 and up

Employment Prospects: Good

Advancement Prospects: Good

Prerequisites:

Education or Training—Four-year degree in accounting or finance

Experience—Three to five years' auditing experience in public companies

Special Skills and Personality Traits—Strong project management and analytical skills; excellent communication skills; detailed knowledge of federal securities reporting

Special Requirements—Certified Public Accountant (CPA) certification

CAREER LADDER

```
┌─────────────────────────────────────┐
│     Manager, Financial Reporting     │
└─────────────────────────────────────┘

┌─────────────────────────────────────┐
│      Director, Corporate Finance     │
└─────────────────────────────────────┘

┌─────────────────────────────────────┐
│              Controller              │
└─────────────────────────────────────┘
```

Position Description

Public companies have been hiring compliance specialists at a frenetic pace ever since federal securities regulations tightened following accounting scandals at several high-profile companies in 2001–02. The Sarbanes-Oxley Act of 2002 effectively created a new high-level position, the Financial Reporting Manager, who is charged with preparing financial reports and overseeing the internal controls ensuring the integrity of data being reported.

The objective of Sarbanes-Oxley, the most comprehensive revision to federal securities regulations since the 1930s, was to protect investors by improving the accuracy and reliability of financial reports such as 10-K annual reports, 10-K quarterly reports, proxy statements, and other financial reports issued by public companies. Sarbanes-Oxley is named after its main architects, Senator Paul Sarbanes and Representative Michael Oxley. The law has 11 sections, but section 404 is probably the most significant with respect to compliance. Sarbanes-Oxley section 404 says public companies have to evalu-

ate the effectiveness of internal controls to ensure that financial reports present an accurate picture of the company's financial health and do not present any misleading or intentionally false information. Furthermore, the external auditor must certify the effectiveness of these controls once a year, usually when the auditor reviews the company's financial statements.

The Financial Reporting Manager is responsible for financial statements filed with the Securities and Exchange Commission, senior management, the audit committee, and the company's board of directors. The Financial Reporting Manager oversees compliance with financial disclosure regulations issued by the SEC, the Financial Accounting Standards Board, and the Public Company Accounting Oversight Board—the regulatory board created to oversee Sarbanes-Oxley compliance.

The Financial Reporting Manager coordinates the activities of internal audit staff and external auditors and issues progress reports to senior management. The manager also works closely with the corporate controller's group by preparing technical accounting research, performing special projects, and analyzing financial reports for compliance with applicable federal or state regulations.

Specific duties may include the following:

- documenting and testing financial reporting controls
- coordinating quarterly reviews of financial reporting activities
- assisting in coordinating, with the chief financial officer and internal audit, the review of controls by all departments
- overseeing month-closing financial reports to the SEC
- coordinating preparation of monthly financial reports, including consolidated financial statements and cash flow statements
- assisting in preparation of quarterly and annual board of directors reports
- performing research on technical accounting issues
- maintaining records of accounting policies and procedures
- serving as a accounting liaison to corporate tax, treasury, and other internal departments
- assisting in communication with external auditors along with internal audit staff and the chief financial officer
- providing education and training to senior management on important accounting issues

Salaries

Salaries are commensurate with experience and company size. The middle 50 percent of Financial Reporting Managers earned salaries of $66,500 to $100,000 in 2005, according to the Association for Financial Professionals. More-experienced individuals can earn higher salaries. The compensation package usually includes performance bonuses and incentive awards for meeting departmental and corporate goals, plus an initial signing bonus when a reporting manager is hired from outside the company. Prior experience in financial reporting by public companies, specifically, Sarbanes-Oxley reporting, is usually a requirement.

Employment Prospects

There is continuing strong demand for corporate accountants with financial reporting experience. By 2006, the largest public companies have had ample experience with Sarbanes-Oxley compliance and have staffed their accounting departments to handle compliance and reporting requirements of the law. Initially, because of a lack of qualified candidates, some firms turned to internal auditors to fill compliance reporting positions. Individuals with auditing or financial reporting experience in specific industries, such as insurance or financial services, will find their prior experience advantageous in a job search.

Advancement Prospects

This position reports to the corporate controller or director of financial reporting. Financial Reporting Managers can move into more senior positions, such as director of financial reporting, director of finance, or eventually corporate controller. Other advancement options are in Sarbanes-Oxley consulting with a Big 4 accounting firm or a financial consulting firm specializing in financial reporting compliance.

Education and Training

The position requires a four-year degree in accounting or finance. Some firms prefer candidates with Masters of Business Administration (M.B.A.) degrees. A solid knowledge of Securities and Exchange Commission regulations, generally accepted accounting principles (GAAP), and Public Company Accounting Oversight Board (PCAOB) regulations is usually a requirement. Most people in this field acquire the necessary background through a combination of college-level courses and continuing professional education after graduation.

Special Requirements

A Certified Public Accountant (CPA) license is usually a requirement.

Experience, Skills, and Personality Traits

This is not an entry-level position. Most firms require some previous experience, anywhere from three years to 10 years, in internal auditing or financial reporting in public companies. Financial Reporting Managers should have strong organizational and team leadership skills, strong analytical skills, and excellent verbal and written communication skills. Prior experience delivering board-level and senior management-level presentations is often a requirement.

Unions and Associations

Financial Reporting Managers can become members of professional associations such as the Institute of Internal Auditors, the Institute of Management Accountants, or the Financial Executives Institute.

Tips for Entry

1. Financial reporting positions are often filled through executive search firms. Develop contacts with one or more search firms to improve your chances of being hired.
2. Internet job boards and bulletin boards are another source of job leads.
3. Networking in professional associations can also lead to an interview at a hiring firm.

FINANCIAL WRITER

CAREER PROFILE

Duties: Writes editorial copy to support marketing activities of mutual fund distributors and investment managers

Alternate Title(s): Investment Writer, Marketing Writer, Writer/Editor

Salary Range: $40,000 to $70,000 and up

Employment Prospects: Good

Advancement Prospects: Good

Prerequisites:

Education or Training—Four-year college degree

Experience—Two to five years

Special Skills and Personality Traits—Excellent written and verbal communication skills

Special Requirements—M.B.A. or CFA designation usually required for advancement to more senior positions

CAREER LADDER

```
┌─────────────────────────────┐
│       Senior Writer         │
└─────────────────────────────┘

┌─────────────────────────────┐
│     Marketing Director      │
└─────────────────────────────┘

┌─────────────────────────────┐
│   Junior Financial Writer   │
└─────────────────────────────┘
```

Position Description

Twenty years ago most people who invested in the stock market were professional investors who managed money for their company or their clients. Today, nearly everyone with an investment or savings account has some money in the stock market. Individual participation in the financial markets is extraordinarily high compared with what it was 10 or 15 years ago. Individuals born in the "Baby Boom" generation are saving more for their retirement years. Employer-sponsored 401(k) plans and other salary-reduction plans are replacing company-funded pension plans. Investment decisions are being driven toward the end-user investor.

An outgrowth of the soaring rate of individual investor participation in the financial markets is the unprecedented demand for information about the financial markets and about the investment products available in today's market. Wall Street investment banks are very good at creating new financial products—mutual funds, index funds, enhanced index funds, exchange traded funds, and so on—and then finding ways to market these products to investors.

The Financial Writer is responsible for producing the marketing copy, fund performance reports, market analysis, and other collateral materials supporting the sponsoring organization's marketing of those products. All of these products—how they work, the reasons for owning them—have to be explained to the investor. It is the Financial Writer's job to present that information—not in Wall Street's jargon, but in language the average individual can readily understand.

Financial Writers occupy different niches in a money management firm, depending on their specialization. Some Financial Writers produce performance reviews telling retail investors where they made money and where they lost money. Promotional writers tell investors why they should invest in a particular fund. The writer works closely with investment analysts, portfolio managers, and marketing staff on a daily basis to maintain a high level of familiarity with market and portfolio trends.

The writer may edit or write monthly or quarterly reports written for institutional (pension fund, endowment fund, etc.) and individual investors.

Responsibilities may include the following:

- writing monthly or quarterly fund commentaries for retail or institutional clients
- writing position papers (white papers), marketing brochures, and commentaries on industry trends and investment strategy; portfolio commentary for investors; and commentary on market or portfolio events for internal as well as external audiences.
- editing or writing various newsletters, both equity and fixed-income, to ensure compliance with SEC rules
- organizing and leading portfolio video presentations

- preparing press releases and arranging interviews
- answering media requests for information or interviews
- writing speeches for senior executives
- writing market commentary and content for Web sites
- writing investment strategy for mutual fund reports to investors and technical articles for strategy publications

The investment field is highly specialized because of the research-intensive nature of the work and the industry's focus on specific client groups. Besides mutual funds, there are hedge funds (private investment pools that have authority to invest in a wide range of financial assets) and real estate investment conduits (REITS), to name a few of the leading players. Each may have its own requirements for Financial Writers, but for the most part, they are looking for people who can speak the language of the investment community and who can effectively communicate strategy and investment performance to their primary audience.

Salaries

Starting salaries of $40,000 to $45,000 are fairly common for individuals entering the field after a year or two learning the business at a financial industry publication. More experienced Financial Writers can earn anywhere from $70,000 to $100,000 plus an annual bonus for meeting departmental or company sales goals. The Financial Writer earning more than $100,000 in base salary has plenty of writing experience with mutual fund distributors and may also have an M.B.A. degree.

Employment Prospects

There is a growing need for Financial Writers and investment writers who can communicate effectively to a general audience. Entering the field directly from college is rather challenging because employers prefer to hire people who have some prior experience as Financial Writers. However, one to two years' work at a daily newspaper or financial magazine writing about mutual funds, developing personal financial goals, and saving for college expenses or retirement can be a door opener. Investment firms have carved out marketing positions where they did not exist years ago, which means fund distributors employ Financial Writers in several areas within marketing. Brokerage firms and commercial banks also hire Financial Writers for various marketing positions, although the work there may be quite different from writing about investments.

Advancement Prospects

Financial Writers move ahead as they gain experience and demonstrate competence handling a variety of assignments. The junior writer can advance to senior writer, who functions as a project leader, and ultimately to director of marketing. Advancing to a management-level position is more challenging, usually requiring a combination of experience and an advanced business degree such as an M.B.A. degree. Directors of marketing may have as many as 20 to 30 people reporting to them.

Education and Training

There are no specific academic requirements for the position. A four-year college degree with an emphasis in economics, finance, or journalism would be a good start for a career as a Financial Writer. A journalism degree with a minor in finance would be an ideal combination. Financial Writers have to know their markets and be good communicators.

Special Requirements

More-senior positions often require an industry certification or licensing, depending on the firm. Individuals who have one or more investment securities licenses (a Series 7 general brokerage license, for instance) from the National Association of Securities Dealers or have begun work toward their Chartered Financial Analyst (CFA) designation may have an advantage in securing a more senior position. An M.B.A. degree may be a requirement for a management-level position as director of marketing or head of marketing.

Experience, Skills, and Personality Traits

Very few Financial Writers enter the field directly from college. Usually, they have at least a year or two of experience at a financial publication, writing about mutual funds and similar products. More-senior positions require five to 10 years' job-related experience. Successful candidates have a demonstrated ability to absorb and rewrite technical reports into concise, clearly written reports. They know how to manage competing priorities and work under tight deadlines and have some proficiency with standard personal computer software. Beyond that, an interest in learning about investments is important.

Unions and Associations

Investment writers who are employed as financial journalists can become members of professional associations such as the New York Financial Writers Association; writers involved in marketing may want to join the Financial Communications Society for networking and career advancement opportunities.

Tips for Entry

1. Check listings in online job boards for current openings. A good place to start is the Financial Communications Society Web site (www.fcsinteractive.com).
2. Finding the most qualified candidate can often be challenging; companies frequently use search firms or executive recruiters to fill these positions. Contact search firms specializing in financial communication.
3. Informal networking contacts may also lead to interviews with hiring companies.

REQUEST FOR PROPOSAL WRITER

CAREER PROFILE

Duties: Writes responses to bid offers from companies or organizations requesting competitive bids for new business

Alternate Title(s): RFP Writer, Marketing Proposal Writer

Salary Range: $60,000 to $70,000 and up

Employment Prospects: Good

Advancement Prospects: Fair

Prerequisites:

　Education or Training—Four-year college degree

　Experience— Three to five years' marketing experience in a financial organization

　Special Skills and Personality Traits—Excellent verbal and written communications; working knowledge of PC software

CAREER LADDER

```
┌─────────────────────────────┐
│     Department Manager      │
└─────────────────────────────┘

┌─────────────────────────────┐
│      Senior RFP Writer      │
└─────────────────────────────┘

┌─────────────────────────────┐
│         RFP Writer          │
└─────────────────────────────┘
```

Position Description

Organizations seeking to hire vendors or suppliers often begin the selection process by requesting written business proposals from qualified vendors. By reviewing proposals from competing vendors, a company can select the vendor whose product line, servicing, and pricing best meets its current needs. The selection process often begins with the issuance of a request for information (RFI) or a request for quotations (RFQ) to a large number of vendors. After the initial responses are reviewed, a more detailed request for proposals (RFP) is usually issued to a smaller group of vendors requesting answers to a more detailed questionnaire about their capabilities, staffing, and other qualifying criteria. The Request for Proposals Writer produces marketing proposals in response to these formal solicitations for business.

Selecting vendors through an RFP is very common in financial services. Some companies use RFP projects as a means to control their bank service costs. Others issue an RFP when they want to add services unavailable from their current vendor, are considering a technology upgrade, or are dissatisfied with their current vendor. Some organizations routinely put their banking services out to bid every three to five years. This is more common in the public sector, where it may be required by statute. In the investment world, the majority of money manager selections are done through the

issuance and completion of RFP documents. The process has recently spread to alternative investments such as hedge funds, which have experienced explosive growth since 2000, heightening market demand for experienced RFP Writers.

The RFP Writer is a skilled communicator with detailed knowledge of the company's objectives, practices, and position in the industry. As a member of the company's marketing team, the RFP Writer works closely with the appropriate department managers to produce clearly written and concise responses to requests for proposals. The RFP Writer edits written answers to an RFP for clarity and content, working to ensure that the response document has sufficient quantitative information, such as tables or graphs, and that all questions have been answered. This role requires frequent contact with both the product development teams and the sales managers so the writer can stay up to date on the company's product offerings and sales efforts. Because the turnaround time for gathering information for and delivering a completed RFP may be quite limited, RFP Writers work under very tight production deadlines.

Full-time RFP Writers wear many hats. An RFP Writer's skills can easily translate into other tasks, such as technical writing or in-house communications. Some RFP Writers have extensive backgrounds in marketing or corporate communications, which can come in handy when they are creating new advertising or marketing materials or when they are asked to assist in creating new sales or marketing initiatives.

Other duties of RFP Writers include the following:

- responding to ad hoc information requests from client service or marketing
- analyzing RFP requirements to write, organize, and edit proposal content
- maintaining a database of common RFP questions and answers
- researching product information to update RFP responses

Salaries

Starting salaries of $60,000 to $75,000 are fairly common, and higher salaries are paid to more experienced RFP Writers. Employers in the financial services field often require some previous experience producing marketing materials for an investment management firm, hedge fund, investment bank, or other financial company. Compensation packages often include annual incentive or performance bonuses for attaining department or company goals.

Employment Prospects

There is good demand for RFP Writers, especially in the mutual fund and investment management industry. Individuals with some experience writing financial reports for investment firms or a strong background in financial journalism will find ample opportunities as RFP Writers. More-senior positions usually require some previous experience writing RFP documents. As RFP-format requests for bids are widely used in financial services, RFP Writers with solid experience can find opportunities working at hedge funds, commercial banks, insurance companies, and other firms. Specific opportunities and job requirements will vary by industry.

Advancement Prospects

REP Writers usually advance by moving to more senior positions, such as team leader. The lead RFP manager is responsible for a team of marketing writers. Individuals with a postgraduate degree, such as an M.B.A. degree, which is not usually a requirement for entry, can move into management-level positions such as director of marketing. Some individuals can move laterally into related fields such as client servicing and client support.

Education and Training

A four-year college degree with a concentration in business, economics, or a related field is a basic requirement for entry to the field. As with the financial writer position, some academic background in finance will also be a useful asset. A degree in journalism with a minor in finance would be a good academic background. RFP Writers have to know their markets and be able to explain complex topics in concise, readable copy. Most of this industry knowledge is gained through on-the-job experience after graduation from college. A working knowledge of standard PC office software and some familiarity with database software are very useful in this position.

Experience, Skills, and Personality Traits

RFP Writers have to be adept at absorbing a large amount of information quickly and preparing concisely written responses to detailed questions. Excellent verbal and written communication skills, plus an interest in writing about technically challenging subjects, are important skills. RFP Writers need to be assertive in obtaining required information from department managers, often working under tight production deadlines. An ability to make decisions quickly and work as part of a marketing team is a useful job-related skill.

Unions and Associations

RFP Writers can become members of professional associations such as the Financial Communications Society for career advancement and networking opportunities.

Tips for Entry

1. Check online job boards such as the Financial Communications Society Web site (http://www.fcsinteractive.com) for current openings.
2. Executive search firms specializing in financial services are a good source of job leads.
3. College courses in finances, economics in business are helpful.

SUPERVISORY AGENCIES

BANK EXAMINER

CAREER PROFILE

Duties: Reviews the records and operating procedures of banking institutions to ensure compliance with applicable federal and state laws and regulations; ensures that the bank is operating in a safe and sound manner and depositors' assets are adequately protected

Alternate Title(s): Compliance Examiner

Salary Range: $33,000 to $95,000

Employment Prospects: Good

Advancement Prospects: Excellent

Prerequisites:

Education or Training—Four-year college degree with courses in accounting or finance

Experience—Prior banking industry experience in management or supervision

Special Skills and Personality Traits—Excellent written communication and organizational skills; computer literacy with word processing and spreadsheet accounting programs; strong negotiating skills; detailed understanding of banking regulation and supervision is a job requirement

Special Requirements—Industry certification is not required but is preferred

CAREER LADDER

```
┌─────────────────────────────┐
│      Bank Examiner          │
└─────────────────────────────┘

┌─────────────────────────────┐
│     Associate Examiner      │
└─────────────────────────────┘

┌─────────────────────────────┐
│      Examiner Trainee       │
└─────────────────────────────┘
```

Position Description

Bank Examiners work for federal and state regulatory agencies and Federal Reserve Banks. They review the records and operating procedures of commercial banks and savings institutions to ensure compliance with applicable federal and state laws and regulations. Examiners have the authority to enter a bank's premises without prior notice, and gain access to all documents and records. Examiners verify cash on hand and review the documentation of bank loans and loan collateral, investments, and other assets. They review loan accounts to make sure the bank has properly classified problem loans (nonperforming loans), and reported these in financial statements. They review procedures for asset-liability management, internal auditing, and risk management. They review the institution's investment decisions and loans approved by the board of directors.

Examiners at the Office of the Comptroller of the Currency, the federal agency supervising nationally chartered banks, may work as generalist examiners or in one of several specialty areas, including asset management, bank information systems, capital markets, consumer compliance, credit, and mortgage banking. Generalists are the largest group of examiners. They evaluate banking practices and financial soundness of the institutions they supervise. The examination process focuses on activities posing the greatest risk to the institution. Specialist examiners conduct more intensive examinations of specific banking activities. The Federal Deposit Insurance Corporation and state banking departments also have examination staffs. State banking departments perform similar audits of state-chartered financial institutions.

Bank Examiner's duties include:

- evaluating the adequacy of financial institution compliance with consumer protection laws
- compiling and analyzing data, developing, conclusions, and making recommendations

- using word processing, spreadsheet, and database software to present information
- managing and reviewing the work of subordinates and evaluating their performance
- conducting or leading Community Reinvestment Act audits of banking institutions
- developing strategies for administering audits of consumer, Bank Secrecy Act and Community Reinvestment Act fair lending programs, including recommendations for corrective action when weaknesses or deficiencies are identified
- making presentations to bank regulators, boards of directors, or committees
- obtaining commitments for corrective action of deficiencies through effective negotiating skills when necessary

Salaries

Bank Examiners can expect to earn salaries ranging from $33,000 to $95,000 at the federal level. Bank Examiners working for state banking departments earn slightly lower salaries. Annual compensation normally includes paid health and life insurance.

Employment Prospects

Banking regulatory agencies have continuing needs for qualified, experienced Examiners. The Office of the Comptroller of the Currency hires examiners for a range of specialty audits, ranging from data processing and electronic security to audits of international banking operations.

Advancement Prospects

Advancement in the field is generally to a position of increased responsibility, such as examining larger financial institutions. Bank examiners with leadership ability can move into management positions and direct a team of Bank Examiners during routine audits of financial institutions.

Education and Training

Banking regulatory agencies require a four-year bachelor's degree with a major field of study in accounting, banking, business administration, commercial or banking law, economics, finance, or another business-related field. Alternatively, beginning examiners must have at least three years experience providing knowledge of accounting and auditing principles and practices. This prior work experience may include employment in a financial institution reviewing, recommending, or approving bank loans or investments, accounting, or auditing work in a financial

institution, or reviewing or recommending investments in a bank trust department. If you have a business-related master's degree, or additional experience as a bank officer, financial analyst, or accountant, or similar experience, you may qualify for a higher-level bank examiner position. New Bank Examiners participate in a one-year training program that combines classroom instruction and on-the-job training.

Special Requirements

Industry certification is not required. However, a financial industry certification designating expertise in a specific field will enhance the bank examiner's competency and ability to perform on the job.

The Office of the Comptroller of the Currency, the chief regulator of nationally chartered banks, has determined the following certifications enhance the overall expertise of its examining workforce. These include: Certified Public Accountant and Certified Fraud Examiner, Certified Information Systems Auditor, Certified Financial Planner, Certified Financial Analyst, and Certified Regulations Compliance Manager.

Experience, Skills, and Personality Traits

Prior experience in financial services, such as bank lending or management, is necessary to become a Bank Examiner. Important job-related skills are strong verbal and written communication, good organizational skills, and good negotiating skills.

Unions and Associations

As professional employees, Bank Examiners are usually not members of labor unions. They can become members of professional associations such as the Conference of State Bank Supervisors for networking and career development.

Tips for Entry

1. Bank supervisory agencies are continually hiring examiners. Applying directly to an agency can lead to an interview.
2. Check the Comptroller of the Currency's Web site and the Federal Deposit Insurance Corporation's Web site for information about currently available jobs.
3. Networking with members of state banking associations can also produce job leads.
4. Develop a specialty expertise in such areas as fraud control and e-commerce to increase your chances of getting hired.

INSURANCE EXAMINER

CAREER PROFILE

Duties: Examines the financial condition of licensed insurance companies; enforces compliance with applicable laws and regulations; may verify the authenticity of insurance company records

Alternate Title(s): Field Examiners

Salary Range: $400,000 to $75,000

Employment Prospects: Good

Advancement Prospects: Good

Prerequisites:

Education or Training—Four-year degree with courses in accounting, finance, or business administration

Experience—One or more years' experience as an auditor or accountant or equivalent academic qualifications

Special Skills and Personality Traits—Knowledge of accounting or auditing principles; strong oral and written communication skills; a working knowledge of spreadsheet accounting and word processing computer software

Special Requirements—Pass written Civil Service examination; certification by the Society of Financial Examiners required in some states

CAREER LADDER

```
┌─────────────────────────────┐
│      Senior Examiner        │
└─────────────────────────────┘

┌─────────────────────────────┐
│     Insurance Examiner      │
└─────────────────────────────┘

┌─────────────────────────────┐
│  Insurance Examiner Trainee │
└─────────────────────────────┘
```

Position Description

Insurance Examiners carry out the financial review and audit of regulated insurance companies licensed to do business or seeking approval to do business. Field examiners who travel to an insurance company's home office and audit its financial records do much of the work performed by Insurance Examiners. Starting Insurance Examiners work under the guidance of experienced examiners, while becoming familiar with the business practices unique to the insurance industry. They assist the examiner-in-charge during on-premise examinations of regulated insurance companies.

In addition to field examiners, state insurance departments have several other types of Insurance Examiners. Some examiners work in the market conduct bureau, where they investigate policyholder complaints against insurance companies or insurance agents and brokers. Insurance fraud investigators conduct investigations of alleged insurance fraud and recommend criminal prosecutions if violations of state laws are suspected. Department staff attorneys work in the office of general counsel and prepare insurance-related legislation and litigation. Insurance department actuaries review insurance company applications for approval to sell specific lines of insurance.

Specific duties of Insurance Examiners include the following:

* examining and verifying the assets and liabilities of insurance companies
* assisting a group of examiners in auditing the records of large insurance companies
* reviewing the financial reserves and insurance rates of regulated insurance companies
* compiling statistics on individual insurance companies from annual financial statements and insurance company records

- preparing statements of capital, securities, assets, and liabilities to determine compliance with state law
- participating in preparing reports for complex, large examinations
- assisting in in-office audits of insurance companies' financial statements, premium taxes, and other fees payable by regulated insurance companies.

Insurance Examiners work long hours and have extensive overnight travel. Field examiners may spend more than 50 percent of their time working on the premises of regulated insurance companies. Some state insurance departments employ contract examiners, who are self-employed professionals working exclusively as employees of state insurance departments.

Salaries

Qualifications and experience determine salaries. Salaries in 2004 ranged from $40,000 to $75,000, according to the U.S. Department of Labor. A senior-level examiner, such as a bureau chief managing an insurance department's field examiner staff, can earn up to $120,000 a year. Examiner salaries are set by state regulations; salary increases (and advancement) are tied to successful completion of civil service examinations. Examiner compensation in addition to salary includes health and dental insurance and participation in public employee pension plans. Field examiners receive an allowance for travel and mileage expenses. Contract examiners receive a daily stipend, or per diem allowance, for work performed for a state insurance department.

Employment Prospects

Employment opportunities for financial examiners will grow about as fast as for other occupations, according to the U.S. Department of Labor's Bureau of Labor Statistics. There is good demand for Insurance Examiners in most states. Individuals who have insurance industry experience as actuaries, accountants, or who have a professional certification are sought-after candidates for Insurance Examiner positions. Som job openings will occur as experienced examiners reach retirement age or move into positions in private industry. Expected growth in the amount of insurance-related products sold to the public will create additional demand for field examiners.

Advancement Prospects

Examiners usually start their careers as junior examiners, advancing to examiner after two years of in-service training. Further advancement is contingent on passing state civil service exams. Insurance Examiners successfully completing a promotional exam can move up to become a senior exam-

iner and manage examinations of large, complex insurance companies.

Another option is moving into private industry and working for a regulated insurance company. An examining actuary could, for instance, move into the compliance department of an insurance company and use their regulatory experience in getting new insurance products approved by a state insurance department. Experienced examiners can also move into careers with accounting firms or professional service firms and conduct financial examinations of insurance companies.

Education and Training

Education requirements for Insurance Examiners vary by state. Applicants should have a four-year college or university degree with an emphasis in accounting, finance, business administration, insurance or actuarial science, or a closely related field, and have a basic understanding of business law, finance, and overall business administration. New York State's insurance department, one of the largest in the country, requires starting examiners to have 24 college credits in accounting, or relevant job experience and a qualifying grade point average.

Experience, Skills, and Personality Traits

Generally, one year of professional accounting, auditing, or general financial service industry experience is required. Starting Insurance Examiners should have some knowledge of accounting and auditing principles and practices, state regulations, and laws pertaining to insurance companies, insurance theory, and the operations of insurance companies. Examiners should have the ability to analyze accounts, records, and documents for irregularities.

A working knowledge of spreadsheet accounting and word processing software is useful in performing the work of an examiner. Also important are good interpersonal communication skills, which are useful in establishing effective working relationships with associates, insurance company officials, and the general public.

Special Requirements

Candidates for Insurance Examiner positions must pass a written Civil Service examination, personal background check, and other parts of the selection process. Examiners employed as independent contractors, a practice in some states, should have certification by the Society of Financial Examiners. Field examiners should have a valid driver's license. Available certifications include the following: Certified Financial Examiner (CFE), from the Insurance Regulatory Examiners Society; Accredited Financial Examiner (AFE), and Certified Public Accountant (CPA).

Unions and Associations

Insurance Examiners can become members of the Insurance Regulatory Examiners Society or the Society of Financial Examiners for networking and career advancement opportunities. Both organizations offer continuing education seminars through state chapters or association-sponsored career advancement seminars.

Tips for Entry

1. While in college, take courses in accounting, business, or mathematics to get the required academic background

2. Computer skills are becoming important job-related skills for examiners. Get a good background in personal computer application software, especially spreadsheet accounting software.

3. Check state insurance departments for internship or summer employment opportunities to gain on-the-job insight into the job functions of Insurance Examiners.

4. To learn about job openings, apply directly to state insurance departments or check online job postings at the National Association of Insurance Commissioners' Web site, http://www.naic.org.

APPENDIXES

APPENDIX I
COLLEGE AND UNIVERSITY
DEGREE AND NON-DEGREE PROGRAMS

The preferred minimum educational requirement for the majority of positions discussed in this book is a four-year college degree. Of the nearly 4,000 accredited four-year colleges, universities, and community colleges, more than 1,000 offer degree programs in financial studies.

This section contains the names, mailing addresses, and contact information for more than 500 four-year colleges and universities that offer programs with an emphasis in banking, finance, insurance, and related fields of study. Included here are the names of educational institutions with four-year programs of study in actuarial science, auditing, banking or finance, financial planning, and insurance. Also included are the names of colleges and universities offering postgraduate programs in finance or business. Space limitations preclude the listing of all such colleges and universities.

Information about these colleges and universities can be obtained by contacting them directly. You can get additional information about these and other colleges by talking to school and career counselors and industry prefessionals in your region. Other sources of information are college directories published by Peterson's, Barron's, and others, which can be found in school or public libraries.

A. ACTUARIAL SCIENCE

ARIZONA

Northern Arizona University
University Admissions
P.O. Box 4084
Flagstaff, AZ 86011
Phone: (928) 523-5511
Fax: (928) 523-6023
E-mail: undergraduate.admissions@nau.edu
http://www.nau.edu

CALIFORNIA

The Master's College and Seminary
Director of Admissions
21726 Placerita Canyon Road
Santa Clarita, CA 91321
Phone: (661) 259-3540
E-mail: enrollment@masters.edu

COLORADO

Colorado State University
University Admissions, Spruce Hall
Fort Collins, CO 80523-0015
Phone: (970) 491-6909
Fax: (970) 491-7799
E-mail: admissions@colostate.edu

CONNECTICUT

Central Connecticut State University
University Admissions
1615 Stanley Street
New Britain, CT 06050-4010
Phone: (860) 832-2278
Fax: (860) 832-2295
E-mail: admissions@ccsu.edu

Quinnipiac University
University Admissions
275 Mount Carmel Avenue
Hamden, CT 06518
Phone: (203) 582-8600 or
    (800) 462-1944
Fax: (203) 281-8906
E-mail: admissions@quinnipiac.edu
http://www.quinnipiac.edu

University of Connecticut
University Admissions
2131 Hillside Avenue, U-3088
Storrs, CT 06268-3088
Phone: (860) 486-3137
Fax: (860) 486-1476
E-mail: beahusky@uconn.edu
http://www.uconn.edu

University of Hartford
University Admissions
200 Bloomfield Avenue
West Hartford, CT 06117
Phone: (860) 768-4296
Fax: (860) 768-4961
E-mail: admission@mail.hartford.edu
http://www.hartford.edu

FLORIDA

Florida Agricultural and Mechanical University
University Admissions
Suite G-9 Foote-Hilyer Administration
    Center
Tallahassee, FL 32307
Phone: (850) 599-3796
Fax: (850) 599-3069
E-mail: adm@famu.edu
http://www.famu.edu

Florida State University
University Admissions
2500 University Centre, Building A
Tallahassee, FL 32306-2400
Phone: (850) 644-6200
Fax: (850) 644-0197
E-mail: admissions@admin.fsu.edu
http://www.fsu.edu

GEORGIA

Georgia State University
University Admissions
P.O. Box 4009
Atlanta, GA 30302-4009
Phone: (404) 651-2365
Fax: (404) 651-4811
E-mail: admissions@gsu.edu
http://www.gsu.edu

ILLINOIS

Bradley University
1501 West Bradley Avenue
Peoria, IL 61625
Phone: (309) 677-1000
Fax: (309) 677-2797
E-mail: admissions@bradley.edu
http://www.bradley.edu

DePaul University
University Admissions
1 East Jackson Boulevard
Chicago, IL 60604-2287
Phone: (312) 362-8300
Fax: (312) 362-5749
E-mail: admitdpu@depaul.edu

Elmhurst College
190 Prospect Avenue
Elmhurst, IL 60126
Phone: (630) 617-3400
Fax: (630) 617-5501
E-mail: admit@elmhurst.edu
http://www.elmhurst.edu

North Central College
30 North Brainerd Street
P.O. Box 3063
Naperville, IL 60540
Phone: (800) 411-1861
Fax: (630) 637-5819
E-mail: ncadm@noctrl.edu
http://www.northcentralcollege.edu

Saint Xavier University
3700 West 103rd Street
Chicago, IL 60655
Phone: (773) 298-3000
Fax: (773) 298-3076
E-mail: admissions@sxu.edu
http://www.sxu.edu

University of Illinois at Urbana–Champaign
901 West Illinois Street
Urbana, IL 61801
Phone: (217) 333-0302
Fax: (217) 244-0903
E-mail: undergraduate@admissions.uiuc.
    edu

University of St. Francis
500 Wilcox Street
Joliet, IL 60435
Phone: (800) 735-7500
Fax: (815) 740-4285
E-mail: information@stfrancis.edu
http://www.stfrancis.edu

INDIANA

Ball State University
Office of Admissions
2000 University Avenue
Muncie, IN 47306-1099
Phone: (765) 285-8300
Fax: (765) 285-1632
E-mail: AskUs@wp.bsu.edu

Butler University
Office of Admissions
4600 Sunset Avenue
Indianapolis, IN 46208-3485
Phone: (317) 940-8100
Fax: (317) 940-8150
E-mail: admissions@butler.edu
http://www.butler.edu

Indiana University Northwest
3400 Broadway, Hawthorn 100
Gary, IN 46408-1197
Phone: (219) 980-6991
Fax: (219) 981-4219
E-mail: admit@iun.edu
http://www.indiana.edu

IOWA

Drake University
Office of Admissions
2507 University Avenue
Des Moines, IA 50311-4505
Phone: (515) 271-3181 or (800)
    44DRAKE
Fax: (515) 271-2831
E-mail: admission@drake.edu
http://www.drake.edu

The University of Iowa
University Admissions
107 Calvin Hall
Iowa City, IA 52242
Phone: (319) 335-3847
Fax: (319) 333-1535
E-mail: admissions@uiowa.edu
http://www.uiowa.edu

KANSAS

Washburn University of Topeka
University Admissions
1700 Southwest College Avenue
Topeka, KS 66621
Phone: (785) 231-1030
Fax: (785) 296-7933
E-mail: admissions@washburn.edu

KENTUCKY

Bellarmine University
2001 Newburg Road
Louisville, KY 40205
Phone: (502) 452-8131
Fax: (502) 452-8002
E-mail: admissions@bellarmine.edu
http://www.bellarmine.edu

MARYLAND

Frostburg State University
Office of Admissions
101 Braddock Road
Frostburg, MD 21532-1099
Phone: (301) 687-4201
Fax: (301) 687-7074
E-mail: fsuadmissions@frostburg.edu

MASSACHUSETTS

Worcester Polytechnic Institute
Office of Admissions
100 Institute Road
Worcester, MA 01609
Phone: (508) 831-5286
Fax: (508) 831-5875
E-mail: admissions@wpi.edu

MICHIGAN

Central Michigan University
University Admissions
105 Warriner Hall
Mt. Pleasant, MI 48859
Phone: (989) 774-3076
Fax: (989) 774-7267
E-mail: cmuadmit@cmich.edu
http://www.cmich.edu

Eastern Michigan University
University Admissions
400 Pierce Hall
Ypsilante, MI 48197
Phone: (734) 487-3060
Fax: (734) 487-1484
E-mail: admissions@emich.edu
http://www.emich.edu

University of Michigan—Flint
University Admissions
303 East Kearsley Street
Flint, MI 48502-1950
Phone: (810) 762-3300
Fax: (810) 762-3272
E-mail: admissions@flint.umich.edu

MINNESOTA

Saint Cloud State University
Office of Admissions
720 4th Avenue South
St. Cloud, MN 56301-4498
Phone: (320) 308-2244
Fax: (320) 308-2243
E-mail: scsu4u@stcloudstate.edu
http://www.stcloudstate.edu

University of Minnesota—Duluth
Office of Admissions
23 Solon Campus Center
1117 University Drive
Duluth, MN 55812
Phone: (218) 726-7171
Fax: (218) 726-7040
E-mail: umdadmis@d.umn.edu
http://www.d.umn.edu

**University of Minnesota—Twin Cities
   Campus**
Office of Admissions
240 Williamson Hall
231 Pillsbury Drive SE
Minneapolis, MN 55455-0213
Phone: (612) 625-2008
Fax: (612) 626-1693
E-mail: admissions@tc.umn.edu
http://www.umn.edu/tc

University of St. Thomas
2115 Summit Avenue
St. Paul, MN 55102-1096
Phone: (651) 962-6150
Fax: (651) 962-6160
E-mail: admissions@stthomas.edu
http://www.stthomas.edu

MISSOURI

Central Missouri State University
Office of Admissions
Administration Building, WDE 1401
Warrensburg, MO 64093
Phone: (660) 543-4290 or
   (800) 956-0117
Fax: (660) 543-8517
E-mail: admit@cmsuvmb.cmsu.edu
http://www.cmsu.edu

Maryville University
13550 Conway Road
St. Louis, MO 63141-7299
Phone: (314) 529-9350
Fax: (314) 529-9927
E-mail: admissions@maryville.edu
http://www.maryville.edu

NEBRASKA

University of Nebraska at Kearney
Office of Admissions
905 West 25th Street
Kearney, NE 68849-0001
Phone: (308) 865-8441
   or (800) 532-7639
Fax: (308) 865-8987
E-mail: admissionsug@unk.edu
http://www.unk.edu

University of Nebraska—Lincoln
Office of Admissions
313 North 13th Street
Lincoln, NE 68588-0417
Phone: (402) 472-2023
   or (800) 742-8800
Fax: (402) 472-0670
E-mail: nuhusker@unl.edu
http://www.unl.edu

NEW HAMPSHIRE

Plymouth State University
17 High Street MSC 52
Plymouth, NH 03264-1595
Phone: (603) 535-2237
Fax: (603) 535-2714
E-mail: plymouthadmit@plymouth.edu
http://www.plymouth.edu

NEW JERSEY

New Jersey Institute of Technology
University Heights
Newark, NJ 07102
Phone: (973) 596-3300
Fax: (973) 596-3461
E-mail: admissions@njit.edu
http://www.njit.edu

Rider University
Office of Admissions
2083 Lawrenceville Road
Lawrenceville, NJ 06848-3099
Phone: (609) 896-5042
   or (800) 257-9026
Fax: (609) 895-6645
E-mail: admissions@rider.edu
http://www.rider.edu

NEW YORK

**Bernard M. Baruch College—City
   University of New York**
One Bernard Baruch Way
New York, NY 10010
Phone: (646) 312-1400

Fax: (646) 312-1361
E-mail: admissions@baruch.cuny.edu
http://www.baruch.cuny.edu

College of Insurance
101 Murray Street
New York, NY 10007
Phone: (212) 815-9232
Fax: (212) 964-3381
http://www.elearners.com

Dominican College
470 Western Highway
Orangeburg, NY 10962
Phone: (845) 359-3533
Fax: (845) 365-3150
E-mail: admissions@dc.edu
http://www.dc.edu

Mercy College
555 Broadway
Dobbs Ferry, NY 10522
Phone: (914) 674-7324
Fax: (914) 674-7382
E-mail: admissions@mercy.edu
http://www.mercy.edu

New York University
Office of Admissions
22 Washington Square North
New York, NY 10011
Phone: (212) 998-4500
Fax: (212) 995-4902
E-mail: admissions@nyu.edu
http://www.nyu.edu

State University of New York at Albany
1400 Washington Avenue
Albany, NY 12222
Phone: (518) 442-5435
Fax: (518) 442-5383
E-mail: ugadmissions@albany.edu
http://www.albany.edu

NORTH CAROLINA

**University of North Carolina—
   Asheville**
CPO # 2210, 117 Lipinsky Hall
Asheville, NC 28804-8510
Phone: (828) 251-6481
Fax: (828) 251-6482
E-mail: admissions@unca.edu
http://www.unca.edu

NORTH DAKOTA

Jamestown College
608 College Lane

Jamestown, ND 58405-0001
Phone: (701) 252-3467
Fax: (701) 253-4318
E-mail: admissions@jc.edu
http://www.jc.edu

North Dakota State University
Office of Admissions
P.O. Box 5454
Fargo, ND 58105
Phone: (701) 231-8643 or (800) 488-NDSU
Fax: (701) 231-8802
E-mail: ndsu.admission@ndsu.edu
http://www.ndsu.edu

OHIO

Bowling Green State University
Office of Admissions
110 McFall Center
Bowling Green, OH 43403
Phone: (419) 372-2478
Fax: (419) 372-6955
E-mail: admissions@bgnet.bgsu.edu
http://www.bgsu.edu

Ohio State University
Office of Admissions
110 Enarson Hall, 154 West 12th Avenue
Columbus, OH 43210-1200
Phone: (614) 292-3980
Fax: (614) 292-4818
E-mail: askabuckeye@osu.edu
http://www.osu.edu

Ohio University
Office of Admissions
120 Chubb Hall
Athens, OH 45701-2979
Phone: (740) 593-4100
Fax: (740) 593-0560
E-mail: admissions@ohiou.edu
http://www.ohiou.edu

OKLAHOMA

University of Central Oklahoma
Office of Admissions
100 North University Drive
Edmond, OK 73034
Phone: (405) 974-2338
Fax: (405) 341-4964
E-mail: admituco@ucok.edu
http://www.ucok.edu

OREGON

Oregon State University
104 Kerr Administration Building
Corvallis, OR 97331-2106

Phone: (541) 737-4411
Fax: (541) 737-2482
E-mail: osuadmit@orst.edu
http://www.oregonstate.edu

PENNSYLVANIA

Lebanon Valley College
101 North College Avenue
Annville, PA 17003-0501
Phone: (717) 867-6181
Fax: (717) 867-6026
E-mail: admissions@lvc.edu
http://www.lvc.edu

Lycoming College
700 College Place
Williamsport, PA 17701
Phone: (570) 321-4026
Fax: (570) 321-4317
E-mail: admissions@lycoming.edu
http://www.lycoming.edu

Mansfield University of Pennsylvania
Office of Admissions
Alumni Hall
Mansfield, PA 16933
Phone: (570) 662-4243
Fax: (570) 662-4121
E-mail: admissions@mansfield.edu
http://www.mansfield.edu

Mercyhurst College
501 East 38th Street
Erie, PA 16546
Phone: (814) 824-2202
Fax: (814) 824-2071
E-mail: admissions@mercyhurst.edu
http://www.mercyhurst.edu

Millersville University of Pennsylvania
P.O. Box 1002
Millersville, PA 17551-0302
Phone: (717) 872-3371
Fax: (717) 872-2147
E-mail: admissions@millersville.edu
http://www.millersville.edu

Pennsylvania State University—University Park
Office of Admissions
201 Shields Building
University Park, PA 16802-3000
Phone: (814) 865-5471
Fax: (814) 863-7590
E-mail: admissions@psu.edu
http://www.psu.edu

Seton Hill College
1 Seton Hill Drive
Greensburg, PA 15601
Phone: (724) 838-4255
Fax: (724) 830-1294
E-mail: admit@setonhill.edu
http://www.setonhill.edu

Temple University
Office of Admissions
1801 North Broad Street
Philadelphia, PA 19122-6096
Phone: (215) 204-7200
Fax: (215) 204-5694
E-mail: tuadm@mail.temple.edu
http://www.temple.edu

Thiel College
75 College Avenue
Greenville, PA 16125
Phone: (724) 589-2345
Fax: (724) 589-2013
E-mail: admission@thiel.edu
http://www.thiel.edu

University of Pennsylvania
Office of Admissions
1 College Hall, Levy Park
Philadelphia, PA 19014
Phone: (215) 898-7507
Fax: (215) 898-9670
E-mail: info@admissions.ugao.upenn.edu
http://www.upenn.edu

University of Pittsburgh—Bradford
Office of Admissions
Hanley Library, 300 Campus Drive
Bradford, PA 16071
Phone: (814) 362-7555
Fax: (814) 362-7578
E-mail: admissions@upb.pitt.edu
http://www.upb.pitt.edu

RHODE ISLAND

Bryant University
Office of Admissions
1150 Douglas Pike
Smithfield, RI 02917-1284
Phone: (401) 232-6100 or (800) 622-7001
Fax: (401) 232-6741
E-mail: admission@bryant.edu
http://www.bryant.edu

TENNESSEE

Southern Adventist University
P.O. Box 370
Collegedale, TN 37315

Phone: (423) 236-2844
Fax: (423) 236-1844
E-mail: admissions@southern.edu
http://www.southern.edu

WISCONSIN

University of Wisconsin—Madison
Office of Admissions

716 Langdon Street
Madison, WI 53706-1481
Phone: (608) 262-3961
Fax: (608) 262-7706
E-mail: onwisconsin@admissions.wisc.edu
http://www.wisc.edu

University of Wisconsin—Stevens Point
Student Services Center
Stevens Point, WI 54481

Phone: (715) 346-2441
Fax: (715) 346-3957
E-mail: admiss@uwsp.edu
http://www.uwsp.edu

B. BANKING AND FINANCE

ALABAMA

Alabama A&M University
University Admissions
4107 Meridian Street
Normal, AL 35762
Phone: (256) 851-5245 or (800) 553-0816
Fax: (256) 851-5249
E-mail: aboyle@.aamu.edu
http://www.aamu.edu

Alabama State University
University Admissions
915 South Jackson Street
Montgomery, AL 36104
Phone: (334) 229-4291 or (800) 253-5037
Fax: (334) 229-4984
E-mail: admission@alasu.edu
http://www.alasu.edu

Auburn University—Main Campus
University Admissions
202 Mary Martin Hall
Auburn, AL 36849
Phone: (334) 844-4080
Fax: (334) 844-6179
E-mail: admissions@auburn.edu
http://www.auburn.edu

Auburn University—Montgomery
University Admissions
7300 University Drive
Montgomery, AL 36117-3596
Phone: (334) 244-3611 or
    (800) 227-2649
Fax: (334) 244-3795
E-mail: vsamuel@mail.aum.edu
http://www.aum.edu

Jacksonville State University
University Admissions
700 North Pelham Road

Jacksonville, AL 36265
Phone: (256) 782-5268
Fax: (256) 782-5953
E-mail: info@jsu.edu
http://www.jsu.edu

Troy State University—Main Campus
University Admissions, Adams
Administration Building
University Avenue
Troy, AL 36082
Phone: (334) 670-3179
Fax: (334) 670-3733
E-mail: admit@troyst.edu
http://www.troyst.edu

Troy State University—Montgomery
University Admissions
P.O. Drawer 4419
231 Montgomery Street
Montgomery, AL 36103-4419
Phone: (334) 241-9506
Fax: (334) 241-5448
E-mail: admit@tsum.edu
http://www.tsum.edu

Tuskegee University
University Admissions
101 Old Administration Building
Tuskegee, AL 36088
Phone: (334) 727-8500
    or (800) 622-6531
Fax: (334) 727-5750
E-mail: admit@tuskegee.edu
http://www.tuskegee.edu

University of Alabama
University Admissions
P.O. Box 870132
Tuscaloosa, AL 35487-0132
Phone: (205) 348-5666
    or (800) 933-BAMA

Fax: (205) 348-9046
E-mail: admissions@ua.edu
http://www.ua.edu

University of Alabama at Birmingham
Office of Undergraduate Admissions
1530 Third Avenue South
Birmingham, AL 35294-1150
Phone: (205) 934-8221
Fax: (205) 975-7114
E-mail: undergradadmit@uab.edu
http://www.uab.edu

University of Alabama in Huntsville
University Admissions
301 Sparkman Drive
University Center 119
Hunstville, AL 35899
Phone: (256) 824-6070
    or (800) UAH-CALL
Fax: (256) 824-6073
E-mail: admitme@email.uah.edu
http://www.uah.edu

University of North Alabama
Office of Admissions
P.O. Box 5011
University Station
Florence, AL 35632-0001
Phone: (256) 765-4318
Fax: (256) 765-4329
E-mail: admissions@una.edu
http://www.una.edu

University of South Alabama
Office of Admissions
182 Administration Building
Mobile, AL 36688-0002
Phone: (334) 460-6141 or (800) 872-5247
Fax: (334) 460-7023
E-mail: admiss@usouthal.edu
http://www.southalabama.edu

ALASKA

University of Alaska—Anchorage
University Admissions
3211 Providence Drive
Anchorage, AK 99508-8046
Phone: (907) 786-1480
Fax: (907) 786-4888
E-mail: enroll@uaa.alaska.edu
http://www.uaa.alaska.edu

ARIZONA

Arizona State University—Main Campus
University Admissions
P.O. Box 870112
Tempe, AZ 85287
Phone: (480) 965-7788
Fax: (480) 965-3610
E-mail: ugrading@asu.edu
http://www.asu.edu

Northern Arizona University
University Admissions
P.O. Box 4084
Flagstaff, AZ 86011
Phone: (928) 523-5511 or
   (888) MORE-NAU
Fax: (928) 523-0226
E-mail: undergraduate.admissions@nau.
   edu
http://www.nau.edu

University of Arizona
University Admissions
P.O. Box 210040
Tucson, AZ 85721
Phone: (520) 621-3237
Fax: (520) 621-9799
E-mail: appinfo@arizona.edu
http://www.arizona.edu

ARKANSAS

Arkansas State University
University Admissions
P.O. Box 1630
State University, AR 72467
Phone: (870) 972-3024 or (800) 643-0080
Fax: (870) 910-8094
E-mail: admissions@astate.edu
http://www.astate.edu

Harding University
University Admissions
900 East Center
P.O. Box 11255
Searcy, AR 72149-0001
Phone: (501) 279-4407 or (800) 377-8632

Fax: (501) 279-4129
E-mail: admissions@harding.edu
http://www.harding.edu

University of Arkansas at Fayetteville
University Admissions
200 Silas H. Hunt Hall
Fayetteville, AR 72701-1201
Phone: (479) 575-5346 or (800) 377-8632
Fax: (479) 575-7515
E-mail: uofa@uark.edu
http://www.uark.edu

University of Arkansas at Little Rock
Office of Admission and Records
2801 South University Avenue
Little Rock, AR 72204-1099
Phone: (501) 569-3127 or (800) 482-8892
Fax: (501) 569-8915
E-mail: admissions@ualr.edu
http://www.ualr.edu

University of Central Arkansas
University Admissions
201 Donaghey Avenue
Conway, AR 72035-0001
Phone: (501) 450-3128 or
   (800) 243-8245
Fax: (501) 450-5228
E-mail: admissions@ecom.uca.edu
http://www.uca.edu

CALIFORNIA

California Baptist University
8432 Magnolia Avenue
Riverside, CA 92504
Phone: (951) 343-4212
Fax: (951) 343-4525
E-mail: admissions@calbaptist.edu
http://www.calbaptist.edu

**California State Polytechnic
   University—Pomona**
3801 West Temple Avenue
Pomona, CA 91768
Phone: (909) 869-3210
Fax: (909) 869-4529
E-mail: admissions@csupomona.edu
http://www.csupomona.edu

**California State University—
   Los Angeles**
5151 State University Drive
Los Angeles, CA 90032
Phone: (323) 343-3901
Fax: (323) 343-6306
E-mail: admission@calstatela.edu
http://www.calstatela.edu

**California State University—
   Northridge**
P.O. Box 1286
Northridge, CA 91328-1286
Phone: (818) 677-3773
Fax: (818) 677-4665
E-mail: lorraine.newlon@csun.edu
http://www.csun.edu

**California State University—
   Sacramento**
6000 J Street, Lassen Hall
Sacramento, CA 95819-6048
Phone: (916) 278-3901
Fax: (916) 278-5603
E-mail: admissions@csus.edu
http://www.csus.edu

**California State University—
   San Bernardino**
5500 University Parkway
San Bernardino, CA 92407-2397
Phone: (909) 880-5188
Fax: (909) 880-7034
E-mail: moreinfo@mail.csusb.edu
http://www.csusb.edu

Chapman University
University Admissions
One University Drive
Orange, CA 92866
Phone: (714) 997-6711
Fax: (714) 997-6713
E-mail: admit@chapman.edu
http://www.chapman.edu

Golden Gate University
University Admissions
536 Mission Street
San Francisco, CA 94105-2968
Phone: (415) 442-7200 or (800) 448-4968
Fax: (415) 442-7807
E-mail: info@ggu.edu
http://www.ggu.edu

The Master's College
21726 Placerita Canyon Road
Santa Clarita, CA 91321-1200
Phone: (661) 259-3540
Fax: (661) 288-1037
E-mail: enrollment@masters.edu
http://www.masters.edu

Notre Dame du Namun University
1500 Ralston Avenue
Belmont, CA 94002
Phone: (650) 508-3600
Fax: (650) 508-3426

E-mail: admissions@ndnu.edu
http://www.ndnu.edu

Pacific Union College
One Angwin Avenue
Angwin, CA 94508
Phone: (800) 862-7080
Fax: (709) 965-6432
E-mail: enroll@puc.edu
http://www.puc.edu

St. Mary's College—California
Office of Admissions
P.O. Box 4800
Moraga, CA 94556-4800
Phone: (925) 631-4224
Fax: (925) 376-7193
E-mail: smacadmit@stmarys-ca.edu
http://www.stmarys-ca.edu

San Diego State University
5500 Campanile Drive
San Diego, CA 92182
Phone: (619) 594-7800
Fax: (619) 594-1250
E-mail: admissions@sdsu.edu
http://www.sdsu.edu

San Francisco State University
1600 Holloway Avenue
San Francisco, CA 94132
Phone: (415) 338-6486
Fax: (415) 338-7196
E-mail: ugadmit@sfsu.edu
http://www.sfsu.edu

Santa Clara University
University Admissions
500 El Camino Real
Santa Clara, CA 95053
Phone: (408) 554-4700
Fax: (408) 554-5255
E-mail: ugadmissions@scu.edu
http://www.scu.edu

Stanford University
Old Union 232
Stanford, CA 94305-3005
Phone: (650) 723-2091
Fax: (650) 723-6050
E-mail: admissions@stanford.edu
http://www.stanford.edu

United States International University
10455 Pomerado Road
San Diego, CA 92131
Phone: (619) 635-4772
Fax: (619) 635-4739

E-mail: admissions@usiu.edu
http://www.usiu.edu

University of California—Berkeley
Office of Undergraduate Admissions
110 Sproul Hall, #5800
Berkeley, CA 94720-5800
Phone: (510) 642-3175
Fax: (510) 642-7333
E-mail: ouars@uclink.berkeley.edu
http://www.berkeley.edu

University of California—Davis
Undergraduate Admissions
175 Mrak Hall, 1 Shields Avenue
Davis, CA 95616
Phone: (530) 752-2971
Fax: (530) 752-1280
E-mail: undergradadmissions@ucdavis.edu
http://www.ucdavis.edu

University of California—Irvine
Office of Admissions
204 Administration Building
Irvine, CA 92697-1075
Phone: (949) 824-6703
Fax: (949) 824-2711
E-mail: admissions@uci.edu
http://www.uci.edu

University of California—Los Angeles
405 Hilgard Avenue
Los Angeles, CA 90095
Phone: (310) 825-3101
Fax: (310) 206-1206
E-mail: ugadm@saonet.ucla.edu
http://www.ucla.edu

University of California—Riverside
1120 Hinderaker Hall
Riverside, CA 92521
Phone: (951) 829-3411
Fax: (951) 827-6344
E-mail: discover@ucr.edu
http://www.ucr.edu

University of California—San Diego
9500 Gilman Drive
La Jolla, CA 92093
Phone: (858) 534-4831
Fax: (858) 534-5723
E-mail: admissionsinfo@ucsd.edu
http://www.ucsd.edu

University of California—Santa Barbara
Office of Admissions
1210 Cheadle Hall
Santa Barbara, CA 93106

Phone: (805) 893-2881
Fax: (805) 893-2676
E-mail: appinfo@sa.ucsb.edu
http://www.ucsb.edu

University of California—Santa Cruz
Office of Admissions
Cook House, 1156 High Street
Santa Cruz, CA 95064
Phone: (831) 459-4008
Fax: (831) 459-4452
E-mail: admissions@ucsc.edu
http://www.ucsc.edu

University of Southern California
University Park
Los Angeles, CA 90089
Phone: (213) 740-1111
Fax: (213) 740-6364
E-mail: admitusc@usc.edu
http://www.usc.edu

COLORADO

Colorado State University
University Admissions
Spruce Hall
Fort Collins, CO 80523-0015
Phone: (970) 491-6909
Fax: (970) 491-7799
E-mail: admissions@colostate.edu
http://www.colostate.edu

Metropolitan State College of Denver
Office of Admissions
P. O. Box 173362, Campus Box 16
Denver, CO 80217-3362
Phone: (303) 556-3058
Fax: (303) 556-6345
E-mail: askmetro@mscd.edu
http://www.mscd.edu

Regis University
University Admissions
3333 Regis Boulevard
Denver, CO 80221-1099
Phone: (303) 458-4900 or (800) 388-2366
Fax: (303) 964-5534
E-mail: regisadm@regis.edu
http://www.regis.edu

University of Denver
University Hall, Room 110
2197 South University Boulevard
Denver, CO 80208
Phone: (303) 871-2036 or (800) 525-9495
Fax: (303) 871-3301
E-mail: admission@du.edu
http://www.du.edu

CONNECTICUT

Central Connecticut State University
University Admissions
1615 Stanley Street
New Britain, CT 06050-4010
Phone: (860) 832-2278
Fax: (860) 832-2295
E-mail: admissions@su.edu
http://www.ccsu.edu

Fairfield University
University Admissions
1073 North Benson Road
Fairfield, CT 06430-5195
Phone: (203) 254-4100
Fax: (203) 254-4199
E-mail: admis@mail.fairfield.edu
http://www.fairfield.edu

Quinnipiac University
Office of Admissions
275, Mount Carmel Avenue
Hamden, CT 06518
Phone: (203) 582-8600 or (800) 462-1944
Fax: (203) 281-8906
E-mail: admissions@quinnipiac.edu
http://www.quinnipiac.edu

Sacred Heart University
Undergraduate Admissions
5151 Park Avenue
Fairfield, CT 06825
Phone: (203) 371-7999
Fax: (203) 365-7607
E-mail: enroll@sacredheart.edu
http://www.sacredheart.edu

Southern Connecticut State University
Admissions House
131 Farnham Avenue
New Haven, CT 06515-1202
Phone: (203) 392-5656 or (888) 500-SCSU
Fax: (203) 392-5727
E-mail: adminfo@scsu.ctstateu.edu
http://www.southernct.edu

University of Connecticut
University Admissions
2131 Hillside Road, Unit 3088
Storrs, CT 06268
Phone: (860) 486-3137
Fax: (860) 486-1476
E-mail: beahusky@unconn.edu
http://www.uconn.edu

University of Hartford
University Admissions
200 Bloomfield Avenue
West Hartford, CT 06117
Phone: (860) 768-4296 or (800) 947-4303
Fax: (860) 748-4961
E-mail: admission@mail.hartford.edu
http://www.hartford.edu

University of New Haven
University Admissions
300 Orange Avenue
West Haven, CT 06516
Phone: (203) 932-7319 or
 (800) DIALUNH
Fax: (203) 931-6093
E-mail: adminfo@newhaven.edu
http://www.newhaven.edu

Western Connecticut State University
Undergraduate Admissions
181 White Street
Danbury, CT 06810
Phone: (203) 837-9000 or (877) 837-9278
Fax: (203) 837-8320
E-mail: admissions@wcsu.edu
http://www.wcsu.edu

DELAWARE

Delaware State University
1200 North Dupont Highway
Dover, DE 19901
Phone: (302) 857-6361
Fax: (302) 857-6362
E-mail: admissions@dsc.edu
http://www.dsc.edu

University of Delaware
University Admissions
116 Hullihen Hall
Newark, DE 19716
Phone: (302) 831-8123
Fax: (302) 831-6905
E-mail: admissions@udel.edu
http://www.udel.edu

Wilmington College—New Castle
320 DuPont Highway
New Castle, DE 19720-6491
Phone: (302) 328-9401 or (877) 967-5464
Fax: (302) 328-5902
E-mail: mlee@wilm.coll.edu
http://www.wilcoll.edu

DISTRICT OF COLUMBIA

American University
University Admissions
4400 Massachusetts Avenue NW
Washington, D.C. 20016-8001
Phone: (202) 885-6000
Fax: (202) 885-1025
E-mail: admissions@american.edu
http://www.american.edu

Catholic University of America
University Admissions
620 Michigan Avenue NE
Washington, D.C. 20064
Phone: (202) 319-5305 or (800) 673-2772
Fax: (202) 319-6533
E-mail: cua-admissions@cua.edu
http://www.cua.edu

George Washington University
Office of Undergraduate Admissions
2121 I Street NW
Washington, D.C. 20052
Phone: (202) 994-6040 or
 (800) 447-3765
Fax: (202) 994-0325
E-mail: gwadm@gwu.edu
http://www.gwu.edu

Georgetown University
Office of Undergraduate Admissions
Thirty-seventh and O Streets
Washington, D.C. 20057-1002
Phone: (202) 687-3600
Fax: (202) 687-5084
E-mail: guadmiss@georgetown.edu
http://www.georgetown.edu

Howard University
University Admissions
2400 Sixth Street NW
Washington, D.C. 20059
Phone: (202) 806-2700 or
 (800) HOWARD-U
Fax: (202) 806-4467
E-mail: admission@howard.edu
http://www.howard.edu

Southeastern University
Admissions Office
501 I Street SW
Washington, D.C. 20024
Phone: (202) COLLEGE
E-mail: admissions@admin.seu.edu
http://www.seu.edu

University of the District of Columbia
University Admissions
4200 Connecticut Avenue NW
Washington, D.C. 20008
Phone: (202) 274-6110
Fax: (202) 274-5552
E-mail: cflannagan@udc.edu
http://www.udc.edu

FLORIDA

Clearwater Christian College
3400 Gulf-to-Bay Boulevard
Clearwater, FL 33759-4595
Phone: (727) 726-1153
Fax: (727) 726-8597
E-mail: admissions@clearwater.edu
http://www.clearwater.edu

Florida Atlantic University
University Admissions
777 Glades Avenue
P. O. Box 3091
Boca Raton, FL 33431-0991
Phone: (561) 297-3040 or (800) 299-4FAU
Fax: (561) 297-2758
E-mail: admisweb@fau.edu
http://www.fau.edu

Florida International University
University Admissions
University Park
Miami, FL 33199
Phone: (305) 348-2363
Fax: (305) 348-3648
E-mail: admiss@fiu.edu
http://www.fiu.edu

Florida State University
Office of Admissions
2500 University Center
Tallahassee, FL 32306-2400
Phone: (850) 644-6200
Fax: (850) 644-0197
E-mail: admissions@admin.fsu.edu
http://www.fsu.edu

Northwood University—Florida
2600 North Military Trail
West Palm Beach, FL 33409-2911
Phone: (561) 478-5500
Fax: (561) 640-3328
E-mail: fladmit@northwood.edu
http://www.northwood.edu

University of Central Florida
University Admissions
P.O. Box 16011
Orlando, FL 32816
Phone: (407) 823-3000
Fax: (407) 823-5665
E-mail: admission@mail.ucf.edu
http://www.ucf.edu

University of Florida
Office of Admissions
P.O. Box 114000
Gainesville, FL 32611-4000
Phone: (352) 392-1365
Fax: (904) 392-3987
E-mail: freshman@ufl.edu
http://www.ufl.edu

University of Miami
University Admissions
P.O. Box 248025
Coral Gables, FL 33146-4616
Phone: (305) 284-4323
Fax: (305) 284-2507
E-mail: admissions@miami.edu
http://www.miami.edu

University of North Florida
University Admissions
4567 St. Johns Bluff Road South
Jacksonville, FL 32224-2645
Phone: (904) 620-2624
Fax: (904) 620-2414
E-mail: admissions@unf.edu
http://www.unf.edu

University of South Florida—Tampa
University Admissions
4202 East Fowler Avenue—SVC 1036
Tampa, FL 33620-9951
Phone: (813) 974-3350
Fax: (813) 974-9689
E-mail: jglassma@admin.usf.edu
http://www.usfweb.edu

University of Tampa
University Admissions
401 West Kennedy Boulevard
Tampa, FL 33606
Phone: (813) 253-6211 or (800) 733-4733
Fax: (813) 258-7398
E-mail: admissions@ut.edu
http://www.ut.edu

University of West Florida
University Admissions
11000 University Parkway
Pensacola, FL 32514-5750
Phone: (850) 474-2230
Fax: (850) 474-3360
E-mail: admissions@uwf.edu
http://www.uwf.edu

GEORGIA

Augusta State University
University Admissions
2500 Walton Way
Augusta, GA 30904-2200
Phone: (706) 737-1632
Fax: (706) 667-4355
E-mail: admissions@aug.edu
http://www.aug.edu

Clark Atlanta University
Office of Admissions
223 James P. Brawley Drive SW
Atlanta, GA 30314
Phone: (800) 688-3228
Fax: (404) 880-6174
E-mail: admissions@panthernetcau.edu
http://www.cau.edu

Columbus State University
University Admissions
4225 University Avenue
Columbus, GA 31907-5645
Phone: (706) 568-2035
Fax: (706) 568-5091
E-mail: admissions@colstate.edu
http://www.colstate.edu

Georgia Southern University
University Admissions
P.O. Box 8024
Statesboro, GA 30460
Phone: (912) 681-5391
Fax: (912) 486-7240
E-mail: admissions@georgiasouthern.edu
http://www.georgiasouthern.edu

Georgia State University
University Admissions
P.O. Box 4009
Atlanta, GA 30302-4009
Phone: (404) 651-2365 or (800) 651-2365
Fax: (404) 651-4811
E-mail: admissions@gsu.edu
http://www.gsu.edu

Kennesaw State University
University Admissions
1000 Chastain Road
Kennesaw, GA 30144-5591
Phone: (770) 423-6000
Fax: (770) 423-6541
E-mail: ksuadmit@kennesaw.edu
http://www.kennesaw.edu

Mercer University
University Admissions
1400 Coleman Avenue
Macon, GA 31207-0001
Phone: (478) 301-2650 or (800) 637-2378
Fax: (478) 301-2828
E-mail: admissions@mercer.edu
http://www.mercer.edu

State University of West Georgia
University Admissions

1601 Maple Street
Carrolton, GA 30118-0001
Phone: (678) 839-4000
Fax: (678) 839-4747
E-mail: admiss@westga.edu
http://www.westga.edu

University of Georgia
University Admissions, Terrell Hall
Athens, GA 30602
Phone: (706) 542-8776
Fax: (706) 542-1466
E-mail: undergrad@admissions.uga.edu
http://www.uga.edu

Valdosta State University
University Admissions
1500 North Patterson Street
Valdosta, GA 31698
Phone: (229) 333-5791 or (800) 618-1878
Fax: (229) 333-5482
E-mail: admissions@valdosta.edu
http://www.valdosta.edu

HAWAII

Hawaii Pacific University
University Admissions
1164 Bishop Street
Honolulu, HI 96813-2785
Phone: (808) 544-0238 or (800) 669-4724
Fax: (808) 544-1136
E-mail: admissions@hpu.edu
http://www.hpu.edu

University of Hawaii at Manoa
University Admissions
2600 Campus Road, Room 001
Honolulu, HI 96822
Phone: (808) 956-8975 or (800) 823-9771
Fax: (808) 956-4148
E-mail: ar-info@hawaii.edu
http://www.uhm.hawaii.edu

IDAHO

Boise State University
University Admissions
1910 University Drive
Boise, ID 83725
Phone: (208) 426-1156 or (800) 824-7017
Fax: (208) 426-3765
E-mail: bsuinfo@boisestate.edu
http://www.idbsu.edu

Idaho State University
University Admissions
741 South 7th Avenue
Pocatello, ID 83209

Phone: (208) 282-2475
Fax: (208) 282-4231
E-mail: info@isu.edu
http://www.isu.edu

University of Idaho
Undergraduate Admissions Office
P.O. Box 444264
Moscow, ID 83844
Phone: (208) 885-6326 or (888) 884-3246
Fax: (208) 885-9119
E-mail: admappl@uidaho.edu
http://www.uidaho.edu

ILLINOIS

Bradley University
University Admissions
1501 West Bradley Avenue
Peoria, IL 61625-0002
Phone: (309) 677-1000 or
 (800) 447-6460
Fax: (309) 677-2797
E-mail: admissions@bradley.edu
http://www.bradley.edu

Depaul University
University Admissions
1 East Jackson Boulevard
Chicago, IL 60604-2287
Phone: (312) 362-8300 or
 (800) 4DE-PAUL
Fax: (312) 362-5749
E-mail: admitdpu@depaul.edu
http://www.depaul.edu

Eastern Illinois University
University Admissions
600 Lincoln Avenue
Charleston, IL 61920-3099
Phone: (217) 581-2223
 or (800) 252-5711
Fax: (217) 581-7060
E-mail: admissions@eiu.edu
http://www.eiu.edu

Illinois State University
University Admissions
Campus Box 2200
Normal, IL 61790-2200
Phone: (309) 438-2181 or (800) 366-2478
Fax: (309) 438-3932
E-mail: admissions@ilstu.edu
http://www.ilstu.edu

Lewis University
University Admissions
P.O. Box 297
Romeoville, IL 60446

Phone: (815) 836-5250 or (800) 897-9000
Fax: (815) 836-5002
E-mail: admissions@lewisu.edu
http://www.lewisu.edu

Loyola University—Chicago
University Admissions
820 North Michigan Avenue
Chicago, IL 60611
Phone: (312) 915-6500 or (800) 262-2373
Fax: (312) 915-7216
E-mail: admission@luc.edu
http://www.luc.edu

Northeastern Illinois University
University Admissions
5500 North St. Louis Avenue
Chicago, IL 60625
Phone: (773) 442-4000
Fax: (773) 442-4020
E-mail: admrec@neiu.edu
http://www.neiu.edu

Northern Illinois University
University Admissions
Williston Hall 101
DeKalb, IL 60115-2854
Phone: (815) 753-0446 or (800) 892-3050
Fax: (815) 753-1783
E-mail: admissions@niu.edu
http://www.niu.edu

**Southern Illinois University—
 Carbondale**
University Admissions
Carbondale, IL 62901-4710
Phone: (618) 536-4405
Fax: (618) 453-3250
E-mail: joinsiuc@siu.edu
http://www.siuc.edu

University of Illinois at Chicago
University Admissions
P.O. Box 5220
Chicago, IL 60680-5220
Phone: (312) 996-4350
Fax: (312) 413-7628
E-mail: uicadmit@uic.edu
http://www.uic.edu

**University of Illinois—
 Urbana-Champaign**
University Admissions
901 West Illinois Street
Champaign, IL 61801
Phone: (217) 333-0302
Fax: (217) 244-0903
E-mail: undergraduate@admissions.uiuc.
 edu
http://www.uiuc.edu

University of St. Francis
Office of Admissions
500 North Wilcox Street
Joliet, IL 60435
Phone: (815) 740-5037
Fax: (815) 740-5032
E-mail: admissions@stfrancis.edu
http://www.stfrancis.edu

Western Illinois University
University Admissions
1 University Circle, 115 Sherman Hall
Macomb, IL 61455-1390
Phone: (309) 298-3157
Fax: (309) 298-3111
E-mail: wiuadm@wiu.edu
http://www.wiu.edu

INDIANA

Ball State University
Office of Admissions
2000 University Avenue
Muncie, IN 47306-1099
Phone: (765) 285-8300 or
    (800) 482-4BSU
Fax: (765) 285-1632
E-mail: askus@bsu.edu
http://www.bsu.edu

Butler University
University Admissions
4600 Sunset Avenue
Indianapolis, IN 46208-3485
Phone: (317) 940-8100, ext. 8124 or
    (800) 940-8100
Fax: (317) 940-8150
E-mail: admission@butler.edu
http://www.butler.edu

Indiana State University
University Admissions
210 North 7th Street
Terre Haute, IN 47809-1401
Phone: (812) 237-2121 or (800) 742-0891
Fax: (812) 237-8023
E-mail: admissions@indstate.edu
http://www.indstate.edu

**Indiana University—Purdue
    University—Indianapolis**
University Admissions
425 North University Boulevard
Cavanaugh Hall Room 129
Indianapolis, IN 46202-5143
Phone: (317) 274-4591
Fax: (317) 278-1862
E-mail: apply@iupui.edu
http://www.iupui.edu

Indiana Wesleyan University
University Admissions
4201 South Washington Street
Marion, IN 46953-4974
Phone: (765) 677-2138 or (800) 332-6901
Fax: (765) 677-2333
E-mail: admissions@indwes.edu
http://www.indwes.edu

Purdue University—Main Campus
University Admissions
1080 Schleman Hall
West Lafayette, IN 47907-1080
Phone: (765) 494-1776
Fax: (765) 494-0544
E-mail: admissions@purdue.edu
http://www.purdue.edu

University of Evansville
University Admissions
1800 Lincoln Avenue
Evansville, IN 47722-0002
Phone: (812) 479-2468 or (800) 423-8633
Fax: (812) 474-4076
E-mail: admission@evansville.edu
http://www.evansville.edu

University of Notre Dame
University Admissions
220 Main Building
Notre Dame, IN 46556-5612
Phone: (574) 631-7505
Fax: (574) 631-8865
E-mail: admissio-1@nd.edu
http://www.nd.edu

IOWA

Buena Vista University
610 West Fourth Street
Storm Lake, IA 50588-1798
Phone: (712) 749-2235
Fax: (712) 749-1459
E-mail: admissions@bvu.edu
http://www.bvu.edu

Clarke College
University Admissions
1550 Clarke Drive
Dubuque, IA 52001-3198
Phone: (563) 588-6316 or (800) 383-2345
Fax: (563) 588-6789
E-mail: admissions@clarke.edu
http://www.clarke.edu

Drake University
University Admissions
2507 University Avenue
Des Moines, IA 50311-4505

Phone: (515) 271-3181 or
    (800) 44DRAKE
Fax: (515) 271-2831
E-mail: admission@drake.edu
http://www.drake.edu

Iowa State University
University Admissions
100 Alumni Hall
Ames, IA 50011-2011
Phone: (515) 294-5836 or (800) 262-3810
Fax: (515) 294-2592
E-mail: admissions@iastate.edu
http://www.iastate.edu

University of Iowa
University Admissions
107 Calvin Hall
Iowa City, IA 52242
Phone: (319) 335-3847 or (800) 553-4692
Fax: (319) 335-1535
E-mail: admissions@uiowa.edu
http://www.uiowa.edu

University of Northern Iowa
University Admissions
1227 West 27th Street
Cedar Falls, IA 50614-0018
Phone: (319) 273-2281 or (800) 772-2037
Fax: (319) 273-2885
E-mail: admissions@uni.edu
http://www.uni.edu

KANSAS

Emporia State University
University Admissions
1200 Commercial Street
Emporia, KS 66801-5087
Phone: (620) 341-5465 or
    (800) 896-7544
Fax: (620) 341-5599
E-mail: goto@emporia.edu
http://www.emporia.edu

Fort Hays State University
University Admissions
600 Park Street
Hays, KS 67601-4099
Phone: (785) 628-5666 or (800) 432-0248
Fax: (785) 628-4187
E-mail: tigers@fhsu.edu
http://www.fhsu.edu

Kansas State University
University Admissions
119 Anderson Hall
Manhattan, KS 66506
Phone: (785) 532-6250 or (800) 432-8270

Fax: (785) 532-6393
E-mail: k-state@k-state.edu
http://www.ksu.edu

Washburn University of Topeka
University Admissions
1700 Southwest College Avenue
Topeka, KS 66621
Phone: (785) 231-1030 or (800) 332-0291
Fax: (785) 296-7933
E-mail: zzdpadm@washburn.edu
http://www.washburn.edu

Wichita State University
University Admissions
1845 North Fairmount
Wichita, KS 67260
Phone: (316) 978-3085
Fax: (316) 978-3174
E-mail: admissions@wichita.edu
http://www.wichita.edu

KENTUCKY

Eastern Kentucky University
University Admissions
521 Lancaster Avenue
Richmond, KY 40475-3102
Phone: (859) 622-2106 or (800) 465-9191
Fax: (606) 622-8024
E-mail: admissions@eku.edu
http://www.eku.edu

Morehead State University
University Admissions
150 University Boulevard
Morehead, KY 40351
Phone: (606) 783-2000 or (800) 585-6781
Fax: (606) 783-5038
E-mail: admissions@moreheadstate.edu
http://www.moreheadstate.edu

Murray State University
University Admissions
P.O. Box 9
Murray, KY 42071-0009
Phone: (270) 762-3741 or (800) 272-4678
Fax: (270) 762-3780
E-mail: admissions@murraystate.edu
http://www.murraystate.edu

Northern Kentucky University
University Admissions
Administrative Center 400
Highland Heights, KY 41099-7010
Phone: (859) 572-5220 or (800) 637-9948
Fax: (859) 572-6665
E-mail: admitnku@nku.edu
http://www.nku.edu

University of Louisville
Office of Admissions
2211 South Brook
Louisville, KY 40292-0001
Phone: (502) 852-6531 or (800) 334-8635
Fax: (502) 852-4776
E-mail: admitme@louisville.edu
http://www.louisville.edu

University of Kentucky
University Admissions
100 W.D. Funkhouser Building
Lexington, KY 40506-0054
Phone: (859) 257-2000 or (800) 432-0967
Fax: (859) 257-3823
E-mail: admission@uky.edu
http://www.uky.edu

Western Kentucky University
University Admissions, Potter Hall 117
1 Big Red Way
Bowling Green, KY 42101-3576
Phone: (270) 745-2551 or (800) 495-8463
Fax: (270) 745-6133
E-mail: admission@wku.edu
http://www.wku.edu

LOUISIANA

Louisiana State University
University Admissions
110 Thomas Boyd Hall
Baton Rouge, LA 70803-3013
Phone: (225) 578-1175
Fax: (225) 578-4433
E-mail: admissions@lsu.edu
http://www.lsu.edu

Louisiana State University—Shreveport
University Admissions
1 University Place
Shreveport, LA 71115-2399
Phone: (318) 797-5061
Fax: (318) 797-5204
E-mail: admissions@pilot.lsus.edu
http://www.lsus.edu

Louisiana Tech University
University Admissions
University Avenue
P.O. Box 3178
Ruston, LA 71272
Phone: (318) 257-3036
Fax: (318) 257-2499
E-mail: bulldog@latech.edu
http://www.latech.edu

Loyola University—New Orleans
University Admissions

6363 St. Charles Avenue, Box 18
New Orleans, LA 70118-6195
Phone: (504) 865-3240
Fax: (504) 865-3383
E-mail: admit@loyno.edu
http://www.loyno.edu

McNeese State University
University Admissions
P.O. Box 92495
Lake Charles, LA 70609-2495
Phone: (318) 475-5146 or (800) 622-3353
Fax: (318) 475-5189
http://www.mcneese.edu

Nicholls State University
University Admissions
P.O. Box 2004
Thibodaux, LA 70310
Phone: (985) 448-4507
Fax: (985) 448-4929
E-mail: nicholls@nicholls.edu
http://www.nicholls.edu

Tulane University of Louisiana
University Admissions
6823 St. Charles Avenue
New Orleans, LA 70118-5669
Phone: (504) 865-5731 or (800) 873-9283
Fax: (504) 862-8715
E-mail: undergrad.admission@tulane.edu
http://www.tulane.edu

University of New Orleans
University Admissions
Lake Front
New Orleans, LA 70145
Phone: (504) 280-6595 or (888) 514-4275
Fax: (504) 280-5522
E-mail: admissions@uno.edu
http://www.uno.edu

MAINE

Husson College
One College Circle
Bangor, ME 04401
Phone: (207) 941-7100
Fax: (207) 941-7935
E-mail: admit@husson.edu
http://www.husson.edu

MARYLAND

Morgan State University
University Admissions
1700 East Cold Spring Lane
Baltimore, MD 21251

Phone: (800) 332-6674
Fax: (410) 319-3684
E-mail: tjeness@moac.morgan.edu
http://www.morgan.edu

University of Maryland—College Park Campus
University Admissions, Mitchell Building
College Park, MD 20742
Phone: (301) 314-8385 or (800) 422-5867
Fax: (301) 314-9693
E-mail: um-admit@uga.umd.edu
http://www.maryland.edu

MASSACHUSETTS

Babson College
Office of Undergraduate Admissions
Lunder Hall
Babson Park
Wellesley, MA 02457-0310
Phone: (781) 239-5522
Fax: (781) 239-4135
E-mail: ugradadmission@babson.edu
http://www.babson.edu

Bentley College
University Admissions
175 Forest Street
Waltham, MA 02452-4705
Phone: (781) 891-2244 or (800) 523-2354
Fax: (781) 891-3414
E-mail: ugadmission@bentley.edu
http://www.bentley.edu

Boston College
University Admissions, Devlin Hall 208
140 Commonwealth Avenue
Chestnut Hill, MA 02467-3809
Phone: (617) 552-3100 or (800) 360-2522
Fax: (617) 552-0798
E-mail: ugadmis@bc.edu
http://www.bc.edu

Bridgewater State College
Office of Admissions—Gates House
Bridgewater, MA 02325
Phone: (508) 531-1237
Fax: (508) 531-1746
E-mail: admission@bridgew.edu
http://www.bridgew.edu

New England College of Finance
Office of Admissions
Suite 204
10 High Street
Boston, MA 02110
Phone: (617) 951-2350
Fax: (617) 951-2533

E-mail: info@finance.edu
http://www.finance.edu

Northeastern University
University Admissions, 150 Richards Hall
360 Huntington Avenue
Boston, MA 02115-5096
Phone: (617) 373-2200
Fax: (617) 373-8780
E-mail: admissions@neu.edu
http://www.northeastern.edu

Simmons College
Office of Admissions
300 The Fenway
Boston, MA 02115
Phone: (617) 521-2051
Fax: (617) 521-3190
E-mail: ugadm@simmons.edu
http://www.simmons.edu

Suffolk University
University Admissions
8 Ashburton Place
Boston, MA 02108-2770
Phone: (617) 573-8460
Fax: (617) 742-4291
E-mail: admission@admin.suffolk.edu
http://www.suffolk.edu

University of Massachusetts—Amherst
University Admissions
Amherst, MA 01003
Phone: (413) 545-0222
Fax: (413) 545-4312
E-mail: mail@admissions.umass.edu
http://www.umass.edu

University of Massachusetts—Boston
University Admissions
100 Morrissey Boulevard
Boston, MA 02125-3393
Phone: (617) 287-6000
Fax: (617) 287-5999
E-mail: undergrad@umb.edu
http://www.umb.edu

University of Massachusetts—Dartmouth
Office of Admissions
285 Old Westport Road
North Dartmouth, MA 02747-2300
Phone: (508) 999-8605
Fax: (508) 999-8755
E-mail: admissions@umassd.edu
http://www.umassd.edu

Western New England College
University Admissions
1215 Wilbraham Road
Springfield, MA 01119

Phone: (413) 782-1321 or
    (800) 325-1122, ext.1321
Fax: (413) 782-1777
E-mail: ugradmis@wnec.edu
http://www.wnec.edu

MICHIGAN

Andrews University
University Admissions
Berrien Springs, MI 49104
Phone: (269) 471-6343 or (800) 253-2874
Fax: (269) 471-2670
E-mail: enroll@andrews.edu
http://www.andrews.edu

Central Michigan University
Office of Admissions
Warriner Hall
Mount Pleasant, MI 48859
Phone: (989) 774-3076
Fax: (989) 774-7267
E-mail: cmuadmit@cmich.edu
http://www.cmich.edu

Eastern Michigan University
University Admissions
Ypsilante, MI 48197
400 Pierce Hall
Phone: (734) 487-3060 or
    (800) GOTOEMU
Fax: (734) 487-1484
E-mail: admissions@emich.edu
http://www.emich.edu

Ferris State University
University Admissions
1201 South State Street
Big Rapids, MI 49307-2742
Phone: (231) 591-2100
Fax: (231) 591-3944
E-mail: admissions@ferris.edu
http://www.ferris.edu

Grand Valley State University
University Admissions
1 Campus Drive
Allendale, MI 49401-9403
Phone: (616) 331-2025 or (800) 748-0246
Fax: (616) 331-2000
E-mail: go2gvsu@gvsu.edu
http://www.gvsu.edu

Madonna University
36600 Schoolcraft Road
Livonia, MI 48150-1173
Phone: (734) 432-5339
Fax: (734) 432-5393
http://www.madonna.edu

Michigan State University
University Admissions
250 Administration Building
East Lansing, MI 48824-1046
Phone: (517) 355-8332
Fax: (517) 353-1647
E-mail: admis@msu.edu
http://www.msu.edu

Northwood University—Michigan
4000 Whiting Drive
Midland, MI 48640
Phone: (800) 457-7878
Fax: (989) 837-4490
E-mail: admissions@northwood.edu
http://www.northwood.edu

Oakland University
Office of Admissions, 101 North
Foundation Hall
Rochester, MI 48309-4401
Phone: (248) 370-3360
Fax: (248) 370-4462
E-mail: ouinfo@oakland.edu
http://www.oakland.edu

Saginaw Valley State University
University Admissions
7400 Bay Road
University Center, MI 48710
Phone: (989) 964-4200
Fax: (989) 790-0180
E-mail: admissions@svsu.edu
http://www.svsu.edu

University of Michigan—Flint
University Admissions
303 East Kearsley Street
Flint, MI 48502-1950
Phone: (810) 762-3300 or (800) 942-5636
Fax: (810) 762-3272
E-mail: admissions@umflint.edu
http://www.flint.umich.edu

Wayne State University
Office of Admissions
Welcome Center
42 West Warren
Detroit, MI 48202
Phone: (313) 577-3577
Fax: (313) 577-7536
E-mail: admissions@wayne.edu
http://www.wayne.edu

Western Michigan University
Office of Admission and Orientation
1903 West Michigan Avenue
Kalamazoo, MI 49008-5167
Phone: (269) 387-2000 or (800) 400-4968
Fax: (616) 387-2096

E-mail: ask-wmu@wmich.edu
http://www.wmich.edu

MINNESOTA

Augsburg College
Office of Admissions
2211 Riverside Avenue South
Minneapolis, MN 55454-1351
Phone: (612) 330-1001 or (800) 788-5678
Fax: (612) 330-1590
E-mail: admissions@augsburg.edu
http://www.augsburg.edu

Minnesota State University—Mankato
Office of Admissions
122 Taylor Center
Mankato, MN 56001-8400
Phone: (507) 389-1822 or (800) 722-0544
Fax: (507) 389-1511
E-mail: admissions@mnsu.edu
http://www.mnsu.edu

Minnesota State University—Moorehead
University Admissions, Owens Hall
1104 7th Avenue South
Moorhead, MN 56563-0002
Phone: (800) 593-7246
Fax: (218) 477-4374
E-mail: dragon@mnstate.edu
http://www.mnstate.edu

St. Cloud State University
University Admissions
720 4th Avenue South
St. Cloud, MN 56301-4498
Phone: (320) 308-2244
Fax: (320) 308-2243
E-mail: scsu4u@stcloudstate.edu
http://www.stcloudstate.edu

Saint Mary's University of Minnesota
University Admissions
700 Terrace Heights #2
Winona, MN 55987-1399
Phone: (507) 457-1600
Fax: (507) 457-1722
E-mail: admissions@smumn.edu
http://www.smumn.edu

University of Minnesota—Duluth
University Admissions
23 Solon Campus Center
1117 University Drive
Duluth, MN 55812
Phone: (218) 726-7171 or (800) 232-1339
Fax: (218) 726-7040
E-mail: umdadmis@d.umn.edu
http://www.d.umn.edu

University of Minnesota—Twin Cities
University Admissions
240 Williamson Hall
231 Pillsbury Drive SE
Minneapolis, MN 55455-0213
Phone: (612) 625-2008 or (800) 752-1000
Fax: (612) 626-1693
E-mail: admissions@tc.umn.edu
http://www.tc.umn.edu

Winona State University
Office of Admissions
8th and Johnson Street
Winona, MN 55987-0838
Phone: (507) 457-5100
Fax: (507) 457-5620
E-mail: admissions@winona.edu
http://www.winona.edu

MISSISSIPPI

Delta State University
University Admissions
Highway 8
Cleveland, MS 38733-0001
Phone: (662) 846-4020
Fax: (662) 846-4683
E-mail: admissions@deltastate.edu
http://www.deltastate.edu

Jackson State University
University Admissions
1400 John R. Lynch Street
Jackson, MS 39217
Phone: (800) 848-6817
Fax: (601) 979-3445
E-mail: schatman@ccaix.jsums.edu
http://www.jsums.edu

Mississippi State University
Office of Admissions
P.O. Box 6305
Mississippi State, MS 39762
Phone: (662) 325-2224
Fax: (662) 325-7360
E-mail: admit@admissions.msstate.edu
http://www.msstate.edu

University of Mississippi—Main Campus
Office of Admissions
145 Martindale Student Services Center
University, MS 38677
Phone: (662) 915-7226
Fax: (662) 915-5869
E-mail: admissions@olemiss.edu
http://www.olemiss.edu

University of Southern Mississippi
University Admissions

118 College Drive
Hattiesburg, MS 39406-0001
Phone: (601) 266-5000
Fax: (601) 266-5148
E-mail: admissions@usm.edu
http://www.usm.edu

MISSOURI

Central Missouri State University
Office of Admissions
Administration Building Room 104
Warrensburg, MO 64093
Phone: (660) 543-4290 or (800) 956-0177
Fax: (660) 543-8517
E-mail: admit@cmsuvmb.cmsu.edu
http://www.cmsu.edu

Missouri Southern State University
Office of Admissions
3950 East Newman Road
Joplin, MO 64801-1595
Phone: (417) 625-9378
Fax: (417) 659-4429
E-mail: admissions@mssu.edu
http://www.mssu.edu

Northwest Missouri State University
University Admissions
800 University Drive
Maryville, MO 64468
Phone: (800) 633-1175
Fax: (660) 562-1121
E-mail: admissions@mail.nwmissouri.edu
http://www.nwmissouri.edu

St. Louis University—Main Campus
University Admissions
221 North Grand Boulevard
St. Louis, MO 63103-2097
Phone: (314) 977-2500 or (800) 758-3678
Fax: (314) 977-7136
E-mail: admitme@slu.edu
http://www.slu.edu

Southeast Missouri State University
University Admissions
One University Plaza
Mail Stop 3550
Cape Girardeau, MO 63701
Phone: (573) 651-2590
Fax: (573) 651-5936
E-mail: admissions@semo.edu
http://www.semo.edu

Southwest Missouri State University
University Admissions
901 South National Street
Springfield, MO 65804

Phone: (417) 836-5517
Fax: (417) 836-6334
E-mail: smsuinfo@smsu.edu
http://www.smsu.edu

Washington University in St. Louis
University Admissions
Campus Box 1089
One Brookings Drive
St. Louis, MO 63130-4899
Phone: (314) 935-6000 or (800) 638-0700
Fax: (314) 935-4290
E-mail: admissions@wustl.edu
http://www.wustl.edu

MONTANA

Montana State University—Billings
University Admissions
1500 University Drive
Billings, MT 59101-9984
Phone: (406) 657-2158 or (800) 565-6782
Fax: (406) 657-2051
E-mail: cjohannes@msubillings.edu
http://www.msubillings.edu

Montana State University—Bozeman
New Student Services
P.O. Box 172190
Bozeman, MT 59717-2190
Phone: (406) 657-2158 or (800) 565-6782
Fax: (406) 994-1923
E-mail: admissions@msubillings.edu
http://www.msubillings.edu

NEBRASKA

Creighton University
University Admissions
2500 California Plaza
Omaha, NE 68178-0001
Phone: (402) 280-2703 or (800) 282-5835
Fax: (402) 280-2685
E-mail: admissions@creighton.edu
http://www.creighton.edu

University of Nebraska at Kearney
University Admissions
905 West 25th Street
Kearney, NE 68849-0001
Phone: (308) 865-8526 or
    (800) KEARNEY
Fax: (308) 865-8987
E-mail: admissionsug@unk.edu
http://www.unk.edu

University of Nebraska—Lincoln
University Admissions

313 North 13th Street
Lincoln, NE 68588-0256
Phone: (402) 472-2023
    or (800) 742-8800
Fax: (402) 472-0670
E-mail: nuhusker@unl.edu
http://www.unl.edu

University of Nebraska—Omaha
Office of Admissions
6001 Dodge Street
Omaha, NE 68182
Phone: (402) 554-2393 or (800) 856-8648
Fax: (402) 554-3472
E-mail: unoadm@unomaha.edu
http://www.unomaha.edu

NEVADA

University of Nevada—Las Vegas
University Admissions
P.O. Box 451021
Las Vegas, NV 89154-1021
Phone: (702) 774-8658 or
    (800) 334-UNLV
Fax: (702) 774-8008
E-mail: undergraduate.recruitment@
    ccmail.nevada.edu
http://www.unlv.edu

University of Nevada—Reno
University Admissions
Mail Stop 120
Reno, NV 89557
Phone: (775) 784-4700 or (800) 622-4867
Fax: (775) 784-4283
E-mail: asknevada@unr.edu
http://www.unr.edu

NEW HAMPSHIRE

Franklin Pierce College
Admissions Office
P.O. Box 60
20 College Road
Rindge, NH 03461
Phone: (603) 899-4050
Fax: (603) 889-4394
E-mail: admissions@fpc.edu
http://www.fpc.edu

NEW JERSEY

Ramapo College of New Jersey
Office of Admissions
505 Ramapo Valley Road
Mahwah, NJ 07430-1680
Phone: (201) 684-7300, ext. 7601 or
    (800) 9RA-MAPO

Fax: (201) 684-7964
E-mail: admissions@ramapo.edu
http://www.ramapo.edu

Rider University
University Admissions
2083 Lawrenceville Road
Lawrenceville, NJ 08648-3099
Phone: (609) 896-5042 or (800) 257-9026
Fax: (609) 895-6645
E-mail: admissions@rider.edu
http://www.rider.edu

Rutgers University—Newark
College of Arts and Sciences
University Admissions
249 University Avenue
Newark, NJ 07102
Phone: (973) 353-5205
Fax: (973) 353-1440
E-mail: admissions@rutgers.edu
http://www.rutgers.edu

Rutgers University College of Arts and Sciences
Undergraduate Admissions
65 Davidson Road, Room 202
Piscataway, NJ 08854-8097
Phone: (732) 932-4636
Fax: (732) 445-0237
E-mail: admissions@rutgers.edu
http://www.rutgers.edu

Rutgers University—Camden
University Admissions
406 Penn Street
Camden, NJ 08102
Phone: (856) 255-6104
Fax: (856) 225-6498
E-mail: camden@camuga.rutgers.edu
http://www.rutgers.edu

Seton Hall University
Enrollment Services, Bayley Hall
400 South Orange Avenue
South Orange, NJ 07079-2697
Phone: (973) 761-9332 or
    (800) THE HALL
Fax: (973) 275-2040
E-mail: thehall@shu.edu
http://www.shu.edu

Thomas A. Edison State College
Admissions Services
101 West State Street
Trenton, NJ 08608-1176
Phone: (609) 984-1150 or
    (800) 442-8372
Fax: (609) 984-8447

E-mail: info@tesc.edu
http://www.tesc.edu

NEW MEXICO

Eastern New Mexico University
University Admissions
Station #7 ENMU
Portales, NM 88130
Phone: (505) 562-2178 or (800) 367-3668
Fax: (505) 562-2118
E-mail: admissions@enmu.edu
http://www.enmu.edu

New Mexico State University—Main Campus
University Admissions
P.O. Box 30001, MSC 3A
Las Cruces, NM 88003-8001
Phone: (505) 646-3121 or (800) 662-6678
Fax: (505) 646-6330
E-mail: admissions@nmsu.edu
http://www.nmsu.edu

NEW YORK

Adelphi University
Levermore Hall 114
1 South Avenue
Garden City, NY 11530
Phone: (516) 877-3050 or
    (800) ADELPHI
Fax: (516) 877-3039
E-mail: admissions@adelphi.edu
http://www.adelphi.edu

Canisius College
Office of Admissions
2001 Main Street
Buffalo, NY 14208-1098
Phone: (716) 888-2200 or (800) 843-1517
Fax: (716) 888-3230
E-mail: inquiry@canisius.edu
http://www.canisius.edu

Dowling College
Office of Admissions
Idle Hour Boulevard
Oakdale, NY 11769-1999
Phone: (800) 369-5464
Fax: (631) 563-3827
E-mail: admissions@dowling.edu
http://www.dowling.edu

Excelsior College
7 Columbia Circle
Albany, NY 12203-5159
Phone: (518) 464-8500
Fax: (518) 464-8777

E-mail: admissions@excelsior.edu
http://www.excelsior.edu

Hartwick College
Office of Admissions
P.O. Box 4020
Oneonta, NY 13820-4020
Phone: (607) 431-4150 or
    (888) HARTWICK
Fax: (607) 431-4102
E-mail: admissions@hartwick.edu
http://www.hartwick.edu

Hofstra University
Admissions Center
100 Hofstra University
Hempstead, NY 11549
Phone: (516) 463-6700 or
    (800) HOFSTRA
Fax: (516) 463-5100
E-mail: admitme@hofstra.edu
http://www.hofstra.edu

Iona College
Office of Admissions
715 North Avenue
New Rochelle, NY 10801-1890
Phone: (914) 633-2502
Fax: (914) 633-2642
E-mail: icad@iona.edu
http://www.iona.edu

Ithaca College
Office of Admissions, 100 Job Hall
953 Danby Road
Ithaca, NY 14850
Phone: (607) 274-3124 or (800) 429-4274
Fax: (607) 274-1900
E-mail: admission@ithaca.edu
http://www.ithaca.edu

Long Island University—Brooklyn Campus
University Admissions
One University Plaza
Brooklyn, NY 11201-8423
Phone: (718) 548-7526 or
    (800) LIU-PLAN
Fax: (718) 797-2399
E-mail: admissions@brooklyn.liunet.edu
http://www.liunet.edu

Manhattan College
Office of Undergraduate Admissions
4513 Manhattan College Parkway
Riverdale, NY 10471
Phone: (718) 862-7200 or (800) 622-9235
Fax: (718) 862-8019
E-mail: admit@manhattan.edu
http://www.manhattan.edu

New York Institute of Technology—
Old Westbury
Office of Admissions
P.O. Box 8000
Northern Boulevard
Old Westbury, NY 11568-8000
Phone: (516) 686-7520
Fax: (516) 686-7613
E-mail: admission@nyit.edu
http://www.nyit.edu

New York University
University Admissions
22 Washington Square North
New York, NY 10011
Phone: (212) 998-4500
Fax: (212) 995-4902
E-mail: admissions@nyu.edu
http://www.nyu.edu

Pace University
University Admissions
One Pace Place
New York, NY 10038
Phone: (212) 346-1323 or (800) 847-7223
Fax: (212) 346-1040
E-mail: infoctr@pace.edu
http://www.pace.edu

Rochester Institute of Technology
Office of Admissions
60 Lomb Memorial Drive
Rochester, NY 14623-5604
Phone: (585) 475-6631
Fax: (585) 475-7424
E-mail: admissions@rit.edu
http://www.rit.edu

St. Bonaventure University
University Admissions
3261 West State Road
St. Bonaventure, NY 14778-2284
Phone: (716) 375-2400 or (800) 462-5050
Fax: (716) 375-2005
E-mail: admission@sbu.edu
http://www.sbu.edu

St. Johns University
Office of Undergraduate Admissions
8000 Utopia Parkway
Jamaica, NY 11439
Phone: (718) 990-2000 or
(888) 9ST-JOHNS
Fax: (718) 990-5728
E-mail: admhelp@stjohns.edu
http://www.stjohns.edu

Siena College
Office of Admissions

515 Loudon Road
Loudonville, NY 12211
Phone: (518) 783-2423
Fax: (518) 783-2436
E-mail: admit@siena.edu
http://www.siena.edu

Syracuse University
University Admissions
201 Tolley Administration Building
Syracuse, NY 13244-1100
Phone: (315) 443-3611
Fax: (315) 443-4226
E-mail: orange@syr.edu
http://www.syracuse.edu

Touro College
University Admissions
1602 Avenue J
Brooklyn, NY 11230
Phone: (718) 252-7800
Fax: (718) 253-6479
E-mail: lasadmit@touro.edu
http://www.touro.edu

NORTH CAROLINA

Appalachian State University
Office of Admissions
P.O. Box 32004
Boone, NC 28608
Phone: (828) 262-2120
Fax: (828) 262-3296
E-mail: admissions@appstate.edu
http://www.appstate.edu

Meredith College
Office of Admissions
3800 Hillsborough Street
Raleigh, NC 27607-5298
Phone: (919) 760-8581 or
(800) MEREDITH
Fax: (919) 760-2348
E-mail: admissions@meredith.edu
http://www.meredith.edu

North Carolina Central University
Fayetteville Street
Durham, NC 27707
Phone: (919) 560-6298
Fax: (919) 530-7625
E-mail: ebridges@wpo.nccu.edu
http://www.nccu.edu

University of North Carolina
at Greensboro
University Admissions
123 Mossman Building
Greensboro, NC 27402

Phone: (336) 334-5243
Fax: (336) 334-4180
E-mail: undergrad_admissions@uncg.
edu
http://www.uncg.edu

Wake Forest University
University Admissions
P.O. Box 7305
Reynolda Station
Winston-Salem, NC 27109
Phone: (336) 758-5201
Fax: (336) 758-4324
E-mail: admissions@wfu.edu
http://www.wfu.edu

Western Carolina University
University Admissions
242 HFR Administration
Culowhee, NC 28723
Phone: (828) 227-7317
Fax: (828) 227-7319
E-mail: admiss@wcu.edu
http://www.wcu.edu

NORTH DAKOTA

Dickinson State University
Office of Student Recruitment
Box 173
Dickinson, ND 58601-4896
Phone: (701) 483-2175 or (800) 279-4295
Fax: (701) 483-2409
E-mail: dsu.hawks@dsu.nodak.edu
http://www.dickinsonstate.edu

Minot State University
University Admissions
500 University Avenue West
Minot, ND 58707-0002
Phone: (701) 858-3350 or (800) 777-0750
Fax: (701) 858-3386
E-mail: askmsu@minotstateu.edu
http://www.minotstateu.edu

University of North Dakota
University Admissions
P.O. Box 8357
Grand Forks, ND 58202
Phone: (701) 777-3821 or (800) 225-5863
Fax: (701) 777-2721
E-mail: enrollment_services@mail.und.
nodak.edu
http://www.und.edu

OHIO

Ashland University
University Admissions

401 College Avenue
Ashland, OH 44805
Phone: (419) 289-5052 or (800) 882-1548
Fax: (419) 289-5999
E-mail: auadmsn@ashland.edu
http://www.ashland.edu

**Bowling Green State University—
    Main Campus**
University Admissions
110 McFall Center
Bowling Green, OH 43403
Phone: (419) 372-2478
Fax: (419) 372-6955
E-mail: admissions@bgnet.bgsu.edu
http://www.bgsu.edu

Cleveland State University
University Admissions
East 24th Street and Euclid Avenue
Cleveland, OH 44115
Phone: (216) 687-2100
Fax: (216) 687-9210
E-mail: admissions@csuohio.edu
http://www.csuohio.edu

Franklin University
University Admissions
201 South Grant Avenue
Columbus, OH 43215-5399
Phone: (614) 797-4700 or
    (877) 341-6300
Fax: (614) 244-8027
E-mail: info@franklin.edu
http://www.franklin.edu

John Carroll University
University Admissions
20700 North Park Boulevard
University Heights, OH 44118-4581
Phone: (216) 397-4294
Fax: (216) 397-3098
E-mail: admission@jcu.edu
http://www.jcu.edu

Kent State University—Main Campus
University Admissions
161 Michael Schwartz Center
Kent, OH 44242-0001
Phone: (330) 672-2444 or
    (800) 988-KENT
Fax: (330) 672-2499
E-mail: admissions@kent.edu
http://www.kent.edu

Miami University
University Admissions
500 East High Street
Oxford, OH 45056

Phone: (513) 529-2531
Fax: (513) 529-1550
E-mail: admissions@muohio.edu
http://www.muohio.edu

Ohio State University—Columbus
Enarson Hall
154 West 12th Avenue
Columbus, OH 43210-1200
Phone: (614) 292-3980
Fax: (614) 292-4818
E-mail: askabuckeye@osu.edu
http://www.osu.edu

Ohio University
University Admissions
120 Chubb Hall
Athens, OH 45701-2979
Phone: (740) 593-4100
Fax: (740) 593-0560
E-mail: admissions@ohiou.edu
http://www.ohiou.edu

University of Akron
University Admissions
381 Buchtel Common
Akron, OH 44325-2001
Phone: (330) 972-7077 or (800) 655-4884
Fax: (330) 972-7022
E-mail: admissions@uakron.edu
http://www.uakron.edu

University of Cincinnati
University Admissions
P.O. Box 210091
Cincinnati, OH 45221-0091
Phone: (513) 556-1100 or (800) 827-8728
Fax: (513) 556-1105
E-mail: admissions@uc.edu
http://www.uc.edu

University of Dayton
University Admissions
300 College Park
Dayton, OH 45469-1300
Phone: (937) 229-4411 or (800) 837-7433
Fax: (937) 229-4729
E-mail: admission@udayton.edu
http://www.udayton.edu

University of Findlay
University Admissions
1000 North Main Street
Findlay, OH 45840-3653
Phone: (419) 424-4732 or (800) 472-9502
Fax: (419) 434-4822
E-mail: admissions@findlay.edu
http://www.findlay.edu

University of Toledo
University Admissions
2801 West Bancroft
Toledo, OH 43606-3398
Phone: (419) 530-8700 or (800) 5-TOLEDO
Fax: (419) 530-5713
E-mail: enroll@utnet.utoledo.edu
http://www.utoledo.edu

Wright State University—Main Campus
Undergraduate Admissions
3640 Colonel Glenn Highway
Dayton, OH 45435
Phone: (937) 775-5700 or (800) 247-1770
Fax: (937) 775-5795
E-mail: admissions@wright.edu
http://www.wright.edu

Xavier University
University Admissions
3800 Victory Parkway
Cincinnati, OH 45207-2111
Phone: (513) 745-3301
    or (800) 344-4698
Fax: (513) 745-4319
E-mail: xuadmit@xavier.edu
http://www.xavier.edu

Youngstown State University
University Admissions
One University Plaza
Youngstown, OH 44555-0001
Phone: (330) 742-2000 or (877) 468-6978
Fax: (330) 742-3674
E-mail: enroll@ysu.edu
http://www.ysu.edu

OKLAHOMA

Northeastern State University
Office of Admission and Records
600 North Grand
Tahlequah, OK 74464-2399
Phone: (918) 456-5511, ext. 2200 or
    (800) 722-9614
Fax: (918) 458-2342
E-mail: nsuadmis@cherokee.nsuok.edu
http://www.nsuok.edu

Oklahoma Christian University
P.O. Box 11000
Oklahoma City, OK 73136-1100
Phone: (405) 425-5050
Fax: (405) 425-5269
E-mail: info@oc.edu
http://www.oc.edu

Oklahoma City University
University Admissions

2501 North Blackwelder
Oklahoma City, OK 73106-1402
Phone: (405) 521-5050 or (800) 633-7242
Fax: (405) 521-5264
E-mail: uadmissions@okcu.edu
http://www.okcu.edu

Oklahoma State University
Undergraduate Admissions
219 Student Union
Stillwater, OK 74078
Phone: (405) 744-4366
Fax: (405) 744-4300
E-mail: admit@okstate.edu
http://www.okstate.edu

Oral Roberts University
University Admissions
7777 South Lewis
Tulsa, OK 74171
Phone: (918) 495-6518
Fax: (918) 495-6222
E-mail: admissions@oru.edu
http://www.oru.edu

Southeastern Oklahoma State University
University Admissions
1405 North 4th
Durant, OK 74701
Phone: (580) 745-2060 or (800) 435-1327
Fax: (580) 745-4502
E-mail: admissions@suso.edu
http://www.suso.edu

Southwestern Oklahoma State University
100 Campus Drive
Weatherford, OK 73096-3098
Phone: (405) 772-6611
Fax: (405) 774-3795
E-mail: phillic@swosu.edu
http://www.swosu.edu

University of Central Oklahoma
University Admissions
100 North University Drive
Edmond, OK 73034
Phone: (405) 974-2338 or (800) 254-4215
Fax: (405) 341-4964
E-mail: admituco@ocok.edu
http://www.ucok.edu

University of Oklahoma
Admissions
Buchanan Hall 127
1000 Asp Avenue
Norman, OK 73019-4076
Phone: 405-325-2252

Fax: 405-325-7124
E-mail: admrec@ou.edu
http://www.ou.edu

University of Tulsa
University Admissions
600 South College Avenue
Tulsa, OK 74104
Phone: (918) 631-2307 or (800) 331-3050
Fax: (918) 631-5003
E-mail: admission@utulsa.edu
http://www.utulsa.edu

OREGON

Portland State University
Office of Admissions
P.O. Box 751
Portland, OR 97207-0751
Phone: (503) 725-3511 or (800) 547-8887
Fax: (503) 725-5525
E-mail: admissions@pdx.edu
http://www.pdx.edu

University of Oregon
Office of Admissions
Eugene, OR 94704
Phone: (541) 346-3201 or (800) 232-3825
Fax: (541) 346-5815
E-mail: uoadmit@oregon.uoregon.edu
http://www.uoregon.edu

University of Portland
Office of Admissions
5000 North Willamette Boulevard
Portland, OR 97203-7147
Phone: (503) 943-7147 or (888) 627-5601
Fax: (503) 283-7315
E-mail: admissio@up.edu
http://www.up.edu

PENNSYLVANIA

Clarion University of Pennsylvania
Office of Admissions
840 Wood Street
Clarion, PA 16217
Phone: (814) 393-2306 or (800) 672-7171
Fax: (814) 393-2030
E-mail: admissions@clarion.edu
http://www.clarion.edu

Drexel University
University Admissions
3141 Chestnut Street
Philadelphia, PA 19104-2875
Phone: (215) 895-2400 or
    (800) 2-DREXEL

Fax: (215) 895-5939
E-mail: enroll@drexel.edu
http://www.drexel.edu

Duquesne University
Office of Admissions
600 Forbes Avenue
Pittsburgh, PA 15282-0201
Phone: (412) 396-5000 or (800) 456-0590
Fax: (412) 396-5644
E-mail: admissions@duq.edu
http://www.duq.edu

Gannon University
University Admissions
109 University Square
Erie, PA 16541
Phone: (814) 871-7240 or (800) 426-6668
Fax: (814) 871-5803
E-mail: admissions@gannon.edu
http://www.gannon.edu

Indiana University of Pennsylvania
University Admissions
216 Pratt Hall
Indiana, PA 15705
Phone: (724) 357-2230 or (800) 442-6830
Fax: (724) 357-6281
E-mail: admissions-inquiry@iup.edu
http://www.iup.edu

Lasalle University
University Admissions
1900 West Olney Avenue
Philadelphia, PA 19141-1199
Phone: (215) 951-1500 or (800) 328-1910
Fax: (215) 951-1656
E-mail: admiss@lasalle.edu
http://www.lasalle.edu

Lehigh University
University Admissions
27 Memorial Drive West
Bethlehem, PA 18015
Phone: (610) 758-3100
Fax: (610) 758-4361
E-mail: admissions@lehigh.edu
http://www.lehigh.edu

Pennsylvania State University— University Park
University Admissions
201 Shields Building
University Park, PA 16802-1503
Phone: (814) 865-5471
Fax: (814) 863-7590
E-mail: admissions@psu.edu
http://www.psu.edu

Philadelphia University
University Admissions
Schoolhouse Lane and Henry Avenue
Philadelphia, PA 19144-5497
Phone: (215) 951-2800 or (800) 951-7287
Fax: (215) 951-2907
E-mail: admissions@philau.edu
http://www.philau.edu

Robert Morris University
Office of Admissions
881 Narrows Run Road
Moon Township, PA 15108-1189
Phone: (412) 262-8206 or (800) 762-0097
Fax: (412) 299-2425
E-mail: enrollmentoffice@rmu.edu
http://www.rmu.edu

St. Josephs University
University Admissions
5600 City Avenue
Philadelphia, PA 19131-1395
Phone: (610) 660-1300 or
    (888) BEAHAWK
Fax: (610) 660-1314
E-mail: admit@sju.edu
http://www.sju.edu

**Shippensburg University of
    Pennsylvania**
University Admissions
1871 Old Main Drive
Shippensburg, PA 17257-2299
Phone: (717) 477-1231
Fax: (717) 477-4016
E-mail: admiss@ship.edu
http://www.ship.edu

Temple University
University Admissions
1801 North Broad Street
Philadelphia, PA 19122-6096
Phone: (215) 204-7200 or (888) 340-2222
Fax: (215) 204-5694
E-mail: tuadm@mail.temple.edu
http://www.temple.edu

University of Pennsylvania
University Admissions
1 College Hall, Levy Park
Philadelphia, PA 19104
Phone: (215) 898-7507
Fax: (215) 898-9670
E-mail: info@admissions.ugao.upenn.edu
http://www.upenn.edu

University of Pittsburgh
Office of Admissions and Financial Aid

4227 Fifth Avenue, First Floor
Pittsburgh, PA 15213
Phone: (412) 624-7488
Fax: (412) 648-8815
E-mail: oafa@pitt.edu
http://www.pitt.edu

Villanova University
University Admissions
800 Lancaster Avenue
Villanova, PA 19085-1672
Phone: (610) 519-4000 or (800) 338-7927
Fax: (610) 519-6450
E-mail: gotovu@villanova.edu
http://www.villanova.edu

West Chester University of Pennsylvania
University Admissions
Messikomer Hall, Rosedale Avenue
West Chester, PA 19383
Phone: (610) 436-3411
Fax: (610) 436-2907
E-mail: ugadmiss@wcupa.edu
http://www.wcupa.edu

York College of Pennsylvania
University Admissions
Country Club Road
York, PA 17405-7199
Phone: (717) 849-1600 or (800) 455-8018
Fax: (717) 849-1607
E-mail: admissions@ycp.edu
http://www.ycp.edu

RHODE ISLAND

Bryant University
Office of Admissions
1150 Douglas Pike
Smithfield, RI 02917-1284
Phone: (401) 232-6100 or (800) 622-7001
Fax: (401) 232-6741
E-mail: admission@bryant.edu
http://www.bryant.edu

Providence College
Office of Admissions
River Avenue and Eaton Street
Providence, RI 02918
Phone: (401) 865-2535 or (800) 721-6444
Fax: (401) 865-2826
E-mail: pcadmiss@providence.edu
http://www.providence.edu

University of Rhode Island
Undergraduate Admissions Office
19668 Ranger Road Suite 1
Kingston, RI 02881

Phone: (401) 874-7100
Fax: (401) 874-5523
E-mail: uriadmit@etal.uri.edu
http://www.uri.edu

SOUTH CAROLINA

Clemson University
University Admissions
105 Sikes Hall
P.O. Box 345124
Clemson, SC 29634
Phone: (864) 656-2287
Fax: (864) 656-2464
E-mail: cuadmissions@clemson.edu
http://www.clemson.edu

Coastal Carolina University
University Admissions
P.O. Box 261954
Conway, SC 29528
Phone: (843) 349-2026 or (800) 277-7000
Fax: (843) 349-2127
E-mail: admissions@coastal.edu
http://www.coastal.edu

Francis Marion University
Office of Admissions
P.O. Box 100547
Florence, SC 29501-0547
Phone: (843) 661-1231 or (800) 368-7551
Fax: (843) 661-4635
E-mail: admissions@fmarion.edu
http://www.fmarion.edu

University of South Carolina—Aiken
University Admissions
471 University Parkway
Aiken, SC 29801-6309
Phone: (803) 641-3366
Fax: (803) 641-3727
E-mail: admit@sc.edu
http://www.usca.edu

**University of South Carolina—
    Columbia**
Undergraduate Admissions
Columbia, SC 29208
Phone: (803) 777-7700 or (800) 868-5872
Fax: (803) 777-0101
E-mail: admissions@sc.edu
http://www.sc.edu

TENNESSEE

Belmont University
University Admissions
1900 Belmont Boulevard
Nashville, TN 37212-3757

Phone: (615) 460-6785 or
   (800) 56E-NROL
Fax: (615) 460-5434
E-mail: buadmission@mail.belmont.edu
http://www.belmont.edu

Carson-Newman College
University Admissions
1646 Russell Avenue
Jefferson City, TN 37760
Phone: (865) 471-3223 or (800) 678-9061
Fax: (865) 471-3502
E-mail: cnadmiss@cnacc.cn.edu
http://www.cn.edu

East Tennessee State University
University Admissions
P.O. Box 70731
Johnson City, TN 37614-0731
Phone: (423) 439-4213 or (800) 462-3878
Fax: (423) 439-4630
E-mail: go2etsu@etsu.edu
http://www.etsu.edu

Freed-Hardeman University
158 East Main Street
Henderson, TN 38340
Phone: (731) 989-6651
Fax: (731) 989-6047
E-mail: admissions@fhu.edu
http://www.fhu.edu

Middle Tennessee State University
Office of Admissions
Murfreesboro, TN 37132
Phone: (615) 898-2111 or
   (800) 433-6878
Fax: (615) 898-5478
E-mail: admissions@mtsu.edu
http://www.mtsu.edu

Tennessee Technological University
University Admissions
900 North Dixon Avenue
TTU Box 5006
Cookeville, TN 38505
Phone: (931) 372-3888 or (800) 255-8881
Fax: (931) 372-6250
E-mail: admissions@tntech.edu
http://www.tntech.edu

University of Memphis
University Admissions
Central at Patterson
Memphis, TN 38152
Phone: (901) 678-2111
Fax: (901) 678-3053
E-mail: recruitment@memphis.edu
http://www.memphis.edu

University of Tennessee—Knoxville
University Admissions
320 Student Services Building
Circle Park Drive
Knoxville, TN 37996-0230
Phone: (865) 974-2184 or (800) 221-8657
Fax: (865) 974-6341
E-mail: admissions@utk.edu
http://www.utk.edu

TEXAS

Angelo State University
University Admissions
2601 West Avenue North
San Angelo, TX 76909
Phone: (325) 942-2041
Fax: (325) 942-2078
E-mail: admissions@angelo.edu
http://www.angelo.edu

Baylor University
University Admissions
P.O. Box 97056
Waco, TX 76798-7056
Phone: (254) 710-3435 or (800)
   BAYLOR-U
Fax: (254) 710-3436
E-mail: admissions_office@baylor.edu
http://www.baylor.edu

Lamar University—Beaumont
University Admissions
P.O. Box 10009
Beaumont, TX 77710
Phone: (409) 880-8888
Fax: (409) 880-8463
E-mail: admissions@hal.lamar.edu
http://www.lamar.edu

Midwestern State University
University Admissions
3410 Taft Boulevard
Wichita Falls, TX 76308-2096
Phone: (940) 397-4334 or
   (800) 842-1922
Fax: (940) 397-4672
E-mail: admissions@mwsu.edu
http://www.mwsu.edu

Prairie View A&M University
University Admissions
P.O. Box 3089
University Drive
Prairie View, TX 77446
Phone: (936) 857-2626
Fax: (936) 857-2699
E-mail: mary_gooch@pvamu.edu
http://www.pvamu.edu

St. Edwards University
University Admissions
3001 South Congress Street
Austin, TX 78704
Phone: (512) 448-8500 or (800) 555-0164
Fax: (512) 464-8877
E-mail: seu.admit@admin.stedwards.edu
http://www.stedwards.edu

St. Marys University of San Antonio
University Admissions
One Camino Santa Maria
San Antonio, TX 78228-8572
Phone: (210) 436-3126
Fax: (210) 431-6742
E-mail: uadm@stmarytx.edu
http://www.stmarytx.edu

Sam Houston State University
University Admissions
Box 2418
Huntsville, TX 77341
Phone: (936) 294-1828
Fax: (936) 294-3758
E-mail: admissions@shsu.edu
http://www.shsu.edu

Southern Methodist University
University Admissions
P.O. Box 750181
6425 Boaz Street
Dallas, TX 75275-0221
Phone: (214) 768-3417 or (800) 323-0672
Fax: (214) 768-4880
E-mail: enrol_serv@smu.edu
http://www.smu.edu

Stephen F. Austin State University
University Admissions
P.O. Box 13051
SFA Box 13051
Nacogdoches, TX 75962
Phone: (936) 468-2504 or (800) 731-2902
Fax: (936) 468-3849
E-mail: admissions@sfasu.edu
http://www.sfasu.edu

Tarleton State University
Undergraduate Admissions
P.O. Box T-0030
Tarleton Station
Stephenville, TX 76402
Phone: (254) 968-9125
Fax: (254) 968-9951
E-mail: uadmit@tarleton.edu
http://www.tarleton.edu

Texas A&M University
Admissions Counseling

217 John J. Koldus Building
College Station, TX 77843-1265
Phone: (979) 845-3741
Fax: (979) 847-8737
E-mail: admissions@tamu.edu
http://www.tamu.edu

Texas Christian University
Office of Admissions
2800 South University Drive
TCU Box 297013
Fort Worth, TX 76129-0002
Phone: (817) 257-7490 or (800) 828-3764
Fax: (817) 257-7268
E-mail: frogmail@tcu.edu
http://www.tcu.edu

Texas State University—San Marcos
University Admissions
601 University Drive
San Marco, TX 78666
Phone: (512) 245-2364
Fax: (512) 245-8044
E-mail: admissions@txstate.edu
http://www.txstate.edu

Texas Tech University
P.O. Box 45005
Lubbock, TX 79409-5005
Phone: (806) 742-1480
Fax: (806) 742-0062
E-mail: admissions@ttu.edu
http://www.ttu.edu

University of Houston
Office of Admissions
One Main Street
Houston, TX 77002-1010
Phone: (713) 743-1010
Fax: (713) 743-9633
E-mail: admissions@dt.uh.edu
http://www.uh.edu

University of North Texas
P.O. Box 311277
Denton, TX 76203-1277
Phone: (940) 565-2681
    or (800) 868-8211
Fax: (940) 565-2408
E-mail: undergrad@unt.edu
http://www.unt.edu

University of Texas—Austin
John W. Hargis Hall
P.O. Box 8058
Austin, TX 78713-8058
Phone: (512) 475-7440
Fax: (512) 475-7475
E-mail: frmn@ut.cc.utexas.edu
http://www.utexas.edu

UTAH

University of Utah
University Admissions
250 South Student Services Building
Salt Lake City, UT 84112
Phone: (801) 581-7281 or (800) 444-8638
Fax: (801) 585-7864
E-mail: admissions@sa.utah.edu
http://www.utah.edu

Utah State University
Taggard Student Center
0160 Old Main Hill
Logan, UT, 84322-1600
Phone: (435) 797-1129
Fax: (435) 797-3708
E-mail: admit@usu.edu
http://www.usu.edu

Weber State University
Office of Admissions
1137 University Circle
Ogden, UT 84408-1137
Phone: (801) 626-6744 or (800) 634-6568
Fax: (801) 626-6747
E-mail: admissions@weber.edu
http://www.weber.edu

VERMONT

Castleton State College
Office of Admissions
Seminary Street
Castleton, VT 05735
Phone: (802) 468-1213 or (800) 639-8521
Fax: (802) 468-1476
E-mail: info@castleton.edu
http://www.castleton.edu

Norwich University
Office of Admissions
27 I.D. White Avenue
Northfield, VT 05663
Phone: (802) 485-2001 or (800) 468-6679
Fax: (802) 485-2032
E-mail: nuadm@norwich.edu
http://www.norwich.edu

VIRGINIA

George Mason University
University Admissions
4400 University Drive MSN 3A4
Fairfax, VA 22030-4444
Phone: (703) 993-2400
Fax: (703) 993-2392
E-mail: admissions@gmu.edu
http://www.gmu.edu

Hampton University
Office of Admissions
Hampton, VA 23668
Phone: (757) 727-5328 or (800) 624-3328
Fax: (757) 727-5095
E-mail: admit@hamptonu.edu
http://www.hampton.edu

James Madison University
Office of Admissions
Sonner Hall MSC 0101
Harrisonburg, VA 22807
Phone: (540) 568-5681
Fax: (540) 568-3332
E-mail: admissions@jmu.edu
http://www.jmu.edu

Marymount University
University Admissions
2807 North Glebe Road
Arlington, VA 22207
Phone: (703) 284-1500
Fax: (703) 522-0349
E-mail: admissions@marymount.edu
http://www.marymount.edu

Old Dominion University
University Admissions
5215 Hampton Boulevard
108 Rollins Hall Norfolk, VA 23529
Phone: (757) 683-3685 or
    (800) 348-7296
Fax: (757) 683-3255
E-mail: admit@odu.edu
http://www.odu.edu

Radford University
University Admissions
P.O. Box 6903—RU Station
Radford, VA 24142
Phone: (540) 831-5371 or (800) 890-4265
Fax: (540) 831-5138
E-mail: ruadmiss@radford.edu
http://www.radford.edu

Shenandoah University
1460 University Drive
Winchester, VA 22601-5195
Phone: (540) 665-4581
Fax: (540) 665-4627
E-mail: admit@su.edu
http://www.su.edu

University of Richmond
University Admissions
28 Westhampton Way—Maryland Hall
Richmond, VA 23173
Phone: (804) 289-8640 or (800) 700-1662
Fax: (804) 287-6003

E-mail: admission@richmond.edu
http://www.richmond.edu

Virginia Polytechnic Institute and State University
University Admissions, 201 Burrusss Hall
Blacksburg, VA 24061-0202
Phone: (540) 231-6267
Fax: (540) 231-3242
E-mail: vtadmiss@vt.edu
http://www.vt.edu

WASHINGTON

Eastern Washington University
University Admissions
526 Fifth Street MS-148
Cheney, WA 99004-2431
Phone: (509) 359-2397 or (888) 740-1914
Fax: (509) 359-6692
E-mail: admissions@mail.ewu.edu
http://www.ewu.edu

Gonzaga University
University Admissions
East 502 Boone Avenue
Spokane, WA 99258-0102
Phone: (509) 323-6572 or
    (800) 322-2584, ext. 6572
Fax: (509) 324-5780
E-mail: admissions@gonzaga.edu
http://www.gonzaga.edu

WEST VIRGINIA

Marshall University
University Admissions
One John Marshall Drive
Huntington, WV 25755
Phone: (304) 696-3160 or (800) 642-3499
Fax: (304) 696-3135
E-mail: admissions@marshall.edu
http://www.marshall.edu

West Virginia University
Office of Admissions
P.O. Box 6009
Morgantown, WV 26506-6009
Phone: (304) 293-2121 or
    (800) 344-9881
Fax: (304) 293-3080
E-mail: wvuadmissions@arc.wvu.edu
http://www.wvu.edu

WISCONSIN

Concordia University
University Admissions
12800 North Lake Shore Drive
Mequon, WI 53097-2402
Phone: (262) 243-5700
Fax: (262) 243-4545
E-mail: admission@cuw.edu
http://www.cuw.edu

Marquette University
University Admissions
P.O. Box 1881
Milwaukee, WI 53201-1881
Phone: (414) 288-7302 or (800) 222-6544
Fax: (414) 228-3764
E-mail go2marquette@marquette.edu
http://www.marquette.edu

University of Wisconsin—Eau Claire
University Admissions
P.O. Box 4004
Eau Claire, WI 54702-4004
Phone: (715) 836-5415
Fax: (715) 836-2409
E-mail: admissions@uwec.edu
http://www.wwec.edu

University of Wisconsin at Lacrosse
University Admissions
1725 State Street
LaCrosse, WI 54601-3742

Phone: (608) 785-8939
Fax: (608) 785-8940
E-mail: admissions@uwlax.edu
http://www.uwlax.edu

University of Wisconsin—Madison
University Admissions
716 Langdon Street
Madison, WI 53706-1481
Phone: (608) 262-3961
Fax: (608) 262-7706
E-mail: onwisconsin@admissions.wisc.edu
http://www.wisc.edu

University of Wisconsin—Milwaukee
University Admissions
P.O. Box 749
Milwaukee, WI 53201-0413
Phone: (414) 229-3800
Fax: (414) 229-6940
E-mail: uwmlook@des.uwm.edu
http://www.uwm.edu

University of Wisconsin at Whitewater
University Admissions
800 West Main Street
Whitewater, WI 53190
Phone: (262) 472-1440
Fax: (262) 472-1515
E-mail: uwwadmit@uww.edu
http://www.uww.edu

WYOMING

University of Wyoming
University Admissions
1000 East University Avenue, Dept. 3435
Laramie, WY 82071
Phone: (307) 766-5160 or (800) 342-5996
Fax: (307) 766-4042
E-mail: why-wyo@uwyo.edu
http://www.wwyo.edu

C. FINANCIAL PLANNING

CALIFORNIA

Golden Gate University
536 Mission Street
San Francisco, CA 94105
Phone: (415) 442-7800
Fax: (415) 442-7807
E-mail: info@ggu.edu
http://www.ggu.edu

FLORIDA

University of Miami
Office of Admission

P.O. Box 248025
Coral Gables, FL 33124-4616
Phone: (305) 284-4323
Fax: (305) 284-2507
E-mail: admissions@miami.edu
http://www.miami.edu

ILLINOIS

Trinity Christian College
6601 West College Drive
Palos Heights, IL 60463
Phone: (708) 239-4708

Fax: (708) 239-3969
E-mail: admissions@trnty.edu
http://www.trnty.edu

INDIANA

Purdue University
1080 Schleman Hall
West Lafayette, IN 47907
Phone: (765) 494-1776
Fax: (765) 494-0544
E-mail: admissions@purdue.edu
http://www.purdue.edu

MASSACHUSETTS

Merrimack College
Office of Admissions, Austin Hall
North Andover, MA 01845
Phone: (978) 837-5100
Fax: (978) 837-5133
E-mail: admission@merrimack.edu
http://www.merrimack.edu

MICHIGAN

Central Michigan University
University Admissions
105 Warriner Hall
Mt. Pleasant, MI 48859
Phone: (989) 774-3076
Fax: (989) 774-7267
E-mail: cmuadmit@cmich.edu
http://www.cmich.edu

Northern Michigan University
Office of Admissions
1401 Presque Isle Avenue
304 Cohodas
Marquette, MI 49855
Phone: (906) 227-2650
Fax: (906) 227-1747
E-mail: admiss@nmu.edu
http://www.nmu.edu

NEVADA

University of Nevada—Las Vegas
4505 Maryland Parkway, Box 451021
Las Vegas, NV 89154-1021
Phone: (702) 774-8658
Fax: (702) 774-8008
E-mail: undergraduate.recruitment@
    ccmail.nevada.edu
http://www.unlv.edu

NEW JERSEY

Seton Hall University
Enrollment Services, Bayley Hall

400 South Orange Avenue
South Orange, NJ 07079-2697
Phone: (973) 761-9332 or
    (800) THE HALL
Fax: (973) 275-2040
E-mail: thehall@shu.edu
http://www.shu.edu

NEW YORK

The College of St. Rose
423 Western Avenue
Albany, NY 12203
Phone: (518) 454-5150 or
    (800) 637-8556
Fax: (518) 454-2013
E-mail: admit@strose.edu
http://www.strose.edu

Medaille College
18 Agassiz Circle
Buffalo, NY 14214
Phone: (716) 884-3281
Fax: (716) 884-0291
E-mail: jmatheny@medaille.edu
http://www.medaille.edu

PENNSYLVANIA

Widener University
Office of Admissions
One University Place
Chester, PA 19013
Phone: (610) 499-4126
Fax: (610) 499-4676
E-mail: admissions.office@widener.edu
http://www.widener.edu

Marywood University
2300 Adams Avenue
Scranton, PA 18509-1598
Phone: (570) 348-6234
Fax: (570) 961-4763
E-mail: info@csudh.edu
http://www.marywood.edu

RHODE ISLAND

Roger Williams University
One Old Ferry Road
Bristol, RI 02809-7144
Phone: (401) 254-3500
Fax: (401) 254-3557
E-mail: admit@rwu.edu
http://www.rwu.edu

TEXAS

University of Dallas
1845 East Northgate Drive
Irving, TX 75062
Phone: (972) 721-5266
Fax: (972) 721-5017
E-mail: ugadmis@udallas.edu
http://www.udallas.edu

University of Texas at San Antonio
6900 North Loop 1604 West
San Antonio, TX 78249-0617
Phone: (210) 458-4530
Fax: (210) 458-7716
E-mail: prospects@utsa.edu
http://www.utsa.edu

WASHINGTON

City University
11900 N.E. First Street
Bellevue, WA 98005
Phone: (425) 637-1010 or (888) 422-4898
Fax: (425) 637-2437
E-mail: info@cityu.edu
http://www.cityu.edu

D. INTERNAL AUDITING

ALABAMA

University of Alabama—Birmingham
Office of Undergraduate Admissions
1530 Third Avenue South
Birmingham, AL 35294-1150
Phone: (205) 934-8221 or
    (800) 421-8743
Fax: (205) 975-7114

E-mail: undergradadmit@uab.edu
http://www.uab.edu

ARIZONA

Arizona State University West
4701 West Thunderbird Road
Phoenix, AZ 85306-4908
Phone: (602) 543-9378

Fax: (602) 543-8312
E-mail: west-admissions@asu.edu
http://www.west.asu.edu

CALIFORNIA

**California State University—
    Dominguez Hills**
1000 East Victoria Street

Carson, CA 90747
Phone: (310) 243-3600
Fax: (310) 516-3609
E-mail: info@csudh.edu
http://www.csudh.edu

**California State University—
    San Bernardino**
5500 University Parkway
San Bernardino, CA 92407-2397
Phone: (909) 880-5188
Fax: (909) 880-7034
E-mail: moreinfo@mail.csusb.edu
http://www.csusb.edu

San Francisco State University
1600 Holloway Avenue, Adm. 154
San Francisco, CA 94132
Phone: (415) 338-6486
Fax: (415) 338-7196
E-mail: ugadmit@sfsu.edu
http://www.sfsu.edu

DISTRICT OF COLUMBIA

Howard University
University Admissions
2400 Sixth Street, NW
Washington, D.C. 20059
Phone: (202) 806-2700 or
    (800) HOWARD-U
Fax: (202) 806-4467
E-mail: admission@howard.edu
http://www.howard.edu

FLORIDA

Florida Atlantic University
University Admissions
777 Glades Avenue
P.O. Box 3091
Boca Raton, FL 22413-0991
Phone: (561) 297-3040 (800) 299-4FAU
Fax: (561) 297-2758
E-mail: admisweb@fau.edu
http://www.fau.edu

Florida International University
University Admissions
University Park
PC 140
Miami, FL 33199
Phone: (305) 348-2363
Fax: (305) 348-3648
E-mail: admiss@fiu.edu
http://www.fiu.edu

IDAHO

Boise State University
University Admissions

1910 University Drive
Boise, ID 83725
Phone: (208) 426-1177
Fax: (208) 426-3765
E-mail: bsuinfo@boisestate.edu
http://www.boisestate.edu

ILLINOIS

Northern Illinois University
Office of Admissions
DeKalb, IL 60115-2857
Phone: (815) 753-0446
Fax: (815) 753-1783
E-mail: admissions-info@niu.edu
http://www.reg.niu.edu

KANSAS

Pittsburgh State University
1701 South Broadway
Pittsburgh, KS 66762-5880
Phone: (620) 235-4251
Fax: (620) 235-6003
E-mail: psuadmit@pittstate.edu
http://www.pittstate.edu

LOUISIANA

Louisiana State University
University Admissions
110 Thomas Boyd Hall
Baton Rouge, LA 70803-3013
Phone: (225) 578-1175
Fax: (225) 578-4433
http://www.lsu.edu
E-mail: admissions@lsu.edu

MASSACHUSETTS

Bentley College
175 Forest Street
Waltham, MA 02452-4705
Phone: (781) 891-2244
Fax: (781) 891-3414
E-mail: ugadmission@bentley.edu
http://www.bentley.edu

MICHIGAN

Eastern Michigan University
University Admissions
400 Pierce Hall
Ypsilante, MI 48197
Phone: (734) 487-3060 or
    (800) GOTOEMU
Fax: (734) 487-1484
E-mail: admissions@emich.edu
http://www.emich.edu

MISSOURI

Southwest Missouri State University
University Admissions
901 South National Street
Springfield, MO 65804
Phone: (417) 836-5517
Fax: (417) 836-6334
E-mail: smsuinfo@smsu.edu
http://www.smsu.edu

NEW JERSEY

Seton Hall University
400 South Orange Avenue
South Orange, NJ 07679
Phone: (201) 761-9332 or
    (800) THE HALL
Fax: (201) 275-2040
E-mail: thehall@shu.edu
http://www.shu.edu

NEW YORK

New York University
70 Washington Square South
New York, NY 10012
Phone: (212) 998-4500
Fax: (212) 995-4902
E-mail: admissions@nyu.edu
http://www.nyu.edu

State University of New York—Buffalo
17 Capen Hall
Buffalo, NY 14260
Phone: (716) 645-6900
Fax: (716) 645-6411
E-mail: admissions@buffalo.edu
http://www.buffalo.edu

NORTH CAROLINA

**University of North Carolina at
    Charlotte**
9201 University City Boulevard
Charlotte, NC 28223-0001
Phone: (704) 687-2213
Fax: (704) 687-6483
E-mail: unccadm@uncc.edu
http://www.uncc.edu

OHIO

Cleveland State University
East 24 and Euclid Avenue
Cleveland, OH 44115
Phone: (216) 687-2100
Fax: (216) 687-9210
E-mail: admissions@csuohio.edu
http://www.csuohio.edu

SOUTH CAROLINA

Clemson University
University Admissions
105 Sikes Hall
P.O. Box 345124
Clemson, SC 29634
Phone: (864) 656-2287
Fax: (864) 656-2464
E-mail: cuadmissions@clemson.edu
http://www.clemson.edu

TENNESSEE

University of Tennessee
University Admissions
320 Student Services Building
Knoxville, TN 37996-0230
Phone: (865) 974-2184 or (800) 221-8657
Fax: (865) 974-6341
E-mail: admissions@utk.edu
http://www.utk.edu

TEXAS

Texas A&M University
University Counseling
217 John J. Koldus Building
College Station, TX 77843-1265
Phone: (409) 845-3741
Fax: (409) 847-8737

E-mail: admissions@tamu.edu
http://www.tamu.edu

University of Houston
University Admissions
One Main Street
Houston, TX 77002-1001
Phone: (979) 221-8931
Fax: (979) 221-8157
E-mail: admissions@uh.edu
http://www.uh.edu

University of North Texas
P.O. Box 311277
Denton, TX 76203-1277
Phone: (940) 565-2681 or (800) 868-8211
Fax: (940) 565-2408
E-mail: undergrad@unt.edu
http://www.unt.edu

University of Texas—Arlington
Office of Admissions
P.O. Box 19111
Arlington, TX 76019-0111
Phone: (817) 272-6287
Fax: (817) 272-3435
E-mail: admissions@uta.edu
http://www.uta.edu

University of Texas—Austin
John W. Hargis Hall

P.O. Box 8058
Austin, TX 78712-8058
Phone: (512) 475-7440
Fax: (512) 475-7475
E-mail: frmn@uts.cc.utexas.edu
http://www.utexas.edu

UTAH

Brigham Young University
A-153 ASB
Provo, UT 84602
Phone: (801) 422-2507
Fax: (801) 422-0005
E-mail: admissions@byu.edu
http://www.byu.edu

VIRGINIA

Old Dominion University
University Admissions
5215 Hampton Boulevard
108 Rollins Hall
Norfolk, VA 23529
Phone: (757) 683-3685 or (800) 348-7296
Fax: (757) 683-3255
E-mail: admit@odu.edu
http://www.odu.edu

E. INSURANCE AND RISK MANAGEMENT

CALIFORNIA

California State Polytechnic University
Office of Admissions
3801 West Temple Avenue
Pomona, CA 91768
Phone: (909) 869-3210
Fax: (909) 869-4529
E-mail: admissions@csupomona.edu
http://www.csupomona.edu

CONNECTICUT

University of Connecticut
University Admissions
2131 Hillside Road, U-3088
Storrs, CT 06268
Phone: (860) 486-3137
Fax: (860) 486-1476
E-mail: beahusky@uconn.edu
http://www.uconn.edu

University of Hartford
University Admissions

200 Bloomfield Avenue
West Hartford, CT 06617
Phone: (860) 768-4296 or (800) 947-4303
Fax: (860) 768-4961
E-mail: admissions@mail.hartford.edu
http://www.hartford.edu

DISTRICT OF COLUMBIA

Howard University
University Admissions
2400 Sixth Street, NW
Washington, D.C. 20059
Phone: (202) 806-2700 or
    (800) HOWARD-U
Fax: (202) 806-4467
E-mail: admission@howard.edu
http://www.howard.edu

FLORIDA

University of Florida
Office of Admissions

P.O. Box 114000
Gainesville, FL 32611-4000
Phone: (352) 392-1365
Fax: (904) 392-3987
E-mail: freshman@ufl.edu
http://www.ufl.edu

Florida International University
University Admissions
University Park
Miami, FL 33199
Phone: (305) 348-2363
Fax: (305) 348-3648
E-mail: admiss@fiu.edu
http://www.fiu.edu

Florida State University
University Admissions
2500 University Center
Tallahassee, FL 32306-2400
Phone: (850) 644-6200
Fax: (850) 644-0197
E-mail: admissions@admin.fsu.edu
http://www.fsu.edu

GEORGIA

Georgia State University
University Admissions
P.O. Box 4009
Atlanta, GA 30302-4009
Phone: (800) 651-4811
E-mail: admissions@gsu.edu
http://www.gsu.edu

University of Georgia
University Admissions
Terrell Hall
Athens, GA 30602
Phone: (706) 542-8776
Fax: (706) 542-1466
E-mail: undergrad@admissions.uga.edu
http://www.uga.edu

ILLINOIS

Bradley University
University Admissions
1501 West Bradley Avenue
Peoria, IL 61625-0002
Phone: (800) 447-6460
Fax: (309) 677-2797
E-mail: admissions@bradley.edu
http://www.bradley.edu

Illinois State University
University Admissions
Campus Box 220
Normal, IL 61790-2200
Phone: (800) 366-2478
Fax: (309) 438-3932
E-mail: admissions@ilstu.edu
http://www.ilstu.edu

Illinois Wesleyan University
P.O. Box 2900
Bloomington, IL 61702
Phone: (309) 556-3031
Fax: (309) 556-3820
E-mail: iwuadmit@iwu.edu
http://www.iwu.edu

INDIANA

Ball State University
Office of Admissions
2000 University Avenue
Munice, IN 47306-1099
Phone: (765) 285-8300 or
    (800) 482-4BSU
Fax: (765) 285-1632
E-mail: askus@bsu.edu
http://www.bsu.edu

Martin University
2171 Avondale Place
P.O. Box 18567
Indianapolis, IN 46218-3867
Phone: (317) 543-3237
Fax: (317) 543-3257
http://www.martin.edu

IOWA

Drake University
University Admissions
2507 University Avenue
Des Moines, IA 50311-4505
Phone: (515) 271-3181 or
    (800) 44DRAKE
Fax: (515) 271-2831
E-mail: admission@drake.edu
http://www.drake.edu

KENTUCKY

Eastern Kentucky University
University Admissions
521 Lancaster Avenue
Richmond, KY 40475-3102
Phone: (859) 622-2106 or (800) 463-9191
Fax: (606) 622-8024
E-mail: admissions@eku.edu
http://www.eku.edu

LOUISIANA

University of Louisiana at Monroe
700 University Avenue
Monroe, LA 71209
Phone: (318) 342-5252
Fax: (318) 342-5274
E-mail: rhood@ulm.edu
http://www.ulm.edu

MASSACHUSETTS

Northeastern University
University Admissions, 150 Richards Hall
360 Huntington Avenue
Boston, MA 02115-5096
Phone: (617) 373-2200
Fax: (617) 373-8780
E-mail: admissions@neu.edu
http://www.neu.edu

MICHIGAN

Ferris State University
University Admissions
1201 South State Street
Big Rapids, MI 49307-2742

Phone: (231) 591-2100
Fax: (231) 591-3944
E-mail: admissions@ferris.edu
http://www.ferris.edu

Olivet College
320 South Main
Olivet, MI 49076
Phone: (269) 749-7635 or (800) 456-7189
Fax: (616) 749-7170
E-mail: admissions@olivetcollege.edu
http://www.olivetcollege.edu

Western Michigan University
Office of Admission and Orientation
1903 West Michigan Avenue
Kalamazoo, MI 49008-4401
Phone: (269) 387-2000 or (800) 400-4968
Fax: (269) 387-2096
E-mail: ask.wmu@wmich.edu
http://www.wmich.edu

MINNESOTA

Minnesota State University at Mankato
University Admissions
209 Wigley Administration Center
Mankato, MN 56001-8400
Phone: (507) 389-1822 or (800) 722-0544
Fax: (507) 389-1511
E-mail: admissions@mnsu.edu
http://www.mnsu.edu

Saint Cloud State University
University Admissions
720 South Fourth Avenue
St. Cloud, MN 56301-4498
Phone: (320) 255-2244
Fax: (320) 308-2243
E-mail: scs4u@stcloudstate.edu
http://www.stcloudstate.edu

University of Minnesota—Twin Cities Campus
University Admissions
240 Williamson
Minneapolis, MN 55455-0123
Phone: (612) 625-2008 or (800) 752-1000
Fax: (612) 626-1693
E-mail: admissions@tc.umn.edu
http://www.tc.umn.edu

MISSISSIPPI

Delta State University
University Admissions
Highway 8
Cleveland, MS 38733-0001
Phone: (662) 846-4020

Fax: (662) 846-4683
E-mail: admissions@deltastate.edu
http://www.deltastate.edu

Mississippi State University
University Admissions
P.O. Box 6305
Mississippi State, MS 39762
Phone: (662) 325-2224
Fax: (662) 325-7360
E-mail: admit@admissions.msstate.edu
http://www.msstate.edu

**University of Mississippi—
    Main Campus**
Office of Admissions
145 Martindale Student Services Center
University, MS 38677
Phone: (662) 915-7226
Fax: (662) 915-5869
E-mail: admissions@olemiss.edu
http://www.olemiss.edu

MISSOURI

Southwest Missouri State University
University Admissions
901 South National Street
Springfield, MO 65804
Phone: (417) 836-5517
Fax: (417) 836-6334
E-mail: smsuinfo@smsu.edu
http://www.smsu.edu

NEW JERSEY

Thomas A. Edison State College
Admissions Services
101 West State Street
Trenton, NJ 08608-1176
Phone: (609) 984-1150 or (800) 442-8372
Fax: (609) 984-8447
E-mail: info@call.tesc.edu
http://www.tesc.edu

NEW YORK

College of Insurance
101 Murray Street
New York, NY 10017
Phone: (212) 815-9232
Fax: (212) 964-3381
E-mail: admissions@tci.edu
http://www.tci.edu

NORTH CAROLINA

Appalachian State University
Office of Admissions

P.O. Box 32004
Boone, NC 28608
Phone: (828) 262-2120
Fax: (828) 262-3296
E-mail: admissions@appstate.edu
http://www.appstate.edu

OHIO

Ohio State University
Undergraduate Admissions
Enarson Hall
154 West 12th Avenue
Columbus, OH 43210-1200
Phone: (614) 292-3980
Fax: (614) 292-4818
E-mail: askabuckeye@osu.edu
http://www.osu.edu

University of Cincinnati
University Admissions
P.O. Box 210091
Cincinnati, OH 45221-0091
Phone: (513) 556-1100 or (800) 827-8728
Fax: (513) 556-1105
E-mail: admissions@uc.edu
http://www.uc.edu

OKLAHOMA

University of Central Oklahoma
University Admissions
100 North University Drive
Edmond, OK 73034
Phone: (405) 974-2338 or (800) 254-4215
Fax: (405) 341-4964
E-mail: admituco@ucok.edu
http://www.ucok.edu

PENNSYLVANIA

Mercyhurst College
501 East 38th Street
Erie, PA 16546
Phone: (814) 824-2202 or (800) 825-1926
Fax: (814) 824-2071
E-mail: admissions@mercyhurst.edu
http://www.mercyhurst.edu

**Pennsylvania State University—
    University Park**
University Admissions
201 Shields Building
University Park, PA 16802-1503
Phone: (814) 856-5471
Fax: (814) 863-7590
E-mail: admissions@psu.edu
http://www.psu.edu

Temple University
University Admissions
1801 North Broad Street
Philadelphia, PA 19122-6096
Phone: (215) 204-7200 or (888) 340-2222
Fax: (215) 204-5694
E-mail: tuadm@mail.temple.edu
http://www.temple.edu

University of Pennsylvania
University Admissions
1 College Hall
Levy Park
Philadelphia, PA 19104
Phone: (215) 898-7507
Fax: (215) 898-9670
E-mail: info@admissions.ugao.upenn.
    edu
http://www.upenn.edu

SOUTH CAROLINA

**University of South Carolina—
    Columbia**
Undergraduate Admissions
Columbia, SC 29208
Phone: (800) 868-5872
Fax: (803) 777-0101
E-mail: admissions@sc.edu
http://www.sc.edu

TENNESSEE

University of Memphis
University Admissions
Central at Patterson
Memphis, TN 38152
Phone: (901) 678-2111
Fax: (901) 678-3053
E-mail: recruitment@memphis.edu
http://www.memphis.edu

TEXAS

Baylor University
University Admissions
P.O. Box 97056
Waco, TX 76798-7056
Phone: (254) 710-3435 or
    (800) BAYLOR-U
Fax: (254) 710-3436
E-mail: admissions_office@baylor.edu
http://www.baylor.edu

Texas Southern University
3100 Cleburne Street
Houston, TX 77004

Phone: (713) 313-7420
Fax: (713) 313-4317
E-mail: admissions@tsu.edu
http://www.tsu.edu

University of North Texas
P.O. Box 311277
Denton, TX 76203-1277
Phone: (940) 565-2681 or
   (800) 868-8211
Fax: (940) 565-2408
E-mail: undergrad@unt.edu
http://www.unt.edu

WASHINGTON

Washington State University
370 Lighty Student Services
Pullman, WA 99164
Phone: (509) 335-5586
Fax: (509) 335-4902
E-mail: admiss2@wsu.edu
http://www.wsu.edu

WISCONSIN

University of Wisconsin at Madison
University Admissions

716 Langdon Street
Madison, WI 53706-1481
Phone: (608) 262-3961
Fax: (608) 262-7706
E-mail: onwisconsin@admissions.wisc.
   edu
http://www.wisc.edu

APPENDIX II
GRADUATE SCHOOLS:
M.A. AND M.B.A. PROGRAMS

ADMINISTRATION PROGRAMS
GRADUATE SCHOOLS: MASTER OF ARTS AND MASTER OF BUSINESS ADMINISTRATION

A Master of Arts (M.A.) or Master of Business Administration (M.B.A.) degree is increasingly a requirement for advancement in financial careers stressing knowledge of quantitative analytical skills or management ability. If you're just starting your career, having a M.A. or M.B.A. degree on your résumé can help you get more job offers. If you're changing careers a postgraduate degree can open the door to job interviews with employers. And if your plans are to stay with your current employer, an additional degree can improve your job status and advancement potential.

More than 800 U.S. colleges and universities offer graduate-level business education programs. This section contains the names, mailing addresses, and contact information for more than 150 four-year colleges and universities that offer M.A. and M.B.A. programs in accounting, finance, business management, or related fields of study. Due to space limitations, the names of some colleges and universities have been omitted. Many have a variety of academic programs, including executive M.B.A. programs that offer the opportunity to study for an advanced degree without having to take a leave of absence for the two-year period normally required to complete an M.B.A. program.

Graduate schools emphasize teamwork and close interaction in the classroom, often through the case study method of teaching—widely used in M.B.A. programs. Class sizes are kept small to encourage discussion among students. As a result, most graduate schools have very selective admissions policies. A four-year degree or the equivalent from an accredited U.S. college is a minimum requirement. Business schools look at three factors for admissions: college academic record, Graduate Management Admission Test (GMAT) scores, and work experience.

The last factor, work experience, is considered very important; graduate schools look for candidates with at least one to two years full-time experience in business or industry before starting graduate studies. Other admissions requirements can vary quite a bit from one graduate school to another; these may include written essays, letters of recommendation, and information about community involvement, in addition to GMAT scores.

Admissions counselors recommend contacting the graduate department to which you seek admission before submitting an application. Send applications to five to 10 schools to increase your chances of being accepted. Business school rankings, while important, should not be the only factor in deciding where to apply; try to judge the progressiveness of the academic program and how closely the program matches your career and life goals.

ALABAMA

Auburn University College of Business
Office of Admissions
415 West Magnolia Avenue
Auburn, AL 36849
Phone: (334) 844-4080
Fax: (334) 821-4851
E-mail: MBAinfo@business.auburn.edu
http://www.business.auburn.edu

University of Alabama
Office of Admissions
Manderson Graduate School of Business
P.O. Box 870223
Tuscaloosa, AL 35487
Phone: (205) 348-6517 or (888) 863-2622
Fax: (205) 348-4504
E-mail: MBA@cba.ua.edu
http://www.cba.ua.edu/mba

ARIZONA

Arizona State University
College of Business—M.B.A. Program
M.B.A. Program Office—Main Campus
P.O. Box 874906
Tempe, AZ 85287-4906
Phone: (480) 965-3332
Fax: (480) 965-8569
E-mail: wpcareymba@asu.edu
http://www.cob.asu.edu/mba

Thunderbird, The Garvin School of International Management
15249 North 59th Avenue
Glendale, AZ 85306-6000
Phone: (800) 848-9084
Fax: (602) 439-5432
E-mail: admissions@t-bird.edu
http://www.thunderbird.edu

University of Arizona
Karl Eller Graduate School of Management
McClelland Hall Room 210
1130 East Helen Street
Tucson, AZ 85721-0108
Phone: (520) 621-4008
Fax: (520) 621-2606

E-mail: ellernet@bpa.arizona.edu
http://www.ellermba.arizona.edu

ARKANSAS

University of Arkansas—Little Rock
2801 South University Avenue
Little Rock, AR 72204
Phone: (501) 569-3356
Fax: (501) 569-8898
http://www.cba.ualr.edu

CALIFORNIA

Claremont Graduate University
Peter F. Drucker School of Management
1021 North Dartmouth Avenue
Claremont, CA 91711
Phone: (909) 607-7811
Fax: (909) 607-9104
http://www.drucker.cgu.edu

Golden Gate University
Edward S. Ageno School of Business
536 Mission Street
San Francisco, CA 94105-2968
Phone: (415) 442-7800 or (888) 488-4968
Fax: (415) 442-7807
E-mail: info@ggu.edu
http://www.ggu.edu

Loyola Marymount
7900 Loyola Boulevard
Los Angeles, CA 90045-8387
Phone: (310) 338-2721
Fax: (310) 338-6086
E-mail: graduate@lmu.edu
http://www.lmu.edu

Pepperdine University
George L. Graziadio School of Business
   and Management
400 Corporate Pointe
Culver City, CA 90230
Phone: (310) 568-5500
Fax: (310) 568-5779
http://bschool.pepperdine.edu

St. Mary's College
School of Economics and Business
   Administration
1928 St. Mary's Road
P.O. Box 4240
Moraga, CA 94575-4240
Phone: (925) 631-4500
Fax: (925) 376-6521
E-mail: smcmba@stmarys-ca.edu
http://www.stmarys-ca. edu/MBA/index.
   html

San Diego State University
Graduate School of Business
5500 Campanile Drive
San Diego, CA 92182
Phone: (619) 594-7800
Fax: (619) 594-1250
E-mail: gradbus@mail.sdsu.edu
http://www.sdsu.edu

Santa Clara University
Leavey School of Business
500 El Camino Real
Santa Clara, CA 95053
Phone: (408) 554-4700
Fax: (408) 554-5255
E-mail: mbaadmissisons@scu.edu
http://www.scu.edu/business

Stanford University
Stanford Graduate School of Business
518 Memorial Way
Stanford, CA 94305-5015
Phone: (650) 723-2146
Fax: (650) 725-7831
E-mail: mba@gsb.stanford.edu
http://www.gsb.stanford.edu

University of California—Berkeley
Haas School of Business
440 Student Services Building
Berkeley, CA 94720-1902
Phone: (510) 642-4417
Fax: (510) 643-4345
E-mail: mbaadms@haas.berkeley.edu
http://www.haas.berkeley.edu

University of California—Davis
Graduate School of Management
One Shields Avenue
Davis, CA 95616
Phone: (530) 752-7658
Fax: (530) 754-9355
E-mail: gsm@ucdavis.edu
http://www.gsm.ucdavis.edu

University of California—Irvine
The Paul Merage School of Business
GSM 202
Irvine, CA 92697-3125
Phone: (949) 824-4MBA
Fax: (949) 824-2944
http://www.gsm.uci.edu

University of California—Los Angeles
Anderson School of Management
110 Westwood Plaza, Suite B201
Los Angeles, CA 90095-1481
Phone: (310) 285-6944
Fax: (310) 285-8582
E-mail: mba.admissions@anderson.ucla.
   edu
http://www.anderson.ucla.edu

University of California—Santa Cruz
Kerr Hall, Fourth Hall
Santa Cruz, CA 95064
Phone: (831) 459-2510
Fax: (831) 459-4843
E-mail: graddiv@ucsc.edu
http://www.ucsc.edu

University of San Diego
School of Business Administration
5998 Acala Park
San Diego, CA 92110-2492
Phone: (619) 260-4524
Fax: (619) 260-4158
http://www.sandiego.edu/business

University of San Francisco
School of Business and Management
2130 Fulton Street
San Francisco, CA 94117-1080
Phone: (415) 422-2089
Fax: (415) 422-2066
http://www.usfca.edu/sobam

University of Southern California
Marshall School of Business
Popovich Hall 308
Los Angeles, CA 90089-2633
Phone: (213) 740-7846
Fax: (213) 749-8520
E-mail: marshallmba@bus.usc.edu
http://www.marshall.usc.edu

COLORADO

University of Colorado—Denver
Graduate School of Business
Administration
Campus Box 165
P.O. Box 173364
Denver, CO 80217-3364
Phone: (303) 556-5900
Fax: (303) 556-5904
http://www.business.cudenver.edu

University of Denver
Daniels College of Business
2101 South University Boulevard #255
Denver, CO 80208
Phone: (303) 871-3416 or (800) 622-4723
Fax: (303) 871-4466
http://www.daniels.du.edu

CONNECTICUT

Fairfield University
Charles F. Dolan School of Business
1073 North Benson Road
Fairfield, CT 06824

Phone: (203) 254-4070
Fax: (203) 254-4105
http://www.fairfield.edu/mba

University of Connecticut
308 Fairfield Road U41-MBA
Storrs, CT 06269
Phone: (860) 486-2872
Fax: (860) 486-5222
http://www.business.uconn.edu

University of Hartford
Barney School of Business and Public
    Administration
200 Bloomfield Avenue
West Hartford, CT 06117
Phone: (860) 768-4444
Fax: (860) 768-4821
http://www.barney.hartford.edu

Yale University
Yale School of Management
135 Prospect Street
Box 208200
New Haven, CT 06520-8200
Phone: (203) 432-5932
Fax: (203) 432-7004
E-mail: mba.admissions@yale.edu
http://www.mba.yale.edu

DELAWARE

University of Delaware
College of Business and Economics
103 MNBA America Hall
Newark, DE 19716
Phone: (302) 831-2221
Fax: (302) 831-3329
E-mail: mbaprogra@udel.edu
http://www.mba.udel.edu

DISTRICT OF COLUMBIA

American University
Kogod College of Business
    Administration
4400 Massachusetts Avenue NW
Washington, DC 20016
Phone: (202) 885-1913
Fax: (202) 885-1078
E-mail: aumbams@american.edu
http://www.kogod.american.edu

Georgetown University
McDonough School of Business
P.O. Box 571148
Washington, DC 20057
Phone: (202) 687-4200
Fax: (202) 687-7809

E-mail: mba@georgetown.edu
http://www.msb.georgetown.edu

George Washington University
School of Business and Public
    Management
710 21st Street NW, Suite 206
Washington, DC 20052
Phone: (202) 994-6380
Fax: (202) 994-2286
E-mail: sbgrad@gwu.edu
http://www.business.gwu.edu

FLORIDA

Florida International University
Alvah Chapman Jr. Graduate School of
    Business
FIU University Park Campus
Miami, FL 33199
Phone: (305) 348-7398
Fax: (305) 348-2368
http://www.chapman.fiu.edu

Florida State University
Graduate Office
College of Business
Tallahassee, FL 32306
Phone: (850) 644-6458
Fax: (850) 644-0588
http://www.cob.fsu.edu

University of Florida
Warrington College of Business
    Administration
134 Bryan Hall
P.O. Box 117152
Gainesville, FL 32611-7168
Phone: (877) 435-2622
Fax: (352) 392-8791
http://www.floridamba.ufl.edu

University of Miami
School of Business Administration
5250 University Drive, Jenkins 221
Coral Gables, FL 33124
Phone: (305) 284-4607
Fax: (305) 284-1878
E-mail: mba@miami.edu
http://www.bus.miami.edu/grad

University of Tampa
John H. Syke College of Business
401 West Kennedy Boulevard
Tampa, FL 33606
Phone: (813) 258-7409
Fax: (813) 259-5403
E-mail: mba@utampa.edu
http://www.utampa.edu

GEORGIA

Emory University
Goizueta Business School
1300 Clifton Road
Atlanta, GA 30322
Phone: (404) 727-6311
Fax: (404) 727-4612
E-mail: admissions@bus.emory.edu
http://www.goizueta.emory.edu

Georgia Institute of Technology
DuPree School of Management
800 West Peach Street NW
Atlanta, GA 30332-0520
Phone: (404) 894-8722
Fax: (404) 894-4199
E-mail: graduate.questions@mgt.gatech.
    edu
http://www.mgt.gatech.edu

Georgia State University
J. Mack Robinson College of Business
P.O. Box 3988
Atlanta, GA 30302
Phone: (404) 463-4568
Fax: (404) 651-2721
http://www.robinson.gsu.edu

University of Georgia
Terry College of Business
362 Brooks Hall
Athens, GA 30602-6264
Phone: (706) 542-5671
Fax: (706) 542-5351
E-mail: terrymba@terry.uga.edu
http://www.terry.uga.edu/mba

HAWAII

University of Hawaii
College of Business Administration
2404 Maile Way, C-202
Honolulu, HI 96822
Phone: (808) 956-8266
Fax: (808) 956-2657
http://www.cba.hawaii.edu

IDAHO

Boise State University
College of Business and Economics
1910 University Drive, B318
Boise, ID 83725-1600
Phone: (208) 426-1126
Fax: (208) 426-1135
http://cobe.boisestate.edu/graduate

ILLINOIS

Depaul University
Kellstadt Graduate School of Business
1 East Jackson, Suite 7900
Chicago, IL 60604
Phone: (312) 362-8810
Fax: (312) 362-6677
http://www.kellstadt.depaul.edu

Illinois Institute of Technology
Stuart Graduate School of Business
565 West Adams
Chicago, IL 60661
Phone: (312) 906-6521
Fax: (312) 609-6549
http://www.stuart.iit.edu

Loyola University Chicago
Graduate School of Business
1 East Pearson
Chicago, IL 60611
Phone: (312) 915-6164
Fax: (312) 915-7207
E-mail: mba-loyola@luc.edu
http://www.gsb.luc.edu

Northern Illinois University
College of Business
DeKalb, IL 60115-2897
Phone: (866) 648-6221
Fax: (815) 753-1668
http://www.cob.niu.edu/mbaprograms

Northwestern University
Office of Admission
J. L. Kellogg Graduate School of
  Management
2001 Sheridan Road
Evanston, IL 60208-1113
Phone: (847) 491-3308
Fax: (847) 491-4960
http://www.kellogg.northwestern.edu

Southern Illinois University
Campus Box 1786
Edwardsville, IL 62026-1102
Phone: (618) 650-3840
Fax: (618) 650-3979
http://www.siuc.edu/business

University of Chicago
Graduate School of Business
5807 South Woodlawn Avenue
Chicago, IL 60637
Phone: (773) 702-7369
Fax: (773) 702-9085
http://www.chicago.GSB.edu

University of Illinois—Urbana-Champaign
College of Commerce and Business
  Administration
405 David Kinley Hall
1407 West Gregory Drive
Urbana, IL 61801
Phone: (217) 244-7602 or (800) 622-8482
Fax: (217) 333-1156
E-mail: mba@uiuc.edu
http://www.mba.uiuc.edu

University of Illinois—Urbana-Champaign
Department of Finance
340 Commerce West
1206 South Sixth Street
Champaign, IL 61820
Phone: (217) 244-0252
Fax: (217) 244-3102
E-mail: finance@uiuc.edu
http://www.uiuc.edu

INDIANA

Indiana University—Bloomington
Kelley School of Business
1275 East Tenth Street, Suite 2010
Bloomington, IN 47405-1701
Phone: (812) 855-8006
Fax: (812) 855-9039
E-mail: mbaoffice@indiana.edu
http://www.kelley.indiana.edu/mba

Indiana University—Purdue University Indianapolis
Kelley School of Business
801 West Michigan Street
Indianapolis, IN 46202-5151
Phone: (317) 274-2147
Fax: (317) 274-2483
http://www.iupui.edu/~business

Purdue University
Krannert Graduate School of Management
100 South Grant Street
West Lafayette, IN 47907-1310
Phone: (765) 494-0773
Fax: (765) 494-9481
http://www.krannert.purdue.edu

University of Notre Dame
Mendoza College of Business
276 Mendoza College of Business
Notre Dame, IN 46556
Phone: (574) 631-8488
Fax: (574) 631-8800
http://www.nd.edu/~mba

IOWA

Iowa State University
College of Business
1360 Gerdin Business Building
Ames, IA 50111-2063
Phone: (515) 294-8118
Fax: (515) 294-2446
E-mail: busgrad@iastate.edu
http://www.bus.iastate.edu/grad

University of Iowa
Henry B. Tippie School of Management
108 John Pappajohn Business
  Administration Building
Suite C140
Iowa City, IA 52242-1000
Phone: (319) 335-1039
Fax: (319) 335-3604
E-mail: iowamba@uiowa.edu
http://www.biz.uiowa.edu/mba

KANSAS

University of Kansas
School of Business
206 Summerfield Hall
Lawrence, KS 66045
Phone: (785) 864-7596
Fax: (785) 864-5376
http://www.business.ku.edu

KENTUCKY

University of Kentucky
Gatton College of Business and
  Economics
415 Business and Economics Building
Lexington, KY 40506-0034
Phone: (859) 257-7722
Fax: (859) 323-9971
http://www.gatton.uky.edu

LOUISIANA

Louisiana State University
E. J. Ourso College of Business
3170 Ceba Building
Baton Rouge, LA 70803
Phone: (225) 578-8867
Fax: (225) 578-2421
http://www.mba.lsu.edu

Tulane University
A.B. Freeman School of Business
7 McAlister Drive, Suite 401
New Orleans, LA 70118-5669
Phone: (504) 865-5410

Fax: (504) 865-6770
http://www.freeman.tulane.edu

University of New Orleans
College of Business Administration
Admin Building Room 103
New Orleans, LA 70148
Phone: (504) 280-6595
Fax: (504) 280-5522
E-mail: admissions@uno.edu
http://www.uno.edu

MAINE

University of Maine
Maine Business School
5723 Donald P. Corbett Business Building
Orono, ME 04469-5723
Phone: (207) 581-1973
Fax: (207) 581-1930
E-mail: mba@maine.edu
http://www.umaine.edu/business

MARYLAND

Loyola College
Sellinger School of Business and
    Management
4501 North Charles Street
Baltimore, MD 21210-2699
Phone: (800) 221-9107
Fax: (410) 617-2005
E-mail: mba@loyola.edu
http://www.sellinger.loyola.edu

University of Baltimore
Merrick School of Business
4501 North Charles Street
Baltimore, MD 21201
Phone: (410) 617-5020 or (877) 277-5982
Fax: (410) 617-2002
http://www.ubalt.edu/study/graduate/mba.
    html

University of Maryland
Robert H. Smith School of Business
2308 Van Munching Hall
College Park, MD 20742-1871
Phone: (301) 405-2278
Fax: (301) 314-9862
http://www.rhsmith.umd.edu

MASSACHUSETTS

Babson College
F.W. Olin Graduate School of Business
Olin Hall
Babson Park, MA 02457-0310

Phone: (781) 239-4317
Fax: (781) 239-4194
E-mail: mbaadmission@babson.edu
http://www.babson.edu/mba

Bentley College
McCallum Graduate School of Business
175 Forest Street
Waltham, MA 02452
Phone: (781) 891-2108 or (800) 442-4723
Fax: (781) 891-2424
E-mail: gradadm.bentley.edu
http://www.bentley.edu

Boston College
Wallace E. Carroll Graduate School of
    Management
Fulton Hall, 140 Commonwealth Avenue
Chestnut Hill, MA 02467-3808
Phone: (617) 552-3920
Fax: (617) 552-8078
http://www.bc.edu/schools/csom/mba

Boston University
Department of Mathematics and Statistics
Graduate School of Arts and Sciences
705 Commonwealth Avenue
Boston, MA 02215
Phone: (617) 353-0943
Fax: (617) 353-8100
E-mail: mathfn@bu.edu
http://www.bu.edu

Boston University
School of Management
595 Commonwealth Avenue
Boston, MA 02215
Phone: (617) 353-2670
Fax: (617) 353-7368
E-mail: mba@bu.edu
http://www.management.bu.edu

Brandeis University
Graduate School of International
    Economics and Finance
Sachar International Center
Waltham, MA 02454-9110
Phone: (781) 736-2252
Fax: (781) 736-2263
E-mail: admission@lemberg.brandeis.edu
http://www.brandeis.edu

Harvard University
Graduate School of Business
    Administration
M.B.A. Admissions Office
Soldiers Field Road
Boston, MA 02163
Phone: (617) 495-6127

Fax: (617) 496-9272
E-mail: admissions@hbs.edu
http://www.hbs.edu

Massachusetts Institute of Technology
Sloan School of Management
E52-118 50 Memorial Drive
Cambridge, MA 02142
Phone: (617) 258-5434
Fax: (617) 253-6405
http://www.mitsloan.mit.edu

Northeastern University
College of Business Administration
350 Dodge Hall
360 Huntington Avenue
Boston, MA 02115
Phone: (617) 373-5992
Fax: (617) 373-8564
http://www.cba.neu.edu/graduate

Suffolk University
Frank Sawyer School of Management
8 Ashburton Place
Boston, MA 02108
Phone: (617) 573-8302
Fax: (617) 305-1733
http://www.suffolk.edu/business

MICHIGAN

Michigan State University
Department of Finance
315 Eppley Center
East Lansing, MI 48824
Phone: (517) 353-1705
Fax: (517) 432-1080
http://www.msu.edu

Michigan State University
Eli Broad Graduate School of
    Management
215 Eppley Center
East Lansing, MI 48824
Phone: (517) 355-7604 or (800) 467-8622
Fax: (517) 353-1649
http://mba.msu.edu

**Walsh College of Accountancy and
    Business Administration**
3838 Livernois Road
P.O. Box 7006
Troy, MI 48007-7006
Phone: (810) 689-8282 or (800) 925-7401
Fax: (810) 524-2520
E-mail: admissions@walshcollege.edu
http://www.walshcollege.edu

Wayne State University
School of Business Administration

5201 Cass, Room 200
Detroit, MI 48202
Phone: (313) 577-4505 or (800) 910-3276
Fax: (313) 577-5299
http://www.busadm.wayne.edu

University of Michigan—Ann Arbor
Stephen M. Ross School of Business
701 Tappan Street
Ann Arbor, MI 48109-1234
Phone: (734) 763-5796
Fax: (734) 763-7804
E-mail: umbusmba@umich.edu
http://www.bus.umich.edu

MINNESOTA

University of Minnesota
Curtis L. Carlson School of Management
Room 2-210, 321 19th Avenue South
Minneapolis, MN 55455
Phone: (612) 625-5555 or (800) 926-9431
Fax: (612) 626-7785
http://www.carlsonschool.umn.edu

MISSISSIPPI

Mississippi State University
College of Business and Industry
P.O. Box 5288
Mississippi State, MS 39762
Phone: (662) 325-1891
Fax: (662) 325-8161
http://www.cbi.msstate.edu/gsb

**University of Mississippi—School of
    Business Administration**
253 Holman Hall
University, MS 38677
Phone: (662) 915-5483
Fax: (662) 232-5821
E-mail: holleman@bus.olemiss.edu
http://www.olemiss.edu

MISSOURI

Saint Louis University
John Cook School of Business
3674 Lindell Boulevard, Suite 132
St. Louis, MO 63108-3397
Phone: (314) 977-6221
Fax: (314) 977-1416
http://www.mba.slu.edu

University of Missouri—Columbia
College of Business
Ph.D. Program in Finance
303 D Middlebush Hall
Columbia, MO 65221

Phone: (573) 882-6272
Fax: (573) 882-7887
E-mail: finance@missouri.edu
http://www.business.missouri.edu

Washington University
John M. Olin School of Business
One Brookings Drive
Campus Box 1133
St. Louis, MO 63130-4899
Phone: (314) 935-7301
Fax: (314) 935-6309
E-mail: mba@olin.wustl.edu
http://www.olin.wustl.edu

NEBRASKA

University of Nebraska—Lincoln
College of Business Administration
210 College of Business Administration
Lincoln, NE 68588-0488
Phone: (402) 472-2338
Fax: (402) 472-5180
http://www.cba.unl.edu

NEVADA

University of Nevada—Las Vegas
College of Business
4505 Maryland Parkway
P.O. Box 456031
Las Vegas, NV 89154
Phone: (702) 895-3655
Fax: (702) 895-4090
http://www.business.unlv.edu

NEW HAMPSHIRE

Dartmouth College
Tuck School of Business
100 Tuck Hall
Hanover, NH 03755
Phone: (603) 646-3162
Fax: (603) 646-1441
E-mail: tuck-admissions@dartmouth.edu
http://www.tuck.dartmouth.edu

Southern New Hampshire University
Graduate School of Business
2500 North River Street
Manchester, NH 03106
Phone: (603) 668-2211
E-mail: graduateprograms@snhu.edu
http://www.snhu.edu

NEW JERSEY

Rutgers University—Newark
190 University Avenue

Newark, NJ 07102-1813
Phone: (973) 353-1234
Fax: (973) 353-1592
http://www.business.rutgers.edu

Seton Hall University
W. Paul Stillman School of Business
400 South Orange Avenue
South Orange, NJ 07079-2692
Phone: (973) 761-9262
Fax: (973) 761-9208
http://www.business.shu.edu

NEW YORK

Adelphi University
Office of Admissions, Levermore Hall
Graduate Division—School of
    Management and Business
1 South Avenue
Garden City, NY 11530
Phone: (516) 877-3050
Fax: (516) 877-3039
E-mail: admissions@adelphi.edu
http://www.adelphi.edu

**Baruch College of the City University
    of New York**
Zicklin School of Business
One Bernard Baruch Way
Box H-0820
New York, NY 10010
Phone: (646) 312-1300 or (646) 312-1301
Fax: (212) 802-6705
http://www.zicklin.baruch.cuny.edu

**City College of the City University of
    New York**
The College of Liberal Arts and Sciences
160 Convent Avenue
New York, NY 10031-9198
Phone: (212) 650-6977
Fax: (212) 650-6417
E-mail: gradadm@ccny.cuny.edu
http://www.ccny.cuny.edu

Columbia University
3022 Broadway
Columbia Business School
Uris Hall, Room 216
New York, NY 10027
Phone: (212) 854-1961
Fax: (212) 662-6754
http://www.gsb.columbia.edu

Columbia University
Graduate School of Arts and Sciences
535 West 116th Street MC 4304
New York, NY 10027
Phone: (212) 854-4737

Fax: (212) 854-2863
E-mail: gsas.admit@columbia.edu
http://www.columbia.edu

Cornell University
Johnson Graduate School of Management
111 Sage Hall
Ithaca, NY 14853-6201
Phone: (607) 255-4526
Fax: (607) 255-0065
E-mail: mba@cornell.edu
http://www.johnson.cornell.edu

Fordham University
Graduate School of Business
    Administration
33 West 60th Street, 4th Floor
New York, NY 10023
Phone: (212) 636-6200
Fax: (212) 636-7076
E-mail: admissionsgb@fordham.edu
http://www.bnet.fordham.edu

Hofstra University
Frank G. Zarb School of Business
126 Hofstra University
Hempstead, NY 11549
Phone: (516) 463-6700 or (866) 472-3463
Fax: (516) 463-4664
E-mail: mba-emba@hofstra.edu
http://www.hofstra.edu

Iona College
Hagan School of Business
715 North Avenue
New Rochelle, NY 10801
Phone: (914) 633-2256
Fax: (914) 633-2012
E-mail: hagan@iona.edu
http://www.iona.edu/hagan

New York University
Leonard N. Stern School of Business
44 West 4th Street
New York, NY 10012-1126
Phone: (212) 998-0100
Fax: (212) 995-4902
http://www.stern.nyu.edu

Pace University
Lubin School of Business
1 Pace Avenue
New York, NY 10038
Phone: (212) 346-1531
Fax: (212) 346-1585
E-mail: gradwp@pace.edu
http://www.pace.edu/lubin

Polytechnic University—Brooklyn
Office of Graduate Admissions
6 Metrotech Center
Brooklyn, NY

Phone: (718) 260-3600
Fax: (718) 260-3136
E-mail: inqury@poly.edu
http://www.www.poly.edu

Rennselaer Polytechnic Institute
Lally School of Management and
    Technology
110 Eighth Street
Pittsburgh Building
Troy, NY 12180-3590
Phone: (518) 276-6565
Fax: (518) 276-2665
E-mail: management@rpi.edu
http://www.lallyschool.rpi.edu

Rochester Institute of Technology
School of Business
105 Lomb Memorial Drive
Rochester, NY 14623-5604
Phone: (585) 475-2229
Fax: (585) 475-5476
E-mail: gradbus@rit.edu
http://www.ritmba.com

St. John's University
Peter J. Tobin College of Business
111 Bent Hall
8000 Utopia Parkway
Jamaica, NY 11439
Phone: (718) 990-1345
Fax: (718) 990-5242
E-mail: admissions@stjohns.edu/
    tobincollege
http://www.stjohns.edu

State University of New York—Albany
School of Business
361A Business Administration
1400 Washington Avenue
Albany, NY 12210
Phone: (518) 442-4961
Fax: (518) 442-3944
E-mail: busweb@albany.edu
http://www.albany.edu/business

State University of New York—Buffalo
School of Management
206 Jacobs Management Center
Buffalo, NY 14260
Phone: (716) 645-3204
Fax: (716) 645-2341
http://www.mgt.buffalo.edu

Syracuse University
Martin J. Whitman School of
    Management
900 South Crouse Avenue, Suite 100
Syracuse, NY 13244-2130
Phone: (315) 443-9214

Fax: (315) 443-9517
http://www.whitman.syr.edu

University of Rochester
William E. Simon Graduate School of
    Business Administration
305 Schlegel Hall
Rochester, NY 14627
Phone: (585) 275-3533
Fax: (585) 271-3907
http://www.simon.rochester.edu

NORTH CAROLINA

Duke University
The Fuqua School of Business
1 Towerville Drive, A-08 Academic
    Center
Durham, NC 27708-0104
Phone: (919) 660-7705
Fax: (919) 681-8026
http://www.fuqua.duke.edu

**University of North Carolina—
    Chapel Hill**
Kenan-Flagler Business School
CB 3490 McColl Building
Chapel Hill, NC 27599-3490
Phone: (919) 962-3236
Fax: (919) 962-0898
E-mail: mba_info@unc.edu
http://www.kenan-flagler.unc.edu

Wake Forest University
Babcock Graduate School of
    Management
P.O. Box 7659
Winston-Salem, NC 27109
Phone: (336) 758-5422
Fax: (336) 758-5830
E-mail: admissions@mba.wfu.edu
http://www.mba.wfu.edu

NORTH DAKOTA

University of North Dakota
College of Business and Public
    Administration
Gamble Hall
P.O. Box 8098
Grand Forks, ND 58202-8098
Phone: (701) 777-4853
Fax: (701) 777-2019
http://www.business.und.edu/mba

OHIO

Bowling Green State University
Graduate Studies in Business

Room 369 BA
Bowling Green, OH 43404
Phone: (419) 372-2488
Fax: (419) 372-2875
http://www.bgsumba.com

Case Western Reserve University
Weatherhead School of Management
160 Peter B. Lewis Building
10900 Euclid Avenue
Cleveland, OH 44106-7235
Phone: (216) 368-2030
Fax: (216) 368-5548
http://weatherhead.cwru.edu

Cleveland State University
James J. Nance College of Business
  Administration
2121 Euclid Avenue, BU 219
Cleveland, OH 44115
Phone: (216) 687-3730
Fax: (216) 687-5311
E-mail: cba@csuohio.edu
http://www.csuohio.edu/cba/

Ohio State University
Fisher College of Business
100 Gerlach Hall
2108 Neil Avenue
Columbus, OH 43210-1144
Phone: (614) 292-2248
Fax: (614) 292-9006
E-mail: cobgrd@cob.ohio-state.edu
http://www.fisher.osu.edu

University of Toledo
College of Business Administration
2801 West Bancroft
Toledo, OH 43606
Phone: (419) 530-2775
Fax: (419) 530-7260
http://www.business.utoledo.edu

Wright State University
College of Business and Administration
110 Rike Hall, 3640 Col. Glenn
  Highway
Dayton, OH 45435
Phone: (937) 775-2437
Fax: (937) 775-3545
http://www.wright.edu/business

OKLAHOMA

University of Tulsa
College of Business
600 South College Avenue
Tulsa, OK 74104-3189
Phone: (918) 631-2242

Fax: (918) 631-2142
http://www.cba.utulsa.edu

OREGON

University of Oregon
Charles H. Lundquist College of
  Business
300 Peterson Hall
1208 University of Oregon
Eugene, OR 97403-1208
Phone: (541) 346-1462
Fax: (541) 346-0073
http://www.uoregonmba.com

Willamette University
Atkinson School of Management
900 State Street
Salem, OR 97301
Phone: (503) 370-6167
Fax: (503) 370-3011
http://www.willamette.edu/mba

PENNSYLVANIA

Carnegie Mellon University
David A. Tepper School of Business
5000 Forbes Avenue
Pittsburgh, PA 15213
Phone: (412) 282-2272
E-mail: gsfa-admissions@andrew.cmu.edu
http://business.tepper.cmu.edu

Drexel University
Lebow College of Business
3141 Chestnut Street
207 Matheson Hall
Philadelphia, PA 19104
Phone: (215) 895-6804 or
  (800) 2-DREXEL
Fax: (215) 895-1725
http://www.lebow.drexel.edu

Duquesne University
John F. Donahue Graduate School of
  Business
600 Forbes Avenue
Pittsburgh, PA 15282
Phone: (412) 396-6276
Fax: (412) 396-1726
E-mail: grad-bus@duq.edu
http://www.bus.duq.edu/grad/

Lehigh University
College of Business and Economics
621 Taylor Street
Bethlehem, PA 18015
Phone: (610) 758-5280
Fax: (610) 758-5283
http://www.lehigh.edu/mba

**Pennsylvania State University—
  University Park**
Smeal College of Business
  Administration
220 Business Building
University Park, PA 16802-3360
Phone: (814) 863-0474
Fax: (814) 863-8072
http://www.smeal.psu.edu/mba

Temple University
Fox School of Business and
  Management
1810 North 13th Street
Speakman Hall—Room 5
Philadelphia, PA 19122
Phone: (215) 204-5890
Fax: (215) 204-1032
http://www.fox.temple.edu/mbams

University of Pennsylvania
The Wharton School
420 Jon M. Huntsman Hall
3736 Walnut Street
Philadelphia, PA 19104-6340
Phone: (215) 898-6183
Fax: (215) 898-0120
E-mail: mba.admissions@wharton.
  upenn.edu
http://www.wharton.upenn.edu/mba

University of Pittsburgh
Katz Graduate School of Business
276 Mervis Hall
Roberto Clemente Drive
Pittsburgh, PA 15260
Phone: (412) 648-1700
Fax: (412) 648-1659
http://www.katz.pitt.edu

Villanova University
College of Commerce and Finance
800 Lancaster Avenue, Bartley Hall
Villanova, PA 19085
Phone: (610) 519-4336
Fax: (610) 519-6273
E-mail: mba@email.villanova.edu
http://www.mba.villanova.edu

RHODE ISLAND

Bryant University
School of Business Administration
1150 Douglas Pike
Smithfield, RI 02917-1284
Phone: (401) 232-6230
Fax: (401) 232-6494
E-mail: gradprog@bryant.edu
http://www.bryant.edu

University of Rhode Island
College of Business Administration
210 Ballantine Hall
7 Lippett Road
Kingston, RI 02881
Phone: (401) 874-5000
Fax: (401) 874-4312
http://www.cba_uri.edu/mba

SOUTH CAROLINA

Clemson University
College of Business and Public Affairs
124B Sirrine Hall
Clemson, SC 29634-1315
Phone: (864) 656-3975
Fax: (864) 656-0947
http://www.business.clemson.edu/mba

University of South Carolina
Darla Moore School of Business
Columbia, SC 29208
Phone: (803) 777-4346
Fax: (803) 777-0414
http://www.mooreschool.sc.edu

SOUTH DAKOTA

University of South Dakota
414 East Clark Street
Vermillion, SD 57069-2390
Phone: (605) 677-5232
Fax: (605) 677-5058
E-mail: dhoadley@charlie.usd.edu
http://www.usd.edu/mba

TENNESSEE

University of Tennessee—Knoxville
College of Business Administration
527 Stokely Management Center
Knoxville, TN 37996-0552
Phone: (865) 974-5033
Fax: (865) 974-3826
E-mail: mba@utk.edu
http://www.mba.utk.edu

Vanderbilt University
Owen Graduate School of Management
401 21st Avenue South
Nashville, TN 37203
Phone: (615) 322-6469
Fax: (615) 343-1175
E-mail: admissions@owen.vanderbilt.edu
http://www.owen.vanderbilt.edu

TEXAS

Baylor University
Hankamer School of Business

One Bear Place #98013
Waco, TX 76798
Phone: (254) 710-3718 or (800) 583-0622
Fax: (254) 710-1066
http://www.baylor.edu/mba

Rice University
Jesse H. Jones Graduate School of
 Management
6100 Main Street, Suite 109
Houston, TX 77005-1892
Phone: (713) 348-4918
Fax: (713) 348-6147
http://www.jonesgsm.rice.edu

Southern Methodist University
Edwin L. Cox School of Business
P.O. Box 750333
Dallas, TX 75275-0333
Phone: (214) 768-1214
Fax: (214) 768-3956
http://www.mba.cox.smu.edu

Texas A&M University
Lowry Mays College and Graduate
 School of Business
212 Wehner Building
College Station, TX 77843-4117
Phone: (979) 845-4714
Fax: (979) 862-2393
http://www.mba.tamu.edu

Texas Christian University
M. J. Neeley School of Business
P.O. Box 298540
Fort Worth, TX 76129
Phone: (817) 257-7531
Fax: (817) 257-6431
E-mail: mbainfo@tcu.edu
http://www.mba.tcu.edu

Texas Tech University
Rawls College of Business
Finance Department, M.S. 2101
Lubbock, TX 79409
Phone: (806) 742-3184
Fax: (806) 742-3958
http://www.mba.ba.ttu.edu

University of Houston—Clear Lake
School of Business and Public
 Administration
2700 Bay Area Boulevard
Houston, TX 77058
Phone: (281) 283-2521
Fax: (281) 283-2530
http://www.adminuhcl.edu/bpa

University of Texas—Austin
Graduate School of Business

CBA 2.316
Austin, TX 78712
Phone: (512) 471-7612
Fax: (512) 471-4243
E-mail: texasmba@bus.utexas.edu
http://www.texasmba.bus.utexas.edu

University of Texas—Austin
McCombs School of Business
1 University Station
Austin, TX 78712
Phone: (512) 471-7612
Fax: (512) 471-4243
http://www.mba.mccombs.utexas.edu

University of Texas—Dallas
School of Management
2601 North Floyd Road
Richardson, TX 75080
Phone: (972) 883-2750
Fax: (972) 883-6425
http://www.som.udallas.edu

West Texas A&M University
T. Boone Pickens College of Business
 Graduate School
WTAMU Box 60907
Canyon, TX 79016-0001
Phone: (806) 656-2020
Fax: (806) 651-5285
http://www.wtamu.edu

UTAH

Brigham Young University
Mariott School of Management
640 Tanner Building
Provo, UT 84602
Phone: (801) 422-3500
Fax: (801) 422-0513
E-mail: mba@byu.edu
http://www.mariottschool.byu.edu/mba

University of Utah
David Eccles School of Business
1645 East Campus Center Drive, Room
 101
Salt Lake City, UT 84112-9301
Phone: (801) 581-7785
Fax: (801) 581-3666
http://www.business.utah.edu/go/
 masters/39

VERMONT

University of Vermont
School of Business Administration
333 Waterman Building
Burlington, VT 05405

Phone: (802) 656-0655
Fax: (802) 656-4078
http://www.bsad.emba.uvm.edu

VIRGINIA

College of William and Mary
Mason School of Business
P.O. Box 8795
Williamsburg, VA 23187
Phone: (757) 221-2900
Fax: (757) 221-2958
http://www.mason.wm.edu

George Mason University
School of Management
4400 University Drive
Mail Stop 5A2
Fairfax, VA 22030
Phone: (703) 993-2136
Fax: (703) 993-1778
http://www.som.gmu.edu

University of Richmond
E. Claiborne Robins School of Business
Richmond, VA 23173
Phone: (804) 289-8553
Fax: (804) 287-6544
E-mail: mba@richmond.edu
http://www.richmond.edu

University of Virginia
Darden Graduate School of Business
    Administration
P.O. Box 6550
Charlottesville, VA 22906-6550

Phone: (800) 882-6221
Fax: (434) 243-5033
E-mail: darden@virginia.edu
http://www.darden.virginia.edu

Virginia Commonwealth University
School of Business
P.O. Box 844000
Richmond, VA 23284
Phone: (804) 828-4622
Fax: (804) 828-7174
http://www.gsib.bus.vcu.edu

**Virginia Polytechnic Institute and State
    University**
Pamplin College of Business
1044 Pamplin Hall
Blacksburg, VA 24061-0325
Phone: (540) 231-6152
Fax: (540) 231-4487
http://www.mba.vt.edu

WASHINGTON

Seattle University
Albers School of Business and Economics
Broadway and Madison
Seattle, WA 98122-4460
Phone: (206) 296-2000
Fax: (206) 296-5902
E-mail: admissions@seattleu.edu
http://www.seattleu.edu

University of Washington
Graduate School of Business
    Administration

110 Mackenzie Hall
P.O. Box 353200
Seattle, WA 98195
Phone: (206) 543-4661
Fax: (206) 616-7351
E-mail: mba@u.washington.edu
http://www.mba.washington.edu

WEST VIRGINIA

West Virginia University
College of Business and Economics
P.O. Box 6027
Morgantown, WV 26506
Phone: (304) 293-5408
Fax: (304) 293-2385
http://www.be.wvu.edu

WISCONSIN

University of Wisconsin—Madison
Business School
975 University Avenue
Madison, WI 53706
Phone: (608) 262-4000
Fax: (608) 265-3607
http://www.bus.wisc.edu/mba

University of Wisconsin—Milwaukee
School of Business Administration
P.O. Box 742
Milwaukee, WI 53201-0742
Phone: (414) 229-5403
Fax: (414) 229-2372
http://www.uwm.edu/business

APPENDIX III
PROFESSIONAL ASSOCIATIONS
AND ORGANIZATIONS

The associations listed here are all closely related to the careers discussed in this book. Those that are mentioned in the position descriptions are included as well as others that are of importance in banking, finance, and insurance. This section includes the name and address of each organization, plus contact information such as telephone numbers and Internet and e-mail addresses.

You can contact these groups or visit their Web sites on the Internet to learn about career opportunities, professional certification, conferences, and seminars. An organization's Web site is the first place to look to get more information about its activities and contact association executives. A number of the organizations listed here have state or local affiliate chapters. To learn about any professional associations that may be in your area, talk with local professionals or look for that information on an association's Web site.

ACCOUNTING AND AUDITING

Accreditation Council for Accountancy and Taxation
1010 N. Fairfax Street
Alexandria, VA 22314
Phone: (888) 289-7763
Fax: (703) 549-2984
E-mail: info@acatcredentials.org
http://acatcredentials.org

American Accounting Association
5717 Bessie Drive
Sarasota, FL 33423
Phone: (941) 921-7747
Fax: (941) 923-4093
E-mail: office@aahq.org
http://aahq.org

American Institute of Certified Public Accountants
1211 Avenue of the Americas
New York, NY 10036
Phone: (212) 596-6200
Fax: (212) 596-6213
http://www.aicpa.org

American Society of Women Accountants
8405 Greensboro Drive, Suite 800
McLean, VA 22102
Phone: (800) 326-2163
Fax: (703) 506-3265
E-mail: aswa@aswa.org
http://www.aswa.org

Financial Accounting Standards Board
401 Merritt 7
P.O. Box 5116
Norwalk, CT 06856-5116
Phone: (203) 847-0700
Fax: (203) 849-9714
http://www.fasb.org

Financial Executives International
200 Campus Drive
Florham Park, NJ 07932-0674
Phone: (973) 765-1000
Fax: (973) 765-1018
http://www.fei.org

Forensic Accountants Society of North America
4348 Park Glen Road
Minneapolis, MN 60060
Phone: (952) 928-4668
Fax: (952) 929-1318
E-mail: info@fasna.org
http://www.fasna.org

Information Systems Audit and Control Association
3701 Algonquin Road, Suite 1010
Rolling Meadows, IL 60008
Phone: (847) 253-1545
Fax: (847) 253-1443
http://www.isaca.org

Institute of Management Accountants
10 Paragon Drive
Montvale, NJ 07645
Phone: (800) 638-4427

Fax: (201) 474-1600
E-mail: ima@imanet.org
http://www.imanet.org

The Institute of Internal Auditors
249 Maitland Avenue
Altamonte Springs
FL 32701-4201
Phone: (407) 937-1100
Fax: (407) 937-1101
http://www.theiia.org

National Association of State Boards of Accountancy
150 Fourth Avenue North, Suite 700
Nashville, TN 37219-2417
Phone: (615) 880-4200
Fax: (615) 880-4290
http://www.nasba.org

National Conference of CPA Practitioners
22 Jericho Turnpike, Suite 110
Mineola, NY 10501
Phone: (888) 488-5400
Fax: (516) 333-4099
E-mail: info@nccpap.org
http://www.nccpap.org

National Society of Accountants
1010 North Fairfax Street
Alexandria, VA 22314-1574
Phone: (703) 549-6400
Fax: (703) 549-2984
E-mail: nsa@wizard.net
http://www.nsacct.org

APPRAISAL ASSOCIATIONS

The Appraisal Institute
550 Van Buren Street, Suite 1000
Chicago, IL 60607
Phone: (312) 335-4100
Fax: (312) 335-4400
E-mail: web@appraisalinstitute.org
http://www.appraisalinstitute.org

American Society of Appraisers
555 Herndon Parkway, Suite 125
Herndon, VA 20170
Phone: (703) 478-2228
Fax: (703) 742-8471
E-mail: asainfo@appraisers.org
http://www.appraisers.org

Institute of Business Appraisers
P.O. Box 17410
Plantation, FL 33318
Phone: (954) 584-1144
Fax: (954) 954-1184
E-mail: ibahq@go-iba.org
http://www.go-iba.org

BANKING

American Bankers Association
1120 Connecticut Avenue, NW
Washington, DC 20036
Phone: (202) 663-5000 or
   (800) BANKERS
http://www.aba.com

American Institute of Banking
1120 Connecticut Avenue, NW
Washington, DC 20036
Phone: (800) BANKERS, ext. 5191
http://www.aba.com/Conference+and+
   Education/aib_main.htm

America's Community Bankers
900 19th Street, NW, Suite 400
Washington, DC 20006
Phone: (202) 857-3100
Fax: (202) 296-8716
E-mail: info@acbankers.org
http://www.acbankers.org

**Association for Management
   Information in Financial Services**
3895 Fairfax Court
Atlanta, GA 30339
Phone: (770) 444-3557
Fax: (770) 444-9084
E-mail: ami@amifs.org
http://amifs.org

Bank Administration Institute
One North Franklin Street
Chicago, IL 60606
Phone: (312) 683-2464
Fax: (312) 683-2373
E-mail: info@bai.org
http://www.bai.org

Conference of State Bank Supervisors
1155 Connecticut Avenue NW
Washington, DC 20036
Phone: (202) 296-2840
Fax: (202) 296-1928
http://www.csbs.org

Consumer Bankers Association
1000 Wilson Boulevard, Suite 2500
Arlington, VA 22209-3912
Phone: (703) 276-1750
Fax: (703) 528-1290
http://www.cbanet.org

Credit Union National Association
P.O. Box 431
Madison, WI 53701
Phone: (800) 356-9655
Fax: (608) 231-4263
http://www.cuna.org

Electronic Funds Transfer Association
11350 Random Hills Road, Suite 800
Fairfax, VA 22030
Phone: (703) 934-6052
Fax: (703) 934-6058
http://www.efta.org

Institute of International Bankers
299 Park Avenue, 17th Floor
New York, NY 10171
Phone: (212) 421-1611
Fax: (212) 421-1119
E-mail: iib@iib.org
http://www.iib.org

**Independent Community Bankers of
   America**
1 Thomas Circle, NW, Suite 400
Washington, DC 20005
Phone: (202) 659-8111
Fax: (202) 659-9216
E-mail: info@icba.org
http://www.icba.org

**International Financial Services
   Association**
9 Sylvan Way
Parsippany, NJ 07054
Phone: (973) 656-1900
Fax: (973) 656-1915

E-mail: info@intlbanking.org
http://www.intlbanking.org

**Mortgage Bankers Association of
   America**
1919 Pennsylvania Avenue
Washington, DC 20006-3404
Phone: (202) 557-2700
http://www.mbaa.org

**NACHA: The Electronic Payments
   Association**
13665 Dulles Technology Drive,
   Suite 300
Herndon, VA 20171
Phone: (703) 561-1100
Fax: (703) 787-0996
http://www.nacha.org

**National Association of Mortgage
   Brokers**
8201 Greensboro Drive, Suite 300
McLean, VA 22102
Phone: (703) 342-5900
Fax: (703) 342-5905
http://www.namb.org

Risk Management Association
1801 Market Street, Suite 300
Philadelphia, PA 19103-1628
Phone: (800) 677-7621
Fax: (215) 446-4101
http://www.rmahq.org

CORPORATE FINANCE ASSOCIATIONS

ACA International
Association of Credit and Collection
   Professionals
P.O. Box 390106
Minneapolis, MN 55439
Phone: (952) 926-6547
http://www.acainternational.org

American Finance Association
University of California at Berkeley
Haas School of Business
Berkeley, CA 94729-1900
Phone: (800) 835-6770
E-mail: pyle@hass.berkeley.edu
http://www.afajof.org

American Payroll Association
660 North Main Avenue, Suite 100
San Antonio, TX 78205-1217
Phone: (210) 226-4600
Fax: (210) 226-4027
http://www.americanpayroll.org

American Purchasing Society
P.O. Box 256
Aurora, IL 60506
Phone: (630) 859-0250
Fax: (630) 859-0270
E-mail: propurch@aol.com
http://www.american-purchasing.com

Association for Financial Professionals
7315 Wisconsin Avenue, Suite 600 West
Bethesda, MD 20814
Phone: (301) 907-2862
Fax: (301) 907-2864
http://www.afponline.org

Credit Professionals International
525B N. Laclede Station Road
St. Louis, MO 63119
Phone: (314) 961-0031
Fax: (314) 961-0040
E-mail: creditpro@creditprofessionals.
    org
http://www.creditprofessionals.org

**Financial Management Association
    International**
College of Business Administration
University of South Florida
Tampa, FL 33620-5500
Phone: (813) 974-2084
Fax: (813) 974-3318
http://www.fma.org

Financial Managers Society
100 West Monroe Street, Suite 810
Chicago, IL 60603
Phone: (800) 275-4367
Fax: (312) 578-1308
http://www.fmsinc.org

Financial Women International, Inc.
1027 West Roselawn Avenue
Roseville, MN 5513
Phone: (866) 236-2007
Fax: (651) 489-1322
http://www.fwi.org

Institute for Professionals in Taxation
600 Northpark Town Center
1200 Abernathy Road NE, Suite L-2
Atlanta, GA 30328
Phone: (404) 240-2300
Fax: (404) 240-2315
http://www.ipt.org

Institute for Supply Management
P.O. Box 22160
Tempe, AZ 85285-2160
Phone: (800) 888-6276

Fax: (480) 752-7890
http://www.ism.ws

**International Association of Financial
    Engineers**
560 Lexington Avenue, 11th Floor
New York, NY 10022
Phone: (212) 317-7479
Fax: (212) 527-2927
E-mail: main@iafe.org
http://www.iafe.org

Managed Funds Association
2025 M. Street NW
Suite 800
Washington, DC 20036-3309
Phone: (202) 367-1140
Fax: (202) 367-2140
E-mail: hq@mfainfo.org
http://www.mfainfo.org

**National Association of Corporate
    Treasurers**
12100 Sunset Hills Road, Suite 130
Reston, VA 20190
Phone: (703) 437-4377
Fax: (703) 435-4390
E-mail: nact@nact.org
http://www.nact.org

**National Association of Credit
    Management**
8840 Columbia 100 Parkway
Columbia, MD 21045-2158
Phone: (410) 740-5560
Fax: (410) 740-5574
E-mail: nacminfo@nacm.org
http://www.nacm.org

National Association of Enrolled Agents
1120 Connecticut Avenue NW
Suite 460
Washington, DC 20036-3922
Phone: (202) 822-6232
Fax: (202) 822-6270
E-mail: info@naeahq.org
http://www.naea.org

**The National Investor Relations
    Institute**
8020 Towers Crescent Drive, Suite 250
Vienna, VA 22182
Phone: (703) 506-3570
Fax: (703) 506-3571
http://www.niri.org

**Society of Financial Service
    Professionals**
17 Campus Boulevard, Suite 201

Newtown Square, PA 19073-3230
Phone: (610) 526-2500
Fax: (610) 527-1499
http://www.financialpro.org

FINANCIAL PLANNING

**Association of Financial Counseling
    and Planning Education**
1500 West Third Avenue, Suite 223
Columbus, OH 43212
Phone: (614) 485-9650
Fax: (614) 485-9621
http://www.afcpe.org

**Certified Financial Planner Board of
    Standards, Inc.**
1670 Broadway, Suite 600
Denver, CO 80202-4809
Phone: (800) 487-1497
Fax: (303) 860-7388
http://www.cfp-board.org

The Financial Planning Association
4100 East Mississippi Avenue, Suite 400
Denver, CO 80246-3053
Phone: (800) 322-4237
Fax: (303) 759-0749
http://www.fpanet.org

**National Association of Mortgage
    Planners**
3001 LBJ Freeway, Suite 110
Dallas, TX 75234
Phone: (800) 724-2004
Fax: (972) 241-7046
E-mail: memberinfo@namp.org
http://www.namp.org

**National Association of Personal
    Financial Advisors**
3250 North Arlington Heights Road,
    Suite 109
Arlington Heights, IL 60004
Phone: (800) 366-2732
Fax: (847) 483-5415
E-mail: info@napfa.org
http://www.napfa.org

Registered Financial Planners Institute
2001 Cooper Foster Park Road
Amherst, OH 44001
Phone: (440) 282-7176
E-mail info@rfpi.com
http://www.rfpi.com

Society of Certified Senior Advisors
1777 South Bellaire Street, Suite 230
Denver, CO 80222

Phone: (800) 653-1785
Fax: (303) 757-7677
E-mail: society@csa-csa.com
http://csa-csa.org

INSURANCE AND RISK MANAGEMENT

American Academy of Actuaries
1100 17th Street NW, 7th Floor
Washington, DC 20036
Phone: (202) 223-8196
Fax: (202) 872-1948
http://www.actuary.org

**American Association of Managing
    General Agents**
150 South Warner Road
King of Prussia, PA 19406
Phone: (610) 225-1999
Fax: (610) 225-1996
http://www.aamga.org

American Council of Life Insurers
101 Constitution Avenue NW
Washington, DC 20001-2133
Phone: (202) 624-2000
http://www.acli.org

**American Institute for Chartered
    Property Casualty Underwriters
    and Insurance Institute of America**
720 Providence Road
Malvern, PA 19355-0716
Phone: (800) 644-2101
Fax: (610) 640-9576
E-mail: cserv@cpcuiia.org
http://www.aicpcu.org

American Insurance Association
1130 Connecticut Avenue, NW,
Suite 1000
Washington, DC 20036
Phone: (202) 8298-7100
Fax: (202) 293-1219
http://www.aiadc.org

**The American Insurance Marketing
    and Sales Society**
P.O. Box 35718
Richmond, VA 23235
Phone: (804) 674-6466
Fax: (804) 276-1300
E-mail: info@cpia.com
http://www.cpia.com/aims

**American Society of Pension
    Professionals & Actuaries**
4245 North Fairfax Drive, Suite 750

Arlington, VA 22203
Phone: (703) 516-9300
Fax: (703) 516-9308
E-mail: asppa@asppa.org
http://www.asppa.org

American Society of Safety Engineers
1800 East Oakton Street
Des Plaines, IL 60018-2187
Phone: (847) 699-2929
Fax: (847) 768-3434
E-mail: customerservice@asse.org
http://www.asse.org

America's Health Insurance Plans
601 Pennsylvania Avenue NW
South Building, Suite 500
Washington, DC 20004
Phone: (202) 778-3200
Fax: (202) 331-7487
E-mail: ahip@ahip.org
http://www.ahip.org

Associated Risk Managers
Two Pierce Place
Itasca, IL 60143-3141
Phone: (630) 285-4186
Fax: (630) 285-3590
http://www.armiweb.com

Casualty Actuarial Society
1100 North Glebe Road, Suite 600
Arlington, VA 22201
Phone: (703) 276-3100
Fax: (703) 276-3108
E-mail: office@casact.org
http://www.casact.org

**Council of Insurance Agents and
    Brokers**
701 Pennsylvania Avenue, NW, Suite 750
Washington, DC 20004-2608
Phone: (202) 783-4400
Fax: (202) 783-4410
E-mail: ciab@ciab.com
http://www.ciab.com

GAMA International
2901 Telestar Court, Suite 140
Falls Church, VA 22042-1205
Phone: (800) 345-2687
Fax: (703) 770-8182
E-mail: gamamail@gama.naifa.org
http://www.gamaweb.com

**Global Association of Risk
    Professionals**
100 Pavonia Avenue, Suite 405
Jersey City, NJ 07310

Phone: (201) 222-0054
Fax: (201) 222-5022
http://www.garp.com

**Health Insurance Association of
    America**
555 13th Street, NW
Washington, DC 20004-1109
Phone: (202) 824-1600
Fax: (202) 824-1722
http://www.hiaa.org

**Independent Insurance Agents of
    America**
127 South Peyton Street
Alexandria, VA 22314
Phone: (800) 221-7917
Fax: (703) 683-7556
E-mail: info@iiaba.org
http://www.independentagent.com

Insurance Claim Association
One Thomas Circle NW
Tenth Floor
Washington, DC 20005
Phone: (202) 452-0143
Fax: (202) 530-0659
http://www.claim.org

Insurance Information Institute
110 William Street
New York, NY 10038
Phone: (212) 346-5500
E-mail: info@iii.org
http://www.iii.org

**Insurance Regulatory Examiners
    Society**
12710 South Pflumm Road, Suite 200
Olathe, KS 66062
Phone: (913) 768-4700
Fax: (913) 768-4900
E-mail: ireshq@swbell.net
http://www.go-ires.org

Life Office Managers Association
2300 Windy Ridge Parkway, Suite 600
Atlanta, GA 30339-8443
Phone: (770) 951-1770
Fax: (770) 984-0441
E-mail: askloma@loma.org
http://www.loma.org

**The National Alliance for Insurance
    Education & Research**
3630 North Hills Drive
Austin, TX 78731
Phone: (800) 633-2165
Fax: (512) 349-6194

E-mail: alliance@scic.com
http://www.scic.com

National Association of Health
    Underwriters
2000 North 14th Street, Suite 450
Arlington, VA 22201
Phone: (703) 276-0220
Fax: (703) 841-7797
E-mail: info@nahu.org
http://www.nahu.org

National Association of Independent
    Life Brokerage Agencies
12150 Monument Drive, Suite 125
Fairfax, VA 22033
Phone: (703) 383-3081
Fax: (703) 383-6942
http://www.nailba.com

National Association of Insurance and
    Financial Advisors
2901 Telestar Court
Falls Church, VA 22042-1205
Phone: (877) TO-NAIFA
E-mail: membersupport@naifa.org
http://www.naifa.org

National Association of Professional
    Insurance Agents
400 North Washington Street
Alexandria, VA 22314
Phone: (703) 836-9340
Fax: (703) 836-1279
E-mail: piainfo@pianet.org
http://www.pianet.com

Property Casualty Insurers Association
    of America
2600 South River Road
Des Plaines, IL 60018-3286
Phone: (847) 297-7800
Fax: (847) 297-5064
E-mail: pcinet@pciaa.net
http://www.pciaa.net

Public Risk Management Association
500 Montgomery Street, Suite 750
Alexandria, VA 22314
Phone: (703) 528-7701
Fax: (703) 739-0200
E-mail: info@primacentral.org
http://www.primacentral.org

Risk and Insurance Management
    Society, Inc.
1065 Avenue of the Americas
13th Floor
New York, NY 10018

Phone: (212) 286-9292
Fax: (212) 986-9716
http://www.rims.org

Society of Actuaries
475 North Martingale Road, Suite 600
Schaumburg, IL 60173-2226
Phone: (847) 706-3500
Fax: (847) 706-3599
http://www.soa.org

Society of Insurance Trainers and
    Educators
2120 Market Street, Suite 108
San Francisco, CA 94114
Phone: (415) 621-2830
Fax: (415) 621-0889
http://www.insuranceetrainers.org

INVESTMENT MANAGEMENT AND SECURITIES

Bond Market Association
360 Madison Avenue
New York, NY 10017-7111
Phone: (646) 637-9200
Fax: (646) 637-9126
http://www.bondmarkets.com

Center for Futures Education
410 Erie Street
P.O. Box 309
Grove City, PA 16127
Phone: (724) 458-5860
E-mail: info@thectr.com
http://www.thectr.com

CFA Institute
560 Ray C. Hunt Drive
Charlottesville, VA 22903-0668
Phone: (434) 951-5499
Fax: (434) 951-5262
E-mail: info@cfainstitute.org
http://www.cfainstitute.org

Fiduciary & Investment Risk
    Management Association
P.O. Box 48297
Athens, GA 30604
Phone: (706) 354-0083
Fax: (706) 353-3994
E-mail: thefirma@negia.org
http://www.thefirma.org

International Swaps & Derivatives
    Association, Inc.
360 Madison Avenue, 16th Floor
New York, NY 10017

Phone: (212) 901-6000
Fax: (212) 901-6001
E-mail: isda@isda.org
http://www.isda.org

Investment Company Institute
1401 H Street, NW
Washington, DC 20005-2148
Phone: (202) 326-5800
Fax: (202) 326-8309
E-mail: info@ici.org
http://www.ici.org

Investment Management Consultants
    Association
5619 DTC Parkway, Suite 500
Greenwood Village, CO 80111
Phone: (303) 770-3377
Fax: (303) 770-1812
http://www.imca.org

National Association of Securities
    Dealers, Inc.
1735 K Street, NW
Washington, DC 20006-1506
Phone: (202) 728-8000
http://www.nasd.com

National Futures Association
200 West Madison Street, Suite 1600
Chicago, IL 60606
Phone: (312) 781-1300
http://www.nfa.futures.org

New York Society of Security Analysts,
    Inc.
1601 Broadway, 11th Floor
New York, NY 10019-7406
Phone: (800) 248-0108
Fax: (212) 541-4677
http://www.nyssa.org

Securities Industry Association
120 Broadway, 35th Floor
New York, NY 10271-0080
Phone: (212) 608-1500
Fax: (212) 968-0703
http://www.sia.com

APPENDIX IV
PROFESSIONAL CERTIFICATIONS

Professional certifications and credentials indicate that an individual has met educational, experience, and ethical qualifications and has achieved a level of professional competence. Many organizations are continuing to enhance their existing qualification standards, while adding new certifications. The most respected practitioners in the financial services industry often have one or more professional certifications. Many have served as officers of local, regional, or national associations.

This section provides information about some of the more common professional certifications in banking, finance, and insurance. You can get more information about available certifications by going to these organizations' Web sites or by contacting the organizations directly. Remember that attaining professional certification can often take two to three years. Talk to industry professionals in your field of interest about professional certification, and ask them how certification can help advance your career or employability before committing your time and resources to an industry-sponsored certification program.

ACCOUNTING AND AUDITING

Accreditation Council for Accounting and Taxation (ACAT)
1010 North Fairfax Street
Alexandria, VA 22314
Phone: (888) 289-7763
Fax: (703) 549-2512
E-mail: info@acatcredentials.org
http://www.acatcredentials.org
Certifications: Accredited Business Accountant/Adviser, Accredited Tax Adviser, Accredited Tax Preparer, Accredited Tax Adviser, Elder Care Specialist, International Accredited Business Accountant

American College of Forensic Examiners
2750 East Sunshine
Springfield, MO 65804
Phone: (417) 881-8318
Fax: (417) 881-4702
E-mail: info@acfei.com
http://www.acfei.com
Certifications: Certified Forensic Consultant, Certified Forensic Accountant

American Institute of Certified Public Accountants
1211 Avenue of the Americas
New York, NY 10036
Phone: (212) 596-6200
Fax: (212) 596-6213
http://www.aicpa.org
Certifications: Certified Public Accountant (CPA), Personal Financial Specialist

Institute of Management Accountants
10 Paragon Drive
Montvale, NJ 07645
Phone: (800) 638-4427
Fax: (201) 474-1600
E-mail: ima@imanet.org
http://www.imanet.org
Certifications: Certified in Financial Management and Certified Management Accountant credentials

The Institute of Internal Auditors
249 Maitland Avenue
Altamonte Springs, FL 32701-4201
Phone: (407) 937-1100
Fax: (407) 937-1101
http://www.theiia.org
Certifications: Certified Internal Auditor, Certification Self-Assessment, Certified Government Auditing Professional, Certified Financial Services Auditor

The Information Systems Audit and Control Association
3701 Algonquin Road, Suite 1010
Rolling Meadows, IL 60008
Phone: (847) 253-1545
Fax: (847) 253-1443
http://www.isaca.org
Certifications: Certified Information Systems Auditor (CISA)

Institute for Professionals in Taxation
3350 Peachtree Road, Suite 280
Atlanta, GA 30326
Phone: (404) 240-2300
Fax: (404) 240-2315
E-mail: ipt@ipt.org
http://www.ipt.org

Certifications: Certified Member of the Institute (CMI)

ACTUARIAL CERTIFICATIONS

Casualty Actuarial Society
4350 North Fairfax Drive, Suite 250
Arlington, VA 22201
Phone: (703) 276-3100
Fax: (703) 276-3108
E-mail: office@casact.org
http://www.casact.org
Certifications: Casualty Actuarial Society (CAS)

Society of Actuaries
475 North Martingale Road, Suite 600
Schaumburg, IL 60173-2226
Phone: (847) 706-3500
Fax: (847) 706-3599
http://www.soa.org
Certifications: Fellow of the Society of Actuaries (FSA)

BANKING

Bank Administration Institute
One North Franklin Street
Chicago, IL 60606
Phone: (312) 683-2464
Fax: (312) 683-2373
E-mail: info@bai.org
http://www.bai.org
Certifications: Certified Risk Professional, Certified Bank Auditor, BAI Certificate for Loan Review

The Institute of Certified Bankers
1120 Connecticut Avenue
Washington, DC 20036
Phone: (202) 663-5376
Fax: (202) 663-7543
E-mail: hwalesma@aba.com
http://www.aba.com/ICBcertifications
Certifications: Certified Lender
  Business Banker, Certified
  Regulatory Compliance Manager,
  Certified Financial Services Security
  Professional, Certified Trust and
  Financial Adviser, Certified Corporate
  Trust Specialist, Certified IRA Services
  Professional, Certified Retirement
  Services Professional, Certified
  Securities Operations Professional

CORPORATE FINANCE

Association for Financial Professionals
7315 Wisconsin Avenue, Suite 600 West
Bethesda, MD 20814
Phone: (301) 907-2862
Fax: (301) 907-2864
http://www.afponline.org
Certifications: Certified Treasury
  Professional

CREDIT MANAGEMENT

**National Association of Credit
  Management**
8840 Columbia 100 Parkway
Columbia, MD 21045-2158
Phone: (410) 740-5560
Fax: (410) 740-5574
E-mail: nacminfo@nacm.org
http://www.nacm.org
Certifications: Credit Business Associate,
  Credit Business Fellow, Certified
  Credit Executive

EMPLOYEE BENEFITS CERTIFICATIONS

The American College
270 South Bryn Mawr Avenue
Bryn Mawr, PA 19010
Phone: (888) 263-7265
Fax: (610) 526-1465
http://www.theamericancollege.edu
Certifications: Registered Employee
  Benefits Consultant

**International Foundation of Employee
  Benefit Plans**
18700 West Bluemound Road
P.O. Box 69
Brookfield, WI53008

Phone: (262) 786-6700
Fax: (262) 786-8670
E-mail: pr@ifebp.org
http://www.ifebp.org
Certifications: Certified Employee
  Benefits Specialist

FINANCIAL INSTITUTION SUPERVISION

Conference of State Bank Supervisors
1155 Connecticut Avenue NW
Washington, DC 20036
Phone: (202) 296-2840
Fax: (202) 296-1928
http://www.csbs.org
Certifications: Certified Operations
  Examiner, Certified Credit Examiner,
  Certified Examiner-in-Charge,
  Certified Examinations Manager,
  Certified Trust Examiner, Associate
  Certified Information Systems
  Examiner, Certified Information
  Systems Examiner, Certified
  Consumer Compliance Specialist

Society of Financial Examiners
174 Grace Boulevard
Altamonte Springs, FL 32714
Phone: (800) 787-SOFE
Fax: (407) 682-3175
E-mail: info@sofe.org
http://www.sofe.org
Certifications: Accredited Financial
  Examiner, Certified Financial
  Examiner

FINANCIAL PLANNING AND ESTATE PLANNING

**Association for Financial Counseling
  and Planning Education**
1500 West Third Avenue, Suite 223
Columbus, OH 43212
Phone: (614) 485-9650
Fax: (614) 485-9621
E-mail: 411@afcpe.org
http://www.afcpe.org
Certifications: Accredited Financial
  Counselor

**Association of Chartered Senior
  Financial Planners**
8174 South Holly Street #253
Centennial, Colorado 80122
Phone: (866) 94-ACSFP (22737)
Fax: (303) 379-6483
E-mail: info@acsfp.com
http://www.acsfp.com
Certifications: Chartered Senior Financial
  Planner

**Certified Financial Planner Board of
  Standards**
1670 Broadway, Suite 600
Denver, CO 80202-4809
Phone: (303) 830-7500
Fax: (303) 860-7388
E-mail: mail@cfp-board.org
http://www.cfp-board.org
Certifications: Certified Financial
  Planner (CFP)

CMPS Institute
3017 Walnut Ridge Drive
Ann Arbor, MI 48103
Phone: (888) 608-9800
http://www.cmpsinstitute.org
Certifications: Certified Mortgage
  Planning Specialist

The College for Financial Planning
8000 East Maplewood Avenue, Suite 200
Greenwood Village, CO 8011
Phone: (800) 237-9990
Fax: (303) 220-1810
http://www.cffp.edu
Certifications: Accredited Asset
  Management Specialist, Chartered
  Mutual Fund Counselor Chartered
  Retirement Planning Counselor

Estate Planning Institute
5 Learning Park
P.O. Box 669 Luray, VA 22835
Phone: (800) 232 6465
Fax: (703) 852-4444
E-mail: reg@cepp-epi.com
http://www.cepp.epi.com
Certifications: Chartered Estate Planning
  Practitioner

Institute of Business and Finance
7911 Herschel Avenue, Suite 201
La Jolla, CA 92037
Phone: (800) 848-2029
Fax: (858) 454-4660
http://www.icfs.com
Certifications: Board Certified in Estate
  Planning, Board Certified in Mutual
  Funds, Board Certified in Securities,
  Certified Annuity Specialist, Certified
  Fund Specialist, Certified Senior
  Consultant

**International Association of Qualified
  Financial Planners**
P.O. Box 7007
Beverly Hills, CA 90212-7007
Phone: (877) 346-3037
E-mail: info@iaqfp.org

http://www.iaqfp.org
Certifications: Qualified Financial
Planner

**National Association of Estate Planners
& Councils**
1120 Chester Avenue, Suite 470
Cleveland, OH 44114
Phone: (866) 226-2224
Fax: (216) 696-2582
E-mail: admin@naepc.org
http://www.naepc.org
Certifications: Accredited Estate Planner,
Estate Planning Law Specialist

**National Association of Financial and
Estate Planning**
525 East 4500 Street, Suite F-100
Salt Lake City, UT 84107
Phone: (801) 226-9900
Fax: (801) 226-1019
E-mail: nafep@nafep.com
http://www.nafep.com
Certifications: Certified estate Adviser

**National Association of Mortgage
Planners**
3001 LBJ Freeway, Suite 110
Dallas, TX 75234
Phone: (800) 724-2004
Fax: (972) 241-7046
E-mail: memberinfo@namp.org
http://www.namp.org

**National Institute of Certified College
Planners**
P.O. Box 15278
Syracuse, NY 13215-0278
Phone: (315) 487-4567
Fax: (315) 487-2663
http://www.niccp.com
Certifications: Certified College
Planning Specialist

**National Institute of Certified Estate
Planners**
3811 Southland Avenue
Kokomo, IN 46902
Phone: (765) 453-4300
E-mail: cep@nicep.org
http://www.nicep.org
Certifications: Certified Estate Planner

Registered Financial Planners Institute
2001 Cooper Foster Park Road
Amherst, OH 44001
Phone: (440) 282-7176
Fax: (440) 282-8027
E-mail: info@rfpi.com

http://www.rfpi.com
Certifications: Registered Financial
Planner

**Society of Certified Retirement
Financial Advisors**
1700 North Broadway
Walnut Creek, CA 94596
Phone: (888) 880-2732
E-mail: info@crfa.us
http://www.crfa.us
Certifications: Certified Retirement
Financial Adviser

Society for Certified Senior Advisors
1685 South Colorado Boulevard
Denver, CO 80222
Phone: (800) 653-1785
Fax: (303) 757-7677
E-mail: society@csa-csa.com
http://www.csa-csa.com
Certifications: Certified Senior Adviser

INSURANCE AGENTS AND BROKERS

**The American Insurance Marketing
and Sales Society**
P.O. Box 35718
Richmond, VA 23235
Phone: (877) 674-CPIA
Fax: (804) 276-1300
E-mail: info@cpia.com
http://www.cpia.com/aims
Certifications: Certified Professional
Insurance Agent

INSURANCE CLAIMS PROCESSING AND CUSTOMER SERVICE

Insurance Institute of America
720 Providence Road
P.O. Box 3016
Malvern, PA 19355-0716
Phone: (610) 644-2100
Fax: (610) 640-9576
E-mail: cserv@cpuiia.org
http://www.aicpcu.org
Certifications: Accredited Adviser in
Insurance, Associate in Claims

Life Office Managers Association
2300 Windy Ridge Parkway, Suite 600
Atlanta, GA 30339-8443
Phone: (770) 951-1770
Fax: (770) 984-0441
E-mail: education@loma.org

http://www.loma.org
Certifications: Certified Insurance
Representative and Associate, Life
and Health Claims, Associate in
Customer Service (ACS), Professional
in Customer Service

**Independent Insurance Agents of
America**
127 South Peyton Street
Alexandria, VA 22314
Phone: (800) 221-7917
Fax: (703) 683-7556
E-mail: info@iiaba.org
http://independentagent.com
Certifications: Accredited Customer
Service Representative (ACSR)

INSURANCE INVESTIGATORS

**Association of Certified Fraud
Examiners**
716 West Avenue
Austin, TX 78701-2727
Phone: (800) 245-3321
Fax: (512) 478-9297
E-mail: info@acfe.com
http://www.acfe.com
Certifications: Certified Fraud Examiner

INSURANCE UNDERWRITING

The American College
270 South Bryn Mawr Avenue
Bryn Mawr, PA 19010
Phone: (888) 263-7265
Fax: (610) 526-1465
Certifications: Chartered Life
Underwriter, Chartered Adviser for
Senior Living, Registered Health
Underwriter, Registered Employee
Benefits Consultant
http://www.theamericancollege.edu

**American Institute for CPCU and
Insurance Institute of America**
720 Providence Road
P.O. Box 3016
Malvern, PA 19355-0716
Phone: (800) 644-2101
Fax: (610) 640-9576
E-mail: cserv@cpcuiia.org
http://www.aicpcu.org
Certifications: Associate in Commercial
Underwriting, Chartered Property
Casualty Underwriter

Life Office Managers Association
2300 Windy Ridge Parkway, Suite 600
Atlanta, GA 30339-8443
Phone: (770) 951-1770
Fax: (770) 984-0441
E-mail: education@loma.org
http://www.loma.org
Certifications: Associate, Life
    Management Institute; Fellow,
    Financial Services Institute; Certified
    Professional, Life & Health Insurance;
    Certified Professional, Financial
    Services

INTERNATIONAL BANKING

International Financial Services
    Association
9 Sylvan Way
Parsippany, NJ 07054
Phone: (973) 656-1900
Fax: (973) 656-1915
E-mail: info@intlbanking.org
http://www.ifsaonline.org
Certifications: Certified Documentary
    Credit Specialist

PROPERTY APPRAISALS AND MORTGAGE BANKING

The Appraisal Institute
875 North Michigan Avenue, Suite 2400
Chicago, IL 60611-1980
Phone: (312) 335-4100
Fax: (312) 335-4400
http://www.appraisalinstitute.org
Certifications: Master Certified
    Appraiser and Certified International
    Property Specialist

Association of Mortgage Brokers
8201 Greensboro Drive, Suite 300
McLean, VA 22102
Phone: (703) 610-9009
Fax: (703) 610-9005
http://www.namb.org
Certifications: Certified Residential
    Mortgage Specialist, Certified
    Mortgage Consultant National

Institute of Business Appraisers
P.O. Box 17410
Plantation, FL 33318
Phone: (954) 584-1144
Fax: (954) 584-1184
E-mail: ibahq@go-iba.org
http://www.go-iba.org
Certifications: Certified Business
    Appraiser, Master Certified Business

Appraiser, Business Valuator
Accredited for Litigation

Mortgage Bankers Association of
    America
1919 Pennsylvania Avenue
Washington, DC 20006-3404
Phone: (202) 557-2700
http://www.mbaa.org
Certifications: Certified Mortgage Banker,
    Accredited Mortgage Professional,
    Certified Mortgage Servicer, Certified
    Mortgage Technologist, Certified
    Quality Assurance Professional,
    Certified Residential Originator,
    Certified Residential Underwriter

PURCHASING MANAGEMENT

Institute for Supply Management
P.O. Box 22160
Tempe, AZ 85285-2160
Phone: (480) 752-6276 or (800) 888-6276
Fax: (480) 752-7890
http://www.ism.ws.
Certifications: Accredited Purchasing
    Practitioner, Certified Purchasing
    Manager

RISK MANAGEMENT

The Financial Engineering Institute
29399 U.S. Highway 19 North
Suite 350
Clearwater, FL 33761
Phone: (727) 573-0497
Fax: (727) 573-0525
E-mail: nickg@thefei.com
http://www.thefei.org
Certifications: Chartered Financial
    Engineer

Global Association of Risk
    Professionals
100 Pavonia Avenue
Suite 405
Jersey City, NJ 07310
Phone: (201) 222-054
Fax: (201) 222-5022
http://www.garp.com
Certifications: Financial Risk Manager

Risk and Insurance Management
    Society
1065 Avenue, The Americas
13th Floor
New York, NY 10017
Phone: (212) 286-9292
Fax: (212) 986-9716

http://www.rims.org
Certifications: Associate in Risk
    Management, Fellow in Risk
    Management

SECURITIES AND INVESTMENT CERTIFICATIONS

Advisor Certification Services, Inc.
8657 Douglas Avenue, Suite 385
Des Moines, IA 50422
Phone: (866) 299-8368
Fax: (641) 755-4034
E-mail: caa@annuityadvisor.org
http://www.annuityadvisor.org
Certifications: Certified Annuity Advisor

American Academy of Financial
    Management
AAFM™ American Academy of
    Financial Management™
World Trade Center
2 Canal Street, Suite 2317
New Orleans, LA 70130
E-mail: info@financialcertified.com
http.www.financialcertified.com
Certifications: Chartered Asset Manager,
    Chartered Portfolio Manager,
    Chartered Trust and Estate Planner,
    Chartered Wealth Manager, Financial
    Analyst Designate, Master Financial
    Professional, Registered Financial
    Specialist

The American College
270 South Bryn Mawr Avenue
Bryn Maur, PA 19010
Phone: (888) 263-7265
Fax: (610) 526-1465
http://www.theamericancollege.edu
Certifications: Chartered Financial
    Consultant, Chartered Adviser in
    Philanthropy

American Institute of Financial
    Gerontology
1525 NW 3rd Street, Suite 8
Deerfield Beach, FL 33442
Phone: (888) 367-8470
Fax: (954) 698-6825
E-mail: info@aifg.org
http://www.aifg.org
Certifications: Certified Financial
    Gerontologist

Center for Fiduciary Studies
438 Division Street
Sewickley, PA 15143

Phone: (412) 741-8140
E-mail: info@fi360.com
http://www.fi360.com
Certifications: Accredited Investment
    Fiduciary

**American Society of Pension
    Professionals and Actuaries**
4350 North Fairfax Drive, Suite 820
Arlington, VA 22203-1619
Phone: (703) 516-9300
Fax: (703) 516-9308
http://www.aspa.org
Certifications: Certified Pension
    Consultant

**Association of Financial Counseling
    and Planning Education**
2121 Arlington Avenue, Suite 5
Upper Arlington, OH 43221-4339
Phone: (614) 485-9650
Fax: (614) 485-9621
E-mail: sburns@finsolve.com
http://www.afcpe.org
Certifications: Accredited Financial
    Counselor

CFA Institute
560 Ray C. Hunt Drive
Charlottesville, VA 22903-0668
Phone: (434) 951-5499
Fax: (434) 951-5262
E-mail: info@cfainstitute.org
http://www.cfainstitute.org
Certifications: Chartered Financial
    Analyst

**Chartered Alternative Investment
    Analyst Association**
29 South Pleasant Street
Amherst, MA 01002
Phone: (413) 253-7373
Fax: (413) 253-4494
E-mail: info@caia.org
http://www.caia.org
Certifications: Chartered Alternative
    Investment Analyst

Institute of Business and Finance
7911 Herschel Avenue, Suite 201
La Jolla, CA 92037-4413
Phone: (800) 848-2029
Fax: (858) 454-4660
http://www.icfs.com
Certifications: Certified Fund Specialist

**International Association of Registered
    Financial Consultants**
The Financial Planning Building
P.O. Box 42506
Middletown, OH 45042-0506
Phone: (800) 532-9060
Fax: (513) 424-5752
http://www.iarfc.org
Certifications: Registered Financial
    Associate, Registered Financial
    Consultant

**International Foundation for
    Retirement Education**
8201 Greensboro Drive, Suite 215
McLean, VA 22102
Phone: (703) 934-0941

Fax: (703) 934-0965
E-mail: infor@infre.org
http://www.infre.org
Certifications: Certified Retirement
    Counselor, Certified Retirement
    Administrator

Investment Advisor Association
1050 17th Street NW
Suite 725
Washington, DC 20036-5503
Phone: (202) 293-4222
Fax: (202) 293-4223
E-mail: iaa@investmentadvisor.org
http://www.icaa.org

**Investment Management Consultants
    Association**
9101 East Kenyon Avenue, Suite 3000
Denver, CO 80237
Phone: (303) 770-3377
Fax: (303) 770-1812
http://www.imca.org
Certifications: Certified Investment
    Management Consultant

Kaplan University
School of Continuing Education
6301 Kaplan University Avenue
Fort Lauderdale, FL 33309
Phone: (866) 572-5268
Fax: (888) 887-6494
E-mail: infoku@kaplan.edu
http//:www.kaplan.edu
Certifications: Wealth Management
    Specialist

APPENDIX V
PROFESSIONAL PERIODICALS

The following list of important periodicals includes magazines and newspapers reporting on news and events in banking, finance, and insurance. Many of the publications report on news and events in more than one field. For example, banking publications have regular feature articles on marketing of insurance or securities products within the banking industry.

The name, publisher, and contact information for each publication is included below. Readers can obtain more information, including subscription price, from the publication's World Wide Web address. Please note that this list represents a core group of professional publications. There are hundreds more publications covering banking, finance, and insurance, but space limitations preclude listing more than the core group of industry periodicals.

ACCOUNTING

The CPA Journal
New York Society of Certified Public
   Accountants
530 Fifth Avenue, Fifth Floor
New York, NY 10036-5101
Phone: (212) 719-8300
Fax: (212) 919-4755
http://www.cpaj.com

Internal Auditor
249 Maitland Avenue
Altamonte Springs, FL 32701-4201
Phone: (407) 937-1100
Fax: (407) 937-1101
E-mail: iia@iia.org
http://www.theiia.org

Journal of Accountancy
Harborside Financial Center
201 Plaza 3
Jersey City, NJ 07311-3881
Phone: (888) 777-7077
http://www.aicpa.org/pubs/jofa/index.
   htm

Management Accounting Quarterly
10 Paragon Drive
Montvale, NJ 07645-1760
Phone: (800) 638-4427
Fax: (201) 474-1600
http://www.imanet.org

NPA Magazine
1010 North Fairfax Street
Alexandria, VA 22314
Phone: (703) 549-6400
Fax: (703) 549-2984
http://www.nsacct.org

BANKING

ABA Banking Journal
345 Hudson Street
New York, NY 10014
Phone: (212) 620-7200
Fax: (212) 633-1165
http://www.ababj.com

American Banker
One State Street Plaza, 27th Floor
New York, NY 10004
Phone: (212) 803-8200
Fax: (212) 843-9600
http://www.americanbanker.com

Bank Marketing
1120 Connecticut Avenue, NW Third Floor
Washington, DC 20036
Phone: (202) 663-5428
Fax: (202) 828-4540
http://www.aba.com/marketingnetwork

Banking Strategies
One North Franklin Street
Chicago, IL 60606
Phone: (312) 683-2464
Fax: (312) 683-2373
http://www.bai.org

Bank Systems & Technology
825 Third Avenue Ninth Floor
New York, NY 10022
Phone: (212) 600-3000
Fax: (212) 600-3045
http://www.banktech.com

Credit Union Magazine
P.O. Box 431
Madison, WI 53701
Phone: (800) 356-9655 ext. 4076
Fax: (608) 231-4370
http://www.creditunionmagazine.com

Credit Union Times
560 Village Boulevard, Suite 325
West Palm Beach, FL 32402
Phone: (561) 683-8515
Fax: (561) 683-8514
http://www.cutimes.com

RMA Journal
One Liberty Place
1801 Market Street, Suite 300
Philadelphia, PA 19103-1628
Phone: (800) 677-7621
Fax: (215) 446-4101
http://www.rmahq.org

Mortgage Banking
1919 Pennsylvania Avenue
Washington, DC 20006-3404
Phone: (202) 557-2700
http://www.mortgagebankingmagazine.
   com

U.S. Banker
One State Street Plaza
New York, NY 10004
Phone: (800) 221-1809
http://us-banker.com

FINANCIAL

AFP Exchange
Association for Financial Professionals
7315 Wisconsin Avenue, Suite 600 West
Bethesda, MD 20814
Phone: (301) 907-2862
Fax: (301) 907-2864
http://www.afponline.org/exchange

Business Credit
8840 Columbia 100 Parkway
Columbia, MD 21045-2158
Phone: (888) 256-3242
Fax: (410) 423-1845
http://www.fcibglobal.com/services/bcm.
   html

Business Finance
P.O. Box 3438
Loveland, CO 80538
Phone: (970) 203-2926
Fax: (970) 593-1050
http://www.businessfinancemag.com

CFO Magazine
253 Summer Street
Boston, MA 02210
Phone: (617) 345-9700
Fax: (617) 345-9385
http://www.cfonet.com

Financial Analysts Journal
P.O. Box 3668
Charlottesville, VA 22903
Phone: (800) 247-8132
Fax: (434) 951-5262
http://www.cfapubs.org

Financial Executive
200 Campus Drive
Florham Park, NJ 07932-0674
Phone: (973) 765-1000
Fax: (973) 765-1018
http://www.fei.org/magazine

Financial Planning
40 West 57 Street, 11th Floor
New York, NY 10019
Phone: (212) 765-5311
http://www.financial-planning.com

Global Finance
1001 Avenue of the Americas, 21st Floor
New York, NY 10018
Phone: (212) 768-1100
Fax: (212) 768-2020
http://www.gfmag.com

Institutional Investor
488 Madison Avenue
New York, NY 10022
Phone: (212) 224-3300
Fax: (212) 224-3553
http://www.institutionalinvestor.com

Investment Dealers' Digest
40 West 57th Street
New York, NY 10019
Phone: (212) 803-8333
http://www.iddmagazine.com

The New York Times
229 West 43rd Street
New York, NY 10036-3959
Phone: (800) 698-4637
http://www.nytimes.com

Pensions & Investments
711 Third Avenue, Third Floor
New York, NY 10017-4036
Phone: (212) 210-0115
Fax: (212) 210-0117
http://www.pionline.com

Plan Sponsor
125 Greenwich Avenue
Greenwich, CT 06830
Phone: (203) 629-5014
Fax: (203) 629-5024
http://www.assetpub.com

Registered Representative
18818 Teller Avenue
Irvine, CA 92612
Phone: (866) 505-7173
Fax: (949) 851-1636
http://www.registeredrep.com

Treasury & Risk Management
475 Park Avenue South
New York, NY 10019
Phone: (212) 557-7480
Fax: (212) 557-7653
http://www.treasuryandrisk.com

The Wall Street Journal
200 Burnett Road
Chicopee, MA 01020
Phone: (800) 568-7625
Fax: (800) 975-8618
http://www.services.wsj.com

INSURANCE AND RISK MANAGEMENT

Best's Review
Ambest Road
Oldwick, NJ 08858
Phone: (908) 439-2200

Fax: (908) 439-3296
http://www.ambest.com/review

Broker World Magazine
9404 Reeds Road
Overland Park, KS 66207
Phone: (913) 383-9191
Fax: (913) 383-1247
http://www.brokerworldmag.com

Business Insurance
Crain Communications Inc.
360 North Michigan Avenue
Chicago, IL 60601
Phone: (312) 649-5442
http://www.businessinsurance.com

National Underwriter
Property and Casualty
505 Gest Street
Cincinnati, OH 45203
Phone: (800) 543-0874
http://www.nationalunderwriter.com

PIA Connection
400 North Washington Street
Alexandria, VA 22314
Phone: (703) 836-9360
Fax: (703) 836-1279
E-mail: proagent@pianet.org
http://www.pianet.com

Risk & Insurance
747 Dresher Road, Suite 500
P.O. Box 980
Horsham, PA 19044-0980
Phone: (215) 784-0910
Fax: (215) 784-0275
http://www.riskandinsurance.com

Risk Management
Risk and Insurance Management
   Society
1065 Avenue of the Americas,
   13th Floor
New York, NY 10017
Phone: (212) 286-9364
Fax: (212) 922-0716
http://www.rmmag.com

APPENDIX VI
REGULATORY AGENCIES OF THE UNITED STATES GOVERNMENT

Commodity Futures Trading Commission
Three Lafayette Centre
1155 21st Street NW
Washington, DC 20581
Phone: (202) 418-5000
http://www.cftc.gov
Regulates the trading of commodity futures and options contracts

Federal Deposit Insurance Corporation
550 17th Street NW
Washington, DC 20429-9990
Phone: (202) 393-8400
http://www.fdic.gov
Examines banks and savings institutions; responds to consumer complaints about FDIC-insured financial institutions

Federal Reserve Board of Governors
20th & Constitution Avenue NW
Washington, DC 20551
Phone: (202) 452-3215
http://www.federalreserve.gov
Supervises activities of Federal Reserve System member banks and financial holding companies; conducts monetary policy to achieve economic growth targets

Federal Housing Finance Board
1625 I Street NW
Fourth Floor
Washington, DC 20006-5212
Phone: (202) 408-2500
http://www.fhfb.gov
Supervises the 12 regional Federal Home Loan Banks

Federal Trade Commission
600 Pennnsylvania Avenue, Room 130
Washington, DC 20580
Phone: (202) 326-2222
http://www.ftc.gov
Enforces antitrust laws and consumer protection legislation

Internal Revenue Service
1111 Constitution Avenue NW
Washington, DC 20224
Phone: (202) 566-4115
http://www.irs.ustreas.gov
Administers tax rules and regulations of the Treasury Department; collects personal and corporate taxes

National Credit Union Administration
1775 Duke Street
Alexandria, VA 22314
Phone: (703) 518-6300
http://www.ncua.gov
Regulates and insures deposits of federally chartered credit unions

Office of the Comptroller of the Currency
490 L'Enfant Plaza NW
Washington, DC 20219
Phone: (202) 447-1800
http://www.occ.treas.gov
Regulates nationally chartered commercial banks

Office of Thrift Supervision
1700 G Street NW
Washington, DC 20552

Phone: (202) 906-6000
http://www.ots.treas.gov
Charters federal savings and loan associations; examines federally chartered savings institutions

Pension Benefit Guaranty Corporation
1200 K Street NW
Washington, DC 20005-4026
Phone: (800) 400-7242
http://www.pbgc.gov
Ensures that private pension plan participants receive basic retirement benefits; operates the federal pension guarantee fund

U.S. Securities and Exchange Commission
100 F Street NE
Washington, DC 20549
Phone: (202) 551-6551
http://www.sec.gov
Regulates the securities industry; registers issues of securities; supervises accounting firms, investment advisers, and mutual fund companies

Securities Investor Protection Corporation
805 15th Street NW, Suite 800
Washington, DC 20005-2215
Phone: (202) 371-8300
Fax: (202) 371-6728
http://www.sipc.org
Insures brokerage customers' holdings in cases of broker misconduct; helps arrange mergers of failing brokerage firms

APPENDIX VII
INTERNET RESOURCES:
THE WORLD WIDE WEB AND
CAREER PLANNING

The Internet is changing the way people manage their careers. With so much information available on the World Wide Web—the network of linked pages we look at when we "surf" the Internet—career planning has changed completely. College and university Web sites offer useful information about courses offered and career opportunities by field of study. Job seekers post their résumés on Internet job banks or e-mail them directly to employers. There are Internet sites offering career counseling—free of charge—to individuals considering careers in a specific field. A vast amount of education and employment-related information is only a mouseclick away, if you know where to look.

Following are suggestions for making the best use of the Internet while gathering information about education and employment opportunities. Remember that the Internet is a constantly changing source of information, so some of the Internet addresses listed below may have changed by the time you are reading this page. Use the search techniques listed below to collect more information about employers, industry trends, and current opportunities. In most cases, a combination of traditional and online techniques is the best approach to landing that first job or moving on in your career.

1. GENERAL INFORMATION

These Web sites can give you more information about various careers:

Occupational Outlook Handbook (OOH), 2006–07 Edition
Bureau of Labor Statistics
http://stats.bls.gov/oco/home.htm
The U.S. Department of Labor Occupational Outlook Handbook is the most comprehensive guide to careers and employment trends. State labor departments and state universities often have Web sites with state-specific information on career opportunities. Here are three examples:

California Occupational Guides
http://www.labormarketinfo.edd.ca.gov/cgi/career

Learn More Indiana
http://www.learnmoreindiana.org/@adults/adults_jobs/career_
    profiles

Virginia's Career Information System
http://www.careerconnect.state.va.us

2. INTERNET SEARCH ENGINES AND DIRECTORIES

There are two general tools for researching anything on the World Wide Web. Directory services such as Yahoo! (http://www.yahoo.com) compile lists of information categorized by topic. Then there are search engines such as Alta Vista or Google that search for information based on keywords you type in. Search engines allow you to cast the widest net in your research. Typing the search term "banking + careers" yields a long list of Internet job banks or financial institutions with available positions.

Some search engines, including Google (http://www.google.com), have directory services for more targeted searches. For example, you can search for employment opportunities in specific industries, such as banking or insurance.

Use these and other sources to add to your collection of bookmarks.

3. FINDING COLLEGES AND UNIVERSITIES

There are more than 3,000 colleges offering business administration majors. Several hundred educational institutions have four-year degree programs in banking, finance, and related fields of study. The complete list is too extensive to list in an appendix, but here are some suggestions for locating a college matching your career interest.

Published Guides

Printed guides such as *Peterson's Guide to Colleges* or *The Princeton Review Complete Guide to Colleges* have extensive Internet databases on a large number of educational institutions. Starting your search with a published directory is still the most efficient way to collect background information about colleges and universities. Then you can look up a college's Web site for up-to-date information about courses offered, academic schedules, tuition, and financial aid.

Web Guides

Web sites such as Peterson's (http://www.petersons.com) have search engines that will match your keywords to college majors and programs. These Web sites have fairly comprehensive databases. A search on one of these sites can yield names of several dozen colleges or more than 1,000 institutions if you're doing a nationwide search.

You might want to check your search results with college accrediting agencies to see whether your selections are accredited educational institutions. The Association to Advance Schools in Business (http://www.aacsb.edu) is the premier accrediting agency for bachelor's, master's, and doctoral degree programs in business administration and accounting. The Accrediting Commission for Community and Junior Colleges (http://www.accjc.org) performs similar evaluations on community colleges. Names of accredited institutions can be found by visiting their Web sites.

Web Directories
Another way to find the name of a specific college is searching on a Web directory such as Yahoo! or Google Web Directory (http://directory.google.com). Both have organized listings of colleges by state so you can easily find schools matching your interest in your region.

Evaluating Educational Programs
On-campus interviews are always recommended when evaluating colleges. If possible, arrange interviews at several colleges that appear to be good possibilities. Ask about internship programs, work-study programs, or other opportunities to gain practical experience before graduation. Try 1 to compare the printed catalog of courses offered against the job requirements in help wanted advertisements, or the position descriptions in this book.

If you can, get recommendations from people working in your intended career field. If you don't know anyone, don't worry. You will have plenty of opportunities to make connections while in college. Consider the range of academic courses offered by colleges on your selection list. While many of the positions described in this book require some academic background in accounting, finance, or business administration, a liberal and diverse education is an asset in financial services today. Strong verbal and written communication skills are as important in many positions as technical knowledge.

Continuing Education
Education does not end with entry into the workforce. Employers are investing large sums of money in continuing education and training programs for employees at all levels of the organization. These programs help employees maintain, or upgrade, key job-related skills, thereby avoiding skills obsolescence, and are given in a variety of formats. A growing number of organizations offer "distance learning" courses (called "e-learning" or "online learning" if provided via computer network) in addition to conventional classroom instructor-led courses. Distance learning courses are offered by accredited colleges and professional associations.

If your eventual aim is a college degree, it is important to check with state accrediting agencies or a professional accrediting organization before enrolling.

Classroom instruction is still preferred for executive education programs, where group discussion and interaction are important parts of the learning experience. Professional education and training programs can be anywhere from one-day workshops to one-week seminars presented on a college campus or conference center.

4. SEARCHING FOR JOB OPENINGS
After obtaining the necessary academic credentials plus some work experience, it's time to enter the job market. There are many sources of job listings, including the traditional sources—newspaper classified advertisements, trade journals, job fairs, state employment agencies, and college employment centers. Executive recruiting agencies, also known as search firms, are an important source of job leads for professional and management positions. Executive recruiters are paid a fee by employers to fill position vacancies. They place advertisements of current vacancies in professional journals, newspapers, and also on the Internet. You can use recruiters to locate opportunities you wouldn't think of yourself, and also to weed out the unattractive positions.

Searching on the Internet
There are a variety of Internet sites specializing in job listings. Many compile listings submitted by from employers or from other sources such as newsgroups. Some employment-related sites specialize in an industry specialty such as accounting, insurance, or investment banking.

Here are some examples of popular job sites on the Internet:

Jobs in Accounting
http://www.accounting.com
http://www.accountingprofessional.com
http://www.careerbank.com
http://www.jobsinthemoney.com
http://www.taxtalent.com

Jobs in Banking
http://www.nationjob.com/financial
http://www.banking-financejobs.com (sponsored by The National Banking Network, an association of recruiting firms)
http://www.bankjobsearch.com (sponsored by the Bank Administration Institute for BAI members)

Jobs in Insurance
http://www.ultimateinsurancejobs.com
http://www.insurance-jobs-center.com
http://www.insurancejobchannel.com

Jobs in Finance and Investment Banking
http://www.brokerhunter.com
http://www.wallstjobs.com

http://www.fei.org/careers
Sponsored by Financial Executives Institute

GENERAL CAREER SEARCH WEB SITES

America's Job Bank (http:www.ajb.dni.us) lists jobs posted from more than 2,000 state employment offices.

Career Magazine (http://www.careermag.com) has lists of job openings, news on hiring trends, and a discussion forum where users can compare notes.

Hotjobs (http://hotjobs.yahoo.com) has company profiles and résumé help.

The Monster Board (http://www.monster.com) has postings for more than one million jobs, company profiles, and job search tips.

5. GETTING SALARY INFORMATION

Information about salaries isn't hard to get if you know where to look. To prepare yourself for a reasonable salary demand or to evaluate an employer's offer, it's a good idea to check surveys of salaries in the financial services field.

The Riley Guide (http://rileyguide.com) has a collection of links to Web sites with salary information in various occupations. *Career Journal* (http://careers.wsj.com/) has occupational profiles and salary charts from the *National Business Employment Weekly*. Another source of information is the federal government's Bureau of Labor Statistics (http://www.stats.bls.gov), which has government surveys on employment and wages.

Remember that salaries can vary quite a bit, depending on qualifications, experience, and where you happen to live. Employers in high cost-of-living areas on the East Coast or West Coast pay higher starting salaries than in other regions such as the Midwest in order to attract qualified candidates.

Some career Web sites such as CareerBuilder (http://www.careerbuilder.com) include online salary calculators to help manage the cost of living issue. CareerBuilder's Salary Wizard is searchable by postal ZIP code, and it can be used to figure out salary ranges in many U.S. and foreign cities. Online salary calculators are useful, but they usually disclose salary information on only a small number of positions. If the position you are seeking isn't listed, the guide might have data on similar positions, which is still very useful information.

6. OTHER SOURCES OF INFORMATION

Company-based Web sites contain a wealth of information about the company as well as current job opportunities. Company Web sites often have job profiles or interviews with recent college graduates, which offer additional information about career opportunities. It's always a good idea to study a company's products and services, its position in the field, and what employees say about their jobs before going out on a job interview. That's the real value of the Internet as a research tool during a job search. You can find much of the information you need by going to an employer's home page, or by doing a web search using the company name as a keyword.

Public documents such as the annual 10K or quarterly 10q filings with the Securities and Exchange Commission yield plenty of information about a company and its officers. You can search SEC documents on Free Edgar (http://freeedgar.com). Other sites worth checking are Corporateinformation.com (http ://www.corporateinformation.com) and Hoover's (http://www.hoovers.com). Both have extensive directories with links to analyst research reports on both public and private companies.

Professional association Web sites and career-oriented Web sites are excellent places to gather information about specific careers, including advancement opportunities and job entry tips.

GLOSSARY

The following is a list of frequently used terms that you may find useful as you learn more about the financial services industry. These terms, also used in the position descriptions earlier in this book, are terms you should be familiar with before going on a job interview.

accreditation Process that an agency or association uses to grant public recognition to a training institution or university program that meets preset standards.

actuary Insurance specialist trained in mathematics, statistics, and accounting who is responsible for statistical studies such as rate, reserve, and dividend calculations.

analyst Individual who tracks the performance of companies or industries. The analyst recommends whether to buy, sell, or hold securities. Also called *financial analyst*.

auditor Individual given responsibility for examining financial records for accuracy and conformity with generally accepted accounting principles.

broker Registered representative or account executive who executes securities buy or sell orders acting as agent, usually charging a commission.

bulge bracket Informal name for the top-ranked investment banks; these firms share the largest participation in an underwriting of securities.

casualty underwriting Contract of insurance involving legal liability for losses caused by injury to persons or damage to property.

certification Issuance of a formal document that certifies or declares that the holder possesses a set of skills, knowledge, or abilities. Professional designation of competence in the related areas is usually granted after completion of a formal program education or training program.

commercial bank Depository financial institution that accepts deposits, makes loans, and offers a range of financial services to the public.

controller Financial executive given responsibility for analyzing and reporting accounting records for an organization.

employee benefits Benefits offered to an employee such as health and life insurance and employer-sponsored retirement plans.

electronic communications network Computerized system that automatically matches orders between buyers and sellers.

exchange Central location where trading of futures and securities takes place.

financial planner Individual who advises clients on use of investments, insurance, and other strategies to meet financial objectives. Planners tailor their advice to individual circumstances.

floor broker Employee of an exchange member who executes buy or sell orders for the company's public customers on the floor of the exchange.

401(k) plan A type of defined contribution retirement plan. Employees make pre-tax contributions to an employer-sponsored plan in lieu of salary.

403(b) plan Retirement plan for employees of certain non-profit organizations, such as teachers and employees of non-profit hospitals, who make pre-tax contributions to employer-sponsored plans.

457 plan A type of deferred compensation plan for employees of state and local governments. Similar to a 401(k) plan.

hedge fund Private investment partnership open to a limited number of investors, often requiring a large minimum investment. Hedge funds may use a variety of speculative trading strategies to increase investment returns.

industry association Organization of companies that represents the industry and acts as a spokesman for members.

investment banking Financial industry group that underwrites new issues of securities and advises corporate and municipal clients on financial strategy. Many investment banks also operate brokerage divisions.

investment management Management of financial assets allocated to stocks, bonds, and other asset classes to achieve client objectives, such as asset growth or capital preservation. Also called *portfolio management*.

insurance underwriter Insurance professional trained in evaluating risks and determining insurance rates and coverage.

loss control Mitigation of workplace losses by surveying of work areas, identifying hazards, and recommending improvements to eliminate or reduce loss probability.

over-the-counter Securities trading away from the floor of an exchange.

professional association Organization representing members of a professional occupation; it may set standards for education, training, and professional certification.

Public Company Accounting Oversight Board Non-profit organization created by the Sarbanes-Oxley Act of 2002 that regulates auditors of publicly traded companies.

Auditors of a company's financial statements are required to follow strict PCAOB guidelines to protect investors.

Regulation FD   A "fair disclosure" rule passed by the Securities and Exchange Commission banning selective disclosure of financial information to securities analysts nd shareholders. The intent of this rule is to even the playing field between professional investors and the general public.

Sarbanes-Oxley Act   Federal law enacted by Congress in 2002 to protect investors from the possibility of fraudulent accounting activities by public corporations. Key sections of this law, the most sweeping overhaul of securities regulations since the 1930s, created the Public Company Accounting Oversight Board and tightened controls on financial reviews by internal auditors and inspecting accounting firms.

thrift institution   Depository financial institution chartered to originate mortgages, accept deposits, and offer other bank-related services to the public. Savings and loan associations, federal savings banks, and credit unions are thrift institutions.

trader   Individual who buys or sells securities, acting as principal for his or her own account or as a representative of their firm.

training   Acquisition of knowledge or skills to improve performance on the job. Training can occur in the workplace or in an educational program.

trustee   Individual who holds legal title to property, acting as fiduciary. The trustee, for example of a bank trust department, manages the property for the benefit of the trust beneficiary.

BIBLIOGRAPHY

There are many books about job searching. The following titles focus on careers in financial services, the job-searching strategy, résumé writing, and how to effectively use the Internet for career research and job hunting.

Alpert, Gary, and Pollock, Steve. *Investment Banking Interviews: Beat the Street: The Wetfeet Insiders Guide.* San Francisco: Wetfeet Press, 2000.

Alsop, Ronald J., and the Staff of the *Wall Street Journal. The Wall Street Journal Guide to the Top Business Schools.* New York: Free Press, 2003.

Asher, Don. *The Overnight Resume.* Berkeley, Calif.: Ten Speed Press, 1999.

Bhatawedekhar, D. *The Vault Guide to Financial Interviews.* New York: Vault, Inc., 2005.

Bolles, Richard Nelson. *Job-Hunting on the Internet, Fourth Edition.* Berkeley, Calif.: Ten Speed Press, 2005.

Camenson, Blyth. *Real People Working in Finance (On the Job Series).* Lincolnwood, Ill.: NTC Publishing Group, 1999.

Corcodilos, Nick A. *Ask the Headhunter: Reinventing the Interview to Win the Job.* East Rutherford, N.J.: Plume 1997.

Criscito, Pat, and Dee Funkhouser. *Interview Answers in a Flash.* Hauppauge, N.Y.: Barron's Educational Series, 2006.

Curley, Michael T., and Joseph A. Walker. *Barron's How to Prepare for the Stockbrokers Exam: Series 7, Third Edition.* Hauppauge, N.Y.: Barron's Educational Series, 2006.

Dawson, Roger. *Secrets of Power Negotiating, Second Edition.* Franklin Lakes, N.J.: Career Press, 2006.

Delaney, Patrick R., and O. Ray Whittington. *Wiley CPA Examination Review 2006–2007, Outlines and Study Guides.* New York: John Wiley & Sons, 2005.

Dikel, Margaret Riley, and Frances E. Roehm. *Guide to Internet Job Searching 2006–2007.* New York: McGraw-Hill, 2006.

Fisher, Ann B. *If My Career's on the Fast Track, Where Do I Get a Road Map?* New York: William R. Morrow & Co., 2001.

Fournier, Myra, and Jeff Spin. *Encyclopedia of Job-Winning Resumes.* Franklin Lakes, N.J.: Career Press, 2006.

Gilbert, Nedda. *Best 143 Business Schools, 2005 Edition.* New York: Princeton Review, 2005.

Harvard Business School Guide to Careers in Finance. Boston: Harvard Business School Publishing, 2002.

Hunt, Christopher W., and Scott Scanlon. *A Job Seeker's Guide to Wall Street Recruiters.* New York: John Wiley & Sons, 1998.

Kador, John. *201 Best Questions to Ask on Your Interview.* New York: McGraw-Hill, 2002.

Kapadia, Anita, Chris Prior, and Tom Lot. *Vault.com Career Guide to Investment Banking.* New York: Vault, Inc., 2000.

Kessler, Robin. *Competency-Based Interviews.* Franklin Lakes, N.J.: Career Press 2006.

Kirsch, Clifford E., ed. *The Financial Services Revolution: Understanding the Changing Roles of Banks, Mutual Funds and Insurance Companies.* New York: McGraw-Hill Professional Publishing, 1997.

Leanne, Shelly. *How to Interview Like a Top MBA: Job-Winning Strategies from Headhunters, Fortune 100 Recruiters, and Career Counselors.* New York: McGraw-Hill, 2003.

McKinney, Anne, ed. *Real Resumes for Career Changers: Actual Resumes and Cover Letters.* Fayetteville, N.C.: PREP Publishing, 2000.

Naficy, Mariam. *The Fast Track: The Insider's Guide to Winning Jobs in Management Consulting, Investment Banking and Securities Trading.* New York: Broadway Books, 1997.

Oldman, Mark, and Samer Hamadeh. *The Internship Bible, 10th Edition.* New York: Princeton Review, 2005.

Passtrak Series 3: National Commodity Futures Exam: License Exam Manual. Chicago: Dearborn Trade Publishing, 2001.

Peterson's Four Year Colleges 2006. Princeton, N.J.: Peterson's, 2006.

Pollock, Steve. *The Mutual Fund Industry: The Wetfeet.com Insider Guide.* San Francisco: Wetfeet Press, 2000.

Smith, Gordon, and S. David Peeler. *The Adjuster: Making Insurance Claims Pay.* Houston: Cargo Publishing Co., 1998.

Wendleton, Kate, and Wendy Rothman. *Targeting the Job You Want.* Franklin Lakes, N.J.: Career Press, 2000.

Yeager, Neil M., and Lee Hough. *Power Interviews: Job Winning Tactics from Fortune 500 Recruiters, Revised and Expanded.* New York: John Wiley & Sons, 1998.

INDEX